AF870825

The Complete Guide to Creating Professional Videos with TechSmith Camtasia

Learn to Train, Teach, and Communicate Effectively Through Video Without Any Video Production Experience

Damien Bruyndonckx

One2Learn Editions

The Complete Guide to Creating Professional Videos with TechSmith Camtasia

Copyright © 2026 One2Learn Editions.

https://www.one2learn.online

All rights reserved.
No part of this publication may be reproduced, stored in a retrieval system, transmitted, or distributed in any form or by any means, including electronic, mechanical, photocopying, recording, or otherwise, without the prior written permission of the publisher, except for brief quotations used in reviews, scholarly works, or as otherwise permitted by applicable copyright law.
This publication is available in both printed and electronic editions. The purchase of one edition does not grant the right to reproduce, share, distribute, or convert the content into another format.

Disclaimer

Every effort has been made to ensure that the information contained in this book is accurate at the time of publication. However, software products evolve continuously, and features, user interfaces, menus, commands, and workflows may change without notice.
The author and publisher make no warranties, express or implied, regarding the completeness, accuracy, reliability, or suitability of the information contained in this publication. The author and publisher shall not be liable for any loss, damage, or inconvenience arising from the use of the information, techniques, or examples presented in this book.
Readers are responsible for verifying that procedures remain applicable to the version of the software they are using.

Independent Publication

This publication is an independent educational work. It has not been authorized, sponsored, endorsed, or certified by TechSmith Corporation.
Any opinions, recommendations, or workflows described in this book are solely those of the author

Trademarks

TechSmith®, Camtasia®, and any related product names are trademarks or registered trademarks of TechSmith Corporation in the United States and/or other countries.
All other product names, company names, logos, and trademarks mentioned in this publication are the property of their respective owners. Their inclusion does not imply any affiliation with or endorsement by the trademark owners.

Screenshots

Screenshots of the Camtasia (and other) software appearing in this publication were captured by the author for educational and instructional purposes.
These screenshots remain subject to the intellectual property rights and trademark rights of their respective owners.

Published by One2Learn Editions - 103, rue d'Anderlues – 6530 Thuin – Belgium
First edition – August 2026
ISBN (Print): 978-2-9604127-2-7
ISBN (eBook): 978-2-9604127-3-4
Legal deposit : D/2026/16244/02

A. Foreword

You've chosen well!

Camtasia is the software used to create the best tutorials, software demos, and even a pair of Super Bowl commercials. You've also chosen a great guide: Damien, a recognized Camtasia expert with a rare talent for explaining complex concepts in simple terms.

Can I give you a tip?

When I was just 25, I went to my boss (at Cisco Systems) and asked her if we could hire an outside company to make a video for us. When she asked me what I wanted the video to achieve, I couldn't tell her. She kindly asked me to come back once I'd defined my expectations.

So, take five minutes to answer the following two questions:

- How do you want the world to be different because you created this video?
- What does your video need to include to achieve that goal?

Write down your ideas, then continue reading this book.

In the following chapters, Damien won't just show you where to click. He'll help you think like a video creator. Concepts such as non-destructive editing, cursor clarity, audio quality, and animation restraint are explained in a way that gives you the context and confidence you need to create better videos.

Damien also explores the Camtasia suite, including tools such as Audiate, Screencast, and Assets Library, helping you save valuable time and significantly enrich your productions.

Whether you are creating your first tutorial or refining your production process, this book is designed to meet you where you are and take you further. If you follow along, practice the exercises, and apply the techniques thoughtfully, you will finish not just with completed videos—but also with a repeatable, confident workflow you can rely on again and again.

You are in great hands with Damien and Camtasia. Enjoy the journey!

Troy Stein
VP, Customer Advocacy
TechSmith Corporation

B. The Author

Damien Bruyndonckx is the founder and CEO of One2Learn, a Belgian company offering a wide range of services in the field of e-learning. With more than 20 years of experience in the e-learning industry, Damien specializes in virtual classrooms, webinars, instructional videos, interactive content development, and training in the use of e-learning content creation tools. As a TechSmith recommended trainer and recognized Camtasia expert, Damien delivers training sessions on Camtasia, Snagit, and other TechSmith tools for a wide range of customers. He also hosts official customer education webinars in French and English on behalf of TechSmith.

- https://www.one2Learn.online/en
- https://www.linkedin.com/in/damienbkx/

This book holds a very special place in my journey. It is my tenth book—a milestone I never imagined I would reach—and the first English title published by One2Learn Editions, the publishing house dedicated to e-learning professionals that I founded as part of One2Learn SRL.

I'd like to thank everyone who, over the years, has patiently taught me the ins and outs of technical writing, as well as all the contributors who, directly or indirectly, helped bring this book to life.

My very special thanks go to Kirsten and David, my amazing reviewers, and to Sacha, my assistant during the video shoots. Finally, a special thought goes to my partner, Céline, who has to put up with my endless working hours and my ramblings every time I embark on a new writing project.

But above all, thank you, dear readers, for placing your trust in me to guide you as you discover TechSmith Camtasia.

The Reviewers

The author would like to express his deepest gratitude to Kirsten and David for their time, care, and attention in reviewing and proofreading the manuscript. Their thoughtful feedback has greatly contributed to the overall quality of this book.

1. Kirsten Rourke

Kirsten Rourke is an instructional designer and eLearning developer who's been part of the training and development speaking circuit for several years. She met Damien at an eLearning seminar where they were both presenting, and over time that connection turned into a genuine friendship built on sharing ideas, swapping feedback, and encouraging each other's work.

She always enjoyed helping the people around her, especially when it comes to creative and technical projects. Whether a friend is building a course, writing a book, or experimenting with a new tool, Kirsten is usually happy to jump in, take a look, and talk things through. She's reviewed multiple projects over the years and tends to focus on what will make something clearer, more usable, and more helpful for the person on the other end.

Her experience working with tools like Camtasia, Storyline, and Rise gives her a practical perspective, but what really drives her is the collaborative side of the work—figuring things out together and making ideas stronger in the process.

Outside of her L&D work, she spends her time creating hand-painted wearable art, which is just another way she enjoys bringing ideas to life in a more creative, hands-on way.

- https://www.linkedin.com/in/kirstenrourke/

I want to thank Damien for the chance to work with him again. It's always a good time!

David Garcia

David Garcia is an instructional designer and talent development leader with more than a decade of experience creating innovative learning solutions, modernizing training systems, and supporting workforce development. In his current role with Los Angeles Metro, he leads the development of agency-wide e-learning and instructor-led training programs, manages learning systems serving more than 13,000 employees, and partners with senior leaders to advance organizational priorities, regulatory compliance, and employee development.

Before joining Metro, David designed and managed large-scale training initiatives for the United States Navy, Army, and other Department of Defense programs. His experience includes leading multidisciplinary teams, conducting instructional and performance analyses, developing scenario-based courseware, and translating complex technical information into engaging and accessible learning experiences. He holds a Master of Science in Modeling and Simulation, with a focus on human systems and human-centered design, and a Bachelor of Science in Psychology from the University of Central Florida.

- https://www.linkedin.com/in/dgarcia327/
- davidrgarcia327@gmail.com

My sincere thanks to Damien for being a valued colleague over the past few years and, more importantly, a wonderful friend.

D. Table of Contents

E. Obtaining Camtasia

This book is designed as a step-by-step guide to help you create a fictional online course consisting of seven video segments.

To get the most out of this book, we recommend installing Camtasia on your computer and completing the exercises as you work through each chapter.

Camtasia is a commercial video editing and screen recording application for Windows and macOS, developed by TechSmith. TechSmith offers a free edition of Camtasia that is ideal for working through the exercises in this book. The free edition includes all the application's features. However, exported videos contain a watermark, which can only be removed with a paid subscription. For information about subscription options and pricing, visit the official TechSmith website at https://www.techsmith.com/all-products/.

The system requirements for using Camtasia are available on the TechSmith website at: https://www.techsmith.com/camtasia/system-requirements/

F. Other applications

For the best possible learning experience, we recommend installing the following software in addition to Camtasia.

1. Microsoft PowerPoint

Although some activities in this manual require Microsoft PowerPoint, not having access to this application will only affect those specific exercises. You can still complete the remaining activities and continue working through the manual.

2. Camtasia Audiate

Some of the exercises in the final chapter of this book require Camtasia Audiate. A free 7-day trial of is available for download from the TechSmith website at https://www.techsmith.fr/camtasia/audiate/.

G. Software Updates

Because TechSmith regularly updates Camtasia, the version you use while working through this book may differ from the one we used to create the exercises. Minor differences between versions should not affect your progress or your ability to complete the activities. However, be mindful of the following:

- When you open an exercise file, Camtasia may ask you to update the file format. This quick and straightforward process will not interfere with your ability to complete the exercise.
- The user interface elements depicted in the screenshots and the features described in this book are subject to change without notice.

The Camtasia release history, including bug fixes and feature updates, is available on the TechSmith Support website at https://support.techsmith.com/hc/en-us.

When this book was published (August 2026), the latest version of Camtasia Editor was version 2026.1.4 (Mac & Windows).

H. Downloading the Exercise Files

Before you begin reading this book, visit https://link.one2learn.online/camtasia26en to download the exercise files.

Since video files require a large amount of storage space, the exercise files are organized into separate ***.zip*** archives, one for each chapter. Be sure to download and extract the relevant files before starting the corresponding chapter.

If you are using Windows, you **must** extract (unzip) the .zip files before using the exercise files.

1. Right-click the ***.zip*** file you want to extract.
2. Select Extract All... from the context menu.
3. Select the destination folder for the extracted files.
4. Click Extract.

This process is depicted in the following screenshot:

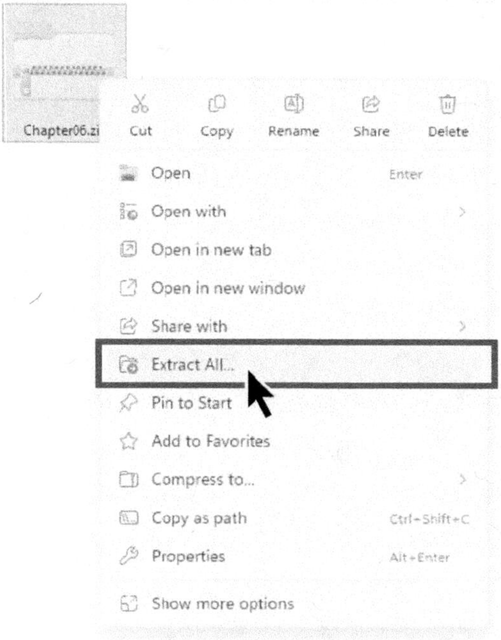

*00_01.png - Right-click and select **Extract All...***

I. A Note on the Images

Unless otherwise indicated, the screenshots in this book are based on a default installation of Camtasia on Windows 11. If you have modified the default settings or are using Camtasia for Mac, some interface elements may appear slightly different.

For technical reasons, the illustrations in this book are reproduced in black and white. Color versions are included in the downloadable resources that accompany the book. The filename of each illustration is provided in its caption.

J. Contact Us

We welcome your questions, comments, and feedback about this book. To contact us, please send your message to editions@one2learn.online and include the book title in the subject line. If you are reporting an erratum, please provide as much detail as possible, including the page number and section title.

Getting Started With TechSmith Camtasia

Over the past two decades, video has radically transformed the way we communicate and consume media. The training and development industry is no exception. Whether in education or in business, the use of video for educational purposes has become a fundamental element of a growing number of training initiatives.

The growing use of online video platforms and social media has further accelerated the rise of video as a learning tool. Platforms such as YouTube and Vimeo offer vast libraries of learning content, covering an astonishing range of subjects. For many of us, YouTube has even become one of the first places we turn to when we need to learn something.

For training and communication professionals, the ability to create this type of video content has become an essential skill. This is where TechSmith Camtasia comes in.

Camtasia is a screen capture and video editing software designed specifically for non-videographers. With Camtasia, trainers, teachers, marketers, communication professionals, influencers, and YouTubers can create highly visual, modern, and engaging content on their own.

A. Objectives of This Book

This book guides you through creating a complete e-learning course composed of seven short video sequences, which is the most common use case for Camtasia. This project-based approach provides you with a hands-on understanding of the tools and features of Camtasia and introduces you to some of the most popular and effective workflows for screen capture and video editing.

Although the exercises in this book focus primarily on creating instructional videos, the core principles apply to all types of video production. The tools and techniques presented here are the same as those used to create promotional videos, corporate communications, product demonstrations, social media content, even movies and TV series. In other words, there's something for everyone!

B. Previewing the Completed Projects

To give you a glimpse of what lies ahead, you will now take a look the final version of the seven video projects featured in this book. These examples are designed to showcase both the power of Camtasia and the skills you'll acquire as you read on.

To do this, you will step into the shoes of a learner and watch these videos in the order defined by the trainer (note that this order does not necessarily correspond to the order in which you will *produce* these videos). In this section, you will simply *watch* the videos, but keep in mind that, in practice, learners must first log in to the learning management system (LMS) where the videos are hosted, before accessing the content. Your experience will, therefore, be slightly different from theirs.

The table of contents for this fictional training course is available in the ***Chapter01/Exercices_TOC.xlsx file*** *of the download.*

1. The Trailer

The first video in the series is a trailer for the training course. It is a promotional tool, optimized for social media and designed to capture attention. Please follow the steps below to view the trailer:

1. Download and unzip the exercises for ***Chapter01*** from https://link.one-2learn.online/camtasia26en
2. Navigate to the ***Chapter01*** folder that you just unzipped.
3. Double-click the file ***Chapter01/00_00_trailer.mp4*** to open it in the default media player installed on your computer.
4. Watch the entire sequence.

This first video is optional content. It is not really part of the training content itself. In fact, it is the only video in the series that will *not* be published on the LMS. Learners are not required to watch it to complete their online training course.

Optimized for mobile viewing, this video adopts the vertical format, typical of smartphones. The subtitles are also typical of videos designed specifically for social media.

2. The Prerequisites

The second video serves as a general introduction to the course and is the first mandatory part of the curriculum. Since the trailer video is optional, you will notice some repetition between this video and the previous one, which is perfectly normal.

1. Double click the ***Chapter01/00_01_prerequisites.mp4*** file to open it in the default media player installed on your computer.
2. Watch the entire video.

Remember that only students enrolled in the course will have access to this video. This has some important consequences:

- The video is not publicly accessible on social media. Learners must first log in to the LMS to access it.
- It is reasonable to assume that learners will watch this video in a place conducive to learning, using a device other than a smartphone (a laptop or desktop computer, or a tablet). That's why this video adopts the traditional landscape layout.
- Because others may be nearby, many learners are likely to use headphones, both to avoid disturbing those around them and to help them concentrate.

These few points illustrate that many of the choices you will have to make as a video content creator depend on your audience and on the context in which your videos are likely to be viewed. It is therefore essential to think through these aspects carefully before getting started on producing videos.

This particular video combines two sources in Camtasia to create the final video.

The first source is the narrator video. It was shot against a green backdrop. In Camtasia, this backdrop was removed and replaced by a transparent layer. You will learn how to manipulate this color removal effect in Chapter 06 - Transitions, Animations, and Visual Effects.

The second source is a PowerPoint presentation that was captured using *Camtasia Recorder*, Camtasia's built-in screen recording tool. You will learn how to record your screen using Camtasia Recorder in Chapter 04 – Recording with Camtasia.

Keep in mind that this is a fictional course. No need to call 8080! The data-analysis platform used in the exercises is also imaginary; it will be included with the exercise files in a later chapter.

3. Logging In and Out

It is now time to watch the third sequence.

1. Double click the file ***Chapter01/01_01_loginLogout.mp4*** to open it in the default media player installed on your computer.
2. Watch the entire sequence.

This third video was produced using *Camtasia Rev*, a streamlined workflow that allows you to capture, edit, and export your videos in three quick and easy steps. You will learn more about Camtasia Rev in Chapter 02 – Your First Video with Camtasia Rev.

Note that this video starts and ends similarly to the previous one. This is because the opening and closing sequences were saved in the *Camtasia library* so they can easily be reused in multiple videos. You'll learn more about customizing Camtasia and using the library in Chapter 09, Extending and Customizing Camtasia.

Also note the presence of closed captions. You will learn how to add closed captions and synchronize them with the narration in Chapter 08 – Working with Audio.

4. Using the Dashboard and Customizing the Platform

The following two videos demonstrate the typical use case of Camtasia. Both were recorded using Camtasia Recorder, which was used to capture the onscreen actions. Follow the steps below to watch these two videos:

1. Double click ***Chapter01/01_02_dashboard.mp4*** to open the file in your computer's default media player
2. Watch the entire sequence.
3. Repeat these steps with the ***Chapter01/01_03_settings.mp4*** file.

In addition to the items already mentioned previously, these two videos showcase a number of additional features.

- Some *zoom and pan* effects created with the built-in animation tool.
- A few *annotations*, such as animated arrows and circles.
- The *Spotlight* effect, which highlights a specific area of the screen by darkening all other areas.
- A series of *click effects* added to the mouse cursor to help the viewer follow the mouse and clearly identify when clicks occur.

These tools and effects will be covered in Chapter 05 – Editing Your Video, Chapter 06 – Transitions, Animations, and Visual Effects, and Chapter 07 – Focus on the Mouse Cursor.

5. The Quiz

Up to this point, the videos you've watched required only passive viewing from learners. The next one is interactive: to progress through the video, learners must answer a series of questions. This is why the steps for playing this video are slightly different.

1. Double-click the ***Chapter01/02_01_Quiz/index.html*** file from the exercises.

Unlike the previous videos, this one opens in your web browser rather than a media player.

2. Watch the entire sequence and answer the quiz questions.

Standard videos do not support this type of user interaction because the ***.mp4*** format does not support interactivity. This is why this video is delivered with the *Smart Player*, a special media player designed to power Camtasia's interactive features . You'll learn more about these interactive features and the *Smart Player* in Chapter 10—Making Your Videos Interactive.

6. The Conclusion

This is the last video of the online training course! Here you summarize the entire course and bid farewell to your learners.

1. Open the ***Chapter01/02_02_conclusion.mp4*** file in the default media player installed on your computer.
2. Watch the entire video.

This sequence is very important from an instructional design standpoint. First, it adds a human touch, which is often missing in many online courses. It also helps learners structure their knowledge by highlighting the key elements they should focus on.

C. An Overview of the Production Process

After watching these videos, you should have a much better idea of the features available in Camtasia and of the content of this book. You will now get a general overview of the process used to produce these videos.

Producing videos with Camtasia is a four-step process: the *pre-production* step, the *recording* step, the *post-production* step (also known as the *editing* step), and the *rendering* step.

1. The Pre-production Step

Any video production, whether it's a basic tutorial or a major Hollywood blockbuster, requires careful preparation. The extent of this preparation varies considerably depending on the complexity and duration of the final video.

For instructional videos, pre-production may only take a few minutes if you have a good grasp of the subject matter and some experience with the recording process. For a major motion picture, it can take months or even years.

Most of the videos you will be making with Camtasia are short, instructional videos. With that in mind, here are some key points you should consider as you enter the pre-production step.

1. Define the Course Outline

Most Camtasia projects are modules within a larger training course. When you embark on such a project, start by defining the overall table of contents for the course.

As a reminder, the outline of the fictional online training course used in these exercises is available in the ***Chapter01/Exercices_TOC.xlsx*** *file.*

2. Script the Videos

Once you have established the general outline for your training course, you can focus on the content of each individual video. Even a basic script will help you stay on topic, ensure you don't forget anything, and stay organized.

You don't need to make it overly complicated. For tutorials such as those found on YouTube, a simple bulleted list of the key points to cover may be enough.

It can be very useful to write down the first few sentences and the conclusion of the narration. Indeed, one of the most difficult aspects of recording this type of content is getting off to a good start and wrapping it up properly. In between, you can afford to improvise and be spontaneous (provided you have a good grasp on the subject matter).

For more complex videos involving several actors and filming locations, it is essential to systematically write out the entire script before filming. This also applies when the trainer appears on camera, in which case a teleprompter can be extremely useful.

A teleprompter is a device that automatically scrolls through the text of a speech or script to help the speaker read it while maintaining eye contact with the camera or with the audience. It is commonly used by TV presenters and politicians so they can speak without having to look at their notes. A teleprompter consists of a horizontal screen on which the text scrolls and a two-way mirror tilted at 45 degrees placed in front of the camera lens. A cost-effective solution is to install a teleprompter app on your tablet, which you can then use as the screen for the teleprompter. See, for example, https://telepromptерpad.com/.

3. Narration, Storyboard, and Shot list

To conclude this section, let's review some documents that you are likely to encounter during your career as an instructional video producer.

The narration

This document contains all the spoken words in the video. For a tutorial based on screen captures, you will also specify the actions to be performed for each sentence.

You can find examples of such narrations in the exercise files of Chapter 2. Feel free to download them now to take a first look.

It is not always necessary to write the entire narration, as in the examples presented in this book. That said, if you plan to appear on camera, even minimal preparation is often essential. Total improvisation will make you waste a lot of time during filming, with results that are far from guaranteed.

The Storyboard

For more advanced videos, it quickly becomes necessary to create a storyboard. A storyboard is essentially a comic strip of your project. You sketch out the scenes to be created in small boxes arranged on the document. To better understand what a storyboard looks like, let's do a quick search on the Internet:

1. Open your favorite browser and search engine.
2. Enter `Storyboard` as the keyword and start the search.
3. Switch to the **Images** tab of the search engine and browse through the storyboard examples.

The storyboard often complements the script and the narration. It is a very effective tool for communicating your intentions visually to the rest of your team and to your client.

The shot list

If your project requires filming in multiple locations, at different times, or with numerous actors, the *shot list* is a critical tool.

It is often just a simple Excel spreadsheet in which you enter all the information about each shot, such as the location, the actors involved, the time of day (day or night), whether it is an indoor or outdoor scene, the camera movement, etc. Thanks to the sorting and filtering tools built into Excel, you can easily group your shots by location, actor, camera type, etc. This makes the *shot list* an extremely valuable tool for organizing and optimizing the production process.

Many resources, including narration and shot list templates, are available for free on the TechSmith Academy website at https://academy.techsmith.com/.

Conclusion

Course outline, narration, script, storyboard, and shot list, none of these documents are mandatory for the success of your project. The number of documents to produce and the level of detail required vary depending on the complexity of the video, its duration, your mastery of the subject matter, the size of your team, the requirements of your customer, your experience in video production, and even your personal preferences.

Either way, you will quickly realize that the pre-production step is essential to the success of your video projects. One of the most common mistakes beginners make is insufficient preparation beforehand.

2. The Recording Step

Once the pre-production step is complete, you can move on to the recording step. At this stage, the goal is to gather all the elements needed to assemble your video. Camtasia supports a wide range of content types, such as:

- **Still images** (photos, illustrations, graphics) either created by you, downloaded from stock image libraries (free or paid), or generated using AI,
- **Video sequences** captured outdoors or in a studio, downloaded from free or paid stock footage libraries, or generated using AI,
- **Animations** made using specialized animation software, downloaded from the Internet, or generated using AI,
- **Screencast videos** recorded with Camtasia Recorder or with an external application,
- **PowerPoint presentations** captured by Camtasia, by an external application, or imported directly into Camtasia,
- **Audio files** with background music, sound effects, or narration for your video.

As you can see, the elements that make up your videos come in different forms, and not all of them require actual *filming*. The main objective of this step is to collect or produce enough high-quality material to ensure the success of the next step (which is the *post-production* step).

In Chapter 03 – Creating a New Project, you will learn how to import these elements into Camtasia, and in Chapter 04 – Recording with Camtasia, you will take a detailed look at *Camtasia Recorder*, the screen capture utility built into the application.

Once the recording step is complete, your video is far from ready. That said, you now have all the material you need to move on to the post-production step (also known as the editing step).

3. The Post-production Step

This step is usually the most time-consuming part of the process. This is also the step where you will use the many tools in Camtasia to:

- Select your shots and remove unwanted parts of your video clips,
- Arrange the components of your video on the timeline,
- Combine multiple media sources to achieve the desired effects,
- Replace backdrops with images or videos of your choosing,
- Add transitions and animations,
- Adjust audio levels between multiple audio clips,
- Create and synchronize subtitles and closed captions.

As you progress through the post-production step, your video will gradually take shape until it eventually reaches its final form. Chapters 5 to 8 are entirely devoted to the post-production step.

At the end of this step, all that remains is to make your work available to the world!

4. The Rendering Step

When post-production is complete, your video still only exists within Camtasia. The rendering step is where you export your project as a video file, which you can share with your learners.

You typically produce an ***.mp4*** file that you can store on your computer and upload to any platform your audience has access to. However, Camtasia offers several additional export options, such as:

- The ability to upload your videos to your YouTube channel,
- Publishing your videos to Screencast, Techsmith's video hosting service,
- Integrating your video into the *Smart Player*, a fully customizable HTML 5 media player designed to leverage Camtasia's interactive features, such as interactive hotspots and quizzes,
- The ability to generate *SCORM* packages that you can easily deploy on your LMS.

Chapter 11 – Producing Your Videos is entirely devoted to the tools used during the rendering phase.

D. Discovering the Camtasia Interface

To wrap up this chapter, let's take a first look at the Camtasia interface. The goal is to give you a general idea of what the software looks like and introduce the terminology that will be used throughout this book.

1. Open Camtasia.
2. Once on the welcome screen, click **Open Project**.
3. Open the ***Chapter01/interface.tscproj/interface.tscproj*** file from the exercises.

This is the project used to generate the conclusion video you watched earlier in this chapter. Once opened, you should see a screen similar to the image below.

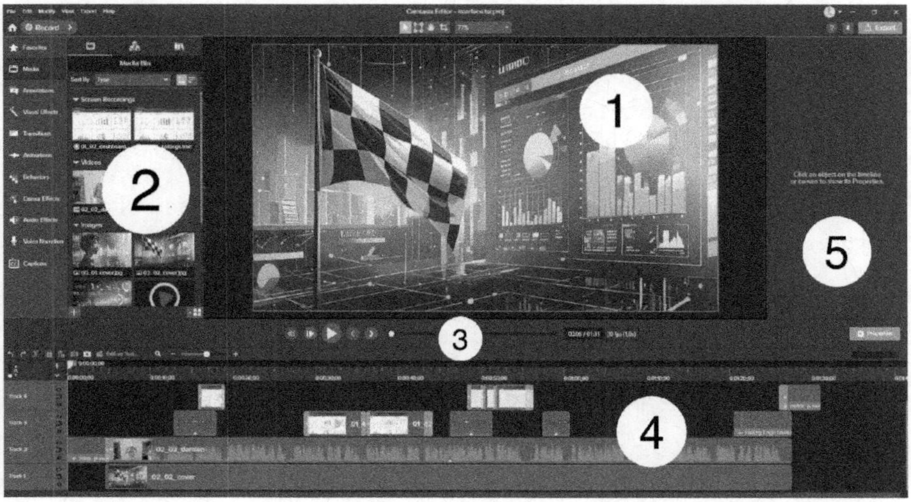

01_01.png – The Camtasia user interface

The Camtasia interface is divided into five areas identified by the numbers 1 to 5 in the above image.

1. The main area is called the *canvas*.
2. The *tool panels* are located on the left side of the canvas.
3. The *playback controls* sit between the canvas and the timeline.
4. The *timeline* spans the bottom of the screen.
5. The *Properties panel* is located on the right side of the canvas and may be closed by default.

You will now take a closer look at each of these five areas.

1. Working with the canvas

The central area of Camtasia is known as the *canvas*. The image visible on the canvas reflects the current position of the playhead on the timeline (you will learn more about the playhead in the Using the Playback Controls section later in this chapter). Right above the canvas is a dropdown menu from which you can adjust the zoom level.

1. Open the dropdown menu located right above the canvas.
2. Set the zoom level to **100%** to see the project in its actual size.
3. Open the same dropdown menu again and select **Fit** at the top of the list.

Fit lets Camtasia determine the best zoom level to display the entire project without generating scroll bars. Another way to set the zoom level of the canvas is to use the mouse wheel.

4. Place the mouse pointer over the canvas, then use the mouse wheel to adjust the zoom level.

This is probably the simplest, fastest, and most intuitive way of adjusting the zoom level of the canvas.

5. Open the **View > Canvas** menu. Here you will find all the commands and keyboard shortcuts used to adjust the zoom level of the canvas.

The dropdown menu located above the canvas offers another very interesting option.

6. Open the dropdown menu above the canvas one more time.
7. Select **Detach Canvas**.

This option turns the canvas into its own floating window that can be moved around independently from the rest of the application. This is especially useful for those working with two monitors. You can position the canvas on one monitor and the rest of the application on the other, which greatly improves the video editing experience.

Note that the playback controls and the dropdown menu controlling the zoom level are integrated into the detached floating window.

8. Open the dropdown menu above the canvas once again.
9. Select **Attach Canvas** to reattach the canvas to the rest of the application and return to the initial state.

And that's it for a first look at the canvas! In the next section, you'll explore the tool panels located on the left side of the interface.

2. Discovering the Tool Panels

In Camtasia, most tools can be accessed using the buttons in the left-hand column. The **Media Bin**, which is part of the **Media** category, should be open by default, as shown in the image below.

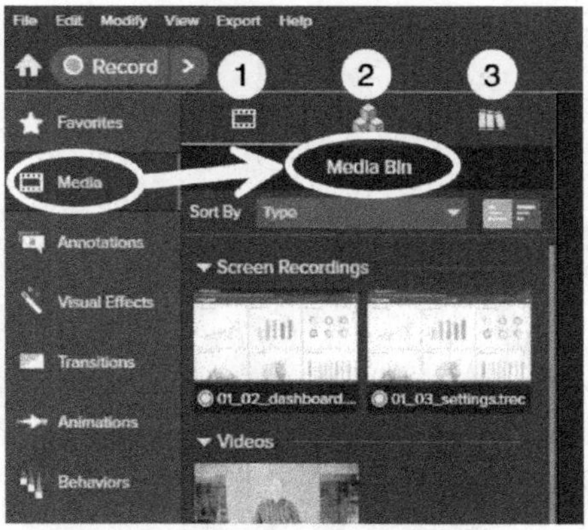

*01_02.png - The **Media Bin** is open by default*

The *Media Bin* is where you find all the multimedia assets used in the project. In this example, it contains two screen recordings, a video recorded against a green background and a few static images in *.jpg* and *.png* format. You will learn more about the *Media Bin* in Chapter 03 – Creating a New Project.

The *Media Bin* is the first of three tabs under the **Media** category. These tabs are numbered from 1 to 3 in the above image.

1. Click the *three-cube* icon (identified by number 2 in the above image) to open the **Camtasia Assets** tab.

Camtasia Assets is a huge resource library hosted by TechSmith. It contains a wide variety of items, such as stock images, video footage, audio tracks, animated elements, title templates, and more. While some of these items are available for free, access to the entire library requires a Camtasia Pro subscription.

2. Click the *books* icon (identified by number 3 in the above image) to open the **Library** panel.

Similar to the Camtasia Assets, the library also provides a collection of items that you can use in your videos. The main difference between the library and the assets is that the library is stored on your computer, while the Camtasia Assets are hosted online by TechSmith. You will learn more about the library in Chapter 09, Extending and Customizing Camtasia.

3. Click the *film* icon (identified by number 1 in the previous image) to return to the **Media Bin**.
4. Click the **Media** button on the left to completely close the tool panels.
5. Position the mouse pointer over the **Media** button without clicking.

Within a few seconds, a tooltip explaining the **Media** section should appear.

6. Briefly hover your mouse over the other buttons in the left column to display the corresponding tooltips.

Depending on the size of your screen, Camtasia may not be able to display all the buttons in the left column. If this happens, Camtasia displays as many tools as possible and adds a **More** button at the bottom of the left column, which gives you access to those tools not shown on smaller screens.

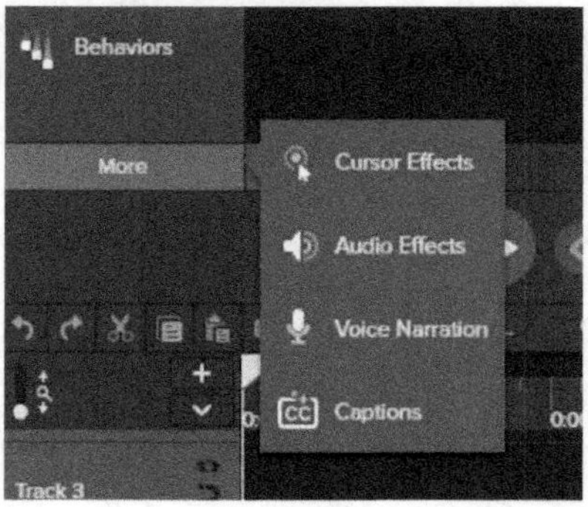

*01_03.png - The **More** button provides access to tools that cannot be displayed on smaller screens.*

Finally, the tool panels can also be accessed using keyboard shortcuts as well as with the application menus.

7. Open the **View > Tools** menu to get a complete list of all the tool panels available in Camtasia, along with the keyboard shortcut for each one.

You'll learn all about these tools as you go through this book, but for now, let's move on to exploring the next area.

3. Using the Playback Controls

The playback controls are located between the canvas and the timeline. They are depicted in the image below.

01_04.png - Camtasia's playback controls.

The most important icon is the play button identified by the arrow in the above image.

1. Click the play button to start playing the video.

Your project starts playing immediately, and the button turns into a pause button. Meanwhile, the playhead starts moving along the timeline.

2. Click the same button again (now the *Pause* button) to pause the video.

The playhead stops on the timeline, and the image on which it stopped freezes on the canvas. The playhead is the vertical bar that crosses the timeline from top to bottom, topped by a triangle, which itself has a green rectangle on the left and a red rectangle on the right.

Since playing and pausing are some of the most common actions you'll perform while editing videos, Camtasia provides a handy keyboard shortcut to instantly play and pause your video.

3. Press the `spacebar` on your keyboard to resume playing the video.
4. Press the `spacebar` again to pause the video.

This is my personal favorite for playing and pausing videos in Camtasia.

These few simple steps clearly demonstrate the importance of the playhead. It is your primary tool for navigating the project. You use it to select a specific moment in the timeline and to determine the image that is visible on the canvas. To work efficiently, it is crucial to always be aware of the playhead's position and to be able to move it with ease.

5. Click anywhere within the ruler along which the playhead moves.

This brings the playhead to the place you clicked. Moving the playhead in this way allows you to jump very quickly from one point to another within your project.

6. Place the mouse pointer on the triangle atop the playhead.
7. Click and drag to move the playhead with the mouse.

This second method allows you to quickly navigate forward or backward in your video.

You can also use the icons on either side of the *Play/Pause* button.

8. Use the two icons on the left side of the play button to move the playhead one frame at a time in either direction. This is the most precise way to move the playhead.
9. Use the two icons on the right side of the play button to navigate between the media items present on the timeline.

You can also use the progress bar located to the right of the playback controls to move the playhead within the project.

10. Click anywhere within the progress bar to move the playhead to that specific location.
11. You can also drag the progress handle with the mouse to scrub through the timeline.

The exact position of the playhead is indicated by a *timecode* displayed right next to it, as shown in the screenshot below.

01_05.png - The timecode marks the exact position of the playhead.

The timecode is expressed in *hours:minutes:seconds;frames*. The timecode shown in the above image indicates that the playhead is positioned on the 18th frame of the 46th second of the project.

The playhead is one of the most widely used tools in Camtasia. For now, it indicates your exact position and lets you select a specific moment in your video.

4. Getting Started With the Timeline

The timeline takes up the lower portion of the screen. While the canvas lets you arrange elements in space, the timeline lets you arrange them in time.

The timeline is divided into tracks, which are layered on top of each other. In this example, there are four tracks on which the elements of the project have been arranged, as shown in the screenshot below.

01_06.png - The timeline for this project contains four tracks.

The timeline has its own zoom feature, which allows you to control how much of the project you see.

1. Increase and decrease the zoom level of the timeline using the slider identified by number 1 in the above image.

There are other methods for adjusting the zoom level of the timeline. Here is the one I use most often:

2. Position the mouse pointer anywhere over the timeline.
3. Hold down the **`Ctrl`** (Windows) or **`Cmd`** (Mac) key of the keyboard and use the mouse wheel to change the zoom level of the timeline.

The timeline allows for an unlimited number of tracks, and it's not unusual to see six, seven, or even more tracks for more complex projects. In such a case, you can use the vertical zoom feature to adjust the height of the tracks on the timeline.

4. Use the small handle identified by number 2 in the previous screenshot to adjust the height of the tracks on the timeline.

You can also adjust the height of the timeline panel itself by following the steps below.

5. Position the mouse over the line between the canvas and the playback controls (Windows) or over the line between the playback controls and the timeline (Mac).
6. When the mouse pointer turns into a double arrow, click and drag up or down to adjust the height of the timeline.

Instead of increasing the height of the timeline (which reduces the space available to the canvas), it is also possible to detach the timeline.

7. Navigate to the **View > Timeline** menu.
8. Take some time to inspect the available commands and their associated keyboard shortcuts.
9. Click **Detach Timeline**.

Just like when you detached the canvas earlier in this chapter, the Camtasia interface is now split into two separate windows. One window displays the timeline, while the other contains the rest of the interface. If you use multiple monitors, you can position the timeline on one monitor and the rest of the interface on another, which is particularly useful when working on complex productions involving a large number of tracks.

10. To revert to the initial view, click the **View > Timeline > Attach Timeline** menu item.

The timeline is one of the most important areas in Camtasia. Throughout this book, you'll have plenty of opportunities to explore its features in detail. But for now, it's time to move on to the next area.

5. Working With the Properties Panel

The *Properties* panel is located on the right side of the screen. Just like the tool panels mentioned earlier, it can be opened or closed.

1. Click the **Properties** button located at the far right of the playback controls several times to open and close the Properties panel.
2. You can also use the `Ctrl + 2` (Windows) or `Cmd + 2` (Mac) keyboard shortcut or the **View > Show/Hide Properties** menu item to toggle the Properties panel on or off.
3. Ensure the Properties panel is visible before continuing with this exercise.

The Properties panel displays the properties of the currently selected object. If nothing is selected, the panel remains empty.

4. In **Track 1** of the timeline, click the item named **02_02_cover** to select it.

Now that you have an active selection, the Properties panel is no longer empty and displays the properties of the **02_02_cover** object. The name of the object is displayed at the top of the panel, as shown in the following screenshot.

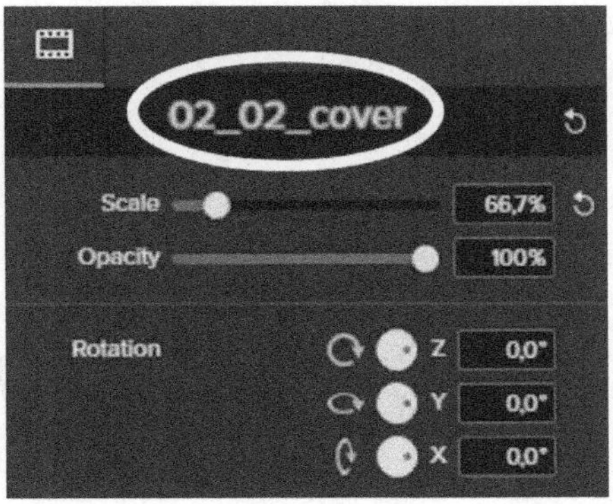

01_07.png - The name of the selected object is displayed at the top of the Properties panel.

The **02_02_cover** item is a still *.jpg* image that is also visible in the *Media Bin* on the left-hand side of the screen.

5. Take a moment to examine the properties available in the Properties panel, but do not change their values.
6. On track 2 of the timeline, click the **02_02_damien** item to select it.

This item is a video sequence recorded in a studio against a green backdrop. Note that the Properties panel now displays the properties of the selected video clip. Since it includes both an audio and a video stream, the Properties panel has two tabs, as shown in the following image.

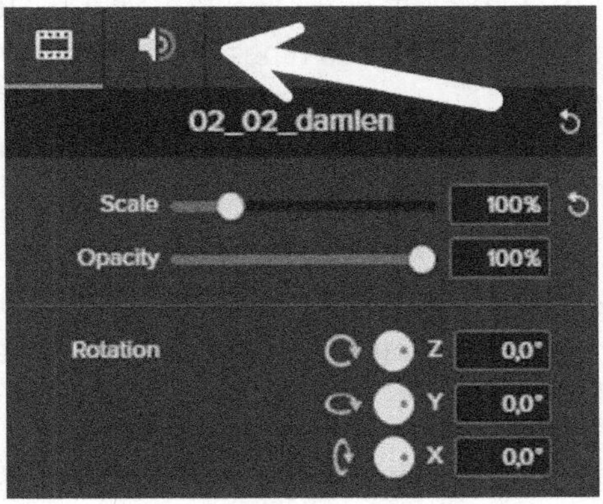

01_08.png – The Properties panel now features two separate tabs.

By default, the *Visual Properties* tab is enabled. It allows you to adjust the properties of the video stream, such as its size, opacity, and rotation.

Two visual effects have already been applied to this video clip: the **Remove a Color** effect and the **Background Removal** effect. You can see the properties of these two effects in the lower section of the Properties panel.

7. Take a moment to inspect the properties currently available in the Properties panel. You may have to scroll down to access the properties associated with the two visual effects.
8. Click the speaker icon at the top of the Properties panel to switch to the audio tab.

The Properties panel now displays properties specific to the audio stream of the selected clip. Two audio effects have been applied: the **Audio Compression** effect and the **AI Noise Removal** effect. The parameters of these two effects are visible in the lower section of the Properties panel.

9. Feel free to select the other elements visible on the timeline to inspect their respective properties.

After completing these few simple steps, you now have a basic understanding of how the Properties panel works. Throughout the rest of this book, you will have plenty of opportunities to explore the properties of each object type in greater detail. For now, just remember that the Properties panel is a *dynamic* panel, meaning it displays the properties of whatever object is selected.

E. Conclusion

At the end of this first chapter, you should have a basic understanding of what Camtasia is and of the various types of projects it allows you to create.

First, you watched the videos that you will reproduce step by step over the course of this book.

Next, you got a general overview of the production process, which always begins with a pre-production step whose duration, complexity and level of detail vary greatly depending on the video you want to create.

To finish off, you explored the five main areas of the Camtasia interface: the *Canvas*, the *Tool Panels*, the *Playback Controls*, the *Timeline*, and the *Properties panel*.

In the next chapter, you will produce your first video using Camtasia Rev, an easy-to-use workflow designed to speed up the production of simple videos.

A First Video With Camtasia Rev

Although Camtasia offers features similar to those found in high-end video editing software, not every project requires complex animations and effects. Sometimes, all you need is to quickly produce a simple, short video with professional-quality audio and visuals. This is where Camtasia Rev comes in.

Camtasia Rev offers a streamlined production workflow, ideal for creating short communication, demonstration or instructional videos on a tight schedule.

This is what you will explore in this chapter. To do so, you will revisit the four steps of the typical video production process as described in the previous chapter, starting with pre-production.

A. Pre-production

The video you will create in this chapter demonstrates how to log in and out of the platform. It is based on a screen recording that also includes the trainer's face, captured with a webcam. Feel free to review the final version of this video one more time to refresh your memory.

1. Open the ***Chapter01/01_01_loginLogout.mp4*** file in the default media player installed on your computer.
2. Watch the entire sequence.

Pre-production for this video has already been completed; all you need to do is review the pre-production documents to prepare for the recording.

1. Explore the Example Application

The dummy training course you are about to develop teaches users how to use a fictional data analysis platform. You will now explore the sample application you'll use for your recordings by completing the following steps:

1. Download and unzip the ***platform.zip*** file.
2. Double click the ***platform/index.html*** file to open it in your default web browser.
3. Make up any username and password and click **Login** (these credentials are not verified on this fictional platform).
4. Take a moment to explore the dashboard. Click the icons to hide, show, and expand / collapse each chart.
5. Click the **Data** link in the main navigation bar and wait for some data to appear on the screen. This is randomly generated data that is refreshed each time the page reloads.
6. Click the icon in the upper right-hand corner of the screen.
7. In the menu that opens, select **My Account**.
8. Fill out the form and click **Save**. A confirmation message appears in the top right corner of the form.
9. Click the icon in the upper right corner of the interface again and explore the remaining options in the menu.
10. Close the browser window when you are done exploring the platform.
11. In preparation for the upcoming recording work, open the ***reset.html*** file from the ***platform*** folder of the exercises.

Now that you are comfortable with the platform, it is time to take a look at the scenario for the first video you will record.

2. Review the Scenario

When preparing for this video tutorial, we created a scenario detailing the actions to be captured and the narration to be recorded. You will now review this scenario, using the following steps.

1. Download and unzip the exercises for ***Chapter02***.
2. Open the ***Chapter02/01_01_loginLogout_scenario.pdf*** file in the default PDF reader installed on your computer.

This document contains a two-column table. The first column contains the narration, or voice-over, that you will read aloud when recording the video. The second column describes the corresponding actions.

You will now practice this scenario until you have a firm grasp on all its aspects.

3. Open the ***platform/index.html*** file in your web browser.
4. Read the narration in the first column aloud while performing the actions described in the second column on the platform open in your browser.

As you are rehearsing the scenario, ensure everything works as expected. After all, you don't want to compromise your recording with incorrectly configured parameters or to capture unexpected error messages. These checks and rehearsals are essential to the success of your recording and should be considered part of your standard workflow.

5. Feel free to rehearse this scenario as many times as needed until you feel comfortable with both the narration and the actions. This will make the actual filming much easier.

Although this scenario is fairly simple, the importance of the preparation phase should be obvious. Beyond guiding the recording process, the scenario also serves as an excellent communication tool between you, your team, and your customer. It is easy for everyone involved to comment on and revise the script using the standard commenting and revision tools available in Microsoft Word or Adobe Acrobat. On the other hand, making changes to a video that has already been recorded often requires re-recording it, and let's face it, no one wants to do that.

The bottom line is simple: there's no reason to skip the preparation step, even for very short and simple videos.

B. Recording

Once the scenario has been finalized, approved, and tested, you can move on to the recording step. In this example, the recording can be carried out entirely using the tools available in Camtasia. This is what you will explore in this section.

1. A First Look at Camtasia Recorder

Most of the time, the raw footage used in your videos, known in the industry as *rushes*, is created outside of the video editing application. This footage may consist of recordings made in a studio or outdoors. It may also include animated sequences produced with specialized animation software or screencasts captured using a dedicated screen capture tool. This raw material is then imported into the video editing application for the post-production step.

You can use Camtasia in this way. You can import footage created outside of the software into Camtasia and use it just as you would with any other video editing application. But Camtasia comes with its own recording tool, which lets you capture *and* edit your footage without ever leaving the application. This is a major difference that sets Camtasia apart from most other video editing software packages.

This built-in recorder is simply called *Camtasia Recorder*. This is what you will discover using the following steps.

1. Open the ***platform/index.html*** file in your web browser.
2. Maximize your browser window.
3. Open Camtasia.
4. Once you are on the welcome screen, click **New Recording**.

This opens Camtasia Recorder, as shown in the following screenshot.

02_01.png –Camtasia Recorder.

For this first exploration, you will simply configure Camtasia Recorder for the video to be recorded in this chapter.

*On Windows, Camtasia Recorder opens as a separate application with a red icon on the taskbar. You therefore have two applications: **Camtasia Recorder** (red icon) and **Camtasia Editor** (green icon). On Mac, however, Camtasia Recorder does not add any additional icons to the dock.*

Camtasia Recorder has four main areas, labeled 1 to 4 in the above image.

The first section, identified by the number 1, relates to screen recording. For this exercise, this section must be enabled.

5. If necessary, turn screen recording on using the toggle button in the first section of Camtasia Recorder.
6. Open the dropdown menu next to this toggle button, then select your screen from the **Full Screen** section of the menu. If you have multiple monitors, select the one displaying the platform you wish to capture.

This action is depicted in the image below.

*02_02.png - Turn screen recording on and choose the **Full Screen** mode.*

The second section of Camtasia Recorder is for your webcam.

7. Make sure webcam recording is enabled in the second section of Camtasia Recorder.
8. If you have multiple webcams, open the dropdown menu and select the webcam you want to use for this recording.
9. Use the preview image as a guide to adjust the position of the webcam.

This exercise also requires recording the narration as defined in the scenario. This is the purpose of the third section of Camtasia Recorder.

10. Make sure you have a working microphone available; the built-in microphone of your computer will do just fine for this first approach.
11. Ensure that audio recording is enabled with the toggle button in the third area of Camtasia Recorder set to green.
12. If you have multiple microphones or audio interfaces, use the corresponding dropdown menu to select the microphone you want to use for this recording.

13. Speak into the selected microphone and check that the green meter moves accordingly.

If you do not see the audio modulating, double check that the correct microphone is selected and that it is working properly. This visual indicator is also useful for adjusting the recording level.

The last area of Camtasia Recorder relates to *System Audio*. These are the sound effects coming from your computer, such as the alert sound you hear when you receive an email. For this exercise, you do not need to record System Audio.

14. Disable recording **System Audio** by toggling the button in the fourth area of Camtasia Recorder to the gray position.

Before you start recording, there is one last option to check out. This is the toggle button in the lower right corner of Camtasia Recorder. This button enables or disables *Camtasia Rev*, the simplified workflow discussed in this chapter.

15. Ensure that **Camtasia Rev** is enabled, with the toggle button in the lower-right corner of Camtasia Recorder set to the green position.

After following these steps, Camtasia Recorder should be configured as shown in the following image.

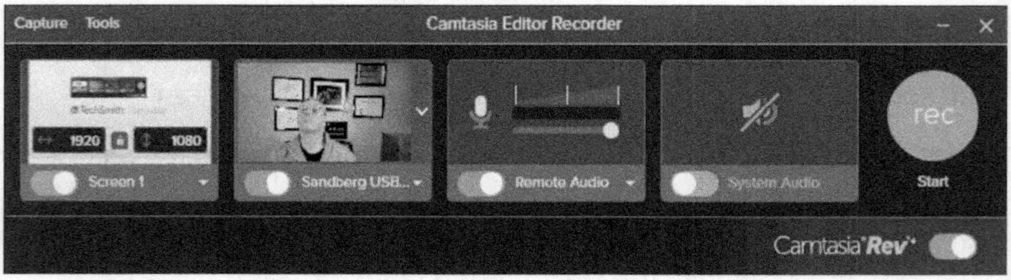

02_03.png - Camtasia Recorder is configured for the recording of your first video.

With Camtasia Recorder properly configured, you can now proceed to the recording step.

2. Recording Your Video

On paper, recording a video tutorial with Camtasia is a breeze. All you have to do is start the recording, complete the actions on screen while delivering the narration, and stop the recording once you're done. In practice, however, things aren't always that simple.

Recording a tutorial is no easy feat. Coordinating step-by-step actions with flawless narration, all while dealing with technical constraints, leaves plenty of room for things to go wrong. It's very likely that you'll have to do several takes before getting it right!

Rest assured that this is completely normal. It is even an integral part of the learning process in which you have embarked!

1. When ready, click the red button on the far right of Camtasia Recorder to start the recording.
2. After a brief three-second countdown, the recording starts.

If you work on Windows, a floating toolbar allows you to control Camtasia Recorder during the recording.

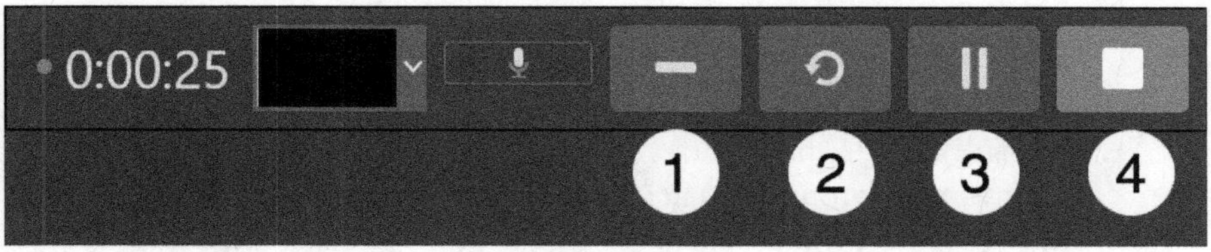

02_04.png - The Camtasia Recorder toolbar (Windows only).

Camtasia *ignores this toolbar during the recording*, so it can remain visible on the screen during the filming. However, any mouse movements you make to move it around or to click its buttons are recorded.

If you work on a Mac, look at the menu bar for an icon that looks like a piece of film strip. Clicking this icon reveals the **Stop Recording**, **Start Recording** and **Start Over** options.

3. After the recording has started, perform the actions described in the script while reading the narration aloud.
4. When done, click **Stop** on the Camtasia Recorder toolbar, identified by the number 4 in the above image. On a Mac, click the red icon in the menu bar and select **Stop Recording**.
5. Within moments, your project automatically opens in Camtasia Rev.

This is how it works if you get it right on the first take, but chances are you won't!

1. Restart the Recording

Errors, stuttering, stammering, or even unexpected external noises can all lead to a failed take. This is nothing to worry about! It's just another day in the life of a video content creator, no matter how experienced you are.

My personal best is around 75 takes before getting the right one! Sure, it was the end of the day, I was tired, and I absolutely had to finish the project! In short, you're not alone!

The creators of Camtasia, themselves content creators, have integrated this reality into the normal recording workflow. If you realize mid-take that it's not going to be the right one, here's what to do.

1. Click the curved arrow icon marked with the number 2 in the previous image. On a Mac, select **Start Over** in the aforementioned icon.
2. Click **Delete** (Windows) or **Start Over** (Mac) to confirm that you want to abandon the current recording.
3. If necessary, navigate back to the login screen of the platform to prepare for the next take.
4. Maximize your chances of success by making the necessary changes to your work environment, such as closing windows, disabling notifications, or putting your phone on silent mode. You can also adjust the Camtasia Recorder configuration if needed.
5. Start recording a new take.

Repeat this process until you get a take you're happy with. Only then can you move on to post-production. But first, here are some tips and tricks to help you nail your first recording.

2. Tips and Tricks for a Successful Recording

If you didn't get it right on the first take, you are in good company! I've been there too, and that's how I slowly figured out what works and what doesn't. Here are some of the strategies I use to maximize my chances of success.

- Take the necessary time to rehearse the scenario multiple times before attempting a first take. The better you master the narration and actions to be recorded, the greater your chances of success, and the more natural your narration will sound.
- If you have multiple screens, position the scenario on one while recording on the other. If this is not possible, consider printing the scenario and taping it to the edge of your screen. There are also many smartphone

and tablet apps you can use to automatically scroll through the scenario during the recording.

- Try placing the scenario somewhere behind the webcam, so that your gaze remains more or less aligned with the camera as you read the lines.
- Reduce external noise sources as much as possible. For example, close all doors and windows during the entire recording session.
- Similarly, close all unnecessary applications, especially your messaging apps, to minimize the risk of unwanted notifications.
- Remember to put your phone on silent mode during the recording.

Eventually, you will get a good enough recording fairly quickly. You can then move on to the post-production step of the process.

C. Post-production with Camtasia Rev

After completing the recording, the project automatically opens in Camtasia Rev, as shown in the image below.

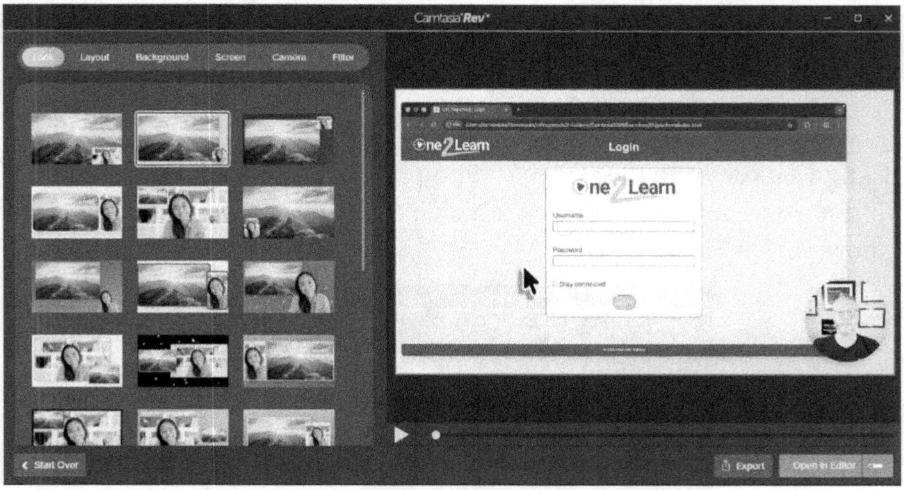

02_05.png – The Camtasia Rev interface.

This window appears because the **Camtasia Rev** switch was enabled in the lower right-hand corner of Camtasia Recorder. Had it been disabled, your recording would have opened directly in the standard Camtasia Editor.

1. Viewing the Project

To begin post-production, simply start by watching the entire video.

1. Click the Play button located below the video on the right side of Camtasia Rev.
2. Watch your video from start to finish.

The goal is to conduct a preliminary quality review to ensure that the footage matches the script, that the actions are consistent, and that the narration flows smoothly. When viewing the video for the first time, it is very common to spot subtle errors that you didn't notice during the recording. Conversely, moments that seemed awkward during the filming may end up working very well on screen.

Once you are done watching the entire video, it is time to make a decision!

- If you feel the recording is good enough, you can move on to the next step, which will be covered in the next section.
- But if you feel the recording is not as good as it should be, click **Start Over** in the lower left-hand corner of Camtasia Rev to start over.

Your efforts will eventually pay off! You will soon obtain *the* take that will get you to post-production.

2. The Camtasia Rev Wizard

Camtasia Rev simplifies video creation through a guided six-step process. These steps are visible on the left side of the Camtasia Rev interface, as shown in the image below.

02_06.png - The six steps of the Camtasia Rev wizard.

The first step is called **Look**. It lets you choose from several predefined templates, with visual effects already applied to your video.

1. If necessary, reposition the playhead (the small white dot moving under the video during playback) to the beginning, so you see the first frame of the video.
2. Click through the **Looks** available in the left panel of Camtasia Rev and choose the one you like the most.

Feel free to explore the features of Camtasia Rev by selecting whatever options you feel appropriate, even if they differ from those featured in the final video you watched at the beginning of this chapter.

Don't worry too much about the colors and animations in the background of the video. Similarly, borders, rounded corners, and other effects applied to the screen recording or to the webcam are not a concern at this stage of the process. You'll have the opportunity to customize these elements at a later stage.

3. Click the **Layout** tab to proceed to the next step of the wizard.
4. Review each of the available layouts and select the one you like the most.

Personally, I chose a layout that focuses on the screen recording rather than on the webcam.

5. Click the **Background** tab to proceed to the next step.
6. Take a moment to review the available backgrounds and choose whichever one you prefer.

Some of these backgrounds are animated, so go ahead and start playing the video to see how the chosen background changes over time.

Don't worry if none of the available backgrounds match your brand colors. Just choose the background that comes closest to what you need. You can fully customize every element, including the color palette, at a later stage.

7. Once you've made a choice, click the **Screen** tab to move on to the next step.

This tab lets you apply special effects to the *screen recording* portion of your video. Unlike the previous steps in the wizard, here you can apply multiple effects simultaneously.

Depending on the choices made previously, many of these effects have already been applied. The active effects are highlighted with a yellow border.

8. Click the available effects to turn them on or off until you find a combination that works for you.

9. You can then proceed to the **Camera** step of the wizard.

This step works in exactly the same way as the previous one, except that you apply effects to the *camera* portion of your recording.

Since the audio track of the narration is associated with the video feed of the camera, the **Camera** tab also contains the **AI Noise Removal** effect, as shown in the image below.

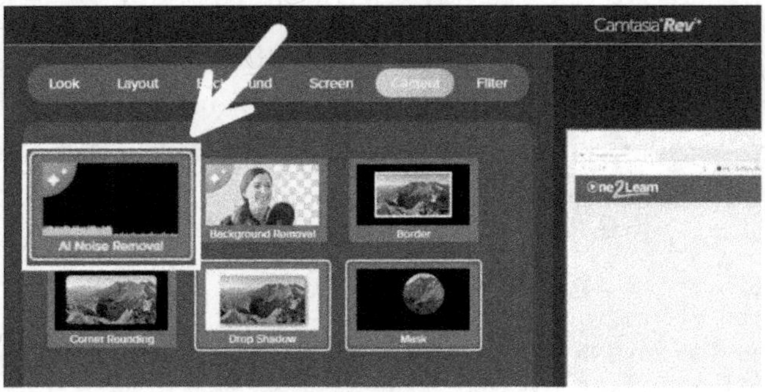

*02_07.png - The **AI Noise Removal** effect in the **Camera** tab of Camtasia Rev.*

I encourage you to always enable this effect, as it significantly improves the audio quality of your video.

10. Toggle the various effects on and off until you find a combination that works for you.
11. Proceed to the final step of the wizard by clicking the **Filter** tab.

This last step lets you apply color correction to the webcam.

12. Browse through the available filters until you find one that you like. You can also choose not to apply any filters at all and leave the webcam in its original state.

You've now reached the end of this wizard, which allowed you to complete the post-production of your video in the blink of an eye! Note that you can return to any previous step at any time and make changes. Once you're happy with the result, you can move on to the rendering phase, which is the final step in the production process.

D. Rendering

At the moment, your video only exists within Camtasia Rev. To share it with the world, you must render the project into a standalone ***.mp4*** file that you can upload to platforms (such as YouTube and Vimeo) or deploy on your LMS.

Once again, you have a choice to make.

- If you are happy with the result, you can export your video directly from Camtasia Rev.
- You can also open your project in Camtasia Editor to continue working on it.

These options can be found at the bottom of the Camtasia Rev window, as shown in the image below.

*02_08.png - **Export**, **Start Over**, or **Open In Editor**. The choice is yours!*

You will now explore each of these possibilities one by one.

1. Export an .MP4 File

First, let's assume that you're happy with the video and want to export it directly from Camtasia Rev.

1. Click **Export** in the lower right-hand corner of Camtasia Rev.
2. Select **Local File**.
3. In the window that opens, enter `01_01_loginLogout` in the **File name** field.
4. Select any folder on your computer as the **Save location**.
5. Leave all other options at their default values.
6. Click **Export**.

This process is illustrated in the image below.

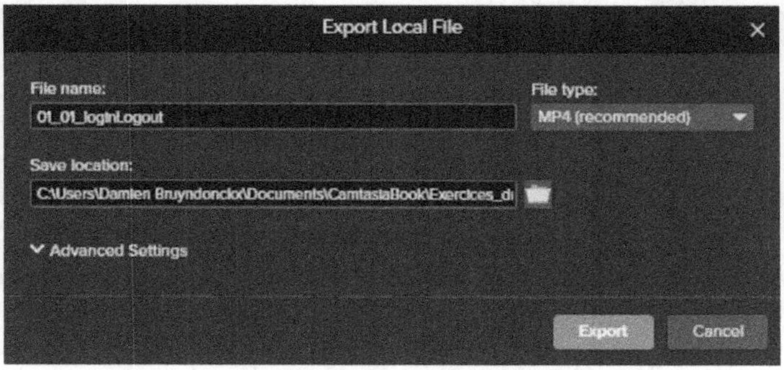

*02_09.png - Select **Local File** to generate an **.mp4** file.*

Depending on the duration and complexity of your project, as well as the processing power of your computer, the rendering step can take anywhere from a few seconds to a few minutes.

7. Once the export is complete, click the **Open File Location** (Windows) or the **Show in Finder** (Mac) button.
8. Double-click the *01_01_loginLogout.mp4* file and watch the resulting video.
9. Return to Camtasia Rev.

This is the option to use if you want to export the final video directly from Camtasia Rev. In the next section, you'll explore how to open the project in Camtasia Editor.

2. Open in Camtasia Editor

Camtasia Rev offers only a subset of the effects and tools available in Camtasia Editor. Fortunately, it's very easy to open your Camtasia Rev project in Camtasia Editor and keep working on your video using the full range of tools available.

1. Back in Camtasia Rev, click **Open in Editor** in the lower right-hand corner of the interface.

After a few moments, your project opens in Camtasia Editor, as illustrated in the following image.

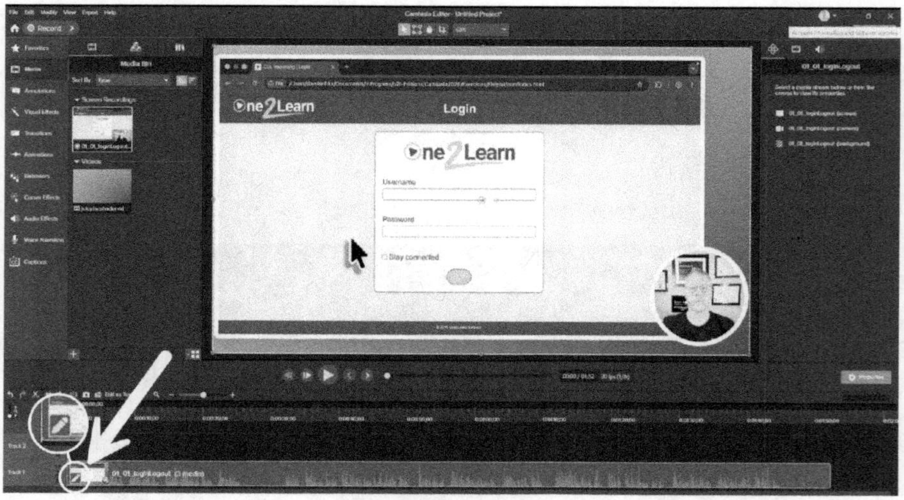

02_10.png - Your Camtasia Rev project opens in the Camtasia Editor.

In the coming chapters, you'll take an in-depth look at many of the tools available in Camtasia Editor. For now, let's focus on the options directly related to Camtasia Rev.

2. Note the presence of a single element on **Track 1** of the timeline.

One way to make changes to this video is to return to Camtasia Rev.

3. Click the pencil icon in the lower left-hand corner of the only media item visible on the timeline as shown by the arrow in the above screenshot.

This reopens the project in Camtasia Rev. It is the same Camtasia Rev you used in the previous section. Take the opportunity to return to the various tabs of the wizard and make changes to your project.

4. Click **Save** or **Cancel** in the lower right-hand corner of Camtasia Rev to return to Camtasia Editor.

Be aware that the ability to click the pencil icon and return to Camtasia Rev is only available for projects originally created using Camtasia Rev.

Also, don't let the simple look of the timeline mislead you. The element you see on Track 1 is actually a composite of three distinct sources: the screen capture, the webcam recording (which includes the audio), and the background you selected in Camtasia Rev. While they appear as a single unit on the timeline, you can view and adjust these elements individually using the Properties panel on the right.

5. Click the media item on **Track 1** of the timeline to select it.
6. If necessary, open the Properties panel on the right side of the interface.

As shown in the following screenshot, the three components embedded in the Rev media element are listed in the Properties panel.

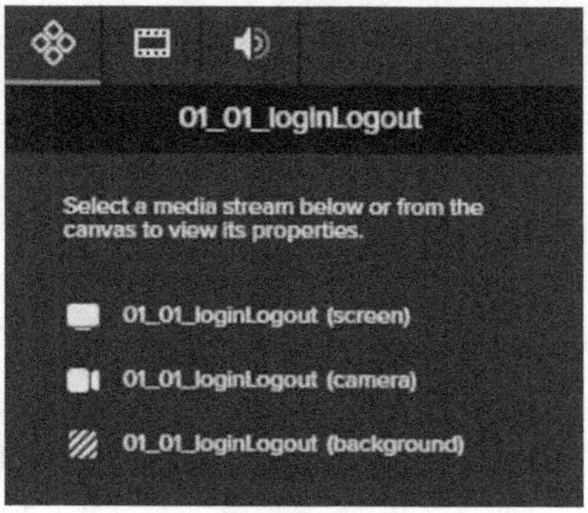

01_11.png - The three components of the Rev project are visible in the Properties panel.

This allows you to access each element independently in order to view and adjust its properties.

7. In the Properties panel, click the third element to open the properties of the **background**.
8. If necessary, adjust these properties (including the colors) in the Properties panel.

To revert to the general properties of the Rev Media element, all you need to do is reselect it in the timeline.

9. Click anywhere on the timeline to deselect the currently selected item.
10. Click the Rev media element on Track 1 to reselect it.

Once the Rev element is reselected, its properties reappear in the Properties panel on the right side of the screen.

Another way to access the individual elements of this project is to unpack the Rev Media element.

11. Right-click the Rev media on **Track 1** of the timeline.
12. In the menu that opens, select **Unpack Rev Media**.

This action unpacks the Rev item and distributes its components across the tracks of the timeline, as shown in the image below.

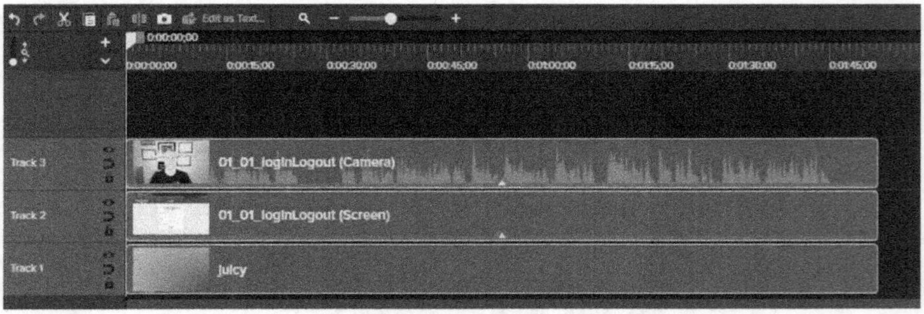

02_12.png - The three components of the Rev media are distributed across the tracks in the timeline.

After unpacking the Rev media, you can select each individual element and arrange them as you wish on the timeline.

Note that this action cannot be undone. After doing this, you will no longer be able to combine these elements into a single Rev media or return to Camtasia Rev to make further changes to this project.

3. Saving the Project

You could have saved your project directly from Camtasia Rev, but since you opened it in Camtasia Editor, this option is no longer available. You will, therefore, use the standard saving process.

1. Open the **File > Save As** menu.
2. Navigate to the ***Chapter02*** folder of the exercises.
3. Type `01_01_loginLogout` as the file name.
4. Leave the other options at their default values.
5. Click **Save**.

This process is depicted in the image below.

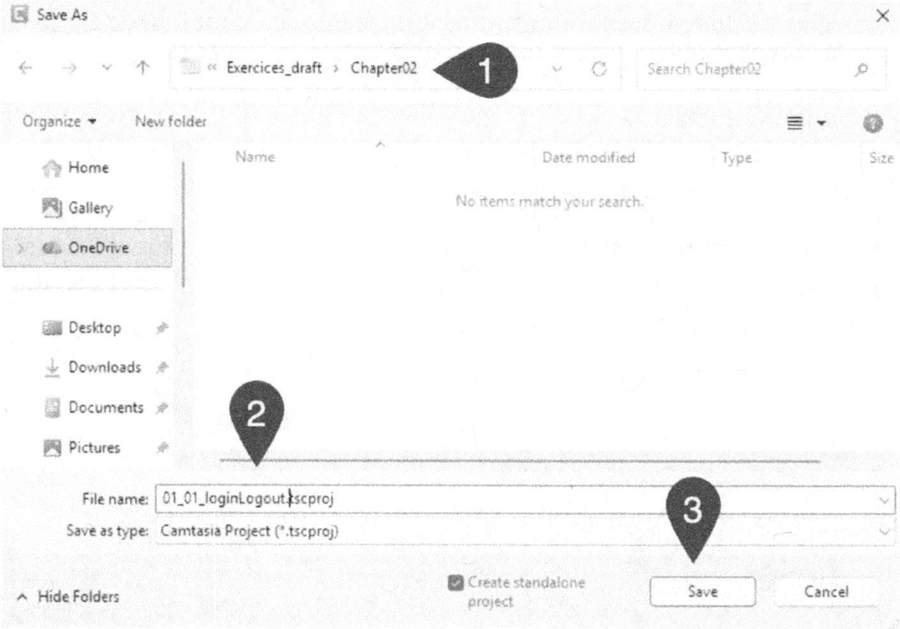

*02_13.png - Leave all the options at their default values and click **Save**.*

In Chapter 3 – Creating a New Project, you'll explore all the methods available in Camtasia for saving your projects, as well as all the options available in this dialog box. For now, just keep in mind that the file extension used to save your project depends on your operating system.

- On Windows, you have created a file with the ***.tscproj*** extension.
- On Mac, you have created a file with the ***.cmproj*** extension.

Your project is now saved, and you can easily reopen it to continue post-production later.

E. Conclusion

Your project isn't quite ready yet; there's still some work left to do before it looks like the result you saw at the beginning of this chapter. For example, you need to add the opening and closing sequences, incorporate branding, and add subtitles. You'll learn how to make these changes as you progress through the next few chapters.

That said, the progress made with Camtasia Rev in this chapter alone is impressive. In fact, you've managed to give your video a near-final look quickly, easily, and with minimal effort.

In many cases, this result is perfectly fine and can be shared as is. Some examples include internal communication videos, content for social media, or educational resources created by teachers for their students.

Although Camtasia Rev is perfectly suited for these specific use cases, it is not designed for every type of video production. As a result, you often need to use many tools that are not available in Camtasia Rev.

You will spend the rest of this book exploring these additional features, starting in the next chapter with a detailed overview of the options available when creating a new project.

Creating a New Project

As a video editing tool, Camtasia's primary purpose is to let you combine various multimedia sources into a single video. These sources encompass a wide range of multimedia content, such as studio and on-location recordings, stock footage, still images, audio tracks, and more. In the video and film industry, these sources are called *rushes*. These *rushes* serve as the raw material for the projects you'll create with Camtasia.

When kicking off a new project, start by importing these *rushes* into Camtasia. Editing can only begin once these assets are available in the Media Bin of the project.

This is what you will learn in this chapter. You will explore the options available when creating a new project and then import the necessary footage.

But first, you need to thoroughly understand two key principles that govern the way Camtasia works: *non-destructive editing* and *linked files*. These two concepts, and the choices they imply, have a significant impact on how you manage your files and how much disk space your projects use.

A. The Non-destructive Editing Principle.

Camtasia follows the *non-destructive editing* principle, which means it treats your raw footage, or *rushes*, as protected assets that can never be modified or overwritten.

1. Exploring the Non-destructive Editing Concept

The aim of this section is to introduce you to the principle of non-destructive editing, a key concept central to most video editing software, including Camtasia. To help you understand this concept, you will import a video into Camtasia and trim out the unnecessary parts. This will also serve as your first steps into video editing.

1. Download and unzip the exercises for Chapter03.
2. Use the File Explorer (Windows) or the Finder (Mac) to navigate to the ***Chapter03/resources*** folder of the exercises.
3. Right-click the ***nonDestructive.mp4*** file.
4. Click **Properties** (Windows) or **Get Info** (Mac) to view the file properties.

This action is depicted in the image below.

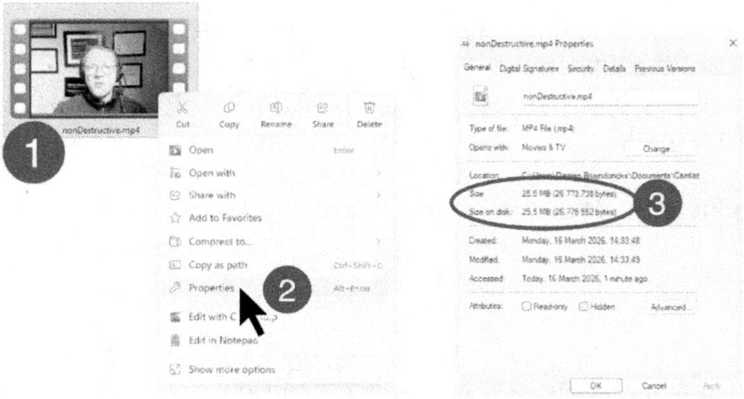

03_01.png - Viewing the properties of a file on Windows.

Note the size of this file (around 25 MB). This is the file you will import into Camtasia for editing.

5. Open Camtasia.
6. Once on the Welcome screen, click **New Project**.
7. Open the **File > Import > Media** menu item.
8. Navigate to the ***Chapter03/resources*** folder and import the ***nonDestructive.mp4*** file into the project.

This action opens the **Media Bin** panel on the left-hand side of the screen, where you can see a thumbnail for the video you just imported. You will now place this video clip on the timeline.

9. In the **Media Bin**, right-click the ***nonDestructive.mp4*** file.
10. Select **Add to Timeline at Playhead**.

This places the video on **Track 1** of the timeline at the playhead position, that is, at the beginning of the project.

11. Use the **View > Timeline > Zoom to Fit** menu item to optimize the zoom level of the timeline.
12. Click the play button located between the canvas and the timeline or press the `spacebar` to start playing the video.

The relevant content in this video starts approximately 16 seconds in and ends around the 30-second mark. Therefore, you need to trim the beginning and end of this video to keep only the useful content.

13. Position the playhead around the 16-second mark in the timeline, which is where the actual content of the video begins.

Use the waveform that appears in the timeline to determine the exact position at which to place the playhead. The waveform represents the variations in audio volume throughout the video, as shown in the image below.

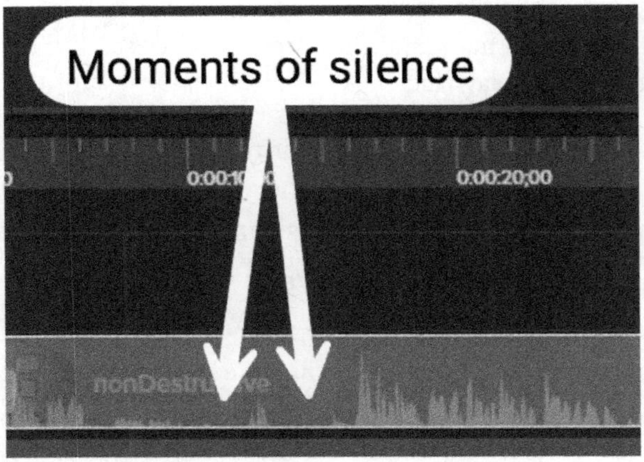

03_02.png - Use the waveform to locate the silent sections.

The higher the peaks of the waveform, the louder the sound. Conversely, flat sections indicate silence. These are often perfect moments to cut your video clip.

14. In the timeline, click the video clip to select it. Camtasia highlights it with a thin yellow border to indicate it is selected.
15. Hover your mouse over the left edge of the video clip until the mouse pointer changes to a double-headed horizontal arrow.
16. Click and drag the start of the video clip to the right up to the current position of the playhead.

This operation is illustrated in the image below.

03_03.png - Click and drag the beginning of the video clip to the current position of the playhead.

By doing so, you have adjusted the start of the video. You will now do the same thing at the end.

17. In the timeline, position the playhead around the 30-second mark in a silent section.
18. Hover your mouse over the right edge of the video clip until the pointer changes to a double arrow.
19. Click and drag the end of the video clip towards the left to the current position of the playhead.

After making these two adjustments, only the desired section of the video remains on the timeline. However, there is now a 16-second gap at the beginning of the project. To fix this, simply drag the entire video clip to the left to place it at the very beginning of the timeline.

20. Position the mouse pointer over the video clip in the timeline.
21. Drag the entire clip to the left and place it at the beginning of the project, removing the 16-second gap.
22. Use the **View > Timeline > Zoom to fit** menu item to adjust the zoom level again. You can also use the **`Ctrl+Shift+7`** (Windows) or **`Command+Shift+0`** (Mac) keyboard shortcut.

Once you've completed this final step, the project should have a duration of approximately 14 seconds, and your timeline should look similar to the following image.

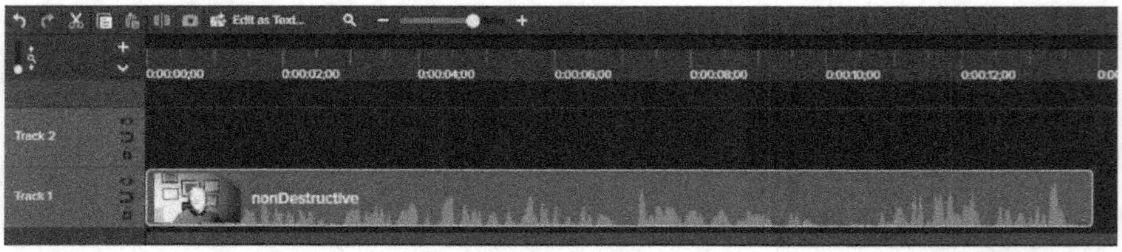

03_04.png - The timeline after trimming the beginning and end of the source video.

You can now move on to the most rewarding part of the process: enjoying the final video.

23. Position the playhead at the very beginning of the project.
24. Click play or hit the `spacebar` to start playback.

Congratulations! You've just taken your first steps into the magical world of video editing. By following these few simple steps, you've successfully trimmed the beginning and end of the original clip, leaving only the relevant content on the timeline.

You will now save this project.

25. Use the **File** > **Save** menu item or the `Ctrl + S` (Windows) or `Cmd + S` (Mac) keyboard shortcut.
26. *Deselect* the **Create standalone project** checkbox. This is a very important step for the rest of this exercise!
27. Navigate to the ***Chapter03*** folder of the exercises.
28. Type `nonDestructive` in the **File name** field.
29. Click **Save**.
30. Click **OK** to dismiss the confirmation message.

Your first Camtasia project has now been saved! To better understand what *actually* happened, you will now close Camtasia and inspect the files you just created.

2. Inspecting the Generated Files

The rest of this experiment takes place in the File Explorer (Windows) or in the Finder (Mac).

1. Close Camtasia.
2. Use the File Explorer (Windows) or the Finder (Mac) to navigate to the ***Chapter03*** folder of the exercises.

There, you should find the ***nonDestructive.tscproj*** (Windows) or ***nonDestructive.cmproj*** (Mac) file generated in the previous section.

3. Right-click the ***nonDestructive.tscproj*** (Windows) or ***nonDestructive.cmproj*** (Mac) file.
4. Click **Properties** (Windows) or **Get Info** (Mac).

Notice the size of this file: it's only a few KB! That's much smaller than the original footage you imported into the project. Remember, that file was about 25 MB.

5. Navigate to the ***Chapter03/resources*** folder of the exercises and double-click the original video file (***nonDestructive.mp4***) to open it in the default video player installed on your system.

Surprise! The original file is intact! It still contains the hesitations at the beginning and the comments at the end. So, what *actually* happened when you trimmed it in Camtasia?

Since Camtasia uses *non-destructive editing*, the imported source files are always left completely untouched! So how can you *trim footage* if you can't modify the source files? Well, here's how it works.

- When you trimmed the beginning of the original video file in Camtasia, the software only took note that the source file should start playing from the 16th second. However, Camtasia did not *actually* remove the first 16 seconds of content from the ***nonDestructive.mp4*** file.
- When you trimmed the end of the original video clip, Camtasia simply took note that playback of the ***nonDestructive.mp4*** file should stop at the 30-second mark, but it did not *actually* delete any content from the original file.
- When you moved the trimmed content to the beginning of the timeline, Camtasia took note that the start of the project corresponds to the 16th second of the source file.
- Finally, when you saved the project, Camtasia saved all these notes into the *.tscproj* (Windows) or *.cmproj* (Mac) file.

This is why the file generated by Camtasia is so small. In fact, it does not contain any multimedia data. The project file only includes a list of all the edits you made in the timeline. To get the final video (*with* the cuts), you need to export the project, which will be covered in Chapter 11 – Exporting Your Videos. This will give you a second ***.mp4*** file, separate from the original raw footage, that includes all the cuts made on the timeline.

The non-destructive editing approach is highly valued by content creators because it allows them to work on a project without bearing the risk of permanent changes. This means you can freely express your creativity and safely experiment with various editing options—including different cuts, effects, transitions, and filters—while ensuring you can always revert to the original footage at any time. It's total creative freedom, with no risk!

B. Understanding the Linked Files Principle

The way Camtasia handles importing multimedia files into a project differs significantly from how applications such as Microsoft Word and PowerPoint handle it. When you import an image or a video into a Word document, the application creates a copy of that item within the ***.doc*** or ***.docx*** file. As a result, the Word document can quickly grow very large. In contrast, Camtasia only records the *location* of the imported source files without importing their content.

In short, the sources you see in the **Media Bin** are not actually *imported* into Camtasia but are merely *linked* to your project. To ensure everything works as expected, it is critical to preserve the integrity of this link throughout the entire editing process. Trivial tasks, such as renaming and moving files, can completely break your video project if they are not performed correctly and with the right tools.

1. Experimenting with Linked Files

There's nothing like a little hands-on experiment to see it for yourself.

1. Close Camtasia.
2. Use the File Explorer (Windows) or the Finder (Mac) to navigate to the ***Chapter03/resources*** folder of the exercises.
3. Rename the ***nonDestructive.mp4*** file to `nonDestructive_source.mp4`.
4. Return to the ***Chapter03*** folder and double-click the ***nonDestructive.tscproj*** (Windows) or the ***nonDestructive.cmproj*** (Mac) file to reopen the project in Camtasia.

When the project reopens, you should see an error message similar to the one pictured below (it looks slightly different on a Mac).

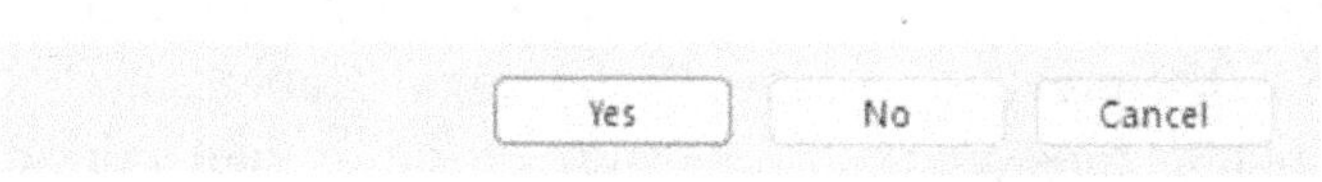

03_05.png - An error message appears when opening the project.

This message appears because Camtasia can no longer locate the source file referenced in the project. When you renamed the ***nonDestructive.mp4*** file, you broke the link between this source and the Camtasia project.

5. On Windows, click **No**, then **OK** to open Camtasia Editor despite the error. On a Mac, click **Close**.
6. Once Camtasia is open, look at the **Media Bin** and notice how the missing file is displayed.

This clearly proves that the source file was *linked* to your Camtasia project rather than *imported*. As a result, you must exercise extra caution when moving or renaming such a file.

Fortunately, the **Media Bin** has the necessary tools to re-establish the link between the project and the renamed or moved source file.

7. In the **Media Bin**, right-click the missing source.
8. Click **Update Media** in the context menu.
9. Navigate to the ***Chapter03/resources*** folder of the exercises.
10. Double-click the ***nonDestructive_source.mp4*** file to restore the link between the file and the Camtasia project.
11. Use the `Ctrl + S` (Windows) or `Cmd + S` (Mac) keyboard shortcut to save the Camtasia project.

The Media Bin also provides a tool to help you *locate* a source file.

12. In the **Media Bin**, right-click the ***nonDestructive_source.mp4*** file once again.
13. In the context menu, click **Open File Location** (Windows) or **Reveal in Finder** (Mac).

This action opens the File Explorer (Windows) or the Finder (Mac) to the location of the selected media file. This feature is very useful for checking on the location of your files or for finding files you may have misplaced.

Thanks to these few simple steps, you should have a better understanding of how important it is to carefully manage the source files imported into the project.

2. Creating a Standalone Project

Every professional video editing application adopts the linked file principle discussed in the previous section. Professional graphics and layout applications (such as those in the Adobe suite, for example) work in the same way. In fact, only productivity applications, such as Word, Excel, and PowerPoint, effectively *embed* a full copy of the imported file.

Microsoft took this approach to ensure document portability and ease of use. But, this convenience comes at a cost in terms of disk space, because the software creates a copy of each imported file. As a result, each imported file takes up twice the disk space: once at its original location and a second time within the Office document into which it is embedded.

As for Camtasia, although it is not, strictly speaking, a consumer-grade software product, one of its main objectives is to make video editing accessible to a wide range of users, including teachers, trainers, communication professionals, and influencers. Consequently, the vast majority of Camtasia users are not video or film professionals and are therefore not necessarily familiar with the idea of linked files. For this reason, TechSmith (the company behind Camtasia) offers the option to create *standalone projects*. A *Standalone* project works in much the same way as a standard Microsoft Office file and effectively includes all imported media sources. Let's explore it in this section.

1. If necessary, reopen the ***Chapter03/nonDestructive.tscproj*** (Windows) or ***Chapter03/nonDestructive.cmproj*** (Mac) project you created in the previous section.
2. Open the **File > Save As** menu item.
3. *Select* the **Create standalone project** checkbox.
4. Navigate to the ***Chapter03*** folder of the exercises.
5. Enter `nonDestructive_standalone` in the **File name** field.
6. Click **Save**.
7. Click **OK** to close the confirmation window.
8. Close Camtasia.

Using these steps, you have created a standalone version of the project developed in the previous section. You will now review the files you just created. These files differ depending on whether you work on a Windows or Mac computer, so feel free to skip directly to the section pertaining to your operating system.

1. Examine the Standalone Project (Windows)

On Windows, you created the ***nonDestructive_standalone.tscproj*** file in the ***Chapter03*** folder of the exercises.

1. Use Windows Explorer to navigate to the ***Chapter03*** folder of the exercises.

2. Open the **View** menu of the File Explorer.
3. Select **Details** to see a more detailed view of the contents of this folder.

As shown in the following screenshot, one of the items in this folder goes by the name of ***nonDestructive_standalone.tscproj***.

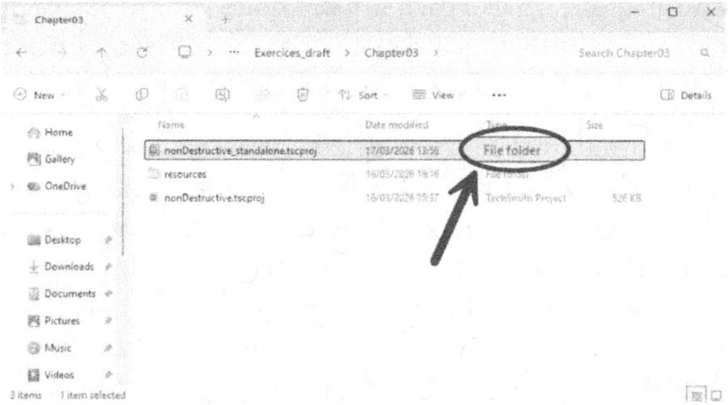

*03_06.png - One of the items is named **nonDestructive_standalone.tscproj**.*

On closer examination, it seems like Windows identifies this item as a **File folder**, rather than as an individual file, as illustrated in the above image.

4. Double-click the ***nonDestructive_standalone.tscproj*** folder to examine its contents.
5. If necessary, reapply the **Details** view to that folder.

You should find the following two items in this folder:

- The ***nonDestructive_standalone.tscproj*** item is identified by Windows as a **TechSmith Project**. It is a very small file, no bigger than a few hundred KB. This is the actual Camtasia project file. As a reminder, this file only contains information about the edits you made on the timeline.
- The ***nonDesctuctive_source.mp4*** file is a *copy* of the original video sequence, which has a size of approximately 25 MB.

On Windows, a standalone project is a *folder* containing both the Camtasia project file (with the ***.tscproj*** file extension) and *a copy* of each source file used in the project. Basically, every time you import a file into the media bin, Camtasia automatically saves a copy of that file in the standalone project folder.

This makes it easier to keep track of your raw footage and helps avoid most of the broken link issues mentioned earlier. On the other hand, it significantly increases the amount of disk space your project uses because Camtasia effectively *creates a copy* of all imported media.

2. Examine the Standalone Project (Mac)

On a Mac, you created the ***nonDestructive_standalone.cmproj*** file in the ***Chapter03*** folder of the exercises.

1. Use the Finder to navigate to the ***Chapter03*** folder of the exercises.
2. Open the **View** menu of the Finder.
3. Select **as List** to see detailed information about the contents of this folder.

One of the items in this folder is the ***nondestructive_standalone.cmproj*** file you created in the previous section. The **as List** view lets you see more information, including the file size, as shown in the image below.

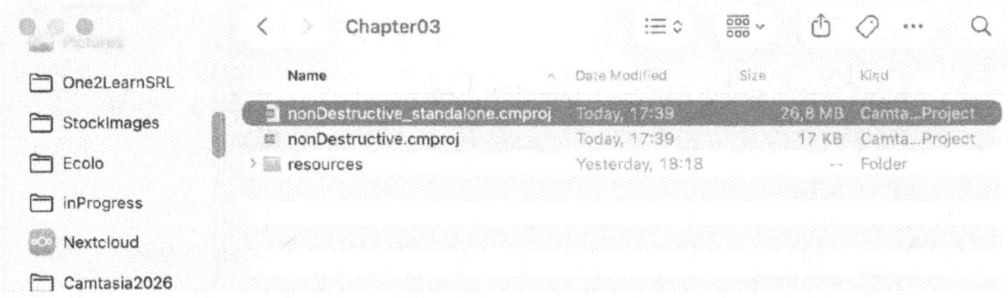

*03_07.png - The **as List** view displays the file size.*

Notice that the ***nonDestcructive.cmproj file***, created earlier in this chapter with the **Create standalone project** option *deselected*, is only a few KB in size. In contrast, the ***nonDestructive_standalone.cmproj*** file is much larger, with a file size of 26.8 MB. This is because the latter includes a copy of the original video footage in addition to the Camtasia project file.

On a Mac, a standalone project is a ***.cmproj*** file containing a copy of each source file used in the project. Basically, every time you import an item into the media bin, Camtasia automatically embeds a copy of that item in the standalone ***.cmproj*** file.

4. Still in the Finder, right-click the ***nonDestructive_standalone.cmproj*** file.
5. Click **Show Package Contents**.

This option allows you to dig into the standalone ***.cmproj*** file and view its inner contents.

- There, you should find the ***project.tscproj*** file. This is the Camtasia project file containing the list of all the edits you made on the timeline.
- You should also locate the ***media*** folder containing a copy of the original video clip.

This is illustrated in the image below.

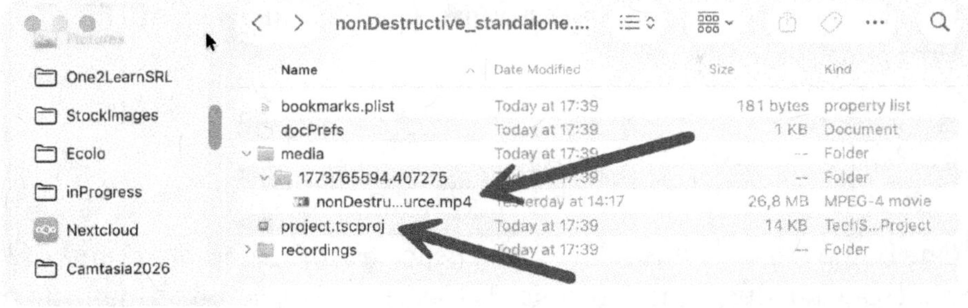

03_08.png - The contents of the ***nonDestructive_standalone.cmproj*** *file on a Mac.*

Interestingly, the ***.cmproj*** *file contains a project file in* ***.tscproj*** *format, which is the same format used on Windows. This means that Camtasia for Mac can open* ***a .tscproj*** *project file created on Windows. However, the opposite is not true. The Windows version of Camtasia cannot open a* ***.cmproj*** *project created with the Mac version.*

On a Mac, a standalone project with a ***.cmproj*** file extension works exactly like a standard Word or PowerPoint document. Since it bundles all the original source files into a single package, it's easy to move, rename, and share the project without worrying about broken links. However, keep in mind that these all-in-one files can quickly take up a lot of disk space.

C. Creating a New Project

Now that you have a better understanding of the inner workings of a Camtasia project file and what it implies for your workflow, it's time to explore the options available when creating a new project.

1. Creating the Conclusion Video Project

In this section, you will create the project file for the closing video of your online training course. You will focus solely on creating the project file and exploring its main parameters. The actual video editing work will take place later.

Before proceeding, consider reviewing the ***Chapter01/02_02_conclusion.mp4*** *video to refresh your memory.*

Follow the steps below to create the project file for this video.

1. Open Camtasia.
2. Once on the welcome screen, click **New Project**.

This action is shown in the image below.

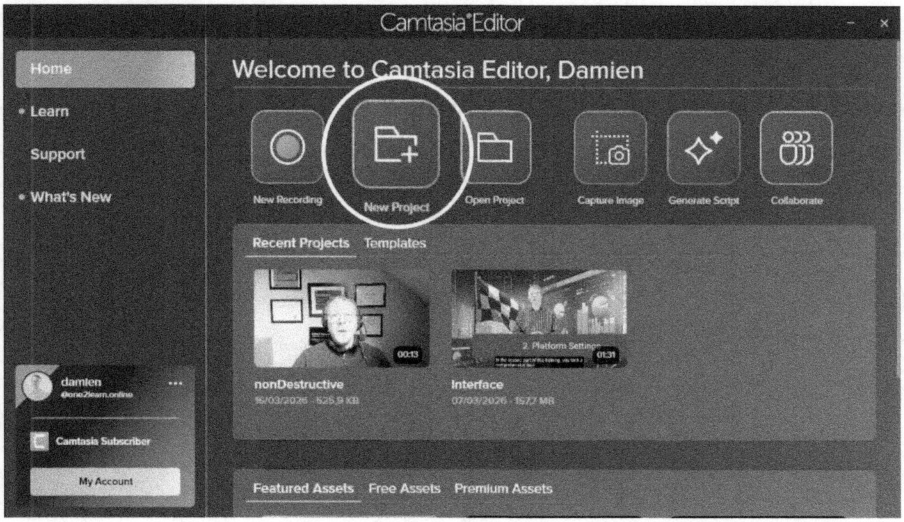

03_09.png – The Camtasia welcome screen

After a short while, Camtasia Editor opens on a blank new project. The next step is to save it.

3. Once in Camtasia Editor, go to the **File** > **Save** menu, or use the `Ctrl + S` (Windows) or `Cmd + S` (Mac) keyboard shortcut.
4. Ensure the **Create standalone project** checkbox is *selected*.
5. Navigate to the ***Chapter03*** folder of the exercises.
6. Enter `02_02_conclusion` in the **File name** field.
7. Click **Save**.

Now that the ***.tscproj*** (Windows) / ***.cmproj*** (Mac) file is properly saved, you can move on to configuring the basic settings for this new project.

1. Selecting the Canvas Size

The canvas size determines the default resolution of the video you will produce at the end of the process. Technically, Camtasia lets you create videos of any size, but in practice, you should use standardized resolutions to make sure your videos remain compatible with the most common video hosting services and streaming platforms.

In the eLearning industry, the two most common resolutions you'll encounter are as follows:

- The *Full HD* resolution (FHD or 1080p) generates a video that is 1920 pixels in width by 1080 pixels in height. This is the resolution selected by default in Camtasia.
- The *HD* resolution (720p) refers to a video that is 1,280 pixels in width by 720 pixels in height.

Both these resolutions feature a 16:9 aspect ratio. This is the most common aspect ratio for most modern computer screens, which display a rectangular image in landscape mode.

For more information about the aspect ratio concept and a list of the most common aspect ratios in use, see the following Wikipedia article: https://en.wikipedia.org/wiki/Display_aspect_ratio.

Other resolutions and aspect ratios are available for different use cases and purposes. For example, the square format (1:1) is popular on LinkedIn and Instagram, while the vertical format (9:16) is widely used on smartphones. When preparing your video project, it is therefore essential to clearly identify the distribution channels you will be using (YouTube, websites, television, social media, etc.) to make an informed decision about the resolution and aspect ratio to choose when creating the project in Camtasia.

You'll often come across buzzwords like 4K and 8K. These ultra-high resolutions are mainly used in television and film production. Since they require a massive amount of disk space, these are very rarely used for videos made for the web, unless there's a compelling reason to do so.

In this example, you will create a high-definition (HD - 1280 x 720) video. This is a standard resolution supported by virtually every modern video platform. It offers an excellent balance between the size of the exported file and the quality of the resulting video.

1. Open the dropdown menu located right above the canvas.
2. Click **Project Settings** at the bottom of the list.

This action opens the **Project Settings** dialog, as shown in the image below.

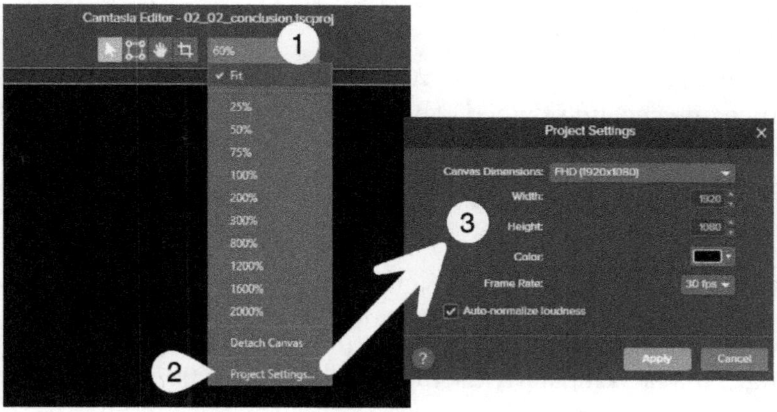

*03_10.png - Open the **Project Settings** dialog.*

Take a moment to examine the options available in this dialog box.

3. Open the **Canvas Dimensions** (Windows) / **Dimensions** (Mac) dropdown menu.

Take some time to review the available choices. Note the **Custom** option at the bottom of the list, which allows you to manually enter custom dimensions for the canvas.

4. Select **HD (1280 x 720)**.
5. Leave the box open for the next section.

You've just made a very important decision that has a significant impact on the rest of the editing process. Although Camtasia lets you change the size of the canvas whenever you want, doing so mid-project can be a real headache. If you change the dimensions of the canvas later on, you'll have to manually resize and reposition every element in the video to fit the new canvas size.

You can find further technical information about the concept of resolution under the following link: https://en.wikipedia.org/wiki/Display_resolution

2. Choosing the Background Color

The **Project Settings** dialog also lets you change the project background color, which appears when your media doesn't fully cover the canvas or during a transition between two clips.

For this example, you can keep the default color (Black). You can easily change this parameter at any time during the editing process.

3. Choosing the Frame Rate

The frame rate determines the number of individual images required to produce one second of video content. Different industries use different standards: 24 frames per second (fps) for motion pictures, and 25 or 30 fps for television. On the Internet, the standard is 30 frames per second, which is also the default value used in Camtasia.

1. Open the **Frame Rate** dropdown menu to view its contents.

A higher frame rate (50 or 60 frames per second) improves motion rendering. This is particularly useful for recording extreme sports, such as footage captured with a GoPro camera.

The frame rate also affects the timecode displayed next to the playhead, which uses the *Hour:Minute:Second;Frame* format.

The last number indicates the frame on which the playhead is located. If you work with a rate of 30 frames per second, this number ranges from 1 to 30. However, if you choose a rate of 60 frames per second, it ranges from 1 to 60.

2. Keep the default frame rate of **30 fps**.
3. Click **Apply** to confirm the changes and close the **Project Settings** dialog.
4. Use the `Ctrl + S` (Windows) or `Cmd + S` (Mac) keyboard shortcut to save the project.
5. Close Camtasia.

Because these initial choices have such a significant impact on your workflow, let's explore them in greater detail in the next section.

4. How These Choices Affect the Final Video

These choices are extremely important. They affect both the technical quality of your video and the weight of the resulting ***.mp4*** file.

A Full HD video has a resolution of 1920 pixels in width by 1080 pixels in height, which means each individual frame is made up of about 2.07 million pixels. When filming at 30 frames per second, the resulting file has to store over 62 million pixels for every second of video! If you increase the frame rate to 60 fps, the amount of pixel data per second doubles.

An HD video has a resolution of 1280 pixels by 720 pixels, for a total of 921,600 pixels per frame.

This is a huge difference! An HD video (720p) uses about 60% fewer pixels than a Full HD video (1080p). This demonstrates how significant an impact the canvas size and the frame rate have on the weight of the resulting ***.mp4*** file. If you want to reduce the size of your videos, start by carefully evaluating the canvas size and frame rate you'll use!

*This explanation has been overly simplified and is therefore not entirely accurate. The aim is to help you understand the close relationship between the dimensions of the canvas in Camtasia and the weight of the resulting video file. However, it is important to keep in mind that the size of the final **.mp4** file also depends on other factors, such as the codec, the compression level, and the bitrate.*

For more information on this important topic, I encourage you to read the following post on the official TechSmith blog: https://www.techsmith.com/blog/how-to-reduce-video-file-sizes/

2. Hands-on Exercise - Creating the Trailer Project File

Unlike the main modules of your course, the trailer is a standalone promotional video designed for social media. As such, it is the only video that will not be published on your learning management system (LMS) along with the rest of the course. As a result, it requires a different resolution and aspect ratio than the other videos.

1. Open Camtasia.
2. Once on the welcome screen, click **New Project**.
3. Open the dropdown menu located above the canvas.
4. Click **Project Settings**.
5. Open the **Canvas Dimensions** (Windows) / **Dimensions** (Mac) dropdown menu.
6. Select **Custom**.
7. Manually enter a width of `720` pixels and a height of `1280` pixels (you may have to click the padlock icon to unlock these two dimensions).
8. Leave all other options unchanged.
9. Click **Apply** to accept these changes and close the **Project Settings** dialog.
10. Use the **File > Save** menu item or the `Ctrl + S` (Windows) or `Cmd + S` (Mac) keyboard shortcut.
11. Ensure the **Create standalone project** option is *selected*.
12. Save this project in the ***Chapter03*** folder as `00_00_trailer.tscproj` (Windows) or `00_00_trailer.cmproj` (Mac).

At the end of this exercise, the Camtasia project file for the trailer is ready and has been properly saved on your computer.

D. Working With the Media Bin

Each Camtasia project has its own Media Bin located on the left side of the interface. It serves as a central repository for all the external resources used in the project. In this section, you'll discover the tools available in the Media Bin by importing the files needed to produce the trailer of your online course.

*The term **Media Bin** goes back to the old days when films were shot on celluloid and edited by hand on editing tables. The **Media Bin** refers to a basket topped with a comb onto which the editor would hang the selected shots; the rejected shots would fall into the bin to be discarded.*

1. Importing Multimedia Assets

In the previous section, you created the Camtasia project file for the trailer. It is now time to gather the multimedia content you'll need to produce this video.

1. If necessary, open the ***Chapter03/00_00_Trailer*** project in Camtasia.

*For the sake of readability, the file extension (**.tscproj** on Windows or **.cmproj** on Mac) will no longer be specified.*

2. Navigate to the **Media** section of the left toolbar.
3. Select the first tab to open the **Media Bin**.

These actions are depicted in the image below.

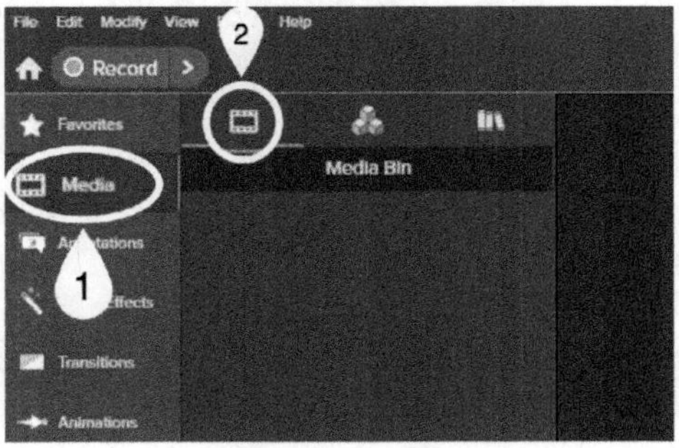

*03_11.png - Opening the project **Media Bin**.*

*To open the **Media Bin**, you can also use the **View > Tools > Media Bin** menu item or press* `B` *on your keyboard.*

With the **Media Bin** panel open in Camtasia, you are now ready to import the necessary files into the project.

4. Click **Import Media** in the middle of the **Media Bin** panel.
5. Navigate to the ***Chapter03/resources/00_00_trailer/rushes*** folder.
6. Select both files in this folder.
7. Click **Open** (Windows) or **Import** (Mac).

This action imports both video clips into the **Media Bin**, as shown in the image below.

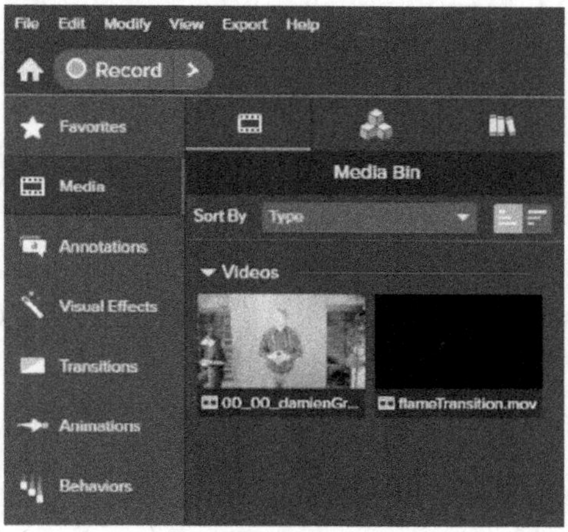

*03_12.png – This action imports two video clips into the project **Media Bin**.*

To produce this video, you also need to import a few static images. But since the media bin is no longer empty, the **Import Media** button is gone! Don't worry, there are many other ways to import things into the project. Here's one of them.

8. Click **+** in the lower left-hand corner of the **Media Bin**.
9. *[Windows only]* Click **Import Media**.
10. Navigate to the ***Chapter03/resources/00_00_trailer/images*** folder.
11. Select all the images in this folder.
12. Click the **Open** (Windows) or **Import** (Mac) button.
13. Use `Ctrl + S` (Windows) or `Cmd + S` (Mac) to save the project.

With two video clips and nine ***.png*** images, the media bin now contains everything you need to complete this project. However, you will import a few additional items in order to explore more import techniques and experiment with other tools available in the media bin.

14. Double-click an empty area within the **Media Bin** panel (i.e., outside of any existing items) to reopen the import window.
15. Navigate to the **Chapter03/resources** folder of the exercises.
16. Select the ***00_01_prerequisites.pptx*** PowerPoint file.
17. Click **Open** (Windows) or **Import** (Mac).
18. *[Mac only]* Choose to import **All** slides and click **Import**.

On a Mac, this process requires having PowerPoint installed on your computer and ensuring PowerPoint has the necessary permissions to access the ***Documents*** *folder in your user profile.*

Camtasia converts your PowerPoint slides into ***.png*** images and saves them in the **Images** section of the **Media Bin**. You can then use them in your video, just like any other static image.

The drawback of this import method is that it does not preserve the animations and transitions from the original PowerPoint file. In Chapter 04 – Recording with Camtasia, you will use Camtasia Recorder to capture all the animations and transitions of the original PowerPoint presentation.

Next, you will discover how to import a PDF file using yet another import method.

19. Use the **File > Import > Media** menu item to reopen the import window.

Note the associated keyboard shortcut: **`Ctrl + I`** on Windows or **`Cmd + I`** on the Mac.

20. Navigate to the ***Chapter03/resources*** folder of the exercises.
21. Select the ***Camtasia_Shortcuts_EN.pdf*** file.
22. Click **Open** (Windows) or **Import** (Mac).

For PDF files, Camtasia imports only the first page and converts it into a static ***.png*** image, which is made available in the **Images** section of the media bin.

You still have one more import method to explore.

23. Use the File Explorer (Windows) or the Finder (Mac) to navigate to the ***Chapter03/resources*** folder of the exercises.
24. Use the mouse to drag the ***music.mp3*** file from the File Explorer (Windows) or the Finder (Mac) and drop it directly into the **Media Bin** of your Camtasia project.

Through this exercise, you discovered different techniques for importing multimedia elements into your project. You should now have sixteen items in the **Media Bin**: two videos, one audio file, and thirteen images in ***.png*** format.

The complete list of file types and formats supported by Camtasia is available on the official TechSmith website at https://support.techsmith.com/hc/en-us/articles/360050165452-Camtasia-Editor-Supported-File-Formats-on-Windows

2. Importing From a Mobile Device

A growing number of users are now relying on their smartphones and tablets to take photos and record videos. As a result, mobile devices have become very popular tools for capturing the raw footage and still images used in Camtasia projects.

To simplify the transfer of data from your smartphone or tablet to Camtasia, TechSmith has developed a mobile app called *TechSmith Fuse*, which is available for iOS and Android.

You won't need this app for the projects featured in this book. To learn more about TechSmith Fuse and how to import media from your mobile device, please visit the TechSmith website at: https://www.techsmith.com/learn/tutorials/mobile-apps/fuse-mobile/.

3. Using the Views of the Media Bin

Throughout your career as a video editor, you will undoubtedly work on projects of varying durations and complexity. Some of these projects may require a large number of multimedia assets, all of which live in the Media Bin. This section introduces you to the tools for sorting, viewing, and efficiently managing these assets.

By default, the imported media items are shown as thumbnails and sorted by **Type** (Windows) or **Media Type** (Mac). This initial view is depicted in the following image.

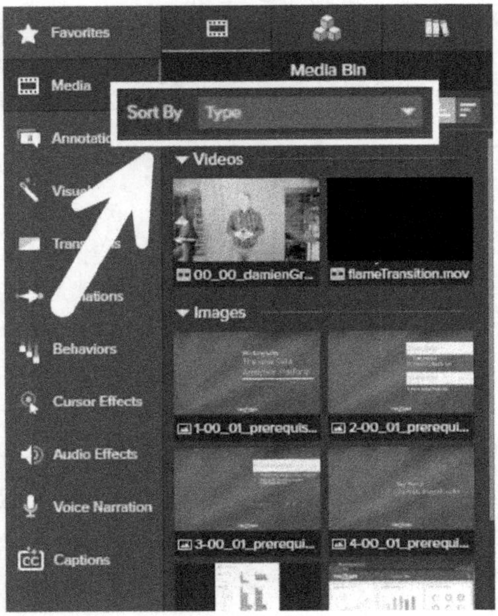

*03_13.png - By default, the items in the **Media Bin** are sorted by **Type**.*

You can use the dropdown menu at the top of the **Media Bin** to change the sorting criteria.

1. Open the **Sort By** dropdown menu, identified by an arrow in the preceding screenshot.
2. Select **Name**.
3. Use the buttons to the right of the **Sort By** dropdown to choose between ascending and descending order.
4. Take a moment to explore the other sorting options available in the menu.
5. Before continuing, revert to the default sorting (**Type** on Windows / **Media Type** on Mac).

You can also use the button in the lower right-hand corner of the Media Bin to change the view.

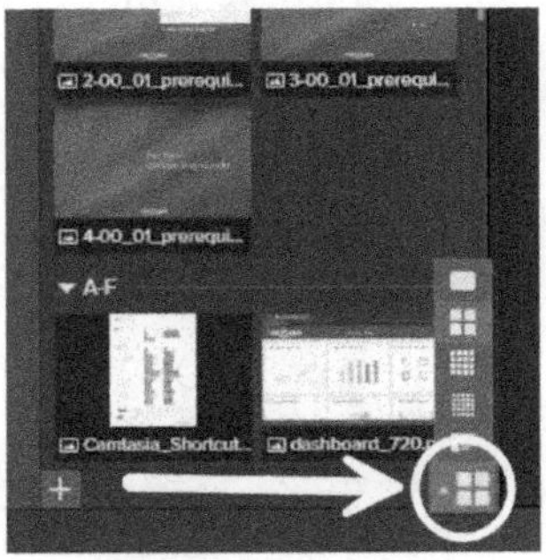

*03_14.png - This button lets you change the **Media Bin** view.*

6. Click the button in the lower right-hand corner of the **Media Bin**, identified by an arrow in the preceding screenshot.
7. Go through each of the available views one by one.

The amount of information displayed in the **Media Bin** depends on the selected view. The following image illustrates the *List* view, which displays the duration of the video and audio clips in addition to their names (it looks slightly different on a Mac).

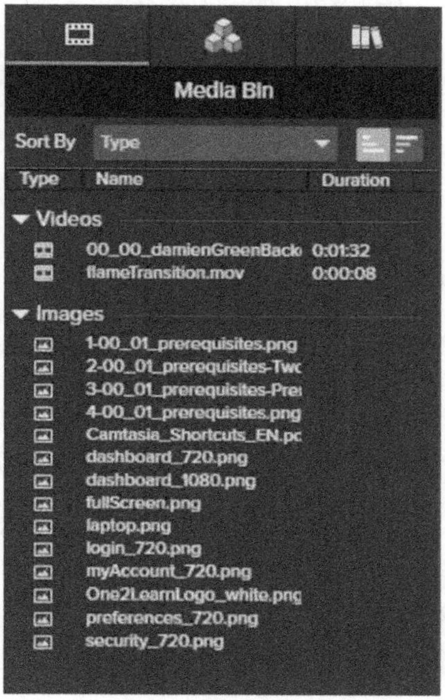

03_15.png - *The List view displays the duration of audio and video clips.*

This handful of tools will quickly become essential for those of you working on larger projects involving numerous multimedia elements.

4. Deleting Items from the Media Bin

It is common to find items in the **Media Bin** that you no longer use in your project. This usually happens when you change your mind about using certain shots or when you test different images before selecting the best one. Regularly cleaning out the **Media Bin** keeps your project tidy and makes it much easier to find the assets you *actually* use.

You will now remove the unnecessary items from this project by completing the following steps.

1. In the **Media Bin**, right-click the ***music.mp3*** audio file you imported earlier.
2. Click **Delete** in the context menu.
3. Repeat this process for the four PowerPoint slides and for the ***Camtasia_Shortcuts_EN.pdf*** file.
4. Use `Ctrl + S` (Windows) or `Cmd + S` (Mac) to save the project.
5. Close Camtasia.

After completing this process, there are eleven items left in the **Media Bin**: two videos and nine images in ***.png*** format.

*When you right-click an item in the Media Bin, notice the **Delete Unused Media** option in the context menu. This option lets you delete, with a single click, all items in the Media Bin that do not appear on the timeline. However, since the timeline of this project is still empty, this option is not applicable here.*

*If you leave the **Create standalone project** option deselected, deleting an item from the Media Bin only breaks the link between the source file and the project. It does not actually delete the media file from your computer.*

5. Hands-On Exercise – Importing Assets

Ready to put your new *Media Bin* knowledge into practice? In this hands-on exercise, you'll go back to the ***02_02_conclusion*** project and import all the multimedia files you'll use during the editing process.

1. Open Camtasia.
2. Once on the welcome screen, click **Open Project**.
3. Navigate to the ***Chapter03*** folder of the exercises.
4. Open the ***02_02_conclusion*** project you created earlier in this chapter.
5. When the project opens in Camtasia, press `B` on your keyboard to open the **Media Bin** if it is not already open.
6. Use any of the methods described earlier to import the two files found in the ***Chapter03/resources/02_02_conclusion*** folder.
7. Use the `Ctrl + S` (Windows) or `Cmd + S` (Mac) keyboard shortcut to save the Camtasia project.
8. Leave Camtasia open for the next exercise.

The **Media Bin** in the ***02_02_conclusion*** project now contains two multimedia files: an ***.mp4*** video and the ***02_02_cover.jpg*** image.

E. Archiving a Project

As discussed earlier, the raw footage and media files associated with your Camtasia projects take up a lot of disk space. Once a project is complete, it's a good idea to archive it to reclaim valuable disk space on your computer.

If you did *not* select **Create standalone project**, you must archive both the Camtasia project file (with the ***.tscproj*** (Windows) or ***.camproj*** (Mac) extension) *and* all the associated media files.

In this section, you'll learn how the built-in archiving feature in Camtasia automatically bundles your project and all associated media files into a compressed ***.zip*** archive. If you're working with standalone projects, you can also take advantage of this feature, as the ***.zip*** compression will help you save disk space.

Use the following steps to archive your project.

1. If needed, open the ***Chapter03/02_02_conclusion*** project in Camtasia.
2. Use the **File > Export > Zipped Project** (Windows) or the **File > Export > Project for Windows** (Mac) menu item.
3. Navigate to your desktop.
4. Click **Save** to export this project as ***02_02_conclusion.zip***.
5. On a Mac, click **Close** to close the confirmation message.
6. Use the File Explorer (Windows) or the Finder (Mac) to navigate to the desktop.
7. Double-click the ***.zip*** file to open it (Windows) or to unzip it (Mac) so you can view its contents.

The generated ***.zip*** file contains both a copy of the ***02_02_conclusion.tscproj*** project file (the ***.tscproj*** extension is used on both Windows and Mac) and a copy of all the original source files, as shown in the image below.

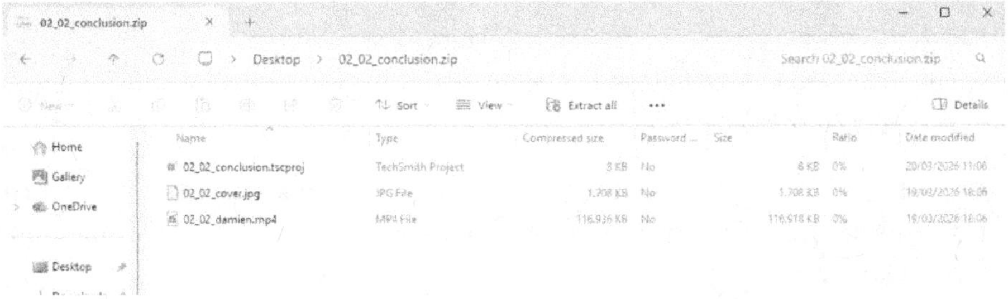

03_16.png - All the required files are part of the ***.zip*** *archive.*

Since all the data needed for your project to run properly is contained in the *.zip* file, you can safely move it to a backup disk, knowing that you haven't missed any source files along the way.

Archiving a project is only useful if you can easily restore it afterwards. Fortunately, the process of restoring a project in Camtasia is extremely simple.

8. Close any open Camtasia project.
9. Return to Camtasia and navigate to the **File > Import > Zipped Project** menu item.
10. [*Windows only*] Click the folder icon right next to the **Zipped project file to import** field.
11. Navigate to your desktop.
12. Select the *02_02_conclusion.zip* file you exported earlier.
13. Click **Open**.
14. [*Windows only*] Click the folder icon next to the **Import into project directory** field.
15. Navigate to where you want to restore the compressed project (for this example, any folder will do).
16. [*Windows only*] Click the **Select Folder** button.
17. Click **Import** (Windows) or **Save** (Mac).

After a short while, the restored project opens in Camtasia.

You can also use this process to transfer a Windows project to a Mac computer, and vice versa.

If the project uses platform-specific features, these will not be restored. When this happens, Camtasia displays a warning listing the features that are not supported on the destination system.

Take good note of this procedure for importing a compressed project, as you will use it repeatedly throughout this book.

F. Conclusion

At the beginning of this chapter, you discovered two key principles governing not only how Camtasia works, but also how most professional video editing software operates.

The *non-destructive editing* principle means that the source files imported into the project are always preserved and never altered, while the *linked files* principle means that the media files used in your video are not actually *imported* into the project but are merely *linked* to it.

Since the source media files are linked to the project rather than imported, it is critical to organize them carefully on your computer. In fact, you must always preserve the integrity of the links between the project and the media files it references to ensure it continues to run properly.

To streamline managing these media assets, Camtasia offers the option of working with *standalone projects*. Such projects actually embed a copy of your raw footage, which avoids most broken link issues. However, keep in mind that this convenience comes at a cost, as it significantly increases disk space usage. The resulting project files have a ***.tscproj*** extension on Windows or a ***.cmproj*** extension on the Mac.

You then reviewed the options available when creating a new project. This helped you understand the close relationship between the size of the canvas in Camtasia and the weight of the ***.mp4*** file you'll generate at the end of the process.

You also discovered the **Media Bin** and the tools available to help you keep track of the multimedia resources used in your projects.

Finally, you've learned how to archive and restore your Camtasia projects. This allows you to free up disk space once a project is complete, and easily share your projects with other users, including those running a different operating system.

After completing this chapter, you still have a few rushes to create before moving on to the actual editing phase. These are the screen recordings you will capture with Camtasia Recorder in the next chapter.

Recording With Camtasia

In the previous chapter, you learned how to create new projects and import multimedia assets into the Media Bin. But before you can start editing, you still need to capture a few more *rushes*.

This chapter focuses on using Camtasia Recorder to capture the necessary footage for the two screencast videos of your online course. You'll also learn how to record the PowerPoint presentation for the introduction video. This corresponds to the recording phase of the video production process described in the first chapter.

At the end of this recording phase, you'll still be a long way from the final result. Keep in mind that the editing phase will follow, which is when your project really comes together. Therefore, your goal in this chapter isn't to produce a finished masterpiece. Instead, focus on capturing enough high-quality material to ensure the success of the editing phase that follows.

With the tools discussed in this chapter, and with a bit of practice, you'll quickly take control of Camtasia Recorder to capture high-quality video tutorials.

A. Recording a PowerPoint Presentation

Recording PowerPoint presentations is a simple and effective way to create online training content. It's also a cost-effective way to turn existing training materials into e-learning content.

Camtasia offers two primary methods for transforming PowerPoint slides into video tutorials.

- As mentioned in the previous chapter, you can import a PowerPoint presentation directly into the media bin. When doing so, Camtasia converts each slide into a ***.png*** image, which can then be used in your project just like any other image. This method has the advantage of being very easy to use. However, since each slide is converted into a static image, the animations and transitions from the original PowerPoint presentation are lost.
- To preserve animations and transitions, the easiest method is to run the slideshow on your computer while recording it with Camtasia Recorder.

This section explores the second option.

These exercises require presentation software that supports ***.pptx*** *files, such as Microsoft PowerPoint, Keynote, or OpenOffice. If you don't have one of these applications, you can still read through this section to get a general idea of the workflow. The files created in this section are included in the exercise files for the following chapters, which will allow you to complete future exercises without issue.*

Before moving on, take a moment to rewatch the final video and refresh your memory.

1. Double-click the ***Chapter01/00_01_prerequisites.mp4*** file to open it in the default media player.
2. Watch the entire video.

With this video fresh in your mind, you now can move on to the next step.

1. Preparing the PowerPoint Presentation

First, let's take a look at the presentation you'll be recording.

1. Download and unzip the exercises for Chapter04.
2. Use the File Explorer (Windows) or the Finder (Mac) to navigate to the ***Chapter04/resources*** folder of the exercises.
3. Double-click the ***00_01_prerequisites.pptx*** file to open it in PowerPoint.
4. On Windows, the **Camtasia PowerPoint Add-in** window may open. If it does, click **OK** to close it.

This opens the presentation in Microsoft PowerPoint, as depicted in the image below.

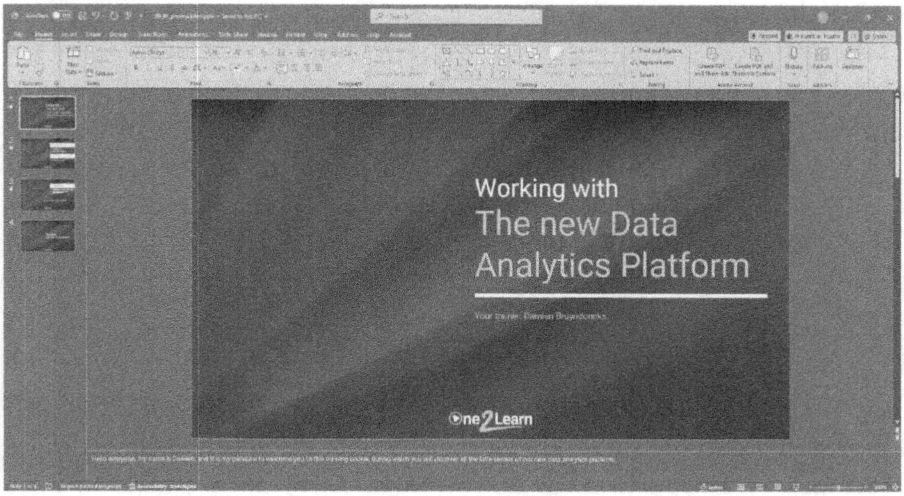

04_01.png – The presentation opens in PowerPoint.

First, notice that the left third of each slide is empty. This is where the video of the narrator will be inserted during the editing process.

This underscores, once again, the crucial importance of the preparation phase. It is essential to have a clear idea of the desired outcome before you even open Camtasia. By planning ahead, you can adapt your existing PowerPoint presentation to the video format and adjust the slide layout accordingly.

Also notice that the spoken lines have been added to the **Notes** panel of PowerPoint.

5. Play the PowerPoint slideshow from the beginning.
6. Take some time to review all four slides, paying close attention to the transitions and animations.
7. Close PowerPoint when done.

If you have two screens, read the narration aloud from one screen while viewing the slideshow on the other. As you do so, try to identify the most appropriate cue points to advance to the next animation or slide.

If you only have one screen, you cannot see the notes while the slideshow is running. In this case, you can print the PowerPoint presentation using a print layout that includes both the slides and the associated notes.

This document is available in the ***Chapter04/resources/00_01_prerequisites_notes.pdf*** *file of the exercises.*

In the upcoming exercise, you will capture both a screen recording of the PowerPoint presentation and your spoken narration. In Chapter 5 – Editing Your Video, you will substitute your voice for that of the narrator featured in the green screen video. You'll need to make a few minor adjustments to perfectly sync the narrator's voice with the animations and transitions you'll record in this section. Your voice recording will serve as a reference track to facilitate this subsequent synchronization process.

2. Using the Camtasia PowerPoint Add-in (Windows only)

On Windows, the **Camtasia PowerPoint Add-in** provides dedicated tools for recording a slideshow directly from Microsoft PowerPoint.

Installing this add-in is part of the standard Camtasia installation process if PowerPoint is installed before Camtasia.

The Camtasia PowerPoint Add-in requires PowerPoint 2013 or later and is available only on Windows. If you work on a Mac, you can skip ahead to the next section, Recording With the Camtasia Recorder (Windows and Mac).

Start by checking whether the add-in is enabled on your Windows PC. It may be missing if PowerPoint was installed after Camtasia or if a technical issue occurred during installation.

1. Open PowerPoint.
2. Once on the PowerPoint home screen, start a new **Blank Presentation**.

Depending on your settings, a welcome window may appear, and an introductory presentation may open automatically in PowerPoint.

3. If necessary, click **OK** to close the welcome window.

Look at the PowerPoint ribbon. If the add-in is installed, you should see the **Add-ins** tab.

4. Open the **Add-ins** tab in the PowerPoint ribbon.

It should contain five buttons, as shown in the screenshot below.

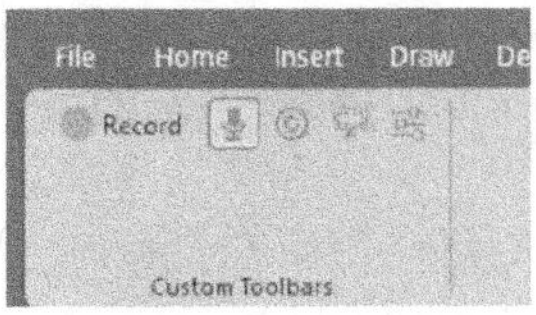

04_02.png - The tools of the Camtasia PowerPoint Add-in.

If you can see these tools in the PowerPoint ribbon, it means the add-in is properly installed and configured. You'll explore these tools in the Recording Your PowerPoint Presentation section later in this chapter.

1. Install or Repair the Camtasia PowerPoint Add-in

If the tools mentioned in the previous section are missing, it means the Camtasia PowerPoint Add-in has not been properly installed or enabled on your system.

Troubleshooting such technical issues, which often depend on a configuration specific to your computer, is beyond the scope of this book. For information on troubleshooting issues related to the Camtasia PowerPoint Add-in, please visit the official TechSmith website at: https://support.techsmith.com/hc/en-us/articles/203728428-Camtasia-PowerPoint-Add-In-Issues.

If you still have trouble installing or activating the add-in after following the instructions on the website above, the easiest workaround is to skip ahead to the Recording with Camtasia Recorder (Mac and Windows) section later in this chapter.

2. Recording your PowerPoint Presentation

With the Camtasia PowerPoint Add-in properly installed and configured, you're ready to record your slideshow directly from within PowerPoint.

1. Open the file ***Chapter04/resources/00_01_prerequisites.pptx*** from the exercises in PowerPoint.
2. If necessary, click **OK** to close the **Camtasia PowerPoint Add-in** welcome screen.
3. Open the **Add-ins** tab of the PowerPoint ribbon.

On the **Add-ins** tab, you should see five tools provided by the Camtasia PowerPoint Add-in, as shown in the screenshot below.

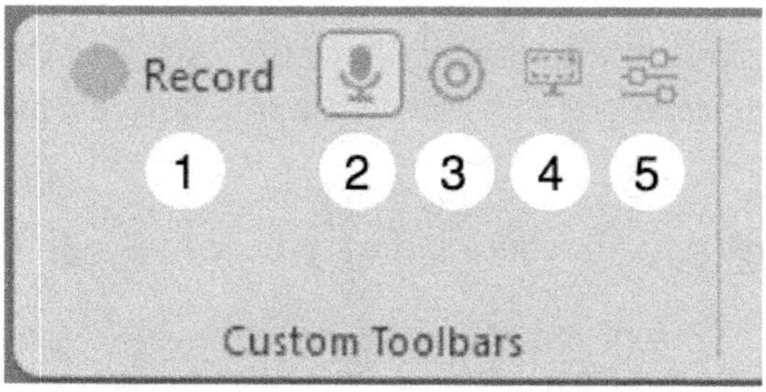

04_03.png - The tools of the Camtasia PowerPoint Add-in.

You will now configure these tools for recording your slideshow.

4. Make sure the **Record Audio** icon (identified by the number 2 in the image above) is *enabled.*
5. Icons 3 and 4 must remain disabled for this recording (they should be disabled by default).

Icon 3 activates webcam recording, which you don't need for this exercise. Icon 4 opens a preview of the camera and is irrelevant when the webcam is disabled.

6. Click icon 5 to examine the **Camtasia Add-in Options**.

This action opens the **Camtasia Add-in Options** window, as shown in the image below.

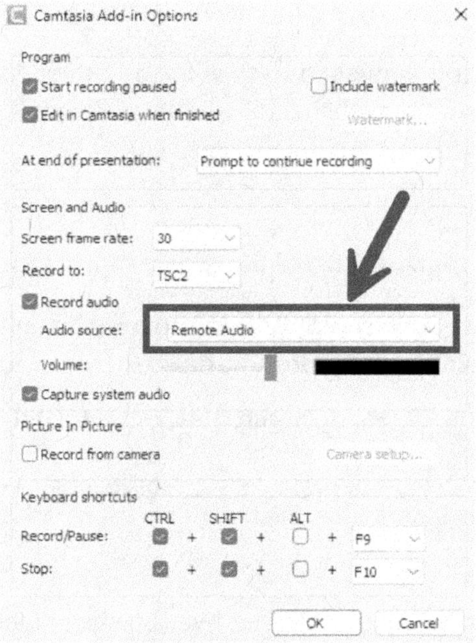

*04_04.png - The **Camtasia Add-in Options** window.*

Take the necessary time to review these options. The defaults should be fine for this exercise. Also notice the keyboard shortcuts listed at the bottom of the window.

There is just one thing to check before proceeding with the recording.

7. If you have multiple microphones available, open the **Audio Source** drop-down identified by an arrow in the above image.
8. Select the microphone you want to use for this recording.

9. Click **OK** to confirm your selection and close the **Camtasia Add-in Options** window.

The Camtasia add-in is now properly configured, and you're all set to start recording your presentation.

10. Click the **Record** button (identified by number 1 in image 04_03) to start the recording.

When clicking **Record**, the slideshow automatically starts and a small yellow status window appears in the lower right-hand corner. Be sure to remember the keyboard shortcut to stop the recording: **`Ctrl + Shift + F10`** or the **`Esc`** key.

11. Use the **Click to begin recording** button in the small yellow window to start the recording.
12. Wait until the mouse pointer and any other onscreen icons disappear.
13. Go through the slideshow while reading the narration aloud into your microphone.

Don't worry if your voice sounds hesitant or if you stumble over a word. Remember that your voice will be replaced by that of the narrator in the final video.

14. When you reach the end of the slideshow, click **Stop Recording** in the window that automatically appears in the center of the screen.
15. If you are satisfied with your recording, save it as ***Chapter04/00_01_prerequisites_ppt.trec***. If you are not satisfied, click **Cancel** and start over.
16. When you have a satisfactory take, select **Edit your recording** and click **OK**.

This last action is illustrated in the image below.

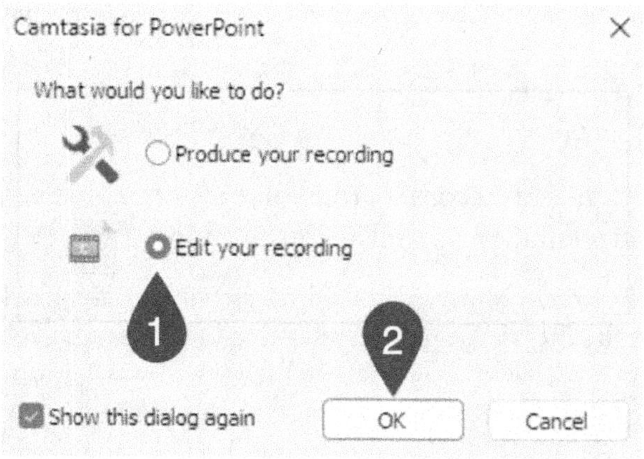

*04_05.png - Select **Edit your recording** and click **OK**.*

Within a few moments, a new project opens in Camtasia Editor, with your recording visible in the Media Bin. The only thing left to do is save the project.

17. Save this project as ***Chapter04/00_01_prerequisites.tscproj***. Be sure to select the **Create standalone project** checkbox.

Congratulations! You just completed your first screen recording with Camtasia. You also saved a new standalone project with your screen recording already imported into the media bin. This project is now ready for the editing phase, which will begin in the next chapter.

3. Recording With Camtasia Recorder (Mac and Windows)

Mac users (as well as Windows users who don't have access to the Add-in) need a different workflow for recording their PowerPoint presentations. Fortunately, the solution is quite simple. You can achieve the same result using Camtasia Recorder.

If you successfully recorded a satisfactory video using the Add-in, there's no need to complete this exercise. Feel free to skip ahead to the next section, Tips and Tricks for Recording Slideshows.

Use the steps below to record the PowerPoint presentation for your course prerequisite video.

This example uses Microsoft PowerPoint, but the process in this exercise works regardless of the presentation software being used.

1. Open the file ***Chapter04/resources/00_01_prerequisites.pptx*** in Microsoft PowerPoint.
2. Open Camtasia.
3. Once on the welcome screen, click **New Recording**.

This opens Camtasia Recorder. You will now configure it to record your PowerPoint presentation as well as the narration.

4. Enable screen recording in the first section of Camtasia Recorder.
5. Open the dropdown menu and select **Full Screen**. If you have multiple monitors, select the screen on which the PowerPoint presentation will play.

This action is illustrated in the image below, which was captured on a Mac.

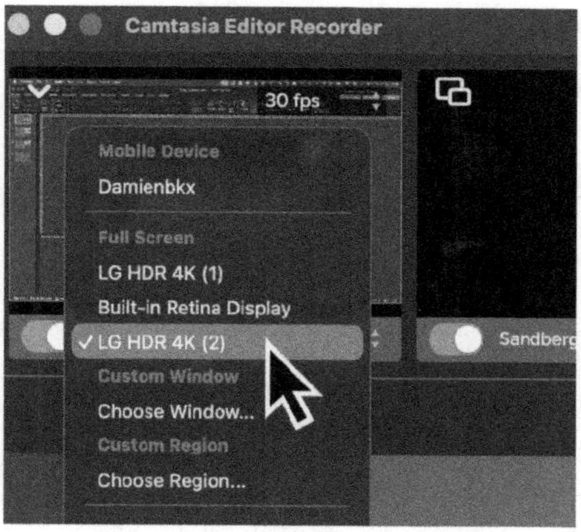

04_06.png - Enable screen recording and select the screen you want to record - Mac

Selecting this option enables full-screen recording. This is indicated by a thin green border around the selected screen.

6. In the second section of Camtasia Recorder, *disable* webcam recording.
7. In the third section of Camtasia Recorder, *enable* audio recording.
8. If you have multiple microphones, open the dropdown menu and select the microphone you want to use for this recording.
9. Speak normally into the microphone and make sure the level meter moves in response to your voice. If necessary, adjust the sensitivity of the microphone using the volume slider.

The sweet spot for the audio level sits between green and orange when talking with a normal voice. Avoid going into the red zone. Red indicates clipping, which significantly reduces the quality of the audio recording.

10. In the fourth section of Camtasia Recorder, *disable* **System Audio.**
11. Finally, make sure to *disable* **Camtasia Rev** in the lower right-hand corner of Camtasia Recorder.

Camtasia Recorder is now properly configured to record both the PowerPoint presentation and the accompanying narration, as depicted in the image below (captured on a Mac).

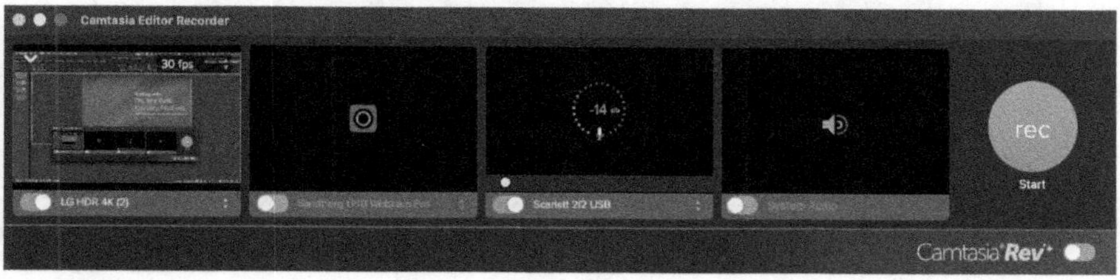

04_07.png - Camtasia Recorder is ready to record the slideshow and accompanying narration.

You are now all set for the actual recording!

12. Click the red button at the far right to start recording.

After a short countdown, the recording begins. From now on, Camtasia captures everything happening on your screen.

13. Return to PowerPoint and start the slideshow from the beginning.
14. Read the narration aloud in your microphone as you play the slideshow.

Don't worry if your voice sounds hesitant or if you stumble over a word. Remember that your voice will be replaced by that of the narrator in the final video.

15. When you reach the end of the slideshow, press the `ESC` key to return to PowerPoint.

Now you need to stop the recording. The process differs depending on whether you're on Mac or Windows.

16. On Windows, click **Stop** on the recording toolbar. On a Mac, use the keyboard shortcut `Opt + Cmd + 2` or the Camtasia icon located on the right side of the Mac menu bar.

This action is depicted in the image below, which was captured on a Mac.

04_08.png - Stop the recording on a Mac

After a short while, a new project opens in Camtasia, with your recording already imported into the media bin. The only remaining task is to save it.

17. Save this project as ***Chapter04/00_01_prerequisites***. Make sure to *select* the **Create standalone project** option.

Congratulations! You just completed your first PowerPoint recording with Camtasia Recorder. You also created a new standalone project with your screen recording already imported into the media bin. This project is now ready for the editing phase, which will begin in the next chapter.

4. Tips and Tricks for Recording Slideshows

Camtasia makes PowerPoint recordings very easy. Nevertheless, here are a few easy-to-follow tips and tricks that will increase your chances of success and improve the overall quality of your recordings.

- When recording your slideshow, you do not need to worry about the resolution of the captured video. By default, PowerPoint displays the presentation in full-screen mode and automatically scales it to fit your screen. As a result, the recorded video has the same resolution as the screen used for the capture. In most cases, this resolution is much higher than what you need. This means that, during editing, you will *reduce* the size of your recording, which will not affect the file size or the quality of the final video.
- Although the resolution of the recording is not important, the aspect ratio does require special attention. In most cases, your Camtasia project uses the standard 16:9 aspect ratio. Make sure that the screen used to capture your slideshow also uses a 16:9 ratio. If it uses a different aspect ratio, black stripes may appear either at the top and bottom or on the sides. If this happens, you may need to adjust your screen resolution before starting the capture.
- Also make sure your PowerPoint presentation uses the same aspect ratio. You can select the aspect ratio for your presentation using the **Slide Size** button located on the **Design** tab of the PowerPoint ribbon, as shown in the image below.

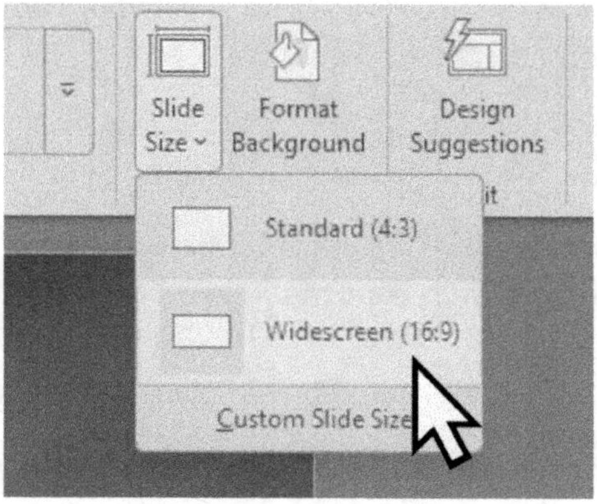

*04_09.png - Changing the **Slide Size** in PowerPoint.*

- When recording, navigate through your presentation slowly enough for Camtasia to properly capture all animations and transitions.
- There is no need to rush! Don't hesitate to pause during the recording. These pauses are very easy to spot and edit out during post-production.

With the tools presented in this section and these few practical tips, you now have everything you need to master the art of recording PowerPoint presentations with Camtasia.

B. Recording Your Screen

Recording a PowerPoint presentation is a specific type of screen recording. Most of the time, you'll be capturing a live demonstration of a software application or an online platform.

This is what you will explore in this section by recording the video of the data dashboard.

1. Use the File Explorer (Windows) or the Finder (Mac) to navigate to the ***Chapter01*** folder of the exercises.
2. As a refresher, double-click the ***01_02_dashboard.mp4*** file and watch the entire video.

You will now go through the process of recording this video. Along the way, you will discover more tools and a wealth of tips and tricks to help you speed up your workflow and improve the quality of your recordings.

1. Preparing Your Computer for Recording

Before you start, take the necessary time to get your computer ready. Doing so serves two main objectives.

- Making sure you only capture the actions you *actually* want to record.
- Making sure you capture a generic computer, not your specific computer.

With these two main objectives in mind, here are a few things you should consider reviewing before recording.

1. Rehearse the Scenario

Several weeks or even months may pass between the writing of the scenario and the actual recording. You should, therefore, take a moment to re-immerse yourself in the scenario and refresh your memory before turning the camera on.

1. Open the ***platform/index.html*** file from the exercises in your web browser.
2. Enter a username and password of your choosing. Remember that this sample application does not verify credentials.
3. Click **Login** to open the **Dashboard** page in your browser.
4. Return to the File Explorer (Windows) or to the Finder (Mac) and open the ***Chapter04/resources/01_02_dashboard_scenario.pdf*** file.
5. Read the scenario in the first column aloud while performing the actions described in the second column.
6. Once you reach the end of the scenario, click the **Dashboard** link to revert to the situation described at the beginning of the scenario.
7. Feel free to repeat these steps as many times as needed to become fully familiar with both the narration and the actions to perform.

Performing such a dry run allows you to remember the steps while making sure your hardware and software are working properly. For example, when creating a tutorial on printing a document in Microsoft Word, rehearsing the scenario provides an excellent opportunity to ensure your printer is properly configured and ready to go. Skipping the rehearsal could lead to capturing unexpected technical issues or even an error message that would force you to scrap the recording and start over.

2. Collect the Necessary Assets

If your recording requires external resources, place them in a dedicated folder on your hard drive before you start recording.

For example, imagine that you want to create a tutorial explaining how to upload an image to your website. In such a case, always select your sample image in advance. Choosing an image on the fly is risky. You might end up with an inappropriate or personal photo, infringe on someone's copyright, or pick an image that won't display properly on your site.

Before you start recording, create a shortcut to the folder containing these resources. Navigating through your folder structure during the recording makes your video unnecessarily long and could reveal confidential information (such as the name of a project or customer, or the location of sensitive files). Above all, it would reveal your lack of preparation!

3. Adjust Your Screen Resolution

When you recorded the PowerPoint presentation in the previous section, you didn't worry about the resolution of your recording. You only made sure that the aspect ratio of the presentation matched that of your screen and the final video.

On the other hand, when recording an application in full-screen mode, you almost always need to adjust your screen resolution before recording. Whenever possible, use the same resolution as the video you're creating.

If this is not possible (for example, if the desired resolution is not supported or if that resolution is too low to display the application being captured), choose the next *highest* resolution offering the same aspect ratio.

If you're using a high-pixel-density display (HiDPI or Retina Display), multiply all dimensions by two:

- Use a resolution of 2560 x 1440 to record a 720p (HD) video.
- Use a resolution of 3840 x 2160 to record a 1080p (Full HD) video.

Picking the right screen resolution is essential. If you don't, you'll often end up with screen recordings whose resolution is much too high. You'll then have to scale down the video during editing, which could make the elements in your screen recording so small that your learners will have trouble seeing or reading them.

This only applies if you are recording in full-screen mode. If you are only capturing a portion of your screen, you probably don't need to adjust the resolution before recording.

4. Anonymize Your Computer

When capturing your screen, you should capture a show-ready computer, not *your* computer. To maintain a professional and anonymous appearance, consider these essential preparation steps before you hit record.

- If your computer desktop appears in the video, consider swapping your custom wallpaper for a system default or company-approved wallpaper. This minor adjustment ensures a neutral look and feel and serves as a prime opportunity to reinforce your brand identity.
- Disable custom mouse cursors and custom sound effects.
- Remove unnecessary icons from your desktop.

On Windows, right-click the desktop and use the ***View > Show desktop icons*** *menu item to show or hide all desktop icons.*

- On Windows, if the Start menu appears in the video, remove any custom shortcuts you don't want to appear.
- Clear any unnecessary icons from the taskbar (Windows), the menu bar (Mac), and various notification areas across your system.

Never forget that your screen recording will be used to create a tutorial. This means you are in an educational context. You are the teacher (the one who knows), and the viewers of the video are your students (those who don't know yet). In this context, students often rely on visual consistency to follow along. Even minor differences between your screen and theirs can cause confusion, which often leads learners to mistakenly attribute their errors to icons and buttons that have nothing to do with the topic of the video! To help prevent this potential confusion, remove any non-essential or customized visual elements to create a clean, focused learning environment.

5. Keep Your Information Confidential

With technology at the heart of all our personal and professional activities, our computers house a critical mix of personal information, sensitive business intelligence, and critical network configurations that require the highest standards of security and confidentiality.

However, when recording a video tutorial, you aim the camera directly at your computer, potentially exposing this confidential information. Here are a few simple tips and tricks to prevent sensitive data from leaking into your recordings.

- If possible, hide any system icons, such as the network icon, during your recording.
- If you plan to capture your web browser, consider hiding your favorites and logging out of any social media accounts. Whenever possible, use an incognito window to strip away personalized data and maintain anonymity. And don't forget to install an ad blocker. The last thing you want is a competitor's pop-up stealing the spotlight in the middle of your tutorial!
- If you need to record something from a social media platform, create a profile specifically for that purpose rather than showing your own personal feed.
- Before you hit record, close any apps you won't need in your video. You might receive an email or message at any time, and the accompanying

notification could reveal private information, such as the sender's identity and the subject of the message.
- In fact, turn off all notifications to avoid any distractions.

There have been instances where cyberattacks and data breaches have been facilitated by freely available online tutorials that inadvertently exposed this type of information.

6. Conclusion

If you are new to the field, you probably won't think about these sorts of things when recording your first tutorials. However, this preparatory step is essential and often marks the difference between an amateur tutorial and a professional-quality one. The time spent setting up your computer before recording is time well spent!

Here are a few additional tips to help you with this process.

- Create a separate computer account just for recording and leave it as neutral and generic as possible. This way, you won't have to reset your personal profile every time you record.
- Another technique is to use virtualization. Virtualization enables a single physical machine to host multiple operating systems simultaneously. For example, you can run Windows on a Mac, run Linux on a PC, or even run a Windows instance within another Windows system.

To fully understand the benefits of virtualization, I recommend watching the following YouTube video: https://youtu.be/nvdnQX9UkMY.

With these few tips and tricks, your computer is now ready to take center stage in your next tutorial.

2. Exploring the Options of Camtasia Recorder

You've already used Camtasia Recorder earlier in this chapter, as well as in the previous chapter. These early experiences provided you with a general understanding of how it works but only with the default settings. This section goes beyond the basics and explores all of Camtasia Recorder's options in detail.

This is an area where the Windows and Mac versions of Camtasia differ quite significantly.

1. On a Windows PC

On Windows, Camtasia Editor and Camtasia Recorder are two separate applications. The main application is Camtasia Editor, which has a green icon, while Camtasia Recorder has a red icon.

1. Open the Windows Start menu.
2. Type `Camtasia` to search the Start menu.

The results of this search help you locate these two apps, as shown in the image below.

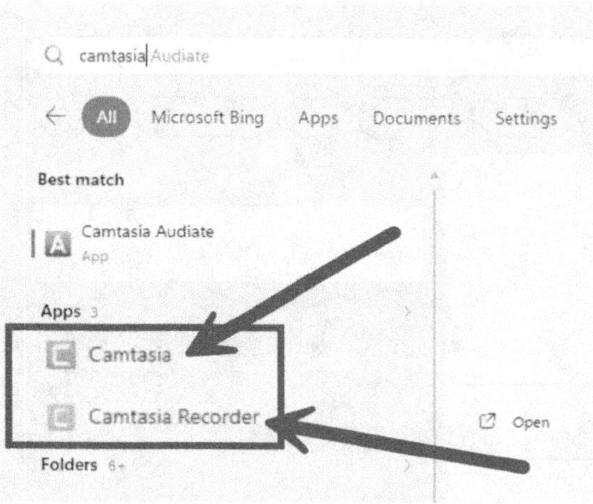

04-10.png - Camtasia and Camtasia Recorder are two separate applications in the Windows Start menu.

Only **Camtasia Recorder** is relevant for this section.

3. Click the Camtasia Recorder icon from the Windows Start menu.

As mentioned earlier, Camtasia Recorder appears as a floating panel with four main sections, as shown in the image below.

04_11.png - Camtasia Recorder on Windows.

Also notice the two menus in the upper-left corner of Camtasia Recorder.

4. Open the **Capture** menu.

The four elements in this menu simply mirror the four main areas of Camtasia Recorder, offering an alternative way to switch them on or off. Since these commands are readily accessible from the main toolbar, this menu is largely redundant and rarely used.

5. Open the **Tools > Preferences** menu item of Camtasia Recorder.

This opens the **Recorder Preferences** window, which features four tabs, as shown in the following image.

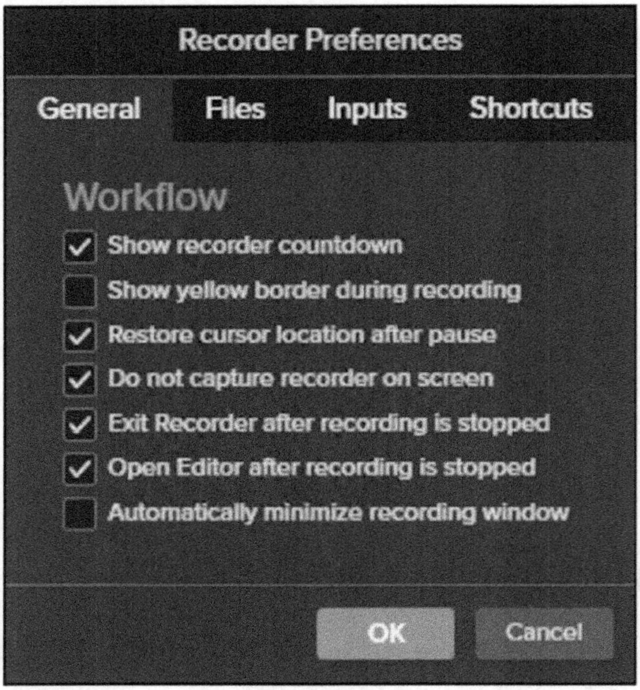

*04_12.png - The **Recorder Preferences** Window.*

While most of these options are self-explanatory, some of them require more detailed explanations.

- The **Restore cursor location after pause** option is enabled by default. It prevents sudden cursor shifts when you resume recording after a pause.
- **Do not capture recorder on screen** hides the Camtasia Recorder toolbar from the recording. This option is enabled by default. You will most likely never disable this option unless you want to create a tutorial on... using Camtasia.

You will now explore the options in the other tabs of this window.

6. Take a moment to review the other options available in the **General** tab, then move on to the **Files** tab.

The **Files** tab lets you define options for saving the captured videos. By default, Camtasia saves them to the ***Documents\Camtasia*** folder of your user profile and automatically determines the file name (based on the date and time of the recording). Enabling the **Prompt for file name** option lets you choose a custom name and destination for each recording.

7. Leave all the options on the **Files** tab at their defaults.
8. Move on to the **Inputs** tab.

The **Inputs** tab contains options related to screen and webcam recording. You likely won't need to change much here, though you might occasionally want to adjust the **Recording dimensions** of the webcam.

9. Open the **Shortcuts** tab of the **Recorder Preferences** window.

This tab lets you customize the keyboard shortcuts of Camtasia Recorder. Here are two examples of when this feature might come in handy.

- When switching from another screen recording application, you can use this tab to assign the same keyboard shortcuts as in your previous tool.
- When you need these hotkeys to interact with the application you want to capture.

Also notice the **Restore Defaults** button, which allows you to restore the original keyboard shortcuts.

10. Click **Cancel** to close the **Recorder Preferences** window without saving any changes.
11. Close Camtasia Recorder.

You now have a solid understanding of the options available in the Camtasia Recorder preferences window. The exercises and step-by-step instructions provided in this book assume you didn't change any of these options.

2. On a Mac

On a Mac, Camtasia Editor and Camtasia Recorder are a single application. Consequently, the recording options are managed directly through the main preferences window.

1. Launch Camtasia on your Mac.

2. Once on the welcome screen, open the **Camtasia** menu in the upper-left corner of the screen.
3. Click **Settings**.
4. At the top of the preferences window, open the **Recording** tab.

This opens the **Recording** Preferences window as pictured below.

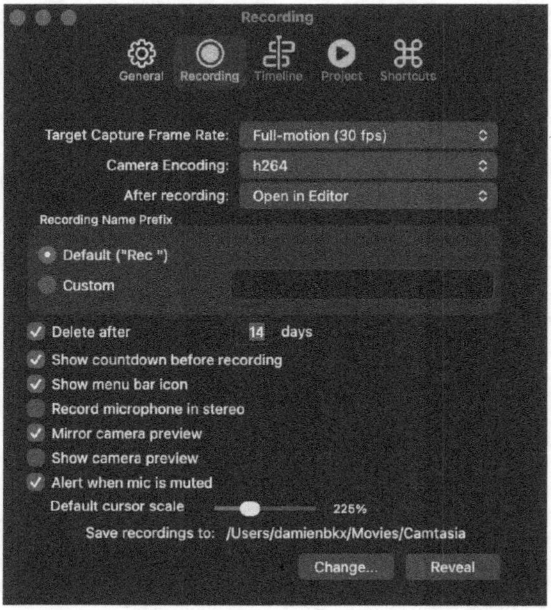

*04_13.png – The **Recording** tab of the Camtasia preferences on a Mac.*

Most of the options available in this dialog box should be self-explanatory.

5. Take a moment to review the available options.
6. Open the **After recording** dropdown and take a moment to review the options it contains.

This dropdown menu lets you choose what happens when the recording is finished. By default, Camtasia saves the file in a predefined location and opens Camtasia Editor. If you select **Prompt to Save**, you'll have to save the recording manually.

7. Turn your attention to the **Default cursor scale** option.

By default, Camtasia enlarges the mouse pointer in your recording to make it easier for your learners to spot and follow. This option lets you adjust the default magnification level for the mouse cursor.

8. Do not change any of these preferences and close the preferences window.

Most of the time, you can leave these preferences at their default values.

You now have a solid understanding of the recording options available in Camtasia for Mac. The exercises and step-by-step instructions provided in this book assume that none of them have been changed.

3. Configuring Camtasia Recorder

It is now time to get Camtasia Recorder ready to capture the data dashboard video. For this project, you need to record both the screen and the audio narration.

1. Open Camtasia.
2. Click **New Recording** to open Camtasia Recorder.
3. Enable screen recording in the first section of Camtasia Recorder.
4. Open the associated dropdown menu.

This action is illustrated in the image below.

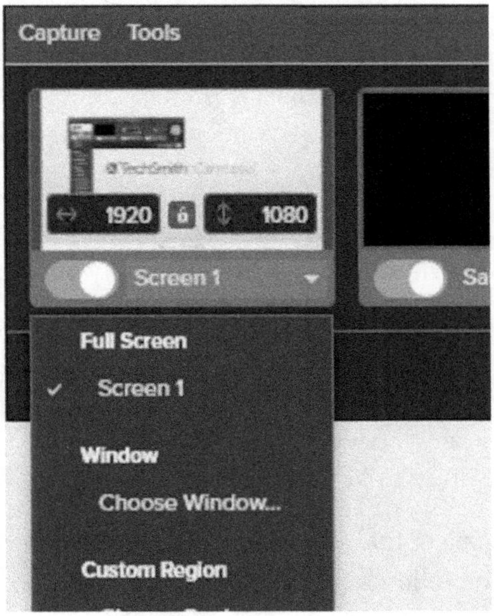

04-14.png - Open the dropdown menu of the screen capture section of Camtasia Recorder.

Your tutorial will use the standard HD resolution of 1,280 pixels wide by 720 pixels high. This resolution provides a 16:9 widescreen aspect ratio. There are a few different approaches you can take to produce this video recording.

For this exercise, we assume that your screen has a resolution of at least 1920 pixels in width by 1080 pixels in height (Full HD). This should be the case for most modern computer screens. If you have a high-pixel-density monitor (HiDPI or Retina Display), remember to multiply all resolutions by two.

A first approach is to select a capture area that is 1280 pixels wide by 720 pixels high and position the window to capture within that area.

5. Select the **HD (1280 x 720)** option (or the **QHD (2560 x 1440)** option if you have a high-density monitor).

You should now see a green rectangle that is 1280 pixels wide by 720 pixels high. This is the recording area. During the recording, Camtasia only captures whatever happens inside this rectangle, ignoring everything else.

You can easily move the green rectangle around to target the desired recording area.

6. On Windows, use the handle in the center of the green rectangle to move it around. On Mac, position the mouse pointer anywhere within the green rectangle, then click and drag to move it around.
7. [*Mac only*] Click **OK** to confirm the recording area.
8. Open the ***platform/index.html*** file from the exercises in your web browser.
9. Move and resize the browser window so that it fits *exactly* within the Camtasia recording area.

At this point, you will notice the main drawback of this approach: it is very difficult to position the browser window *exactly* within the capture area. Fortunately, there are other approaches to investigate.

10. Reopen the dropdown menu associated with the first area of Camtasia Recorder.
11. Select **Choose Window**.
12. Select the window you want to capture and click **OK**.

For this exercise, select the window displaying the data analysis platform, as illustrated in the following screenshot.

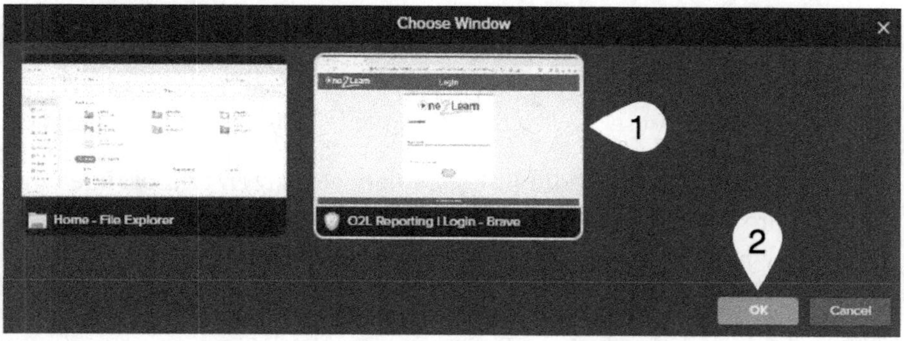

04_15.png - Select the window to capture and click ***OK****.*

When you do this, Camtasia automatically snaps the capture area to the selected window. The downside of this approach is that you lose control over the *exact* dimensions of the capture area, which no longer matches the resolution of the video you want to produce.

A third option is to adjust the resolution of your monitor to the resolution of the video being recorded (1280 x 720). The advantage of this method is that you can record full-screen and obtain a recording of the correct dimensions right away. However, if you decide to zoom in on this footage during editing, a high zoom level will likely result in a pixelated image.

For this exercise, you will adopt a fourth approach. The idea is to record a video that is slightly larger than needed, but with the same aspect ratio (16:9). In this example, you will adjust your screen resolution to Full HD (1920 x 1080) and record in full-screen mode. Since the captured footage will be larger than the Camtasia project, you'll need to scale it down to fit the canvas. The advantage of this method is that it provides headroom for zooming in on your footage. You can zoom in on specific areas during editing without worrying about your image getting pixelated. While the interface may sometimes appear slightly smaller, the improvement in visual quality during close-ups makes this a worthwhile trade-off.

Use the following steps to implement this solution.

13. If necessary, use the tools in your operating system (Mac or Windows) to adjust your screen resolution to 1920 x 1080 (Full HD).
14. Maximize your browser window.
15. Return to Camtasia Recorder and select to record **Full Screen**.
16. *Disable* webcam recording in the second section of Camtasia Recorder.
17. *Enable* audio recording in the third section of Camtasia Recorder.

18. If you have multiple microphones, select the one you want to use from the associated dropdown list.
19. Speak normally and confirm that the level indicator is moving.
20. If necessary, use the slider to adjust the sensitivity of the microphone.

The sweet spot for the audio level sits between green and orange when talking with a normal voice. Avoid going into the red zone. Red indicates clipping, which significantly reduces the quality of the audio recording.

21. *Disable* **System Audio** in the fourth section of Camtasia Recorder.
22. Finally, be sure to *disable* **Camtasia Rev** in the lower right-hand corner of the Camtasia Recorder window.

Camtasia Recorder is now configured as depicted in the image below.

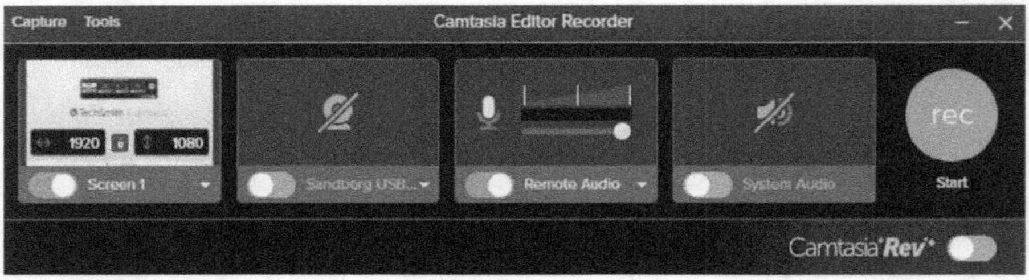

04_16.png - Camtasia Recorder is ready to record your tutorial.

Everything is ready! It's time for you to try a first take.

4. Your First Take

In the previous sections, you've prepared your computer, rehearsed the script, and configured Camtasia Recorder. The time has come to hit *Record* and try a first take.

1. Ensure the **Dashboard** page of the platform is open and that the browser window is in full-screen mode.
2. Click **Rec** at the far right of Camtasia Recorder. After a three-second count-down, the recording begins.
3. Perform the steps outlined in the scenario while reading the corresponding narration aloud.
4. Once the scenario is complete, stop the recording.
5. After a short while, Camtasia generates a new project with your recording already visible on the timeline.
6. Save it as a standalone project under ***Chapter04/01_02_dashboard.***

Don't worry if you do not nail it on the first try; most people don't! Repeat this procedure as many times as needed to obtain the desired take and proceed to the editing phase.

Remember that the goal is to set yourself up for a successful editing process. So don't worry too much about getting a perfect recording; instead, focus on creating high-quality content. During editing, it's easy to remove minor vocal hesitations or overly long pauses. On the other hand, technical issues, typos, or omitted steps are harder to fix and usually warrant a new take.

Back in Camtasia Editor, the first thing to do is watch the entire recording.

7. Click the play button between the canvas and the timeline to start playing the video.
8. Watch your recording from start to finish.
9. Leave the project open for the next section.

After this initial quality assessment, you may realize that you need a new take. Sometimes, it's only when reviewing the raw footage that you notice a problem you missed during the recording.

5. Adjusting the Dimensions of the Screen Recording

In the previous section, you recorded your screen in Full HD (1920 x 1080), but the final output should be in HD (1280 x 720). In this section, you will adjust the canvas size and rescale the screen recording accordingly.

1. If necessary, open the ***Chapter04/01_02_Dashboard*** project generated in the previous section.
2. Open the zoom dropdown menu atop the canvas and select **Project Settings** at the end of the menu.
3. Open the **Canvas Dimensions** (Windows) or the **Dimensions** (Mac) dropdown and select **HD (1280 x 720)**.
4. Click **Apply**.

This adjustment shrinks the canvas but not the screen recording already on the timeline. For now, the screen recording is much larger than the canvas, as shown in the image below.

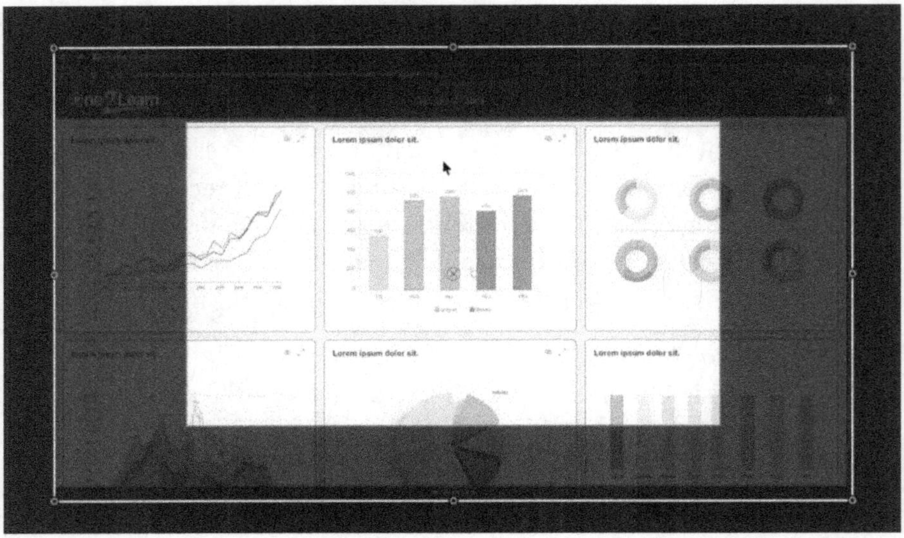

04_17.png – The screen recording is much larger than the canvas.

You will now fit the screen recording into the new canvas.

5. Make sure the screen recording is selected (it is outlined with a thin yellow border in the timeline).
6. If necessary, reduce the zoom level of the canvas to see the resize handles around the screen recording.
7. Use the resize handles to fit the recording into the canvas.

Since the canvas and the screen recording share the same aspect ratio, the recording fits perfectly into the new canvas.

8. Save the project and close Camtasia.

The project is now properly sized and ready for the editing stage, which begins in the next chapter.

6. Tips and Tricks for Successful Screen Captures

Perfect first takes are the exception, not the rule! Here are a few tips and tricks to streamline your process, minimize retakes, and improve the overall quality of your screencasts.

➢ When you start recording, wait an additional three seconds after the Camtasia countdown before you begin, then wait another three seconds once the scenario is complete before stopping the recording. These two pauses will allow you to trim the start and end with great precision during editing.

- If you make a mistake or stumble over a word, you don't necessarily need to start the recording all over again. Just pause for about three seconds before resuming at the beginning of the sentence where you made the mistake. These three-second pauses are very easy to spot and edit out during post-production.
- While recording, move the mouse *only* to perform the actions specified in the script, and take the shortest path between point A and point B. For example, avoid using the mouse to gesture or circle items on the screen. Instead, you will leverage Camtasia's effects and annotations to highlight key elements more effectively during editing.
- Pauses and silences are effortless to remove in post-production. So feel free to stop and refocus as often as you need to. For example, if you need to turn a page in the script, pause for three seconds, turn the page, then wait another three seconds before continuing. These pauses will be edited out, and your page turn will go completely unnoticed in the final video.

With these simple tips and a bit of practice, you'll soon capture the perfect take for a top-quality tutorial.

7. Hands-on Exercise: Recording a Second Tutorial.

You get the idea: it's through practice that you'll master this process and produce recordings of increasingly higher quality. In this section, you will apply this workflow to a second tutorial. This one presents the options for customizing the data analytics platform.

First, take a moment to review the final video to refresh your memory.

1. Double-click the ***Chapter01/01_03_settings.mp4*** file of the exercises to open the video in the default media player.
2. Watch the entire video.

Now that you have a clear idea of the final result, let's proceed with the screen recording for this video.

3. If necessary, adjust your screen resolution to **1920 x 1080** (Full HD).
4. Open the dashboard page of the platform and put your browser in full-screen mode.
5. Open the ***Chapter04/resources/01_03_settings_scenario.pdf*** file.
6. Practice the scenario as many times as needed.
7. Between each rehearsal, remember to open the ***platform/reset.html*** file to reset the platform.

8. Once you are comfortable with the scenario, configure Camtasia Recorder to record in full-screen mode, with audio narration. There is no need to record the webcam or system audio.
9. Disable Camtasia Rev.
10. Click the red button to start recording.
11. Record as many takes as necessary until you have one that meets your expectations. Don't forget to open the ***platform/reset.html*** file in your web browser between each take to reset the platform.
12. As soon as you get the desired take, save the new Camtasia project under ***Chapter04/01_03_settings***.

By the end of this section, you will have gained some hands-on experience with the screen recording process in Camtasia. You will also have two video tutorials ready for editing.

C. Understanding the .trec File Format

After completing the recording in the previous section, Camtasia automatically saved the video in a predefined location using an automatically generated file name. This warrants further investigation.

1. If necessary, open the ***Chapter04/01_03_settings*** project you created in the previous section.

*If you did not manage to get a good recording in the previous section, you can use the **Chapter04/resources/01_03_settings.tscproj/01_03_settings.tscproj** file from the exercises.*

2. In the **Media Bin**, right-click the screen recording you created in the previous section.
3. From the context menu, select **Open File Location** (Windows) or **Reveal in Finder** (Mac).

This action is depicted in the image below.

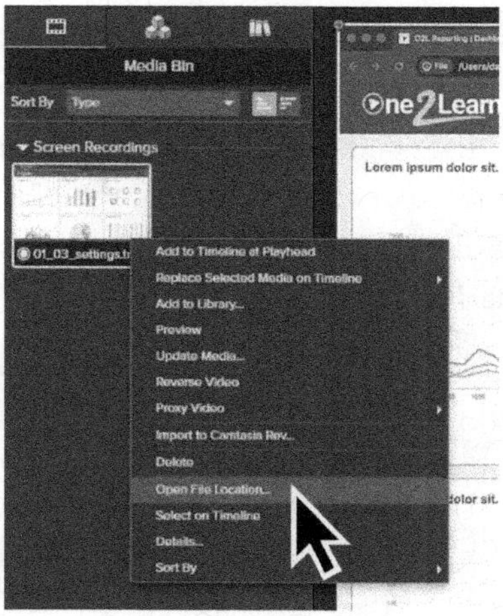

04_18.png - Click ***Open File Location*** *(Windows) or* ***Reveal in Finder*** *(Mac).*

This action opens the folder containing that file. Notice that it uses the ***.trec*** file extension, which stands for *TechSmith Recording*.

The ***.trec*** file extension is a proprietary format developed by TechSmith exclusively for Camtasia, which means it is not supported by any other video editing application.

While a ***.trec*** file stores audio and video data just like any standard ***.mp4*** file, it also captures information about mouse movements, the appearance of the pointer, and the position of the clicks. During editing, this additional metadata allows you to apply special effects to the mouse cursor, change the pointer's appearance, move click locations, and even modify the trajectory of the mouse. These features are unique to Camtasia and to the ***.trec*** format. Standard ***.mp4*** recordings made with third-party software do not include this data layer, making it impossible to use the advanced cursor tools of Camtasia.

You will learn more about these advanced cursor editing options and about the ***.trec*** file format in Chapter 7 – Focus on the Mouse Cursor.

D. Conclusion

In this chapter, you've taken a detailed look at Camtasia Recorder. On Windows, it is a standalone application identified by its red icon; whereas on the Mac, it is part of the main application. However, both platforms offer the same powerful feature set, despite some minor differences in the user interface.

You started out recording a PowerPoint presentation. On Windows, you leveraged the Camtasia PowerPoint Add-in, which is specifically designed for recording PowerPoint presentations. Mac users can achieve the same result using Camtasia Recorder.

Camtasia Recorder also lets you record your webcam, your microphone, as well as system audio, meaning any sound coming from your computer rather than from a microphone.

With the completion of this chapter, you have now completed the recording phase of the production process described in Chapter 1 – Getting Started with TechSmith Camtasia. You have all the raw footage and multimedia elements you need to start editing your videos in the next chapter.

Editing Your Video

In the previous two chapters, you gathered all the multimedia assets you need to create your videos. Whether you've imported external files into the media bin or recorded new footage using Camtasia Recorder, everything is now ready for editing.

This chapter marks the start of the *editing* phase, during which your projects will gradually take their final form. The scope of video editing goes far beyond simple cuts; it is a multifaceted discipline that includes shot sequencing, animations, sound design, and even accessibility features such as subtitling and closed captioning. There is so much to do and discover that we have broken down the editing process into several focused chapters.

This chapter covers the fundamentals, such as organizing media clips on the timeline, trimming the start and end of recordings, removing unwanted segments, and enhancing your projects with annotations.

As you read through these chapters, remember what you've learned in previous chapters. Mastering Camtasia's editing tools will dramatically change the way you approach writing your future scripts and recording your future tutorials.

A. Preparing the Exercises

Although the exercises in this chapter pick up where the previous chapter left off, we strongly recommend using the provided exercise files rather than your screen recordings from the previous chapter. This is because your recordings are unique and will likely not work with the detailed instructions provided below.

Follow these steps to import the first project you'll be using in this chapter into Camtasia.

1. Download and unzip the exercise files for Chapter 05.
2. Open Camtasia.
3. Once on the welcome screen, click **New Project**.
4. When in Camtasia, navigate to the **File > Import > Zipped Project** menu.
5. [*Windows only*] Click the folder to the right of to the **Zipped project file to import** field.
6. Navigate to the ***Chapter05/projects*** folder of the exercises.
7. Double-click the ***01_02_Dashboard.zip*** file to select it.
8. [*Windows only*] Click the folder icon associated with the **Import into project directory** field.
9. Navigate to the ***Chapter05*** folder of the exercises.
10. [*Windows only*] Click **Select Folder**.
11. Click **Import** (Windows) or **Save** (Mac).

This opens the project in Camtasia. On your hard drive, the project is saved under ***Chapter05/01_02_dashboard.tscproj*** (Windows) or ***Chapter05/01_02_dashboard.cmproj*** (Mac).

Make sure you remember this import process; you will return to it often as you progress through this book.

B. Working With the Timeline

In this section, you will start editing the dashboard video. It should now be open in Camtasia, as shown in the following screenshot.

*05_01.png - The **01_02_dashboard** project is open in Camtasia.*

The main editing workspace is the timeline, located at the bottom of the Camtasia interface. Here you can organize your media elements in chronological order.

The timeline is made up of tracks that are layered on top of each other. In this example, there are two tracks: the first one contains the screen recording made in the previous chapter, while the second is currently empty.

One of the most important tools in the timeline is the playhead, which indicates the frame currently displayed on the canvas. By default, the playhead is positioned at the very beginning of the timeline at timecode *0:00:00;00*.

If the playhead is not at the beginning of the project, use the **`Ctrl + Home`** *(Windows) or* **`Cmd + Enter`** *(Mac) shortcut to move it to timecode 0:00:00;00.*

You will now adjust the zoom level of the timeline to get a clear and comfortable view of your recording.

1. Position the mouse anywhere on the timeline.
2. Hold down the **`Ctrl`** (Windows) or **`Cmd`** (Mac) key while scrolling the mouse wheel to adjust the zoom level of the timeline.
3. Adjust the zoom level of the timeline until you see approximately the first thirty seconds of the project.

The next step is to watch the entire video to assess the scope of the work to be done.

4. Click *Play* between the canvas and the timeline or use the **`spacebar`** to start playing the video.

As you watch the video, pay attention to the progress of the playhead. Notice how the audio you hear mirrors the waveform on the timeline, as illustrated in the image below.

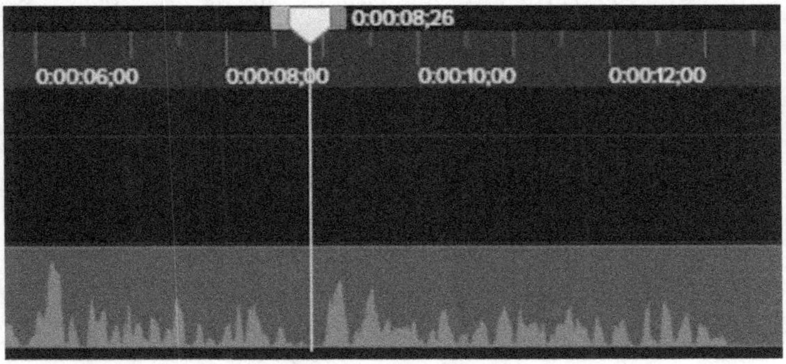

05_02.png - The waveform on the timeline represents the audio recording.

This recording is pretty clean. All you need to do is trim the beginning and end and remove a few hesitations and errors.

1. Trimming the Start and End of a Recording

Keep in mind that you left a three-second buffer at the beginning and at the end of the clip during recording. This means the actual sequence starts slightly after the beginning and ends just before the end of the clip.

1. Use `Ctrl + Home` (Windows) or `Cmd + Enter` (Mac) to bring the playhead back to the beginning of the project.
2. Start playing the video and find the actual beginning of the narration.
3. Position the playhead right before that point, in a silent section of the recording.

In this example, you must position the playhead after the cough about four seconds into the video, as shown in the image below.

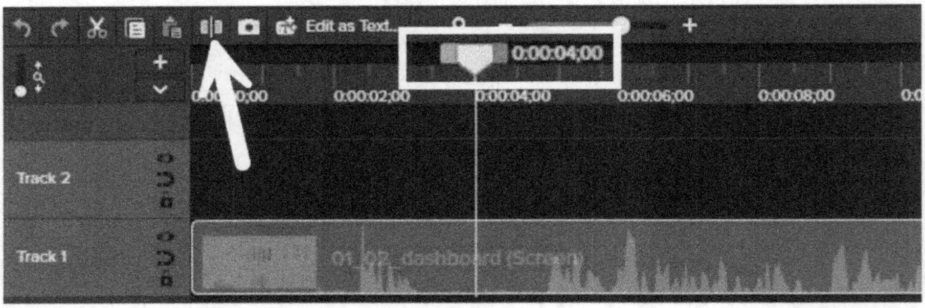

05_03.png - Location of the Playhead and the Split Icon

You need to delete everything before the playhead. There are two ways to do this in Camtasia. By reviewing these two methods, you'll put the non-destructive editing concept (which was covered in Chapter 3 – Creating a New Project) into practice. This will give you a fresh perspective on how Camtasia protects your rushes.

4. In the timeline, click the recording to select it. Camtasia highlights it with a thin yellow border to indicate it is selected.
5. Click the **Split** icon (identified by the arrow in the previous screenshot) or use the `S` key (Windows) or the `Cmd + T` shortcut (Mac).

This splits your recording into two separate video clips on the timeline.

6. Click the video clip preceding the playhead to select it
7. Use the `Delete` key of the keyboard to delete the selected clip.

This effectively removes the first four seconds of your recording, as shown in the image below.

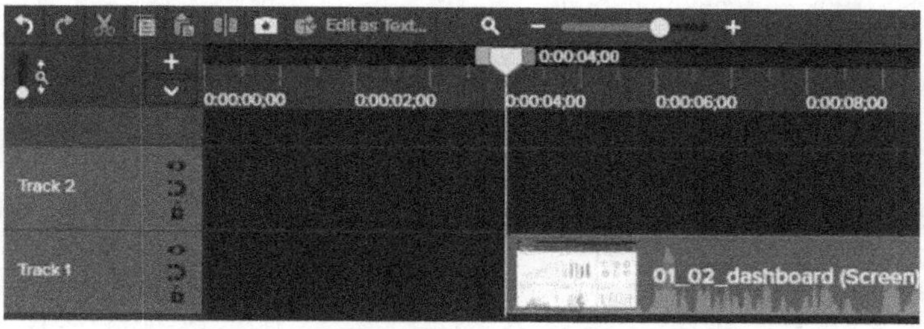

05_04.png - You deleted the first four seconds of the video.

Keep in mind that you are not actually deleting anything. Following the non-destructive editing principle, Camtasia never alters your original footage. It simply remembers to skip the first four seconds during playback. The original file remains completely intact, as demonstrated by the following experiment.

8. Position the mouse over the new start of the video clip until the pointer changes to a double horizontal arrow.
9. Click and drag to move the start of the video clip to the beginning of the project.

This action is shown in the image below.

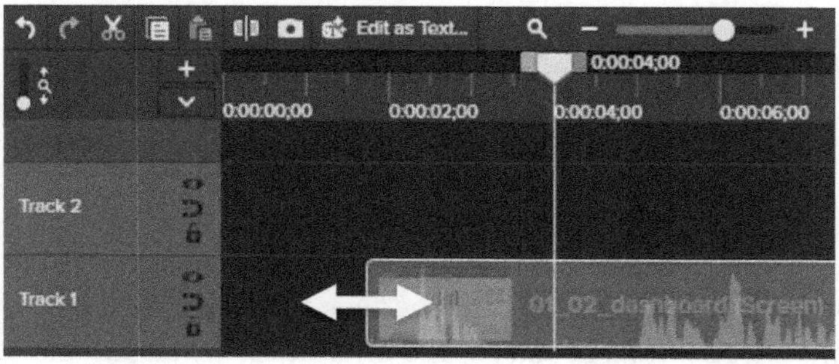

05_05.png - Drag the start of the clip to the left to restore the trimmed footage.

By doing this, you recover all the data you just deleted, which proves that it was never actually erased! With the clip now restored to its original state, let's explore the other way to set the starting point of your clip.

10. Move the mouse pointer to the beginning of the video clip until it changes to a double horizontal arrow (Windows) or a right-pointing black arrow (Mac).
11. Click and drag to move the start of the video clip to the right until it snaps to the playhead.

You can turn this snapping effect on or off in the ***View > Timeline Snapping*** *(Windows) or* ***View > Enable Timeline Snapping*** *(Mac) menu. All snapping effects are enabled by default.*

You will now repeat the same process at the end of the video.

12. Use **`Ctrl + End`** (Windows) or **`Cmd + Shift + Enter`** (Mac) to go to the very end of the project.
13. Position the playhead around timecode *0:02:10;00*.
14. Use the **`spacebar`** to start playing the video from that position.
15. Locate the moment where the narration ends, then position the playhead a little further in a silent section.

In this example, you should position the playhead at timecode *00:02:23;00*.

16. Position the mouse cursor over the right edge of the clip until the pointer changes to a double horizontal arrow (Windows) or a left-pointing black arrow (Mac).
17. Drag the right edge of the clip to the left until it snaps to the playhead.
18. Don't forget to save your project using **`Ctrl + S`** (Windows) or **`Cmd + S`** (Mac).

You've successfully trimmed the beginning and the end of your recording. However, you still need to remove a few hesitations within the body of the clip. You'll take care of that in the next section.

Please refrain from moving the screen recording to the beginning of the timeline, as this would break the step-by-step instructions of the remaining exercises.

2. Cutting In the Middle of a Video Clip

Don't worry if your recording isn't perfect; mistakes, such as hesitations, mispronounced words, missteps, and omissions, are all part of the normal recording process. But even though your raw footage doesn't have to be perfect, your final video does, so you need to edit out those mistakes during post-production.

1. Selecting With the Playhead

First, select the portion of the recording you want to delete.

1. Use **`Ctrl + Home`** (Windows) or **`Cmd + Enter`** (Mac) to move the playhead back to the beginning of the project.

2. Play the video.
3. As soon as you find a section to remove, use the **spacebar** to pause the video.

In this example, the first segment to remove starts around the 17-second mark.

4. Don't hesitate to adjust the zoom level of the timeline to get a better view of the section you're working with.

Note that the view stays centered on the playhead as you adjust the timeline zoom.

5. Position the playhead at the start of the section you want to remove. In this example, position the playhead at the timecode *0:00:17;20.*

The silence left by the narrator during filming makes it easy to spot the end of the section to remove.

6. Expand the selection to timecode *0:00:23;20* by dragging the red handle located on the right side of the playhead.

This action is illustrated in the screenshot below.

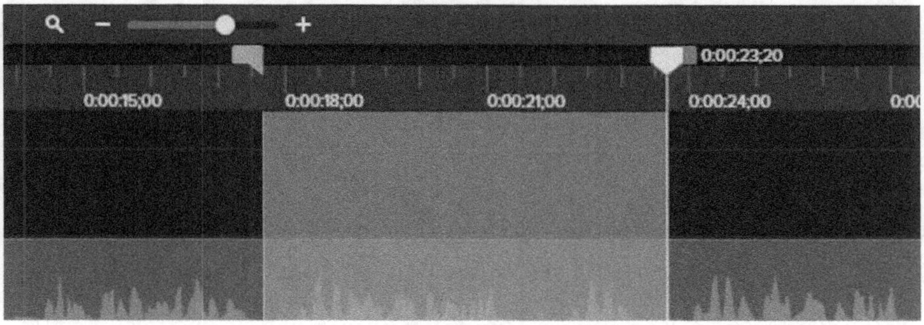

05_06.png - Drag the red handle to select the segment you want to remove.

Selecting segments using the playhead is very convenient and extremely popular among Camtasia users.

- The green handle marks the beginning of your selection.
- The red handle marks the end of the selection.
- The blue rectangle between the handles marks the selected segment.

You can also make this selection by positioning the playhead *at the end* of the section to delete, then dragging the green handle to the left.

7. Use the **spacebar** to start playing the video.

When a selection is active, Camtasia only plays the selected portion of the video. This is very useful for double-checking the selection before removing it.

To deselect, double-click the gray triangle above the playhead to reset the green and red markers to their default positions. You can also manually drag these handles along the timeline to refine an existing selection.

2. Cutting Out Hesitations

After selecting the desired area, you can proceed with its deletion. Camtasia gives you a few different ways to get this done. Let's review them now.

1. Make sure the section to delete is correctly selected.
2. Use the `Delete` key on your keyboard to delete the selected area.

You should now see two video clips on the timeline with a gap in between, as shown in the image below.

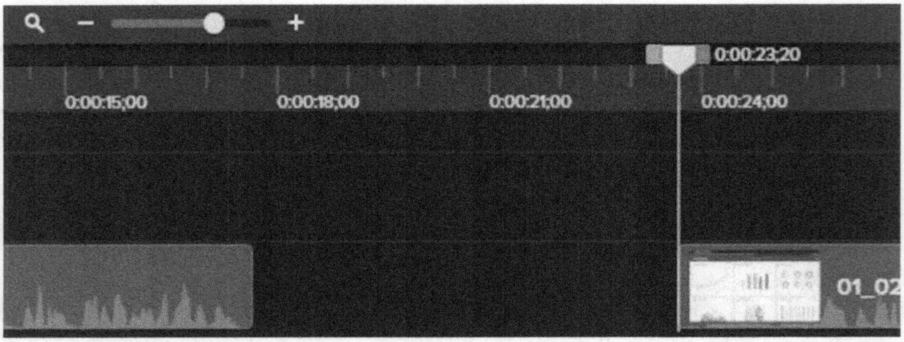

05_07.png - You end up with two separate clips separated by a small gap.

You will now fill that gap using the following steps.

3. Select the clip to the right of the cut.
4. Drag it to the left to fill the gap.
5. Position the playhead a few seconds before the cut.
6. Press the `spacebar` to play the video.

Ensure the video flows naturally, and that the edit goes unnoticed.

Congratulations on your first hesitation removal! Note that this type of edit requires a lot of clicking. More importantly, each cut splits the original video clip into two clips on the timeline. When you only have a few edits to make, this isn't a big deal, but if you need to make many cuts within a single clip, it quickly creates a cluttered and fragmented timeline. This fragmentation significantly complicates the rest of the editing process. So, let's explore another way to achieve the same result.

7. Press **`Ctrl + Z`** (Windows) or **`Cmd + Z`** (Mac) twice to undo the last two actions and return to the original state.
8. If necessary, reselect the area you want to delete.
9. Right-click inside the selection.
10. Select **Ripple Delete** (Windows) or **Ripple Delete Range** (Mac). You can also use **`Ctrl + Backspace`** (Windows) or **`Cmd + Backspace`** (Mac) .

This action does a lot more than deleting the selection! It also fills in the gap and *stitches* the resulting clips together, as shown in the image below.

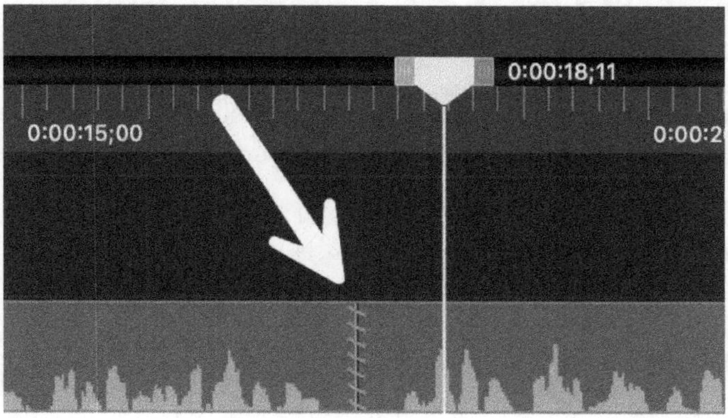

05_08.png - Camtasia stitches the two resulting clips together (Mac). On Windows, the stitch mark is slightly darker, making it a bit harder to see.

The main advantage of this technique is that it leaves only a single video clip on the timeline, making it the preferred method for cleaning up your raw footage.

You will now make sure this cut goes unnoticed.

11. Position the playhead slightly before the cut.
12. Use the **`spacebar`** to start playing the video.
13. Make sure the cut goes unnoticed.

If you're not satisfied with the result, right-click the stitch mark and select **Remove Stitch**. You can then repeat the process with a different selection until you achieve the desired result.

14. Repeat this process to remove the section between timecode *0:00:56;00* and timecode *00:01:10;00*.
15. Save and close the project when done.

By the end of this section, you will have successfully cleaned up a video recording made with Camtasia Recorder in the previous chapter.

3. Hands-on Exercise: Clean Up a Raw Recording

In this section, you will practice cleaning up a recording using the ***01_03_settings*** project. Follow these steps to complete this hands-on exercise.

1. Import the ***Chapter05/projects/01_03_settings.zip*** project into the ***Chapitre05*** folder of the exercises using the import process described at the beginning of this chapter.
2. Trim the beginning and the end of this recording.
3. Clean up the recording by cutting out any hesitations or errors. Use only **Ripple Delete** (Windows) or **Ripple Delete Range** (Mac) to maintain a single video clip on the timeline.

Watch out! Errors and hesitations are not limited to audio narration. During editing, make sure that form field entries and mouse movements remain consistent.

4. Also remove any unnecessary pauses to help your video flow smoothly.
5. Test your edits as you go to ensure they are seamless.
6. Don't forget to save your project regularly.
7. Keep this project open for the next exercise.

By the end of this exercise, the recording should have a total duration of around 2 minutes and 50 seconds. You should have made between four and eight cuts, not counting the trimming at the beginning and at the end of the project.

4. Tips and Tricks for Cleaning Up Your Screen Recordings

With a little bit of practice, cleaning up your recordings will soon become a breeze! To help you get there faster, here are some of my favorite practical tips and tricks.

- Whenever possible, always use **Ripple Delete** (Windows) or **Ripple Delete Range** (Mac) to keep only a single video clip on the timeline.
- To make clean cuts, use the visual audio spikes on the waveform to identify where the unwanted sections start and end.
- Don't hesitate to zoom in and out of the timeline. This will help you precisely position the start (green) and end (red) selection markers.

- Do not edit out the breathing of the narrator. Over-editing these moments often creates a suffocating and uncomfortable listening experience. These pauses maintain a human touch and help the narration feel more natural.
- When reviewing your edits, don't forget to also pay attention to the image continuity. For example, make sure the cursor doesn't jump around the screen because of a cut. Avoiding unnecessary mouse movements during recording makes this aspect of editing a lot easier.
- When cutting within a clip where the narrator is visible on screen, your cuts will most likely be noticeable. This isn't always a problem. Viewers are used to this type of cut, especially in news reports. Later in the process, you can eventually hide these cuts with a framing change or a short transition.
- Remember that you can easily remove a cut by right clicking the stitch marker and selecting **Remove Stitch**. If you'd like to start all over again, click **Remove All Stitches** to instantly restore your footage to its original state.

With these tips and a little bit of practice, you'll soon master the art of cleaning up your recordings in Camtasia.

3. Working With the Timeline Tracks

In this section, you will assemble the final sequence of the ***01_03_settings*** video, which you cleaned up in the previous section.

Feel free to watch the ***Chapter01/01_03_settings.mp4*** *video again to refresh your memory. Pay special attention to the final sequence.*

1. Understanding the Timeline Tracks

In the final sequence of this video, you want to highlight the key takeaways using text annotations. Since you want these text elements to appear in sync with the narration, you must keep the original recording in place so that its audio track continues playing. This means you cannot *remove* the screen recording and replace it with text boxes. Instead, you'll use the tracks in the timeline to *overlay* these text annotations over the screen recording.

The sequence you will be working with begins when the narrator says, *"In this video, you discovered the options available in the icon located..."* This happens around timecode 00:03:30;00, although the exact moment varies depending on the cuts you made in the previous section.

1. If necessary, open the ***Chapter05/01_03_settings*** project in Camtasia.
2. Position the playhead around timecode 00:03:30;00, in the silence preceding *"In this video, you discovered the options available in the icon located..."*

You'll start by adding a background image over the screen recording.

3. Import the ***Chapter05/resources/01_03_cover.jpg*** image into the **Media Bin**.
4. Right-click the **01_03_cover** image you just imported in the **Media Bin**.
5. Select **Add to Timeline at Playhead**.

This action is illustrated in the image below.

*05_09.png - Select **Add to Timeline at Playhead.***

To fully understand the effect of this action, you need to check both the canvas and the timeline.

On the canvas, the ***01_03_cover.jpg*** image covers the screen recording. This is possible because the following three conditions are met.

- The image has the same aspect ratio as the video (16:9).
- The image is at least as large as the canvas. Had it been smaller, Camtasia would have centered it on the canvas, but without scaling it up. Therefore, the image would have only partially covered the screen recording.
- In the timeline, the playhead is positioned over the image. Remember that the position of the playhead in the timeline defines what you see on the canvas.

This perfect match between the image and the Camtasia project does not happen by accident. It is the result of careful preparation before you even open Camtasia. Let's take this opportunity to reinforce, once again, the importance of the preparation step.

When it comes to the timeline, note the following points.

- Camtasia places the image on the first available track. Since **Track 1** is already occupied by the screen recording, Camtasia places the image on **Track 2**.
- The image begins at the playhead position.
- The image remains visible for a default duration of five seconds.

This situation is illustrated in the image below.

05_10.png - The image remains visible for five seconds on Track 2.

Unlike a screen recording, an image has no intrinsic duration. For this reason, Camtasia automatically applies a default duration of five seconds to any images you add to the project.

*This default duration can be adjusted in the preferences. Go to the **Edit > Preferences** (Windows) or **Camtasia > Settings** (Mac) menu, and navigate to the **Timing** (Windows) or **Timeline** (Mac) tab. The remaining exercises assume that the default value has not been changed.*

You will now extend the duration of this image, so it remains visible until the end of the project.

6. In the timeline, position the mouse over the right edge of the image until the cursor changes to a horizontal double arrow.
7. Drag the end of the image to the right until it aligns with the end of the screen recording.

The result of this action is shown in the image below.

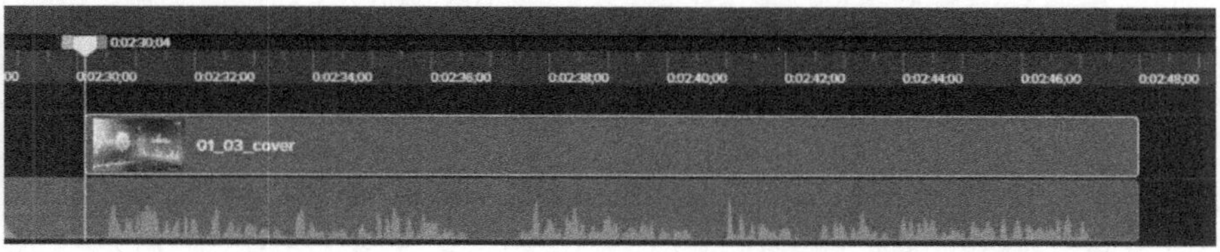

05_11.png - Align the end of the image with the end of the screen recording.

You will now add another element to this project using the following steps.

8. Make sure the playhead is still positioned at the beginning of the final sequence of the project (i.e., where the image you just inserted begins).
9. Open the **Annotations** panel on the left side of the screen.
10. Open the **Shapes** tab, as shown in the image below.

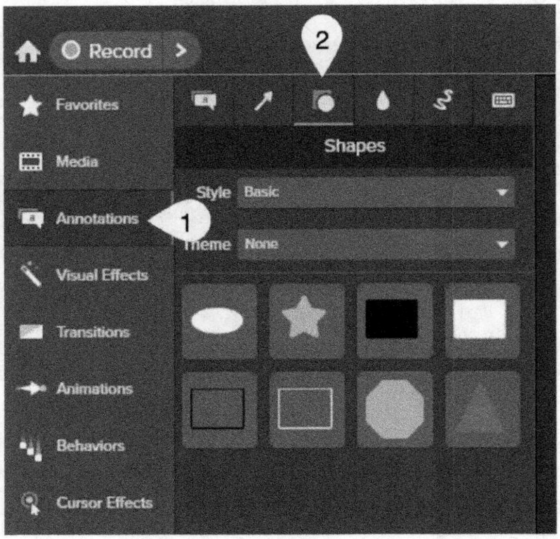

*05_12.png - Open the **Shapes** tab of the **Annotations** panel.*

11. In the **Annotations** panel, right-click the white rectangle.
12. Select **Add to Timeline at Playhead**.

Just as before, Camtasia adds this item to the first available track in the timeline. But this time, both tracks are already occupied. No problem! Camtasia simply creates an additional track to accommodate the new item. So, you now have *three* tracks in your project.

On the canvas, Camtasia places the rectangle at the center of the screen, with a preset size.

13. In the timeline, extend the duration of the white rectangle all the way to the end of the project.
14. Remember to save your work on a regular basis.

The timeline tracks allow you to layer multiple multimedia elements. As the playhead progresses through the project, it displays all the layers along its path simultaneously, merging them into a single image visible on the canvas.

You can have an unlimited number of tracks in a Camtasia project.

2. Changing the Track Order

The stacking order of the elements on the canvas matches the layering order of the tracks in the timeline. So, you can change the stacking order of the elements in your project by reordering the tracks in the timeline.

1. Make sure the white rectangle from the previous section is still visible on the canvas. If it is not, position the playhead accordingly.
2. Position the mouse pointer over the **Track 2** label at the far left of the timeline.
3. Drag **Track 2** down and drop it below **Track 1**.

As a result, the screen recording reappears on the canvas and covers the background image. Note that Camtasia has renamed the tracks: former **Track 2** is now **Track 1**, and vice versa.

4. Drag what is now **Track 1** up one level to restore the original arrangement.

In this section, you learned how to reorder tracks in the timeline, which also changes the stacking order of elements on the canvas.

3. Renaming tracks

Camtasia allows you to rename the tracks to help you stay organized. This feature only affects your working experience in Camtasia and has no impact on the final result.

1. Double-click the **Track 1** label at the far left of the timeline.
2. Type `Screen` and press `Enter` to confirm.

The result of this action is illustrated in the image below.

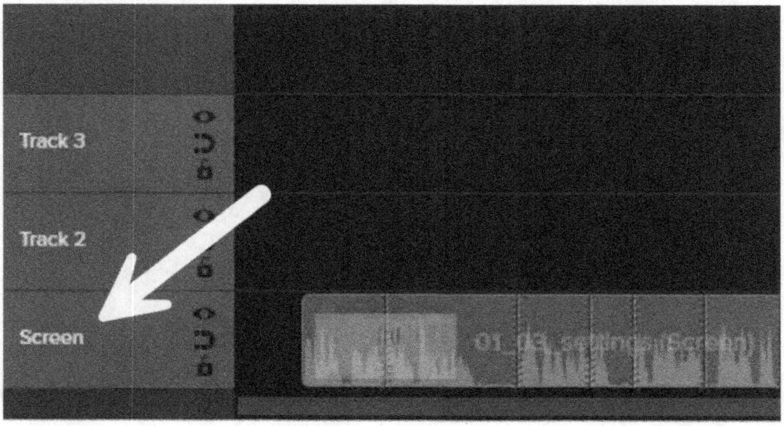

*05_13.png – **Track 1** was renamed **Screen** in Camtasia.*

4. Controlling Track Visibility

At the far left of the timeline, each track is associated with a vertical row of three icons. Use the *eye* icon to toggle track visibility. You can use this to hide layers that are blocking your view so you can access the elements underneath, or to exclude certain tracks from your final export.

1. Position the playhead towards the end of the project so you can see both the image and the white rectangle on the canvas.
2. Click the eye icon for Track 2 (the track with the image) or right-click the track header and select **Turn Track Off**.

When you click this icon, your screen recording reappears on the canvas, with the white rectangle still visible in the center of the screen. Notice that the icon you just clicked has now changed to a crossed-out eye, as illustrated below.

05_14.png - A crossed-out eye indicates a hidden track.

3. Click the crossed-out eye icon to bring track 2 back into view. You can also right-click the track header and select **Turn Track On**.
4. Press and hold `Alt` (Windows) or `Option` (Mac) and click the eye icon for Track 3 (the track containing the white rectangle). You can also right-click the track and select **Enable Solo Track**.

This action sets the corresponding track to solo, as shown in the image below.

05_15.png - All tracks are disabled, except Track 3.

Only the white rectangle is visible on the canvas, making it very easy to select and adjust its properties in a clutter-free workspace.

5. Hold down **`Alt`** (Windows) or **`Option`** (Mac) and click the same icon again. You can also right-click the track 3 header and select **Disable Solo Track**.

All tracks are now back in sight. In this section, you learned how to toggle track visibility using the eye icon in the track headers at the far left of the timeline.

5. Expanding and Collapsing Tracks

You can also adjust the height of the timeline tracks. These adjustments are solely for your convenience and do not affect the final video.

1. Position your mouse on the dividing line between the **Screen** track and **Track 2** in the track header area.
2. When the cursor turns into a double vertical arrow (Windows only), click and drag upward to increase the height of the **Screen** track.

This process is illustrated in the image below.

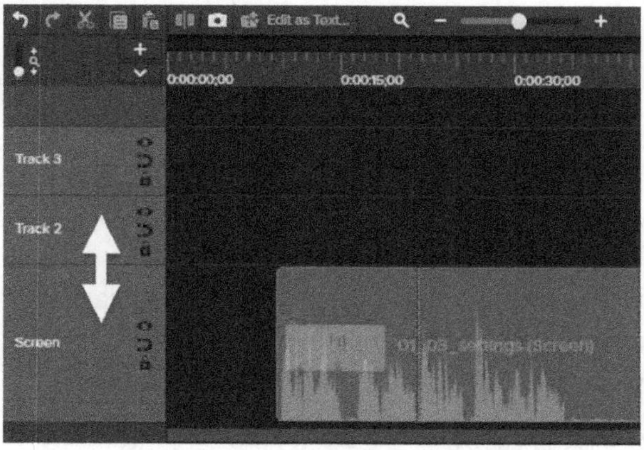

*05_16.png - Increase the height of the **Screen** track.*

To reduce the height of the track, either reverse the previous steps or use the second method described below.

3. Right-click the header for the **Screen** track.
4. Click **Minimize Track** (Windows) or **Minimize** (Mac).

This action collapses the **Screen** track to the smallest possible size.

5. Right-click the **Screen** track header again.

6. Click **Maximize Track** (Windows) or **Maximize** (Mac) to expand the **Screen** track to the maximum possible size.

This view is particularly useful when working with audio, as it offers the most detailed rendering of the waveform.

You can also adjust the height of all tracks at once using the handle in the upper-left corner of the timeline.

7. Drag the handle in the upper-left corner of the timeline up and down to make all tracks the same height.

In this section, you've learned several ways to adjust the height of tracks in the timeline. This feature is very useful when working on complex projects with many tracks, as well as when working with audio data.

C. Working With Annotations

In the previous section, you inserted a white rectangle into the project's final sequence. Unlike other elements on the timeline, this rectangle is a native Camtasia annotation, not an imported media file visible in the Media Bin.

In this section, you'll learn more about this rectangle, explore its properties, and discover other annotations available in Camtasia.

1. Adjusting the Properties of the Rectangle

To begin your exploration of annotations in Camtasia, you will now adjust the properties of the white rectangle, which currently is the only annotation on the timeline.

1. Open the ***Chapter05/01_03_settings*** project if necessary.
2. Position the playhead towards the end of the project so that you can see the white rectangle on the canvas.
3. Click the white rectangle to select it.

It doesn't matter whether you click the white rectangle in the timeline or on the canvas. In either case, you select the same object. Your selection is highlighted by a thin yellow border in the timeline and by resize and selection handles on the canvas.

4. Make sure the Properties panel is open at the right side of the screen. If necessary, click **Properties** to open it.

This panel displays the properties of the currently selected object, which, in this case, are those of the white rectangle. They are distributed across two tabs at the top of the Properties panel, as illustrated in the image below.

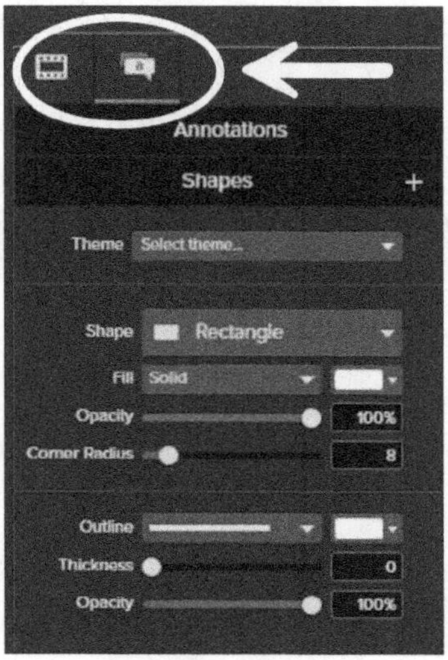

05_17.png - The Properties panel displays the properties of the white rectangle.

The *Annotation Properties* tab is currently open in the above image, as indicated by the thin green underline. Use it to edit properties such as the fill color, the border style, and the roundness of the corners.

5. Open the other tab to examine its properties.

This tab contains the visual properties of the selected object. Use it to adjust the size, position, tilt, rotation, and opacity.

6. Use the resize handles on the canvas to enlarge the white rectangle.

As you scale the rectangle up, keep an eye on the Properties panel to see how the visual properties evolve as you manipulate the object.

7. In the Properties panel, enter a width of `1080` pixels and press `Enter`.

See how this operation makes the rectangle wider on the canvas.

8. In the Properties panel, enter a height of `589` pixels and press `Enter`.

You may need to disable the padlock linking the width and height to edit these two properties separately.

The next step is to position the white rectangle *exactly* at the center of the screen.

9. Drag the white rectangle across the canvas while monitoring the **Position** properties in the Properties panel.
10. Move the rectangle towards the center of the canvas until it snaps into position.
11. Save the project when done.

The white rectangle should now be centered on the canvas, as shown in the image below.

05_18.png - The white rectangle is exactly at the center of the canvas.

The **X** and **Y** coordinates of the rectangle in the Properties panel are both at 0, which confirms the rectangle is perfectly centered.

*The snapping feature you used to center the rectangle on the canvas is enabled by default in Camtasia. You can turn it on and off using the **View > Enable Canvas Snapping** menu item.*

2. Adding Text Annotations

Another type of annotation available in Camtasia is *Text Annotations*. In this section, you will place three of these annotations over the white rectangle you've positioned in the previous section. They must appear in sync with the narration, so your first task is to position the playhead exactly when the first annotation should appear.

1. Open the ***Chapter05/01_03_settings*** project if necessary.
2. Position the playhead just before the image and the white rectangle come into view.
3. Use the `spacebar` to start playing the video.
4. Pause the video when the narrator says, *"... manage your user profile"* and position the playhead exactly at that point.
5. Don't hesitate to zoom in on the timeline and replay the video several times until you find the perfect position for the playhead.

Once the playhead is correctly positioned, you can add a first text annotation over the white rectangle.

6. Open the **Annotations** panel on the left side of the interface.
7. If necessary, select the **Callouts** tab.
8. Open the **Theme** dropdown and select **Default**.

These steps are illustrated in the image below.

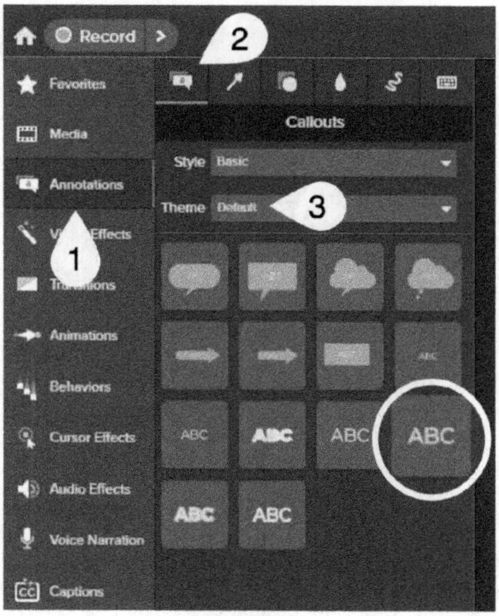

*05_19.png - The **Annotations** panel is open on the **Callouts** tab.*

In this tab, you will find several caption styles that you can easily add to your project. For this exercise, you need a simple text box, such as the one highlighted with a white circle in the above image.

9. Drag the highlighted caption from the **Annotations** panel onto the canvas.

*Using a Mac? The location of this particular caption style in the **Annotations** panel is slightly different.*

Remember that every element in your project must be positioned both in space (on the canvas) and in time (in the timeline). On the canvas, the new text annotation appears where you dropped it; on the timeline, the new annotation:

- starts at the playhead position on the first available track
- appears for a default duration of five seconds.

If no track is available, Camtasia seamlessly creates a new one to accommodate the new object.

10. Double-click inside the new text annotation to switch to edit mode.
11. Type `Edit your user profile`.
12. Click anywhere outside the annotation to exit edit mode.

You will now adjust the formatting properties of the text annotation.

13. Make sure the text annotation is selected.
14. If necessary, click **Properties** to open the Properties panel on the right side of the screen.
15. Open the **Callout** tab of the **Properties** panel by clicking the **a (font)** icon, as illustrated in the image below.

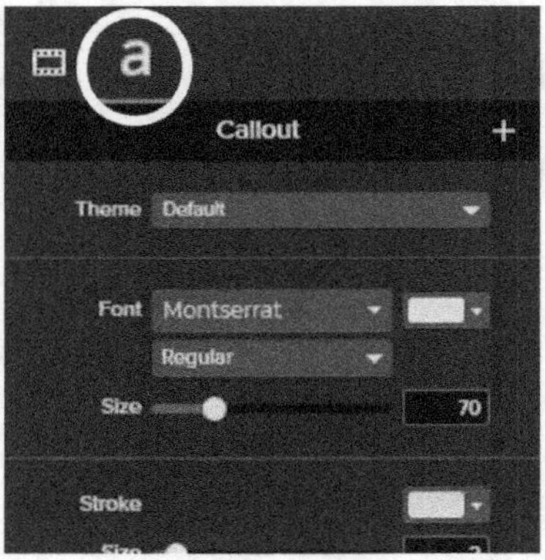

*05_20.png - Open the **Callout** tab of the Properties panel.*

This tab is specific to text annotations. You can use it to change the font, font size, color, and text alignment.

16. Click the color swatch next to the font dropdown to open the color palette.
17. Choose any dark color. This color is applied to the text in the caption.
18. Reduce the **Size** to 60.
19. Reduce the **Stroke Size** to 0.
20. Align the text left.
21. Use the mouse to position the text caption as shown in the image below.

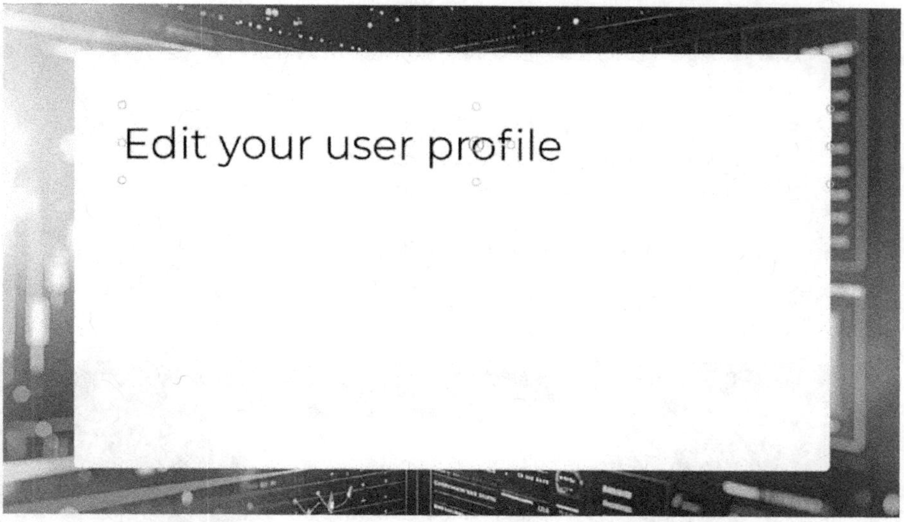

05_21.png - Position your first text annotation.

The first text caption is now correctly positioned on the canvas. The next step is to adjust its duration in the timeline.

22. In the timeline, extend the duration of the text caption to the end of the project.

You will now add the remaining two annotations. To speed up the process, you will duplicate the existing annotation and make the necessary changes.

23. In the timeline, position the playhead when the narrator says, *"...update your password"*.
24. Select the first annotations and use `Ctrl + C` (Windows) or `Cmd + C` (Mac) to copy it.
25. Press `Ctrl + V` (Windows) or `Cmd` + V (Mac) to paste the second text annotation.

In the timeline, the duplicated annotation is placed at the playhead position on the first available track, or on a new track if none is available.

26. On the canvas, move the new text caption and position it roughly in the center of the screen.
27. Double-click the new caption and type `Change your password`. Click anywhere when done.
28. In the timeline, position the playhead exactly when the narrator says, *"... and choose the language..."*.

29. Repeat the above steps to create a third annotation. Type **`Choose the language (FR/EN)`** and position it towards the bottom of the white rectangle.
30. In the timeline, adjust the duration of the two new annotations so that they remain visible until the end of the project.
31. Adjust the position of the annotations as shown below.

As you move the annotations into position, yellow guides will automatically appear to help you align them precisely. The result is shown in the image below.

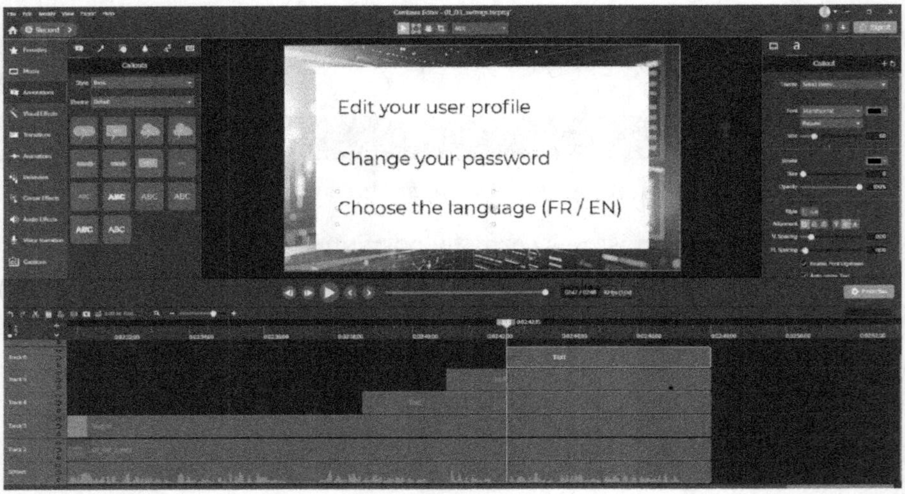

05_22.png - The three text annotations are positioned both on the canvas and in the timeline.

You will animate these annotations in Chapter 6 – Transitions, Animations, and Visual Effects and you will finalize their formatting with a custom theme in Chapter 9 – Extending and Customizing Camtasia. But for now, your work on these annotations is complete, so you can save and close the project.

32. Use **`Ctrl + S`** (Windows) or **`Cmd + S`** (Mac) to save this project.
33. Close Camtasia.

In this section, you learned about shapes and text annotations. You also gained hands-on experience with the **Annotations** panel on the left and the **Properties** panel on the right. In the next section, you'll take a closer look at the canvas tools.

D. Working With the Canvas

When editing video, you need to position elements both in space and in time. In Camtasia, the canvas is the stage where you organize the elements of your projects in space.

In this section, you will revisit the ***00_01_prerequisites*** project you recorded in the previous chapter and integrate the studio recording of the narrator. Before you begin, use these steps to set up your workspace.

1. Import the ***Chapter05/projects/00_01_prerequisites.zip*** project in the ***Chapter05*** folder of the exercises using the process covered at the beginning of this chapter.
2. Press the **`spacebar`** to play the video.
3. Watch the entire video as a refresher.

This project includes the slideshow recording captured in the previous chapter. Remember that the narration in this project is only a reference track intended to help synchronize the slideshow with the green screen video of the narrator that you will shortly import into the project.

To speed things up, the unwanted sections at the beginning and end of the recording have already been trimmed. You can now import the narrator video.

4. Import the ***Chapter05/resources/00_01_damienGreenScreen.mp4*** video into the **Media Bin**.
5. Use **`Ctrl + Home`** (Windows) or **`Cmd + Enter`** (Mac) to reposition the playhead at the beginning of the project.
6. Drag the **00_01_ damienGreenScreen** video from the **Media Bin** onto the canvas.

Because the video has the same aspect ratio as the project (16:9), it aligns seamlessly with the canvas and fully covers the PowerPoint recording. In the timeline, the new video includes its own audio and is a bit longer than the slideshow recording.

This situation is illustrated in the image below.

05_23.png - On the canvas, the new video covers the PowerPoint slideshow. In the timeline, it is a bit longer than the slideshow recording.

In the final video, the narrator is positioned on the left side of the screen and does not take up the entire frame. In this section, you will use the tools of the canvas to resize the video of the narrator and reposition it over the PowerPoint presentation.

To do so, the canvas offers several operating modes, which can be activated using the icons next to the zoom dropdown menu at the top of the screen.

1. Using the Edit Mode

By default, the canvas works in *Edit* mode, identified by the arrow icon highlighted in the image below.

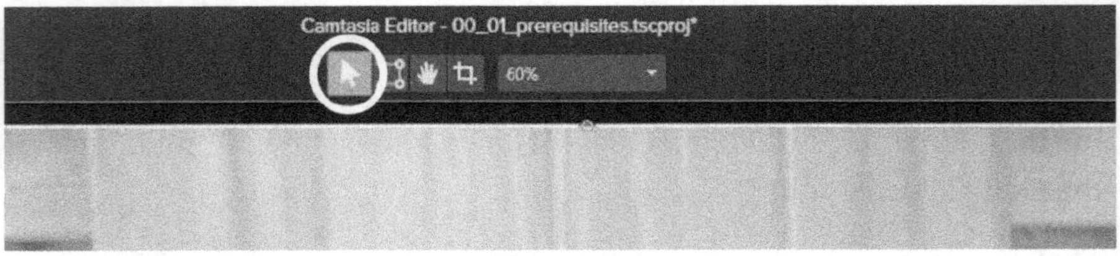

05_24.png - The edit mode is identified by the arrow icon.

In edit mode, you can select, resize, and move objects on the canvas.

1. Click the video of the narrator on the canvas to select it.

On the canvas, a bounding box with eight resize handles encloses the selection. Remember that the object is also selected in the timeline, where it is outlined by a thin yellow border.

2. Use a corner handle to reduce the size of the narrator's video. Doing so reveals the PowerPoint slideshow underneath.

In Camtasia, using a corner handle to resize an item *maintains* its aspect ratio: the narrator's video is *not* distorted after being resized in this way.

3. Hold down the `Shift` key and continue resizing the video of the narrator using a corner handle.

When the **`Shift`** key is pressed, Camtasia no longer preserves the aspect ratio of the resized element. As a result, the footage will most likely appear stretched or squashed after resizing.

Be careful, as this behavior in Camtasia is the opposite of what is observed in many other applications, where `Shift` *is used to maintain the aspect ratio of the resized object.*

4. Use `Ctrl + Z` (Windows) or `Cmd + Z` (Mac) to undo the last action and restore the original aspect ratio of the narrator.
5. Use the mouse to move the narrator to the left.

As a result, the video of the narrator extends beyond the boundaries of the canvas, as shown in the image below.

05_25.png - The video of the narrator extends beyond the canvas.

The edit mode also allows you to rotate the selected object(s).

6. Make sure the video of the narrator is selected.

When an object is selected on the canvas, Camtasia displays two handles in the center of the selection, in addition to the eight resize handles mentioned earlier.

- The leftmost central handle marks the center of the object. It is the point around which the object spins when you apply a rotation.
- Use the rightmost central handle to set the rotation angle.

You will now use these two handles to apply a rotation to the narrator's video.

7. Make sure the Properties panel is visible on the right side of the screen and ensure the Visual Properties tab is active.
8. Drag the rightmost center handle with the mouse to rotate the selected video clip.

The onscreen handle lets you apply simple rotations. But Camtasia also supports advanced 3D rotations, which you can configure in the Properties panel.

Within the Visual Properties tab, notice the **X**, **Y**, and **Z** dials in the **Rotation** section, as shown in the image below.

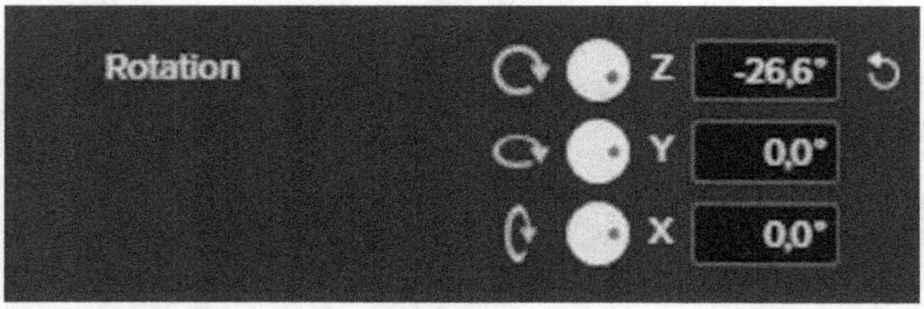

05_26.png - *The **X**, **Y**, and **Z** dials in the **Rotation** section are used to apply three-dimensional rotations.*

The names of these three properties refer to the axes of three-dimensional space. The x-axis is the horizontal axis running from left to right, the y-axis is the vertical axis going up and down, and the z-axis is the depth axis coming out of the screen towards you. These three axes intersect at the rotation point, which, in Camtasia, is the center of the object.

You will now experiment with these three dials.

9. Rotate the **Z** dial in the **Rotation** section of the Properties panel.

This action rotates the video of the narrator around the z-axis, which is the depth axis. Camtasia provides two methods for performing this type of rotation: you can either drag the central handles directly on the canvas or use the **Z** dial in the **Rotation** section of the Properties panel.

10. Take a moment to experiment with the **Y** and **X** dials and see how they affect the video of the narrator on the canvas.
11. Before continuing, reset the **Z**, **Y**, and **X** values in the **Rotation** section of the Properties panel to **0**.

You can adjust these settings in three different ways. You can:

- turn the dials with your mouse,
- type 0 for each value in the Properties panel,
- or click the curved reset arrow next to each option.

In Chapter 06 – Transitions, Animations, and Visual Effects, you'll remove the green screen behind the narrator. Since our studio (which is actually my garage, converted into a makeshift studio for this project) was a bit cramped, the green screen doesn't cover the entire frame.

To prepare for the background removal process in the next chapter, you will now crop out any parts of the video that are not covered by the green screen. But because the clip extends beyond the boundaries of the canvas (see image ***05_25.png***), some of the handles needed to perform this operation are currently out of reach. You will address this situation in the next section.

2. Using the Pan Mode

The second operating mode for the canvas is the *Pan* mode, identified by the hand icon.

1. Enable Pan mode by clicking the hand icon above the canvas.

This action is shown in the image below.

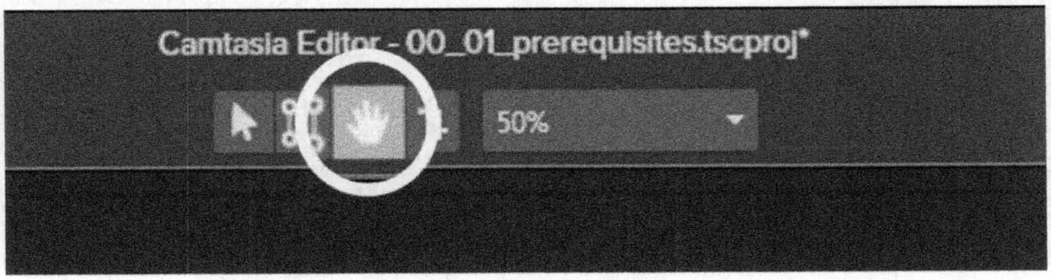

05_27.png - Click the hand icon to enable Pan mode.

2. Hover the mouse over the canvas and notice that the pointer has changed to an open hand.
3. Use this hand pointer to click and drag the whole canvas to the right.

With the Pan mode active, this action shifts the entire canvas to the right, revealing the areas of the narrator's video that were previously off-screen.

Clicking the hand icon every time you need the Pan mode is inefficient. Fortunately, Camtasia offers a convenient keyboard shortcut that lets you pan on the fly without interrupting your creative flow.

4. Return to edit mode by clicking the arrow icon above the canvas.
5. Position the mouse pointer over the canvas.

Now that you're back in edit mode, the mouse pointer reverts to its default appearance.

6. Press and hold the `spacebar`. You should see the cursor change to an open hand.
7. Click and drag to move the canvas around.
8. When done, let go of the mouse, then the spacebar.

Holding down the spacebar temporarily activates the Pan mode. As soon as you release it, you return to Edit mode. This shortcut is extremely convenient, as it allows you to quickly switch between modes without breaking your workflow.

Before moving on, make sure you've panned the canvas so that the video of the narrator is fully exposed, as shown in the image below.

05_28.png - Use the pan mode to move the canvas so you can see the video of the narrator.

3. Using the Crop Mode

The *Crop* mode can be accessed by clicking the rectangle icon next to the zoom dropdown menu. In this section, you'll use it to isolate the narrator by removing any parts of the frame not covered by the green screen.

1. Make sure the video of the narrator is selected.

This reveals the resize handles, some of which are off canvas.

2. Enable the crop mode by clicking the rectangle icon above the canvas.

This action is illustrated in the image below.

05_29.png - Enable the crop mode of Camtasia.

The narrator's video is now surrounded by a *blue* border, and the resize handles have turned into crop handles.

3. Slide the left crop handle inwards until the area not covered by the green screen disappears.

This action is depicted in the image below.

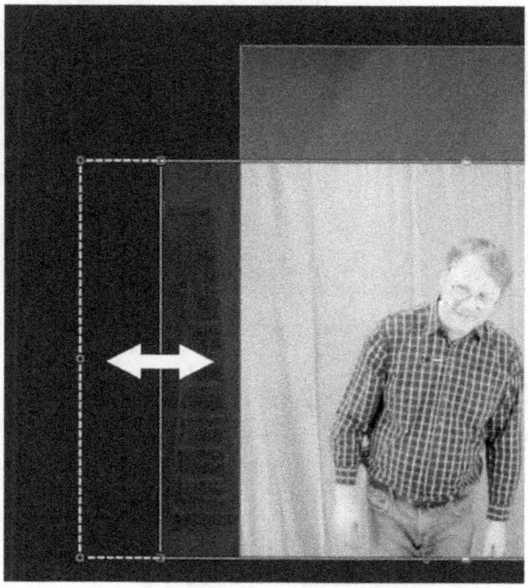

05_30.png - Drag the left crop handle to the right.

With the crop mode enabled, this action removes the unwanted parts of an image or video, helping you get the framing exactly right.

Just like with the Pan tool, you can use a handy shortcut to toggle the crop mode on or off at any time. Let's give it a try!

4. Return to edit mode by clicking the arrow icon above the canvas.
5. Hold down `Alt` (Windows) or `Option` (Mac) to temporarily enable crop mode.
6. Drag the crop handle on the right side of the narrator's video to the left until all areas not covered by the green screen are removed.
7. Let go of the mouse before releasing `Alt` (Windows) or `Option` (Mac).

With this shortcut, you can easily switch from edit to crop mode without interrupting your workflow.

Lastly, you will reset the zoom level and recenter the view on the canvas.

8. Open the zoom dropdown menu and select **Fit**.

The canvas should now look like the image below.

05_31.png - The narrator's video is positioned over the PowerPoint slideshow.

In this section, you used the crop mode to remove the unwanted parts of the narrator's video.

4. Using the Corner Pin Mode

The last operating mode for the canvas is the *Corner Pin* mode, which you will practice using the ***00_00_trailer*** project.

1. Save and close any currently open projects.
2. Import the ***Chapter05/projects/00_00_trailer.zip*** file into the ***Chapter05*** folder of the exercises using the import process described at the beginning of this chapter.
3. Once the project is open in Camtasia, adjust the height of the timeline so that all six tracks are visible.

This step is illustrated in the image below.

05_32.png - Increase the height of the timeline to see all six tracks.

Welcome back to this project! Since your last visit, we've added a few images as well as the narrator's video.

4. Review the entire project to refresh your memory and get acquainted with the new elements.

In this section, you will use the corner pin mode to seamlessly integrate the platform screenshots into the laptop frames.

5. In the timeline, position the playhead at timecode *0:00:11;00* so that both the laptop and the first screenshot are visible.
6. In the **Track 4** header, at the far left of the timeline, click the eye icon to hide the video of the narrator.

This element isn't necessary for the current task. Hiding it ensures it is left untouched all the while reducing visual clutter, which makes your workflow more comfortable.

7. Feel free to zoom in on the canvas to get a clear view of both the laptop image and the first screenshot.

8. Use the **Edit** mode to slightly rotate the screenshot and position it roughly over the laptop image.

Your goal is to position the screenshot roughly along the same axis as the laptop screen in the background. The result of this action is shown in the image below.

05_33.png - Slightly rotate the screenshot to align it with the laptop screen.

No matter how hard you try, you won't be able to position the screenshot *exactly* within the laptop screen. This is where *Corner Pin* mode steps in.

9. Click the icon showing the four corners of a rectangle to enable corner pinning.

This action is depicted in the image below.

05_34.png – Enable Corner Pin mode.

Once this mode is enabled, a thin red border wraps around the screenshot. Corner Pin mode lets you manipulate each corner of the selected element separately, allowing you to distort the image and create a 3D perspective effect.

10. Individually align each corner of the screenshot with the corresponding corner of the laptop screen in the background.
11. Don't hesitate to zoom in and out on the canvas to achieve maximum accuracy.
12. When done, click the arrow icon to switch back to edit mode.

When all four corners are aligned, the screenshot fits perfectly within the laptop screen, as shown in the following image.

05_35.png - When all four corners are aligned, the screenshot fits perfectly within the laptop.

Now you need to apply exactly the same changes to the other screenshots in this project. To ensure consistency and save time, you will simply copy the properties of the image you just worked with and apply them directly to the other screenshots.

13. In the timeline, right-click the image you just worked with.
14. In the context menu, click **Copy Properties**.
15. Move the playhead so that the second screenshot is visible on the canvas.
16. In the timeline, right-click the second screenshot.
17. In the context menu, click **Paste Properties**.

On the canvas, the second screenshot positions itself *exactly* like the first one and fits perfectly onto the laptop screen.

18. Paste the properties again onto the third screenshot.

After applying the properties to the third screenshot, it won't fit exactly on the computer screen like the previous two screenshots did. This is normal and expected; you'll fix this issue in Chapter 06—Transitions, Animations, and Visual Effects. For now, just paste the properties onto the remaining four screenshots.

19. Paste those properties onto the remaining four screenshots in this project.
20. Save and close the project when done.

By the end of this exercise, six of the seven screenshots are perfectly aligned within the laptop frame; only the third one remains a work in progress.

E. Synchronizing Video and Audio

When you use Camtasia Recorder to record a tutorial, you typically capture audio and video together. This saves you a lot of time during editing, since the two tracks are naturally synchronized. The same applies when the narrator appears on screen: recording audio and video simultaneously ensures perfect lip-syncing.

That said, there are many situations in which audio and video must be recorded separately. Here are a few examples.

- When you hire a professional voice actor or use text-to-speech software to record (generate) the narration.
- In multilingual projects where each language version is recorded by a different person (or generated separately using text-to-speech).
- For complex onscreen demonstrations, it may be easier to record the video first and add the voiceover later.
- If you are not satisfied with the quality of the original audio recording, you may want to re-record the narration during post-production.

In this section, you will return to the ***00_01_prerequisite*** project you already worked with earlier in this chapter.

1. Open the ***Chapter05/00_01_prerequisites*** project in Camtasia.
2. Use **`Ctrl + Home`** (Windows) or **`Cmd + Enter`** (Mac) to reposition the playhead at the beginning of the project.

In this project, the audio track comes from the video of the narrator that you imported earlier in this chapter. That clip was filmed in a studio, while the PowerPoint slideshow was recorded separately using Camtasia Recorder. You will now ensure that the animations in the captured slideshow play in sync with the narration in the narrator's video.

3. Use the **`spacebar`** to start playing the video.

What a mess! Since both clips in the timeline include their own audio, you hear both voiceovers at the same time. This overlap makes it impossible to isolate and clean up the narrator's track. Fortunately, there's an easy fix!

1. Separate Audio and Video

In the final video, you won't need the audio track from the PowerPoint slideshow recording. Its purpose was to help you establish the right pace. As a result, the animations and the voiceover should already be more or less in sync, which significantly reduces the necessary adjustments.

The problem is that the audio and video of the PowerPoint recording are merged into a single clip on Track 1 of the timeline. The question is: how do you remove the audio track without removing the video?

1. Right-click the PowerPoint slideshow recording on track 1 of the timeline.
2. In the context menu, select **Separate Audio and Video** (Windows) or **Separate Video and Audio** (Mac).

As a result, the PowerPoint video and the corresponding audio have been split into two independent tracks on the timeline, as shown in the image below.

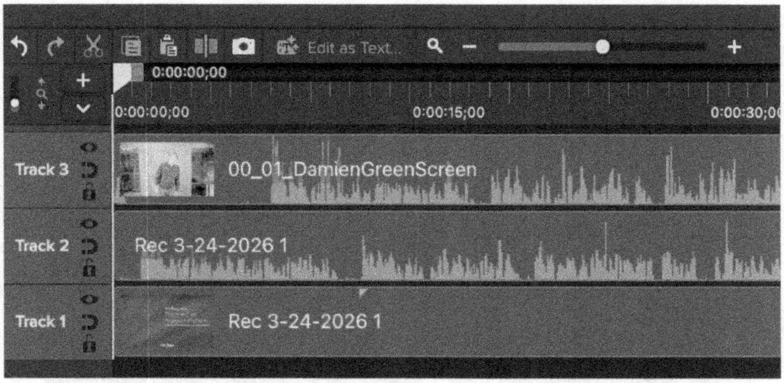

05_36.png - The audio and video occupy two separate tracks in the timeline.

The last step is to delete the audio on track 2.

3. Right-click the **Track 2** header at the far left of the timeline.
4. Select **Remove Track** from the context menu.
5. Confirm your intention to delete the track.

After performing these steps, the audio is gone, but the corresponding PowerPoint video remains exactly as it was.

2. Locking Tracks

You will now clean up the narrator's video using the selection and editing techniques discussed earlier.

1. Trim the beginning and the end of the video using the techniques you learned in the Trimming the Start and End of a Recording section earlier in this chapter.
2. Reposition the narrator's video at the very beginning of the timeline.
3. Reposition the playhead at the beginning of the project to prepare for the next steps.

You have now established the beginning and the end of the narration track. The next step is to remove any hesitations present in the recording.

4. Use the `spacebar` to start playing the video.
5. Pause playback as soon as you notice the first hesitation.
6. Use the green and red handles on either side of the playhead to select the first section to remove (approximately between timecodes *0:00:49;00* and *0:01:00;00*).
7. Right-click within the selected area and select **Ripple Delete** (Windows) or **Ripple Delete Range** (Mac). You can also use `Ctrl + Delete` (Windows) or `Cmd + Delete` (Mac).

And that's when disaster strikes! This action removes the selection from both tracks at once, as illustrated in the following screenshot.

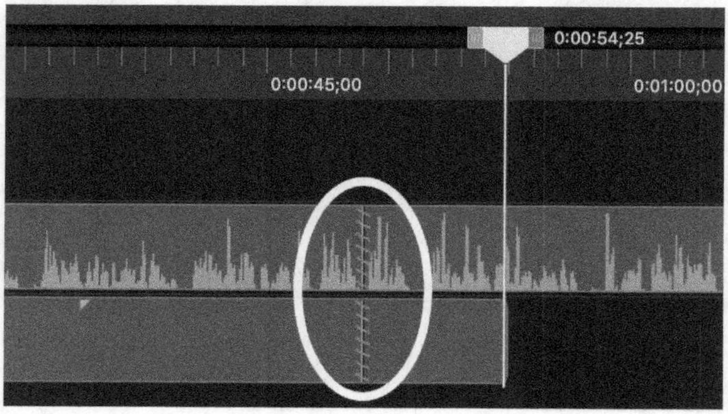

05_37.png - This action cuts across both tracks.

You need to find a way to clean up the narration, but without affecting the PowerPoint recording on track 1.

8. Use `Ctrl + Z` (Windows) or `Cmd + Z` (Mac) to undo the **Ripple Delete** action.

9. In the header of track 1 (which contains the PowerPoint recording), click the padlock icon. You can also right-click the track 1 header and select **Lock Track**.

This action locks track 1, as shown in the image below.

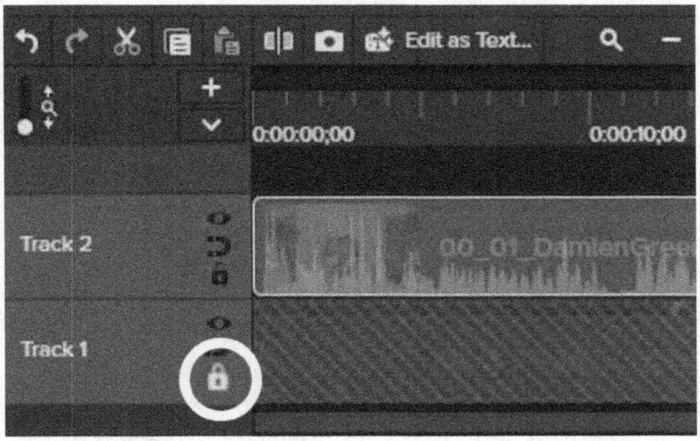

5_38.png - Track 1 is locked.

With this lock enabled, all multimedia elements on Track 1 are protected against any changes. You can't even select these elements unless you first unlock the track.

10. Reselect the portion of the video you want to delete.
11. Use `Ctrl + Delete` (Windows) or `Cmd + Delete` (Mac) to ripple delete the selected section.
12. Repeat these steps for each segment you want to remove from the narrator's video.

With track 1 locked, these changes only affect the video of the narrator, leaving the PowerPoint recording untouched. After making these edits, the narrator's video and the PowerPoint recording should have roughly the same duration.

3. Finalize the Syncing

Thanks to the work done in the previous sections, the video and the PowerPoint recording should already be mostly in sync. But you still need some fine-tuning to ensure the animations and the voiceover are *perfectly* aligned.

For this task, you will assume that the narrator's video is final (at least for now); you will therefore use it as a reference as you adjust the PowerPoint recording.

1. In the track header area, unlock track 1 (the one containing the PowerPoint recording).
2. Lock track 2 (containing the video of the narrator).

From now on, the narrator's video is protected from any changes, whereas the PowerPoint recording can be selected and edited at will.

Only slight modifications are necessary, but their exact timing depends on the cuts made in the previous section, so you will need to adapt the following exercise to your specific situation.

You may encounter the following two situations when performing this type of precise alignment work.

- Either the PowerPoint animation is slightly *ahead* of the narration,
- or the animation is slightly *behind* the narration.

In the next two sections, you'll learn how to handle each of these situations

1. The Animation is Slightly Ahead

If the PowerPoint animation starts slightly ahead of the narration, you need to delay the animation by adding extra material before it begins.

For example, say you want to slightly delay the appearance of the **Two Parts** Header on the second slide of the presentation. To do this, start by splitting the PowerPoint video just before the animation begins.

1. Position the playhead just before the **Two Parts** header appears on the screen and while the first slide is still visible (around timecode *0:00:11;20*).

Notice the tiny blue triangles along the timeline; they mark the transition between two slides. You should position the playhead just before the first blue triangle. Feel free to zoom in on the timeline to position the playhead precisely.

2. Click the PowerPoint recording to select it.
3. Click the **Split** icon in the upper-left corner of the timeline. You can also use the `S` key (Windows) or the `Cmd + T` shortcut (Mac).

This operation creates two separate video clips on track 1, as shown in the image below.

05_39.png - Click the Split icon to divide the selected clip into two parts.

The next step is to position the animation *exactly* as desired.

4. In the timeline, position the playhead exactly when the narrator says, "... *two main parts*".
5. On track 1, drag the second video clip to the right until it snaps to the playhead.

As a result, the **Two Parts** header animation is now perfectly synchronized with the voiceover. However, there is a gap between the two video clips on track 1, as shown in the image below.

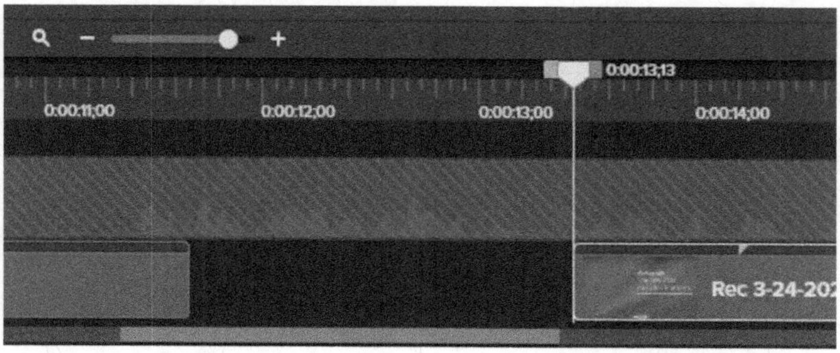

05_40.png - There is a gap between the two video clips on track 1.

You will now fill this gap by extending the duration of the leftmost clip.

6. In the timeline, select the video clip to the left of the gap.
7. Extend its right edge until the gap is completely closed.
8. Rewind the playhead by a few seconds, then play the video to make sure the edit goes unnoticed.

And that's when you notice a big problem! The *"Two Parts"* header is animated twice! How on earth did that happen?

Remember the *Non-destructive Editing* principle? When you drag the edge of the left clip to the right, you actually reveal the video frames that come after the cut! So, you've effectively reintroduced the animation of the *«Two Parts»* heading. Since this animation is also present in the second clip, it now ends the first clip and starts again immediately in the second.

To fill the gap, you must not reveal the video frames after the cut but rather extend the last frame of the left clip into the gap.

9. Use `Ctrl + Z` (Windows) or `Cmd + Z` (Mac) to undo your last action.
10. Hold down `Alt` (Windows) or `Option` (Mac) while extending the right edge of the first clip into the gap.
11. Jump back a few seconds and play the sequence to ensure the transition is seamless.

That's it! By holding down the **`Alt`** (Windows) or **`Option`** (Mac) key, you've extended the last frame of the first video clip. On the timeline, you can see a stitch mark where the first video clip ended before you made this adjustment.

This trick is very useful in many situations, such as when you need to sync audio and video in a Camtasia project.

2. The Animation is Slightly Behind

If the PowerPoint animation starts slightly behind the narration, you must delete a few frames before the animation so that it starts a bit early.

For example, you want the *1. Data analytics* heading on the second slide of the PowerPoint presentation to appear slightly sooner.

1. In the timeline, position the playhead just before the *1. Data Analytics* heading appears.
2. Make sure the PowerPoint recording is selected.
3. Use the **Split** icon, the `S` key (Windows), or the `Cmd + T` shortcut (Mac) to split the selected video clip at the playhead.
4. Now, position the playhead exactly when the narrator says, *"...the basics of data analytics..."*.
5. Drag the right edge of the left clip to the current position of the playhead.
6. Move the right clip to the left to close the gap.
7. Jump back a few seconds and play the video to ensure the edit is seamless.

Great job! You've successfully moved a PowerPoint animation forward that was slightly behind the narration. You've also ensured that the viewer never notices this edit.

3. Practical Exercise

You can now handle both situations: when the PowerPoint animation is slightly ahead, and when it is slightly behind.

- You can now apply these adjustments to the entire project, ensuring that all PowerPoint animations are perfectly synchronized with the voiceover.
- When done, make sure the PowerPoint recording ends at the same time as the narrator's video. To do this, either shorten the PowerPoint recording or extend its final frame.

At the end of this exercise, you'll have a number of short video clips on track 1 of your project, as shown in the image below.

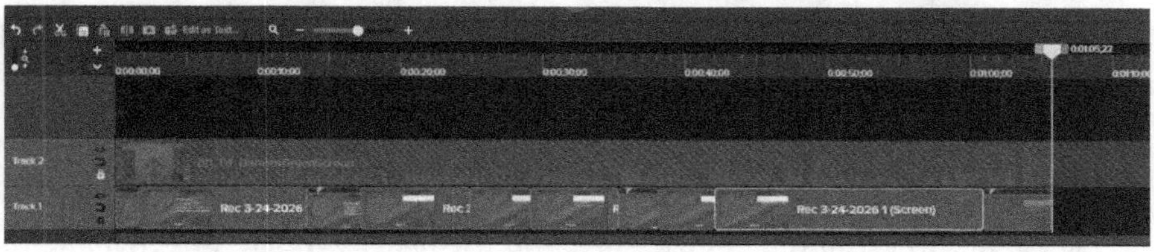

05_41.png - You get a lot of short video clips on track 1.

4. Grouping Clips on the Timeline

The cuts themselves won't be visible to your audience, but splitting the PowerPoint recording into multiple small segments can turn simple tasks, such as applying visual effects, animations, transitions, and behaviors, into a real headache. To streamline your workflow, you'll now group these small pieces into a single, easy-to-manage item on the timeline.

1. Right-click the **Track 1** header at the far left of the timeline.
2. In the context menu, click **Select All Media on Track** (Windows) or **Select All on Track** (Mac).
3. In the timeline, right-click any selected video clip and select **Group** from the context menu. You can also use the `Ctrl + G` (Windows) or `Cmd + G` (Mac) keyboard shortcut.
4. Right-click the newly created group.

Take a moment to explore the options available in the context menu. Notice the **Ungroup** option to split the group, as well as the **Open Group** option, which lets you access nested items without ungrouping.

5. In the context menu, click **Rename Group**.
6. Type `PowerPoint Slideshow` and press `Enter`.

The result of these steps is illustrated in the image below.

05_42.png - The clips making up the PowerPoint slideshow are grouped.

These syncing strategies work perfectly for this exercise, because, aside from animations, a PowerPoint presentation is mostly static. This makes it easy to trim or extend slides without making it noticeable in the final video.

For screen recordings featuring a lot of mouse movements and actions, other techniques are available, such as speeding up or slowing down video playback. Sometimes, you can even delete entire sections and hide the edit with a simple transition. For example, instead of forcing viewers to watch you fill out a long form, you can completely remove that sequence and use a simple fade transition to make the video flow smoothly.

These techniques will be covered in the next chapter: Transitions, Animations, and Visual Effects.

F. Conclusion

In this chapter, you've taken your first steps into the fascinating craft of video editing. The tools you've explored have helped you transform your raw footage into something far more compelling. Even though your projects are still far from finished, the progress you've made is unmistakable.

You have learned some fundamental concepts, such as working with the playhead, managing tracks in the timeline, trimming unwanted parts from your video clips, as well as the significance of positioning your elements both in space (on the canvas) and in time (in the timeline).

You've also experimented with some of the annotations available in Camtasia. Because these objects are created entirely within Camtasia, you don't need to import them into the media bin. These are powerful tools you can use to enhance your videos. In the following chapters, you'll discover other types of annotations and learn how to leverage their many benefits.

These fundamentals form the foundation of all your future editing work and involve some of the most commonly used tools in Camtasia. Don't hesitate to take some time and practice with your own projects and recordings.

In the next chapter, you'll build on these editing skills by adding transitions, animations, and behaviors to your video projects. You'll also discover some of the visual effects available in Camtasia, including the background removal tool, which you'll use to remove the green screen behind the narrator.

Transitions, Animations and Visual Effects

In the previous chapter, you learned about some fundamental editing tools, such as using the timeline and the playhead, the operating modes of the canvas, and how to add simple annotations to your project. This chapter takes your post-production skills to the next level by exploring special effects, transitions, behaviors, and animations.

First, you will customize how elements in your video appear and disappear using Camtasia's built-in transitions. Then, you will learn various animation techniques using the built-in animations and behaviors available in Camtasia. Whether you're rotating, resizing, or moving elements across the screen, these tools will help you create dynamic video tutorials that boost engagement and retention.

Finally, you'll explore some more advanced visual effects, such as the spectacular green-screen removal tool, which is widely used both in traditional video and in online training production.

While transitions, animations, behaviors, and special effects can significantly enrich your videos, they are easily overdone. Always keep in mind that the goal is to support and reinforce your message, not to showcase the full range of features available in Camtasia or your mastery of the software. Sometimes, the key to a polished and effective tutorial lies in simplicity.

A. Preparing the Exercises

As in previous chapters, the step-by-step instructions provided here are based on the supplied exercise files.

These exercises are provided as compressed projects that you must first import into Camtasia using the import process described at the beginning of the previous chapter.

1. Download and unzip the exercises for Chapter 06.
2. Import the ***Chapter06/projects/02_02_conclusion.zip*** project into the ***Chapter06*** folder of the exercises.

You are now ready to start exploring Camtasia's transitions.

B. Using Transitions

You can apply transitions at the beginning and end of any item in your project. Use transitions to control how elements:

- appear on the canvas,
- disappear from the canvas, and
- transition into one another.

In this section, you will explore some of the built-in transition effects and apply them to the elements in the ***02_02_conclusion*** project.

1. Make sure the ***Chapter06/02_02_conclusion*** project is open in Camtasia.
2. Watch the entire video.

The post-production phase of this project is already well underway, and the timeline contains most of the elements present in the final video. These include a static background image, studio footage filmed against a green backdrop, a few text annotations, and several excerpts from screen recordings. After reading through the previous chapters, you should be familiar with these elements and understand how to arrange them on the timeline.

As you watch the video, focus on how these elements appear, disappear, and flow into one another. For now, you shouldn't notice anything special.

1. Choosing a transition

Camtasia offers dozens of built-in transitions available in the **Transitions** panel on the left side of the screen.

1. Click **Transitions** on the left side of the screen to open the transitions panel. You can also press `T` on your keyboard.
2. Open the **Type** dropdown.

These actions are depicted in the image below.

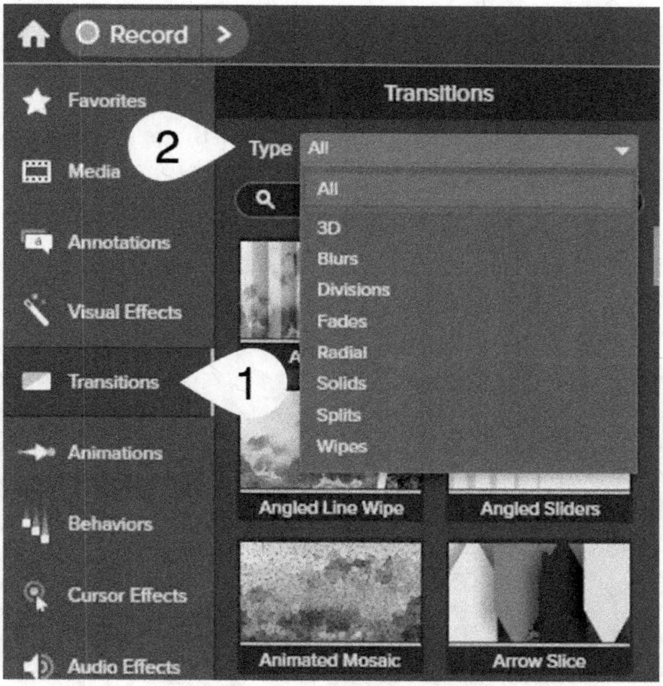

06_01.png - Camtasia offers several types of transitions.

To help you navigate this vast library, Camtasia organizes transitions into several distinct types.

3. Select any type from the **Type** dropdown.
4. Pass the mouse over the transition thumbnails in the panel to get a quick preview.
5. Take some time to explore the available transitions and types.

The ability to preview a transition by simply moving the mouse over the corresponding thumbnail makes it easy to find the right one. If you know the name of the transition you're looking for, you can also use the search field at the top of the **Transitions** panel.

2. Applying Transitions

Now that you have a better idea of the available built-in transitions, it's time to start using them. In this exercise, you'll apply a simple fade effect to the screen recording snippets scattered throughout this project.

1. Position the playhead around timecode *0:00:12;00*.
2. Zoom in on the timeline so that you can see roughly 30 seconds worth of the video.
3. In the **Transitions** panel, open the **Type** dropdown and select **Fades.**

You will now apply a fade transition to the ***01_02_dashboard*** clip on track 4 of the timeline.

4. Drag the **Fade** transition from the **Transitions** panel and move it over the ***01_02_dashboard*** clip on Track 4 of the timeline. *Do not let go of the mouse yet.*

As you move the transition over elements in the timeline, you'll notice green and yellow (Windows only) rectangles appearing at the ends of the element you hover over, as shown in the following image.

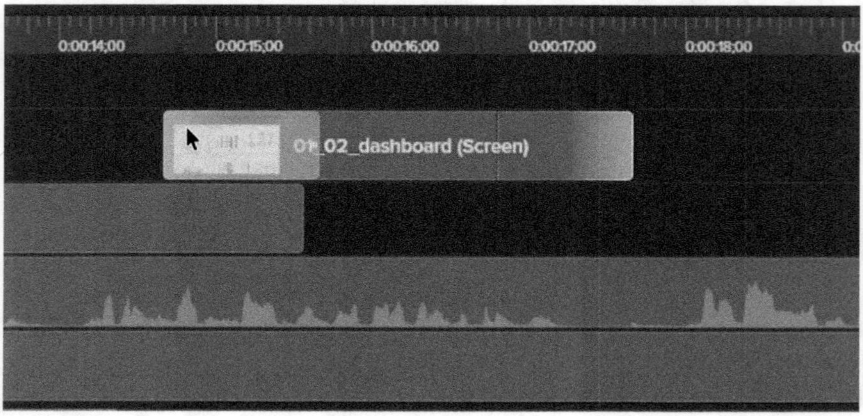

06_02.png – Greenish rectangles appear on the ends of the hovered element.

These rectangles mark possible drop zones for the transition. Hovering over the left, right, or center of an item determines where the transition will be applied.

- Hovering over the left edge of the item would apply an entrance transition only.
- Hovering over the right edge of the item would apply an exit transition only.
- Hovering over the center of the item would apply both transitions.

The highlighted transition is applied when you release the mouse button.

5. Position the mouse over the center of the element so that both green rectangles are displayed simultaneously.
6. Let go of the mouse to apply both transitions.

This action is illustrated in the image below.

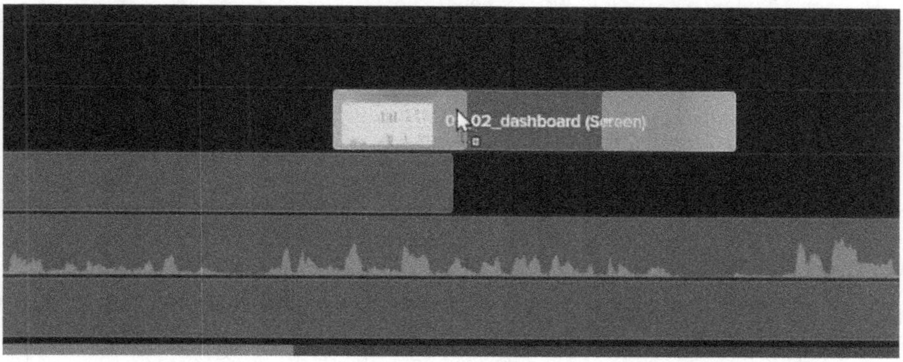

06_03.png - Let go of the mouse when both green rectangles are displayed.

You just applied a fade-in transition at the beginning of this element and a fade-out transition at the end. In the timeline, these two transitions are represented by the two green rectangles visible on either side of the element. Now, let's see them in action.

7. Position the playhead a few seconds ahead of the transition.
8. Use the `spacebar` to play the video.
9. As you watch, pay close attention to how the ***01_02_dashboard*** element appears and disappears.

Congratulations! You've just added your first Camtasia transition to one of the elements in this project.

3. Changing the Transition Duration

The default duration for a transition is one second, which seems a bit slow in this example.

*You can change the default transition duration in the **Timing** (Windows) or **Timeline** (Mac) tab of the preferences.*

In the timeline, the width of the green rectangles determines the duration of the transitions.

1. In the timeline, click the green rectangle at the beginning of the ***01_02_dashboard*** clip.

Clicking this green rectangle selects the fade-in transition. In the timeline, the rectangle turns yellow to indicate it is selected.

2. Use the mouse to shorten the transition (reduce the width of the green rectangle) to about half a second.

Remember that the project plays at 30 frames per second; therefore, half a second corresponds to 15 frames worth of video.

3. Do the same with the fade-out transition at the end of this clip.
4. Move the playhead back a few seconds and hit the `spacebar` to test the new transitions.

You have now successfully reduced the duration of these two transitions, as shown in the image below.

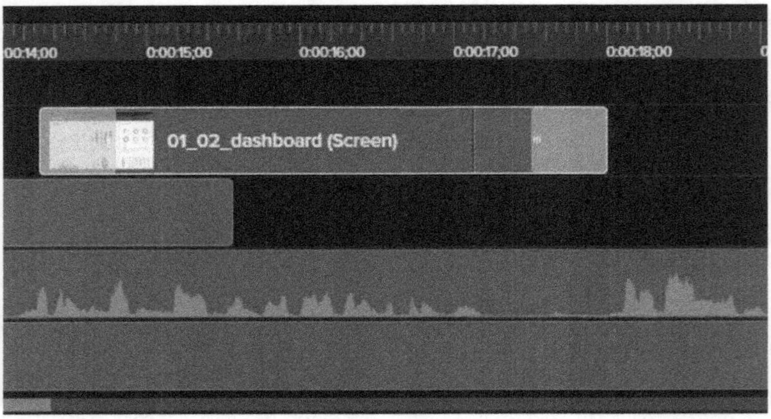

06_04.png - The transitions have been shortened.

4. Practical Exercise: Applying Transitions

In this hands-on exercise, you will apply the same fade transition to the other screen recording excerpts in the project.

The first two are located on track 3 between timecodes *0:00:26;00* and *0:00:42;00*. For this exercise, you will complete the following tasks.

- Add a fade-in transition to the first clip.
- Add a fade-out transition to the second clip.
- Shorten the duration of the transitions to approximately 0.5 seconds.

After completing these tasks, this section of the timeline should look like the following image.

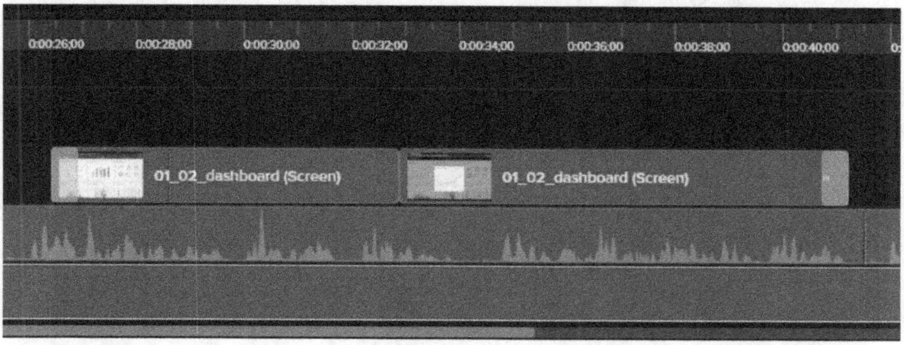

06_05.png - Adding fade-in or fade-out effects.

Next, do the same with the three clips on track 4 of the timeline between timecodes *0:00:46;00* and *0:00:55;00*: apply a fade-in only transition to the first clip and a fade-out only transition to the last one.

In total, you have applied four transitions in this exercise: two fade-ins and two fade-outs.

5. Applying a Transition Between Two Clips

It is very easy to establish a transition between adjacent clips in the timeline. Let's explore this feature using the following steps.

1. Position the playhead around timecode *0:00:45;00*.
2. Start playing the video and observe how the three consecutive video clips on track 4 flow together.

For now, there is no transition between these clips. They are said to appear *cut* on the canvas.

3. Go back to the **Transitions** panel on the left side of the screen and select **Fades** in the **Type** dropdown.
4. Drag the **Burn Through Fade** transition from the **Transitions** panel and move if over the three adjacent clips on track 4– *do not let go of the mouse yet.*

As in the previous section, small yellow (Windows only) and green rectangles mark the possible drop zones for the transition.

06_06.png - It is easy to apply a transition between two adjacent elements on the timeline.

5. Release the mouse once a green rectangle appears *between* the first and the second clips.

This applies the **Burn Through Fade** transition *between* these two clips. On the timeline, the green rectangle spans both clips.

6. Repeat the same actions to apply a **Burn Through Fade** transition between the second and the third clip.
7. Position the playhead slightly ahead of this sequence and play the video to test these new transitions.
8. Feel free to adjust the transition duration by changing the width of the green rectangles in the timeline.

In doing so, note that Camtasia evenly adjusts the transition on both sides of the split.

After completing these steps, this section of the timeline should look like the following image.

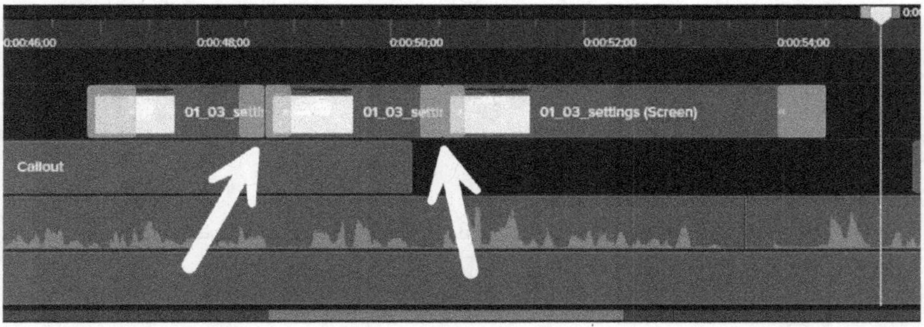

06_07.png - You have added two transitions between items in the timeline.

6. Editing an Existing Transition

Finding the perfect transition often takes a bit of trial and error. This section introduces two different techniques for modifying existing transitions, allowing you to iterate until you find the right one.

A first approach is to drag another transition directly onto the existing one.

1. Select any transition from the **Transitions** panel.
2. Drag and drop it onto an existing transition in the timeline (on Windows, Camtasia highlights the existing transition in red).
3. Rewind the playhead by a few seconds and play the video to review the new transition.

Another way to edit a transition is to select it in the timeline and use the Properties panel to make the necessary changes.

4. Click any transition (any green rectangle) in the timeline. The selected transition turns yellow.
5. If necessary, open the Properties panel on the right side of the screen.

The Properties panel always displays the properties of the currently selected item. In this case, it displays the properties of the selected transition, as shown in the following image.

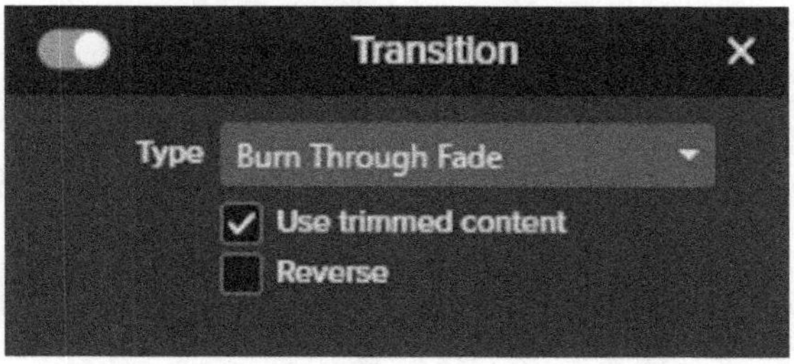

06_08.png - The properties of the ***Burn Through Fade*** *transition.*

Take some time to examine the available properties.

- The toggle button in the upper-left corner lets you enable or disable the transition.
- The **Type** dropdown lets you select another transition.
- The **Use trimmed content** checkbox only applies to *between* transitions and is selected by default. This setting uses frames from either side of the cut to create the transition. Most of the time, this isn't a problem, but in some cases, it can inadvertently expose the mistake or hesitation you are trying to hide with that transition.
- The **Reverse** checkbox changes the direction of the transition.

These options are also available when you right-click the selected transition in the timeline.

The wide variety of built-in transitions, combined with these few options, gives you everything you need to give your transitions a polished and professional finish.

7. Transitions: Use Cases and Best Practices

So far in this chapter, you explored the most common use cases for transitions. You used them to

- bring elements into view on the canvas,
- remove elements from the canvas,
- and change the way two adjacent elements transition from one to the next.

Another use of transitions is creating *time ellipses*. For example, if your tutorial involves a lengthy process (such as downloading a large file, performing a complex calculation, or filling out a lengthy form), you can edit out the wait time and use a transition to show that time has passed. You can also use a transition to hide a cut in a video in which the narrator appears on screen.

Sometimes, the best solution is to not use any transition at all! And don't be intimidated by Camtasia's extensive transition library. In practice, you'll end up using the same few transitions most of the time. Remember that the golden rule is *moderation*. The most effective transitions are often the most subtle.

C. Exploring Animations

Unlike transitions, which can only be applied at the beginning and end of a clip, animations can be added anywhere.

In this section, you will revisit the ***01_02_dashboard*** project you already worked with in the previous chapter. Use the following steps to get ready.

1. Save and close the ***02_02_conclusion*** project from the previous section.
2. Import the ***Chapter06/projects/01_02_dashboard.zip*** project into the ***Chapter06*** folder of the exercises using the import process described at the beginning of the previous chapter.
3. Watch the entire project to refresh your memory.

At this stage, the timeline of this project only contains the screen recording you captured in Chapter 4 – Recording With Camtasia and cleaned up in Chapter 5 – Editing Your Video. You will now take this project to the next level by adding a few animations as well as some annotations.

1. Applying Predefined Animations

Let's start by applying one of the predefined animations available in Camtasia. The first step is to identify the exact moment when to apply this animation effect.

1. Use `Ctrl + Home` (Windows) or `Cmd + Enter` (Mac) to move the playhead back to the beginning of the project.
2. Press the `spacebar` to start playing the video.
3. Pause the video when the narrator says, *"Each chart has two icons in the upper right-hand corner..."*.
4. If necessary, zoom in on the timeline to get a clear view over this particular sequence.
5. Position the playhead at timecode *0:00:14;00*, immediately before the narrator begins that line.

Now that the playhead is at the right spot, the next step is to select the animation to apply.

6. Click **Animations** on the left side of the screen to open the **Animations** panel. You can also use the `A` key on your keyboard.

The **Animations** panel looks different depending on your operating system. On Windows, you'll find two tabs: **Zoom-n-Pan** and **Animations**. On the Mac, only the **Animations** tab is available.

7. [*Windows only*]. Switch to the **Animations** tab of the **Animations** panel.
8. Drag the **Scale Up** animation from the **Animations** panel and drop it onto track 1 so it begins at the playhead position.

Animations appear as green arrows on the timeline (the arrow turns yellow when the animation is selected), as shown in the image below.

Don't hesitate to zoom in on the timeline to clearly see the animation arrow as shown in the image below.

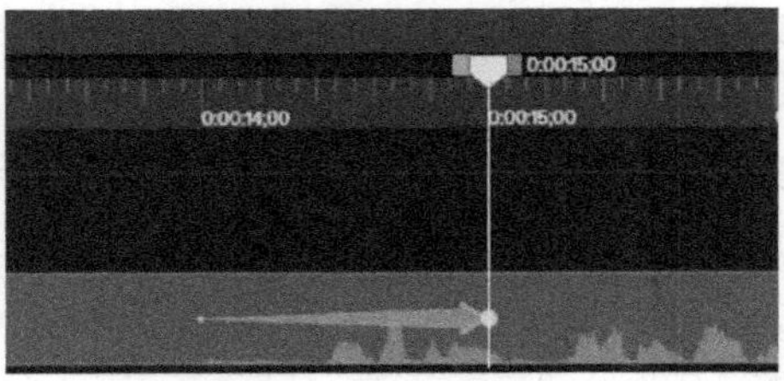

06_09.png – A green arrow represents the animation on the timeline.

9. In the timeline, position the playhead *after* the arrow representing the animation.
10. In the Properties panel, lower the **Scale** of the screen recording to `70%`.
11. On the canvas, move the screen recording downward until the **Dashboard** and **Data** links are visible.

The canvas should now look like the image below.

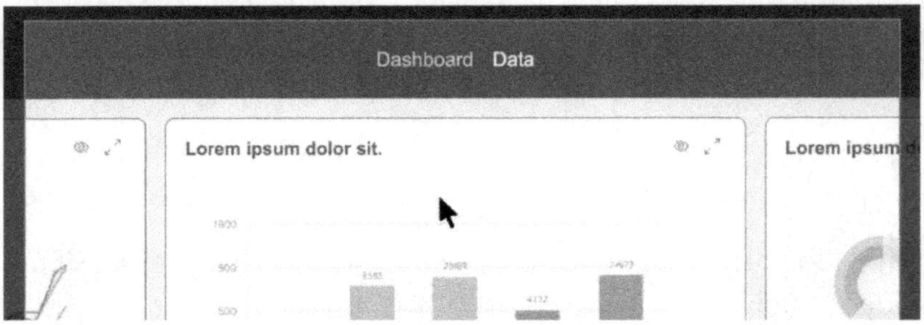

*06_10.png - Reposition the screen recording to see the **Dashboard** and the **Data** links.*

12. In the timeline, position the playhead a few seconds *before* the animation.

On the canevas, notice how the recording resets to its original size and position.

13. Press the `spacebar` to start playing the video.

During playback, watch how the size and the position of the screen recording change as the playhead moves through the animation.

14. Pause the video after the narrator has finished saying, *"...while the second opens the chart in its own enlarged window."*
15. Position the playhead in the silence that follows, at timecode *0:00:25;00*.

Here, you will apply the opposite animation to restore the size and position of the screen recording.

16. Drag the **Restore** animation from the **Animations** panel and drop it onto Track 1 of the timeline so that it starts at the current playhead position.

A second green arrow marks this second animation. When the playhead passes over this second animation, the screen recording reverts to its original size and position on the canvas.

17. In the timeline, reposition the playhead before the *first* animation.
18. Play the video and enjoy the zoom-in effect of the first animation, followed by the zoom-out effect of the second!
19. Don't forget to save your project.

Congratulations on your first Camtasia animations! By adding movement to your project, you've broken up the monotony and made the content a lot more engaging. That's a big win both for your learners and your teaching approach!

2. Understanding Animations

Animations in Camtasia are based on the concept of *keyframes*. Mastering this fundamental concept is essential to truly unlock the full potential of animations in Camtasia.

1. In the timeline, position the playhead *before* the first animation.
2. Click the screen recording to select it.
3. Make sure the Properties panel is open on the right side of the screen and that the first tab (**Visual Properties**) is selected.

As a result, the Properties panel displays the visual properties of the screen recording, as shown in the image below.

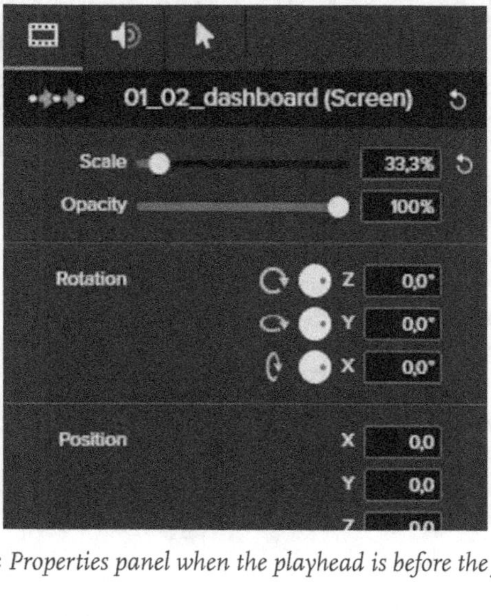

06_11.png - The Properties panel when the playhead is before the first animation.

Take note of the values for the **Scale** (33,3%), the **Position** properties (**X**, **Y**, and **Z** at 0), the **Width** (1280.0), and the **Height** (720.0).

4. In the timeline, position the playhead *between* the two animations.

Take another look at these values in the Properties panel; you'll notice the figures have changed.

You already know that the Properties panel displays the properties of the selected element. You now discover that it displays them *for the current position of the playhead.*

5. In the timeline, reposition the playhead *before* the first animation.
6. As you scrub the playhead forward, keep an eye on the **Scale**, **Position**, **Width**, and **Height** properties within the Properties panel.

As the playhead moves through the first animation, observe how the values of these properties *gradually* change in the Properties panel.

7. In the timeline, zoom in on the first green arrow.

As illustrated below, the green arrow is flanked by two small white dots (if the playhead is past the animation, the ending dot is red instead of white).

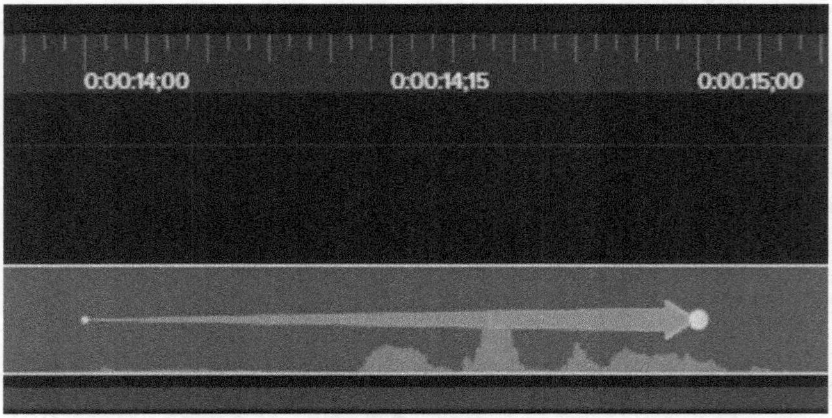

06_12.png - The arrow representing the animation is flanked by two small white dots.

These two dots are the so-called *keyframes*.

- The dot at the beginning of the animation arrow (the first keyframe) represents the object's properties *before* the animation.
- The dot at the end of the animation arrow (the second keyframe) represents the object's properties *after* the animation.
- The arrow itself represents the gradual transition from one set of properties to the next.

An animation can be described as a gradual transition between two sets of properties. In the first keyframe, you set the initial values, while in the second, you specify the final values. The software then generates all the steps needed to transition from one state to the other. The duration of the animation corresponds to the length of the arrow on the timeline (i.e., the distance between the two keyframes).

By leveraging this fundamental principle, you can animate virtually any property within the Properties panel. This opens up a whole new world of creative and storytelling opportunities.

In Chapter 04 – Recording with Camtasia, you recorded this sequence at a 1920 x 1080 resolution (full HD). You can now see the benefits of this choice. After the animation, the video is displayed at only 70% of its original size. In other words, you can zoom in on your screen recording without risking pixelation.

3. Creating Custom Animations

Now that you are familiar with the *keyframe* principle, you're ready to build more complex custom animations. You'll start by adding a new annotation to the ***01_02_dashboard*** project; then you will animate this annotation in sync with the narration.

As usual, the first step is to position the playhead in the timeline.

1. Adjust the timeline zoom so you see approximately 30 seconds worth of video.
2. Position the playhead before the first animation from the previous section.
3. Play the video and locate the moment when the narrator says, *"The first icon allows you to show or hide the chart."*
4. Position the playhead just before that line (around timecode *0:00:18;00*).

The next step is to insert the item you plan to animate. This gives you the opportunity to try out a new type of annotation.

1. Working With Sketch Motions

In the previous chapter, you discovered shapes and text annotations. In this section, you'll explore a third type of annotation known as *Sketch Motion.*

1. Open the **Annotations** panel on the left side of the screen.
2. Open the **Sketch Motion** tab (the fifth tab from the left).

These steps are shown in the image below.

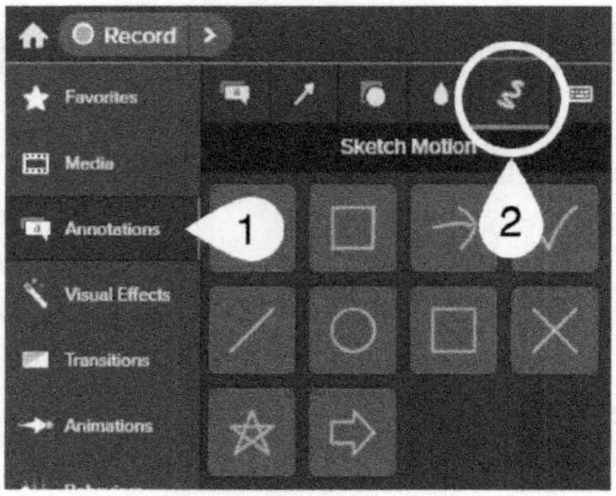

*06_13.png - Open the **Sketch Motion** tab of the **Annotations** panel.*

On a Mac, the available annotations are slightly different, but this doesn't affect the rest of this exercise.

3. Drag an arrow-shaped sketch motion (the third one in the image above) from the annotations panel and drop it onto the canvas.
4. Move the playhead slightly ahead of this annotation and press the `spacebar` to start playing the video.

An arrow should be drawn on the canvas. You will now adjust the properties of this sketch motion using the following steps.

5. In the timeline, position the playhead over the sketch motion so that the arrow is visible on the canvas.
6. Click the arrow to select it.
7. If necessary, open the Properties panel on the right side of the screen.
8. Open the **Annotation Properties** tab.

These actions are depicted in the image below.

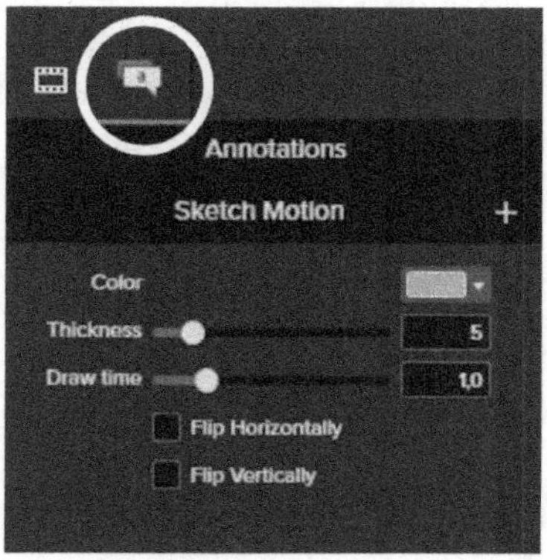

*06_14.png - Open the **Annotation Properties** tab.*

The above image illustrates the default sketch motion properties on Windows. These are slightly different on Mac.

9. Choose any dark color for your sketch motion.
10. Increase the **Thickness** so the object is clearly visible on the canvas.
11. Adjust the sketch motion's size and orientation until it points directly to the eye icon in the top-right corner of the chart.

The result should look like the image below.

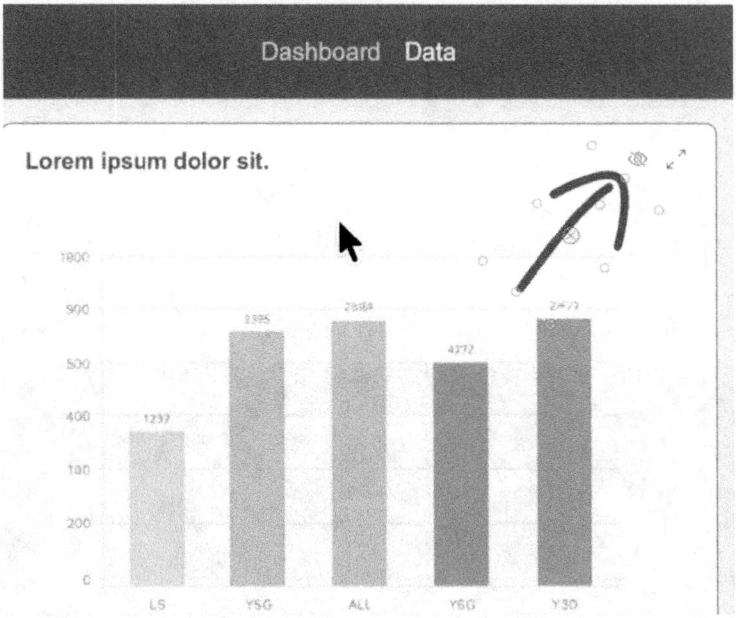

06_15.png - The sketch motion arrow points to the eye icon.

That's it for the canvas! In the timeline, Camtasia places the sketch motion on the first available track (Track 2) for a default duration of five seconds.

On Mac, Camtasia automatically applies a default fade-out transition to any sketch motion annotation.

You will now set the duration of this annotation using the following steps.

12. Position the playhead exactly where the *restore* animation begins (at timecode *0:00:25;00*)
13. Extend the duration of the sketch motion until it snaps to the playhead.

The sketch motion is now correctly positioned both in space (on the canvas) and in time (in the timeline). In the next section, you'll apply a custom animation to this annotation.

2. Animating the Sketch Motion Annotation

The sketch motion arrow you added in the previous section points toward the eye icon, but the voiceover quickly moves on to the other icon.

In this section, you will use an animation to reposition the arrow so that it points to the other icon in sync with the voiceover. As usual, the first step is to position the playhead in the timeline.

1. In the timeline, position the playhead just before the sketch motion.
2. Press the `spacebar` to start playing the project.
3. Pause the video when the narrator says, *"...while the second..."*.
4. Position the playhead in a silence before this line, at timecode *0:00:21:10*.
5. Open the **Animations** panel on the left side of the screen.
6. [*Windows only*] Make sure you are on the **Animations** tab.
7. Drag a **Custom** animation from the **Animations** panel and drop it in the timeline onto the sketch motion annotation so that it starts at the current position of the playhead.

As expected, this action adds a green arrow on track 2 of the timeline.

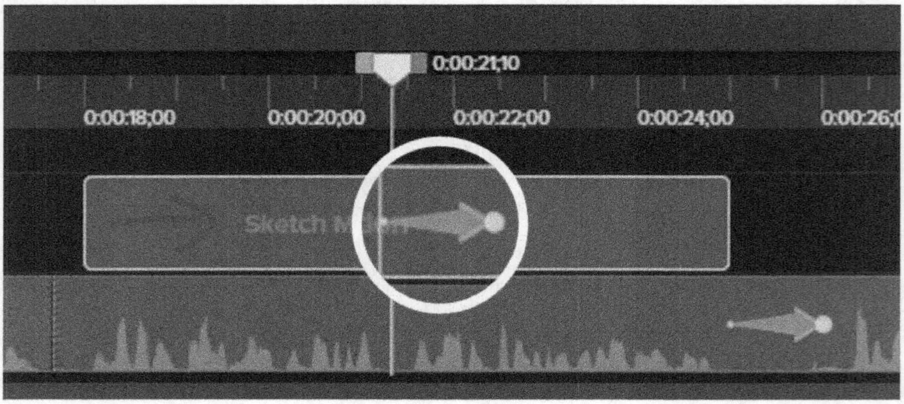

06_16.png - The ***Custom*** *animation on track 2 of the timeline.*

If you rewind the playhead for a few seconds and start playing the video, you won't notice anything special when the playhead reaches this animation. Unlike predefined animations discussed earlier, a custom animation simply establishes two keyframes on the timeline, but without modifying the properties of the animated object. In short, there is currently nothing to animate!

To actually create an animation, you need to modify the properties of the sketch motion to make them different on either side of the green arrow.

8. In the timeline, position the playhead *after* the custom animation.
9. On the canvas, adjust the position and rotation of the arrow to make it point toward the second icon.

The result of this operation is shown in the following image.

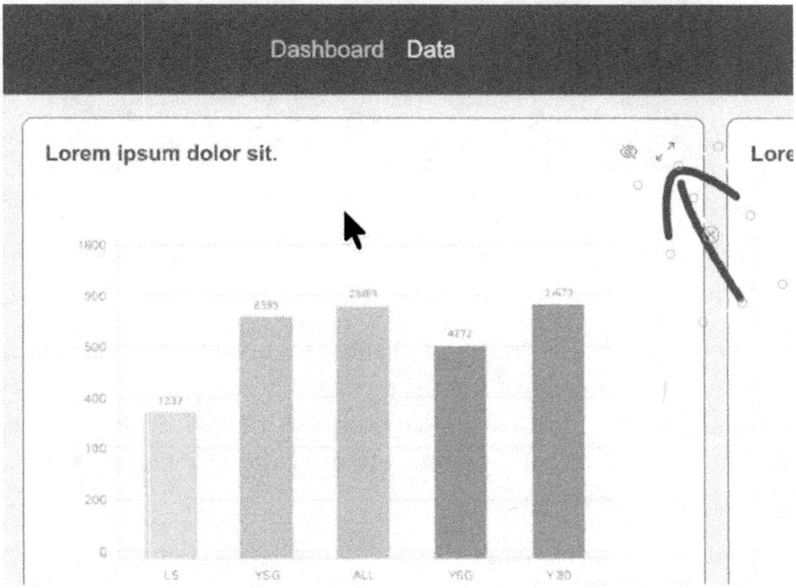

06_17.png – Reposition the arrow so that it points to the second icon.

Now it's time to test this new animation.

10. In the timeline, position the playhead *before* the custom animation.

On the canvas, the arrow reverts to its original position and rotation.

11. Start playing the video.

When the playhead reaches the animation, Camtasia smoothly moves the arrow to its new position.

Here is a brief recap on how this animation works

- Before the animation, the arrow has a certain position and rotation.
- After the animation, the arrow has another position and rotation.
- Camtasia calculates a smooth transition between these two states when the playhead passes over the animation.

You can control the speed of the animation by adjusting the length of the green arrow in the timeline. You can also reposition the animation in the timeline so that it starts at exactly the right moment.

12. [*Windows only*] Add a **Fade** transition to the end of the sketch motion.

This portion of the timeline should now look like the image below.

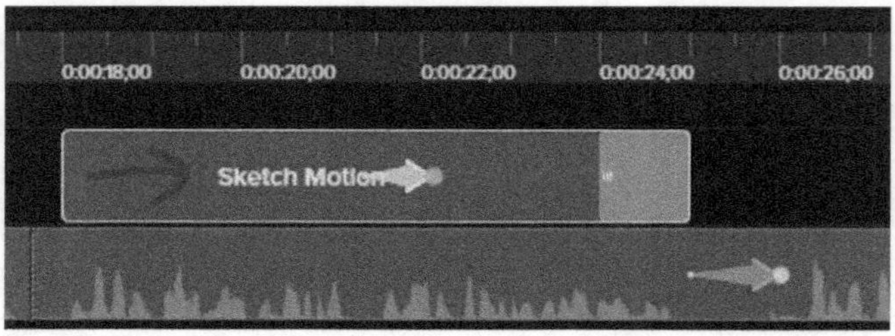

06_18.png - You applied an animation and a transition to the sketch motion annotation.

Congratulations! You've successfully created your first custom animation with Camtasia.

This example clearly illustrates how sketch motions, animations, and transitions can be combined to support your narrative. Not only does this make the tutorial a more enjoyable viewing experience for learners, but it's also an excellent way to boost knowledge retention, thereby increasing the learning effectiveness of your video.

In the next two sections, you'll discover two alternative techniques for creating animations. The first is only available on Windows, and the second only works on a Mac, so feel free to skip directly to the section that applies to your operating system.

4. [Windows] Using the Zoom-n-Pan Tab

On Windows, the **Animations** panel comprises two tabs. So far, you have only used the **Animations** tab. You will now use the **Zoom-n-Pan** tab to create two additional animations.

As usual, start by positioning the playhead in the timeline.

1. Use the `spacebar` to start playing the video.
2. Pause the video when the narrator says: *"At the top of the page, the main navigation bar includes..."*.
3. Position the playhead in the middle of that line, at timecode *0:01:17;15*.
4. Open the **Animations** panel on the left side of the screen and stay on the **Zoom-n-Pan** tab.

This tab contains a thumbnail of the canvas surrounded by eight resize handles.

5. Use the resize handles on the **Zoom-n-Pan** tab to zoom in and reposition the view on the main link bar.

As you make these adjustments, the **Zoom** level shown in the **Zoom-n-Pan** tab changes. On the canvas, the view is reframed and repositioned based on your actions, as shown in the following screenshot.

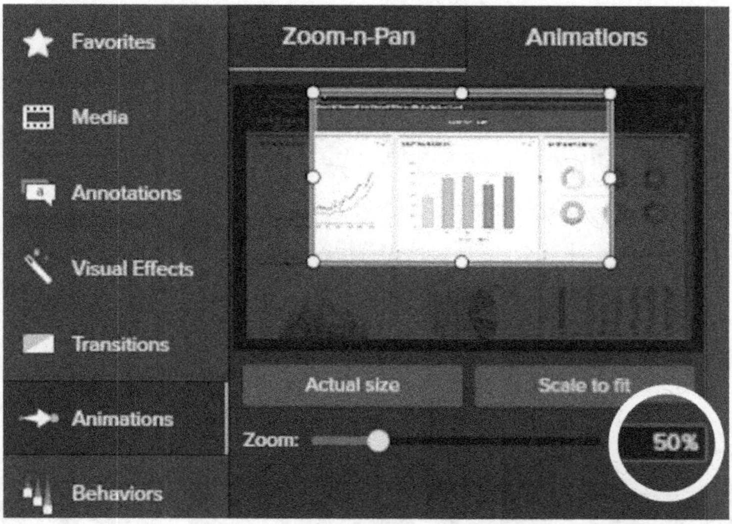

*06_19.png - Use the handles on the **Zoom-n-Pan** tab to reframe and reposition the view.*

In the timeline, Camtasia automatically adds an animation at the current position of the playhead.

6. Reposition the playhead a few seconds ahead of this new animation.
7. Start playing the video to test it.
8. If necessary, you can adjust the duration and the position of the animation in the timeline.

You will now create the opposite animation, which will restore the original view.

9. Start playing the video.
10. Pause the video when the narrator says, *"Selecting Data opens a page..."*.
11. Position the playhead in that sentence at timecode *0:01:22;25*.
12. Click **Scale to fit** in the **Zoom-n-Pan** tab of the **Animations** panel.

This action restores the view on the canvas and inserts a new animation at the current playhead position.

13. In the timeline, reposition the playhead before the two animations you added in this section.

14. Play the video and watch your zoom-in animation, followed by the opposite effect a few seconds later.

On Windows, the **Zoom-n-Pan** tab in the **Animations** panel offers an alternative way to quickly create animations.

5. [Mac] Using Auto Animate

In Chapter 05 – Editing Your Video, you explored the *Edit* mode, the *Pan* mode, the *Crop* mode, and the *Corner Pin* mode of the canvas. This section introduces the *Auto animate* mode, which is specific to Camtasia on Mac.

1. Use the `spacebar` to start playing the video.
2. Pause the video when the narrator says: *"At the top of the page, the main navigation bar includes...".*
3. Position the playhead in the middle of that line, at timecode *0:01:17;15*.
4. Enable **Auto animate** by clicking the icon located just before the zoom dropdown above the canvas.

This action is depicted in the image below.

*06_20.png - Enable **Auto animate** (Mac only).*

5. Click the screen recording to select it.
6. Use the resize handles to enlarge the screen recording and position the view over the main navigation bar.

As you do this, keep an eye on the **Scale** property in the Properties panel and make sure it never exceeds **100%** to avoid any pixelation. After this operation, the canvas should look like the image below.

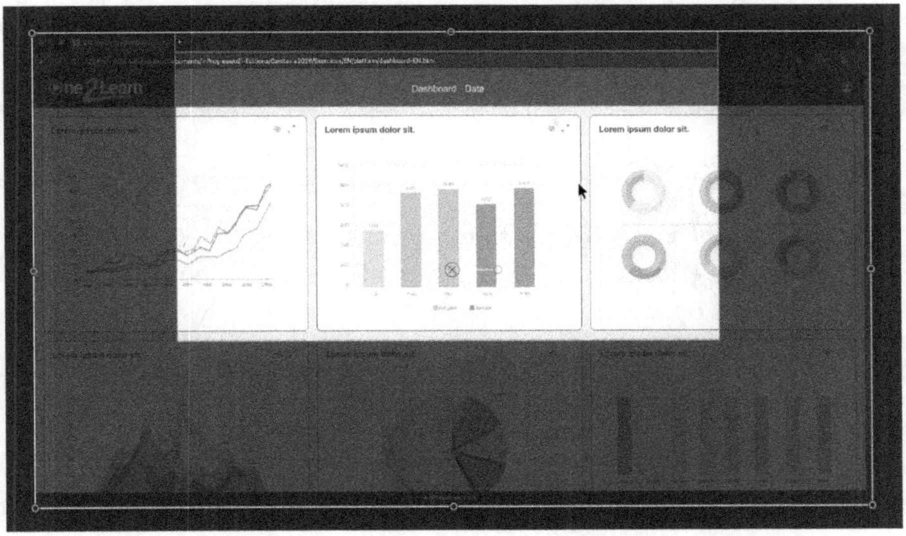

06_21.png - Enlarge the view and position it over the main link bar.

With *Auto animate* enabled, Camtasia automatically adds an animation in the timeline at the playhead position.

7. Position the playhead a few seconds *ahead* of this animation.
8. Start playing the video and carefully monitor what happens when the playhead reaches the animation.
9. If necessary, adjust the duration and position of this animation in the timeline.

You will now create the opposite animation, which will restore the original view.

10. Start playing the video.
11. Pause the video when the narrator says, *"Selecting Data opens a page..."*.
12. Position the playhead in that sentence at timecode *0:01:22;25*.
13. Ensure the screen recording is still selected.
14. Use the resize handles to restore the original view.

Auto animate generates a new animation at the current playhead position.

15. In the timeline, reposition the playhead before the two animations you added in this section.

16. Play the video and watch your zoom-in animation, followed by the opposite effect a few seconds later.
17. Click the arrow icon above the canvas to switch back to edit mode.

On a Mac, *Auto animate* automatically creates animations whenever you make changes to the selected object.

D. Discovering More Annotations

The ***01_02_dashboard*** project is starting to take shape, but it is still possible to improve the effectiveness of this tutorial with a few more annotations. This is a great opportunity to experiment with two types of annotations you haven't worked with yet.

1. Working With the Spotlight Annotation

The *Spotlight* tool is one of the many built-in annotations. It is very effective at drawing the viewer's attention to a specific area of the video.

1. Use `Ctrl + Home` (Windows) or `Cmd + Enter` (Mac) to return the playhead to the beginning of the ***01_02_dashboard*** project.
2. Hit the `spacebar` to start playing the video.
3. Pause the video when the narrator says, *"This reduces visual clutter."*
4. Position the playhead at timecode *0:00:38;00* just before the narrator pronounces that line.
5. Open the **Annotations** panel on the left side of the screen.
6. Select the **Blur and Highlight** tab.

These actions are depicted in the image below, which was captured on a Windows PC. On a Mac, the icons contained in this tab are a bit different.

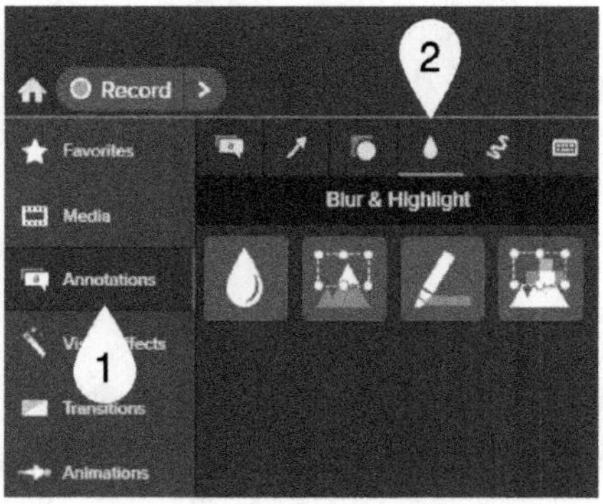

*06_22.png - Open the **Blur and Highlight** tab of the **Annotations** panel.*

In the above image, the *Spotlight* tool is the second from the left (on a Mac, it is the last icon in the first row).

7. Drag the **Spotlight** annotation from the **Annotations** panel and drop it onto the canvas.
8. Adjust the size and position of this annotation to highlight the chart.

In the timeline, Camtasia positions this annotation on the first available track at the playhead position for a default duration of three seconds. You will now add a fade transition on both ends of this element.

9. Open the **Transitions** panel on the left side of the screen.
10. Type `Fade` into the search field.
11. Drag the **Fade** transition from the **Transitions** panel and drop it in the middle of the spotlight annotation, adding both a fade-in and a fade-out transition.
12. Reduce the duration of both transitions to 15 frames.
13. Position the playhead slightly ahead of the spotlight annotation.
14. Play the video and enjoy the new annotation and its transitions.
15. If necessary, adjust the duration of the spotlight to match the voiceover.
16. Don't forget to save your project regularly.

The following image shows the result of these changes, both on the canvas and in the timeline.

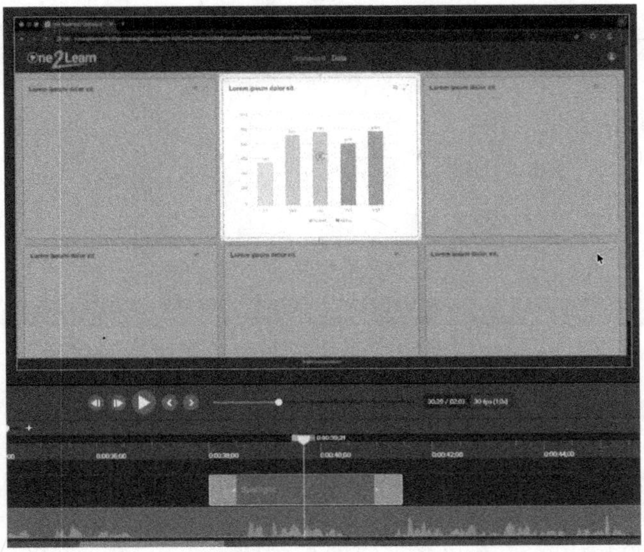

*06_23.png - The **Spotlight** annotation properly positioned on the canvas and in the timeline.*

The spotlight annotation offers a simple yet effective solution for guiding the viewer's attention to a specific area of your video.

2. Adding Arrows and Lines

Arrows and lines are yet another type of annotation available in Camtasia. Let's explore it using the steps below.

1. In the timeline, position the playhead where the narrator says, *"...to compare related charts..."*, around timecode 0:00:43;00.
2. Open the **Annotations** panel and switch to the **Arrows & Lines** tab (the second tab from the left).
3. Drag the orange double arrow from the **Annotations** panel and drop it onto the canvas.

In the timeline, Camtasia positions this annotation on the first available track, at the playhead position, for a default duration of three seconds.

4. In the Properties panel, increase the arrow **Thickness** until it is clearly visible on the canvas.
5. Resize and reposition the double arrow, as shown in the image below.

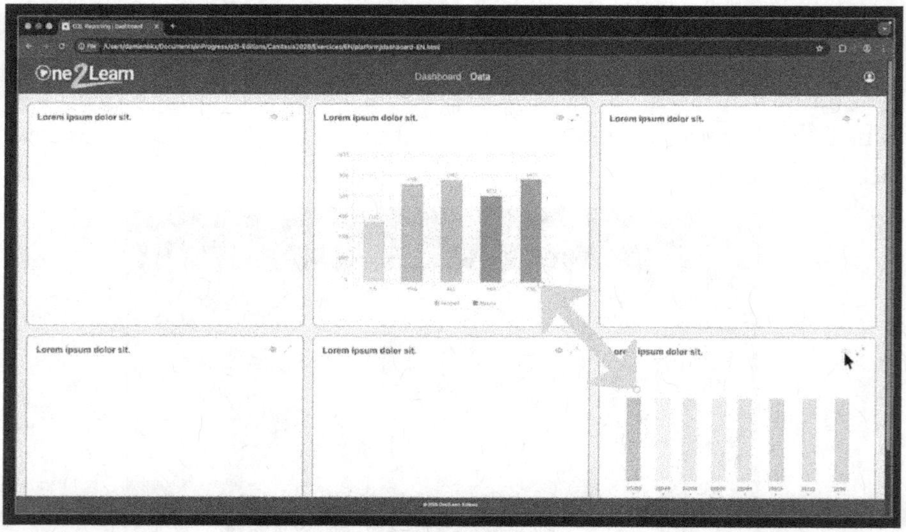

06_24.png - Position the double arrow on the canvas.

6. Position the playhead in the silence that follows *"...to compare related charts without distraction,"* around timecode 0:00:46;00.
7. Adjust the duration of the double arrow to the current position of the playhead.
8. Apply a transition of your choice to both ends of this annotation.

*In the final version of this video, I used the **Blur Zoom** transition, which is available under the **Blur** category in the **Transitions** panel.*

The **Arrow & Lines** annotations are valuable tools for further enhancing your videos and highlighting key points in your message.

3. Practical Exercise – Adding Sketch Motions

It's now time to put your new skills into practice! To wrap up this section, you'll incorporate two additional sketch motion annotations into this project. Since this has already been covered earlier in this chapter, we won't detail all the steps and let you take the lead using the generic instructions below.

- Use a circle sketch motion to outline the cross icon as the narrator says, *"...simply click the X in the upper right-hand corner of the window."* This circle should disappear the moment the click occurs. On a Mac, you'll need to remove the automatic fade-out transition.
- Use a rectangular sketch motion to frame the *Data* link, as the narrator says, *"...includes a 'Data' link next to the 'Dashboard' link."* On Windows, add a fade-out effect to this annotation.
- Apply any dark color and increase the line thickness to make these two annotations clearly visible.
- After testing, save and close the project.

After completing this exercise, post-production of this project is nearly complete. In Chapter 9 - Extending and Customizing Camtasia you will create a custom theme to style these annotations with a specific brand color. But for now, let's explore another Camtasia feature.

E. Working With Behaviors

Behaviors combine animations and transitions into a single effect that you can easily drag and drop on any element in your project. They are particularly well suited for text annotations and are highly customizable.

In this section, you will revisit the ***02_02_conclusion*** project you already worked with earlier in this chapter and apply *behaviors* to the text annotations in this video.

1. Open the ***Chapitre06/02_02_conclusion*** project in Camtasia.

*Since you already worked with this project earlier in this chapter, it might still be present on the **Recent Projects** tab of the welcome screen.*

2. In the timeline, position the playhead just before the *"1. The Basics of Data Analysis"* text annotation, around timecode 0:00:09;00.
3. Play the video and see how the text caption enters and leaves the canvas.

Right now, this annotation isn't affected by any transitions or animations. It appears *cut*, then a screen recording covers it.

1. Applying a Behavior

You will now apply a behavior to this text annotation using the following steps.

1. In the timeline, position the playhead over the *"1. The Basics of Data Analysis"* text annotation so that it is visible on the canvas.

The result of this step is illustrated in the image below.

06_25.png - Position the playhead so you can see the text annotation on the canvas.

Behaviors are accessible through the **Behaviors** panel on the left side of the screen.

2. Click **Behaviors** on the left side of the screen to open the **Behaviors** panel. You can also press O on your keyboard.
3. In the **Behaviors** panel, pass your mouse over each thumbnail to preview the associated behavior.
4. Drag the **Sliding** behavior from the **Behaviors** panel and hover over the timeline. *Do not release the mouse button yet.*

Camtasia identifies eligible elements with a blue outline. On Windows, this highlight changes to green when you hover over an element, as shown in the following image.

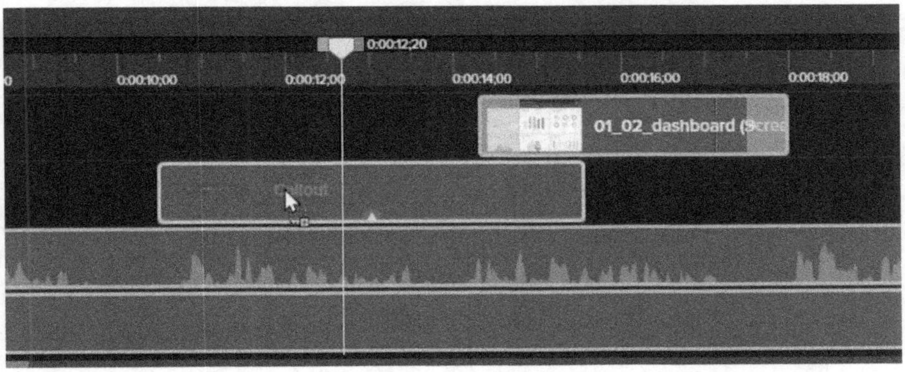

06_26.png - Elements eligible for this behavior are highlighted with a blue border.

You must add this behavior to the *"1. The Basics of Data Analysis."* item.

5. Drop the behavior on the text annotation.
6. In the timeline, position the playhead slightly ahead of the annotation.
7. Play the video and see how the behavior affects it.

Congratulations! You've officially applied your first Camtasia behavior! This built-in behavior may or may not be exactly what you need. For this example, let's assume you don't want the pulse effect after the text annotation slides into place.

2. Editing a Behavior

The behavior slides the text annotation onto the canvas before applying a pulsating opacity effect. In this example, you want to keep the sliding movement but remove the subsequent opacity change.

1. Select the text annotation you just applied the behavior on.
2. Make sure the Properties panel is open on the right side of the screen.
3. Open the **Behavior Properties** tab of the Properties panel

This action is depicted in the image below.

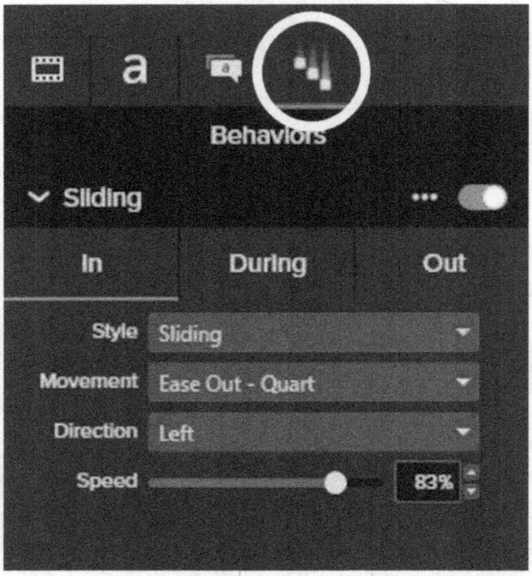

06_27.png – Open the Behavior Properties tab.

Note that the behavior properties are organized into three separate sections.

- **In**: for adjusting how the element enters the canvas.
- **During**: for modifying how the element behaves once the entry animation is complete.
- **Out**: for adjusting how the element exits the canvas.

In this example, you want to remove the **During** behavior, which modifies the opacity of the text annotation.

4. Open the **During** tab of the **Behaviors** properties.
5. Open the **Style** dropdown.
6. Take a moment to review the available options, then select **None**.
7. Position the playhead a few seconds ahead of the text annotation.
8. Play the video to review your adjustments.

During playback, confirm that the opacity of the text annotation no longer changes once the object is positioned on the canvas.

3. Duplicating a Behavior

You will now apply the same behavior to the remaining two text annotations. To ensure consistency and streamline the process; you will simply copy and paste the behavior defined in the previous section.

1. Take a close look at the *"1. The Basics of Data Analysis"* text annotation on the timeline.
2. Click the tiny upward-pointing arrow in the center of the annotation.

This action is shown in the image below

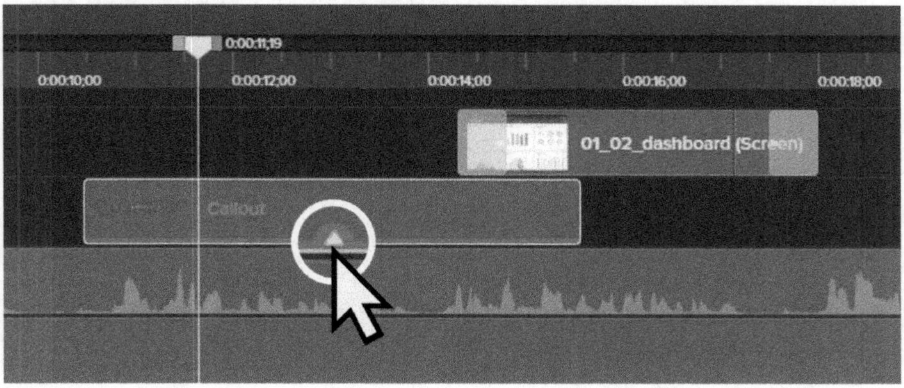

06_28.png – Click the small upward-pointing arrow.

The **Sliding** behavior you applied in the previous section appears as a red bar beneath the text annotation.

3. Click the red bar to select the behavior.

The red bar turns yellow to indicate it is selected. In the Properties panel, only the properties of the behavior are visible.

4. Right-click the behavior (the yellow bar) in the timeline.
5. Take a moment to review the available options then click **Copy Selected Effects** (Windows) or **Copy Effect** (Mac).
6. In the timeline, right-click the *"2. Platform Preferences"* text annotation.
7. Click **Paste Effects** in the context menu.
8. Repeat this process to paste the same effect onto the *"3. The Quiz"* text annotation.
9. In the timeline, position the playhead before the first text annotation.
10. Start playing the video.
11. Watch the entire project and enjoy your newly added sliding behaviors!
12. Save and close this project.

Thanks to these behaviors, your project is a lot more enjoyable to watch. As a trainer and storyteller, you now have a new tool at your disposal to reinforce the key takeaways of your message.

4. Practical Exercise: Adding Behaviors

For this exercise, you will continue working on the final sequence of the ***01_03_settings*** project, which you began to develop in the previous chapter.

1. Import the ***Chapter06/projects/01_03_settings.zip*** project into the ***Chapter06*** folder in the exercises.
2. Watch the entire project and see how it has evolved since you last worked on it. Take some time to check out the new animations, transitions, and annotations.

After reading this chapter, a great exercise is to reopen the project file used in the previous chapter and add these animations, transitions, and annotations yourself.

You will now apply behaviors to the three text annotations located in the final sequence of the project.

3. Position the playhead at the end of the project so all three text annotations are visible on the canvas.
4. Select the first text annotation.
5. Hold down the **`Shift`** key and click the other two text annotations to add them to the selection.

Holding down the **`Shift`** key lets you select multiple elements. You can then apply a behavior to all selected items in a single step.

6. Drag the behavior of your choice from the **Behaviors** panel and drop it onto one of the three selected text annotations.

The selected behavior applies to all three selected text annotations.

7. In the Properties panel, disable the **During** and **Out** effects.
8. Adjust the **In** behavior to your liking.

Don't hesitate to try out several options before making your final decision. This is a great opportunity to explore the full potential of these behaviors.

9. Position the playhead slightly ahead of the final sequence, then play the project to preview the new behaviors.
10. Save the project and leave it open for the next section.

At the end of this exercise, the project isn't quite finished yet, but it's definitely starting to take shape.

F. Applying Visual Effects

Camtasia offers an extensive library of visual effects that you can easily incorporate into your projects. While it's impossible to cover them all in detail, this section explores some of Camtasia's most popular effects. You'll learn how effects work in general so you can continue exploring on your own.

1. Using the Clip Speed Effect

The ***01_03_settings*** project includes several sequences of passive data entry bearing no instructional value. To keep your audience engaged and focused on the essentials, you will use the *Clip Speed* effect to shorten these segments, thereby maintaining a tighter narrative flow in the final production.

1. Open the ***Chapter06/01_03_settings*** project in Camtasia.
2. In the timeline, position the playhead around timecode *0:00:35;00* and start playing the video.

In this sequence, the viewer passively watches as you fill in the **First name** and **Last name** fields of the form. Your task is to speed up this section using the *Clip Speed* effect.

Unfortunately, this effect can only be applied to an entire clip. Before using it, you must first isolate the segment you want to speed up using the *Split* tool.

3. On the timeline, position the playhead just before filling in the **First name** field, at timecode *0:00:37;00*.
4. Click the screen recording to select it.
5. Click the **Split** icon in the upper-left corner of the timeline or use `S` (Windows) or `Cmd + T` (Mac).
6. Repeat the same process *after* filling in the **Last name** field, at timecode *0:00:41;15*.

After completing these steps, you have divided the original clip into three separate segments, thereby isolating the section to speed up, as shown in the image below.

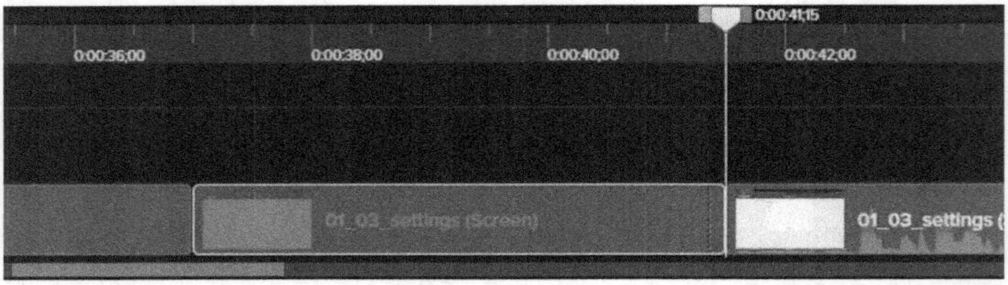

06_29.png - You have divided the original clip into three sections and isolated the segment to accelerate.

You will now apply the *Clip Speed* effect onto the central section.

7. Click **Visual Effects** on the left side of the screen to open the **Visual Effects** panel. You can also press **X** on your keyboard.
8. Take some time to review the available visual effects.
9. Drag the **Clip Speed** effect from the **Visual Effects** panel and drop it onto the segment you isolated earlier.

You must configure the effect before you can see any changes in your video. You can do it using either the Properties panel or the timeline.

10. In the timeline, click the small arrow in the middle of the clip you just applied the effect to.

This action reveals the *Clip Speed* effect. It appears as a blue line underlining the selected clip, with small clock icons on each end.

11. Click the blue line to select the **Clip Speed** effect.

The blue bar turns yellow to indicate it is selected. In the Properties panel, only the properties for the **Clip Speed** effect are visible.

12. In the timeline, drag the right clock icon to the left.

This action is depicted in the following screenshot.

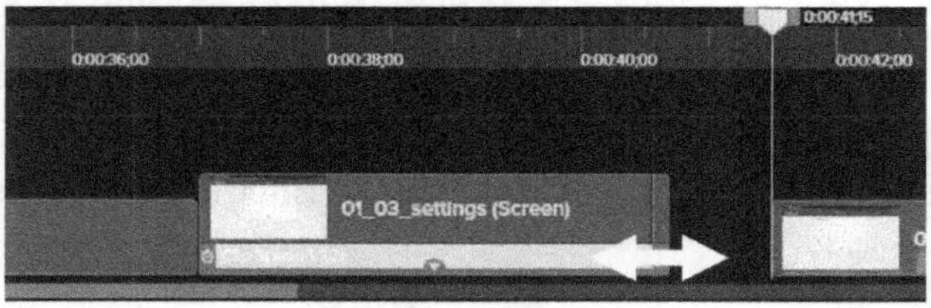

06_30.png - Drag the right clock icon to the left to speed up the selected clip.

As you drag the icon, keep an eye on the **Speed** property in the Properties panel.

13. Let go of the mouse when the **Speed** value is approximately **2.0x**. You can also type 2 directly in the Properties panel.

From now on this section of the video will be played at twice the speed, which reduces the time spent watching the form being filled out!

Unfortunately, this action left a gap of about two seconds in the timeline. To close it, you must shift all subsequent elements to the left, including the screen recording itself, as well as all annotations, animations, and transitions that have already been carefully synchronized.

14. In the timeline, position the playhead before the elements to be moved, at timecode *0:00:41;15*.
15. Hold down the `Shift` key and position the mouse pointer over the white triangle above the playhead.
16. Drag the white triangle to the left until the gap is completely closed.

This action is depicted in the image below.

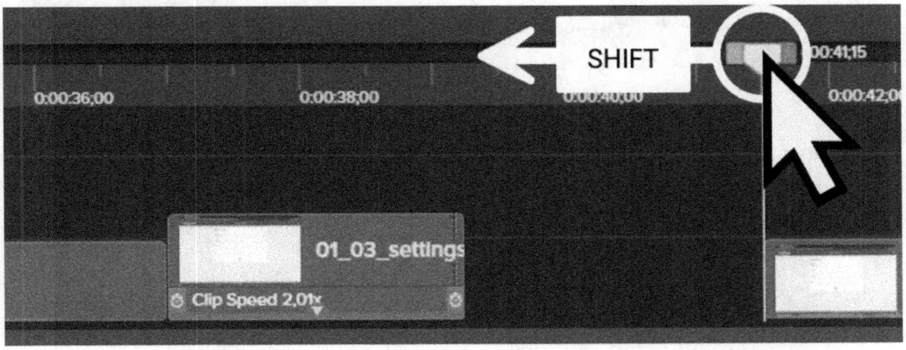

06_31.png - Drag the playhead to the left while holding down the `Shift` *key.*

Shift-dragging the playhead allows you to shift all downstream elements at once. This makes it easy to fill the gap without losing synchronization between elements on different tracks in the timeline.

1. Practical Exercise – Using the Clip Speed Effect

In this hands-on exercise, you will replicate the steps from the previous section to accelerate the typing of the email address on the same form. Here are the general steps for completing this exercise.

- Use the **Split** tool to isolate the segment you want to speed up (between timecodes *0:00:53;00* and *0:00:57;00*).
- Apply the **Clip Speed** effect onto the isolated clip.

- Double the playback speed of this segment.
- Fill the gap by moving all downstream elements to the left without losing their syncing.
- Play the project to ensure this change goes unnoticed.
- Save and close the project when done.

At the end of this exercise, this section of the timeline should look like the following image.

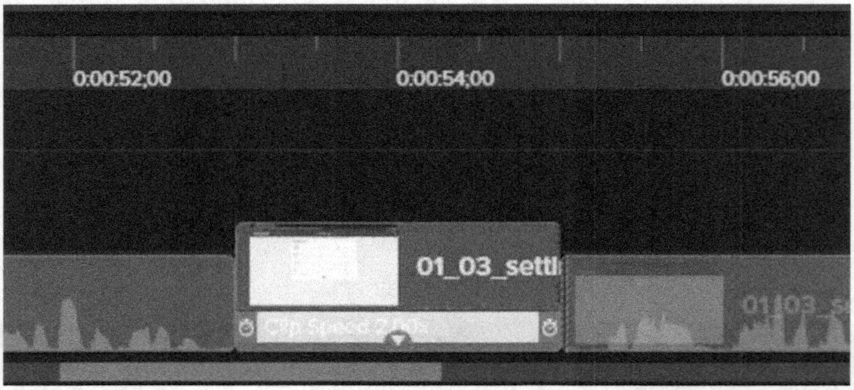

06_32.png - Double the clip speed and fill in the gap in the timeline.

The Clip Speed effect is a versatile tool with a wide range of practical applications. Here are a few examples.

- Speeding up long operations such as filling out long forms or downloading large files.
- Synchronizing the audio with the video when the video contains a lot of movement (such as mouse movements).
- Slowing down complex operations to give viewers time to analyze them in detail.

Although the Clip Speed effect lets you speed up or slow down your videos as much as you like, you should stick to subtle adjustments to avoid overly distorting the original footage.

2. Removing the Background

Of all the visual effects available in Camtasia, the *Color Removal* tool holds a special place. This effect, also known as *Chroma key* or *Green screen*, allows you to remove a color from a video. Although green is the most commonly used color (due to its strong contrast with skin tones), you can use this effect to remove *any* color.

In your data analysis training course, several videos were filmed against a green backdrop. While this situation is ideal, not everyone has access to a fully equipped studio (even a makeshift one). For this reason, Camtasia also offers the AI-powered *Background Removal* effect. This feature attempts to isolate the subject from any environment, eliminating the need for specialized backdrops and complex lighting setups.

In this section, you will first compare these two special effects, and you will use them to remove the green screen around the narrator.

1. Open the **Chapter06/02_02_conclusion** project in Camtasia.
2. In the timeline, position the playhead so that you can see the narrator and the green screen on the canvas.

You are now ready to start exploring the *Background Removal* effect.

1. Using the Background Removal Effect

The background removal effect is designed to eliminate any complex backgrounds without the need for a green screen studio. You will now apply this effect to the video of the narrator and carefully examine the result.

1. Open the **Visual Effects** panel on the left side of the screen.
2. Drag the **Background Removal** effect from the **Visual Effects** panel and drop it onto the video of the narrator.

As shown in the following image, this *automagically* removes the green background.

06_33.png - This automagically removes the green background.

However, upon closer inspection, the background removal isn't quite perfect, as a faint green halo remains visible around the narrator. You can try to fix it using the Properties panel.

3. Click the narrator video to select it.
4. Open the **Visual Properties** tab of the Properties panel.

The properties of the **Background Removal** effect are available at the bottom of the Properties panel, as shown in the image below.

*06_34.png - The properties of the **Background Removal** effect are available at the bottom of the Properties panel.*

5. Experiment with different values to minimize the greenish halo surrounding the narrator.

Applying a slight **Feather** may improve the overall result, but it is most likely not enough to achieve a truly smooth and realistic finish.

You will now remove the **Background Removal** effect, so you can replace it with the **Color Removal** effect in the next section.

6. In the timeline, right-click the video of the narrator.
7. In the context menu, click **Remove > All Effects**.
8. Leave the project open for the next section.

What sets the **Background Removal** effect apart is its remarkable ease of use.

- In post-production all you have to do is drag and drop the effect onto a video clip.
- Filming is also made easier, as the effect does not require any special lighting or green backdrops. The effect works well with most backgrounds, even complex and uneven ones.

This two-fold advantage makes the **Background Removal** effect one of Camtasia's most popular features. It democratizes professional video production, enabling everyone to replicate the look of a high-end green screen studio without the expensive setup.

2. Using the Color Removal Effect

Since this video has actually been shot in a green screen studio, you can use the **Remove a Color** effect to achieve better results.

1. In the timeline, position the playhead so that you can see the narrator and the green screen on the canvas.

Take a moment to examine the green backdrop behind the narrator. During the filming, I did my best to light it evenly, but despite my best efforts, you can still see a few shadows and unevenness due to the limitations of my makeshift home studio.

2. Open the **Visual Effects** panel on the left side of the screen.
3. Drag the **Remove a Color** effect from the **Visual Effects** panel and drop it onto the video of the narrator.

After applying the effect, you won't notice any immediate changes on the canevas. To achieve the desired result, you need to adjust the effect's properties in the Properties panel.

4. Select the narrator video and open the Properties panel on the right side of the screen.

The properties for the **Remove a Color** effect can be found at the bottom of the visual properties tab, as shown in the image below.

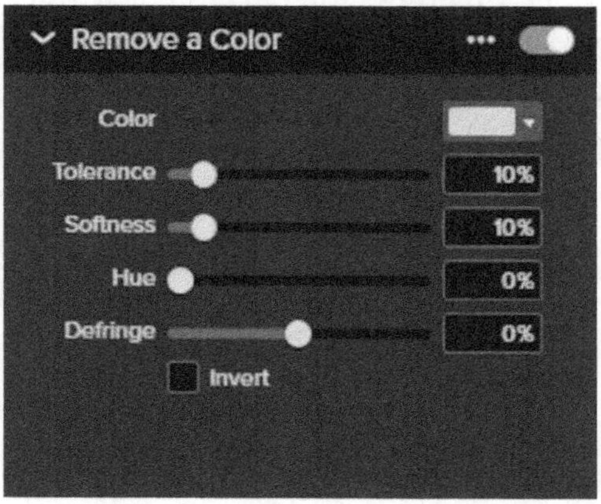

*06_35.png - The properties of the **Remove a Color** effect.*

The most important parameter is the color to remove.

5. Click the green rectangle next to the **Color** property.
6. Click the eyedropper icon in the menu that opens.

Your mouse pointer turns into an eyedropper. With this tool active, simply click anywhere on the screen to pick up the exact color value of the pixel you click on.

7. Click anywhere on the green backdrop using the eyedropper tool (for the best results, click an area near the face of the narrator).

That's where the magic happens! The color you clicked turns transparent, revealing the content of the underlying tracks.

As usual, you can use the Properties panel to fine-tune the effect.

8. Increase the value of the **Tolerance** property and observe the results on the canvas.

By adjusting this value, you remove not just *the* exact shade you selected, but also any adjacent shades of green.

- If the tolerance is too high, you remove too many colors, and the narrator starts to disappear.
- If the tolerance is too low, you don't remove enough colors, and shades of green reappear around the narrator.

For this exercise, the ideal value lies between 10% and 15%.

9. Change the value of the **Softness** property and observe the result on the canvas.

The Softness property feathers the narrator's outline, smoothing harsh edges and neutralizing any leftover green spill from the background.

- If the softness is too low, you'll notice sharp edges around the narrator along with a residual green halo.
- If the softness is too high, the narrator starts to fade into the background.

For this example, the ideal value sits between 7% and 12%.

That's it for the main properties! The canvas should now look similar to the following screenshot.

*06_36.png - The narrator after applying and configuring the **Remove a Color** effect.*

If you have the option to shoot in a green screen studio, the **Remove a Color** effect offers far more granular control and generally produces much better results than the **Background Removal** tool.

3. Tips and Tricks for Successful Background Removal

Having seen the **Background Removal** and the **Remove a Color** effects in action, let's explore how to maximize their impact and make them even easier to use. In this section, you'll find practical tips and tricks to help you get the most out of these tools. Spoiler alert: it all comes down to the filming!

- Try to shoot your video against a uniform background.
- Wear colors that contrast sharply with the background. If you're using a green screen, don't wear green clothes or accessories (unless you're going for an "*Invisible Man*"-style special effect).
- A modest investment in lighting equipment can make a big difference. Even a simple setup will help you achieve an even background and soften shadows.
- Position your light sources to the side rather than head-on so that shadows are cast outside the frame.
- Try to maintain some distance between the subject and the background. When subjects stand too close to the backdrop, they cast shadows that are difficult to eliminate.
- The most challenging part is processing the edges. The more complex the edges, the higher the risk of a residual greenish halo. Long hair is a

typical issue and often produces visible artifacts. If you notice the Background Removal tool is struggling, ask the narrator to tie their hair back during filming, and save time in post!

- Similarly, sudden body movements often cause errors and aberrations. Whenever possible, ask the narrator to avoid sudden movements during filming.
- Finally, the golden rule is to always perform a dry run. Go ahead and shoot a test clip, import it into Camtasia, and apply the **Background Removal** and/or the **Remove a Color** effects. Testing your setup early allows you to identify and troubleshoot lighting issues before you waste time on a take that might not work after all.

Although these tips are easy to implement and don't require any significant investment, they will go a long way toward improving the effectiveness of these effects and will elevate the overall quality of your productions.

You can find more information as well as additional tips and tricks on the official TechSmith website under the following URLs: https://www.techsmith.com/learn/tutorials/camtasia/how-to-remove-a-color/ and https://www.techsmith.com/learn/tutorials/camtasia/video-background-removal/

3. Using the Media Matte Effect

In this section, you'll discover one of Camtasia's most powerful and creative effects. Use the following steps to get ready.

1. Import the ***Chapter06/projects/00_00_trailer.zip*** project into the ***Chapter06*** folder of the exercises.
2. Watch the entire video to refresh your memory.

Since your last visit, this project has been enhanced with new transitions, animations, effects, and behaviors.

3. If necessary, adjust the height of the timeline to see all six tracks.

Notice how animations are used to fade the narrator in and out. When the laptop image is visible, the narrator should disappear, but without losing the associated audio. Since transitions can only be applied at the beginning and end of an element, they cannot be used here. The solution is to use an animation to set the narrator's opacity to 0% when you want to hide it, then back to 100% to make it reappear.

1. Applying the Media Matte Effect

The *Media Mate* effect lets you use an object on an upper track to frame a lower track. When you overlay two clips in the timeline, the effect transforms the upper clip into a dynamic cutout that reveals the track directly underneath. Note that this effect requires two overlapping objects to work.

In this exercise, you will use this technique to craft a unique *entrée* for the narrator at the beginning of the project.

1. In the timeline, position the playhead at timecode *0:00:04;00* to see the narrator on the canvas.
2. Open the **Shapes** tab of the **Annotations** panel (the third tab from the left).
3. Open the **Style** dropdown and select **All**.
4. Right-click the yellow circle.
5. In the context menu, click **Add to Timeline at Playhead**.
6. Slightly shorten the duration of the newly inserted yellow circle so you can move it to track 5 of the timeline.

This last step places the yellow circle directly above the narrator, which is on track 4. The canvas should now look like the following image.

06_37.png - The yellow circle is positioned in the center of the canvas over the narrator.

Both layers for the Media Matte effect are now in place. The narrator will be the masked object, while the yellow circle will serve as the matte.

7. Open the **Visual Effects** panel on the left side of the screen.
8. Drag the **Media Matte** effect from the **Visual Effects** panel and drop it onto the yellow circle.

The effect is spectacular: the narrator appears only within the boundaries of the yellow circle, as shown in the image below.

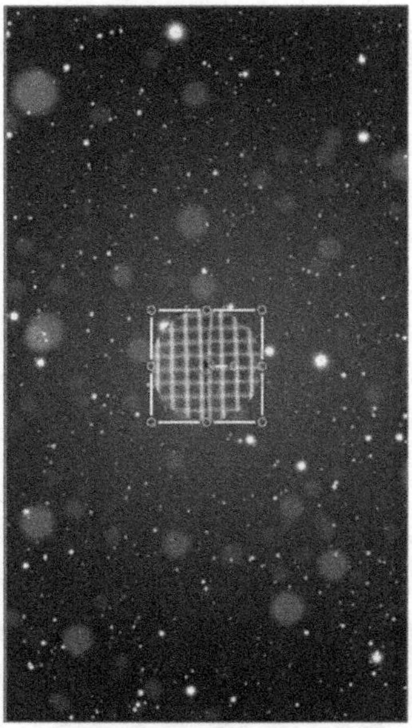

06_38.png - The narrator is visible through the yellow circle.

In other words, the content of Track 5 defines a transparent area, revealing what is directly underneath. Note that this effect has no impact on the background animation, which is lower in the track stack.

*Even though the Media Matte effect removes the yellow color from the circle, it will still be referred to as the "**yellow circle**" for the remainder of this exercise.*

You will now explore the main properties of the Media Matte effect.

9. Click the circle to select it.
10. If necessary, open the Properties panel on the right side of the screen and select the **Visual Properties** tab.

The properties for the **Media Matte** effect can be found at the bottom of the Properties panel. The most important one is the **Mode** property, which defaults to **Alpha**.

11. Open the **Mode** dropdown
12. Select **Alpha Invert**.

This mode reverses the effect: the yellow circle creates a transparent opening in the narrator, revealing the animated starscape in the background.

13. Reopen the **Mode** dropdown and select **Luminosity Invert**.

In this mode the narrator's shirt appears semitransparent within the circular mask. The intensity of the effect now depends on the color brightness of the circle. The lighter the color, the more pronounced the effect. Conversely, a darker color produces a more subtle effect.

For this example, you need the default **Alpha** mode.

14. Open the **Mode** dropdown and reselect **Alpha**.
15. Lower the **Intensity** value.

This property regulates the intensity of the effect outside the yellow circle.

16. For this exercise, restore the intensity to its default value of 100%.

Now that you better understand the basics of the Media Matte effect, you are ready to take it to the next level and combine it with a custom animation.

2. Animating the Matte

In the previous section, you used a yellow circle and the **Media Matte** effect to mask the narrator. You will now animate that circle using a custom animation and create a unique transition.

1. In the timeline, position the playhead at timecode *0:00:05;00* to see the narrator inside the yellow circle.
2. Open the **Animations** panel on the left side of the screen.
3. [*Windows only*] Select the **Animations** tab.
4. Drag a **Custom** animation from the **Animations** panel and drop it in the timeline onto the yellow circle, so it starts at the playhead position.

The result of this action is depicted in the image below.

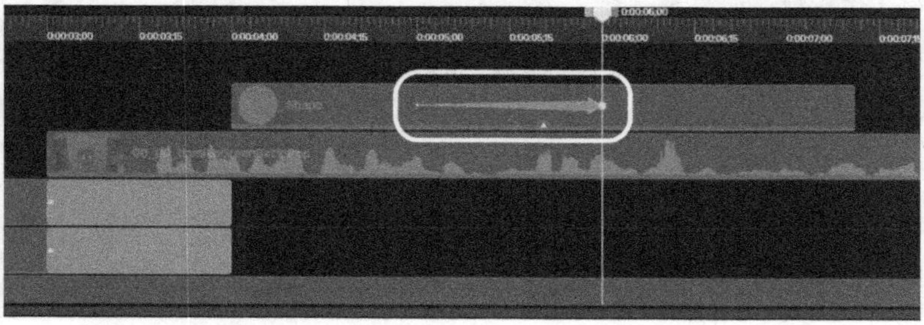

06_39.png - Drop a custom animation on the yellow circle.

To animate the yellow circle, you must now define distinct properties on either side of the animation arrow.

5. In the timeline, position the playhead *before* the animation.
6. Select the yellow circle to view its properties in the Properties panel.
7. Decrease the **Scale** to `1%`.

This makes the circle so small that the narrator disappears.

8. Position the playhead *after* the animation.
9. Hold down **`Ctrl + Shift`** (Windows) or **`Cmd + Shift`** (Mac) and expand the yellow circle using a corner handle until the narrator is completely visible.

Holding **`Ctrl`** (Windows) or **`Cmd`** (Mac) forces the yellow circle to expand outward around its center. Holding **`Shift`** locks the aspect ratio so the circle remains a circle.

10. In the timeline, make the yellow circle appear at the same time as the video of the narrator.
11. Move the animation so it starts exactly when the yellow circle appears.
12. Align the duration of the yellow circle to that of the animation.

This portion of the timeline should now look like the image below.

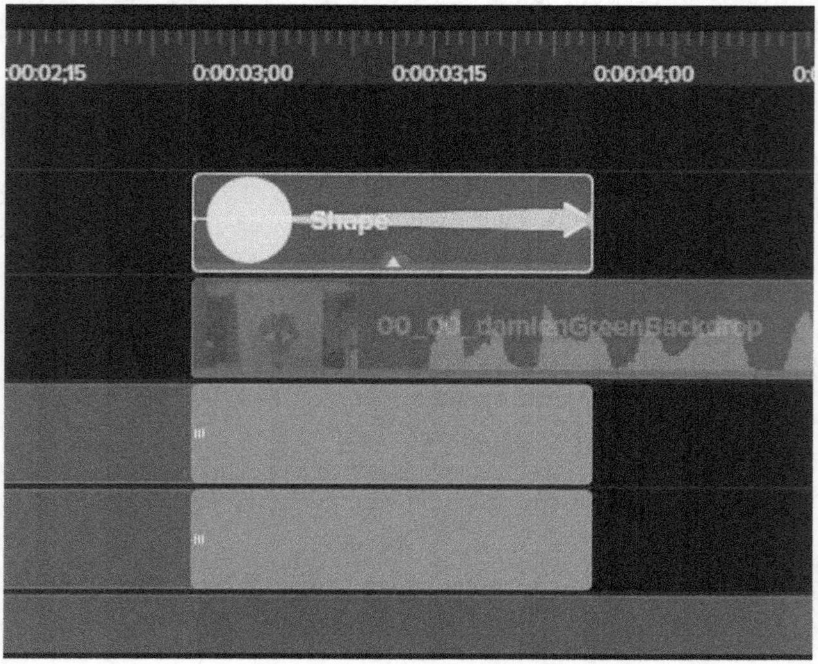

06_40.png - Align the duration of the yellow circle to that of the animation.

It's now time to test the results of your work.

13. Use **`Ctrl + Home`** (Windows) or **`Cmd + Enter`** (Mac) to move the playhead back to the beginning of the project.
14. Play the video and enjoy watching the narrator take center stage!

Congratulations on creating your first custom transition with the Media Matte effect! Before moving on, take a moment to remember the many annotations available in Camtasia and consider all the ways you can animate them. Now imagine how you could combine these annotations and animations with the Media Matte effect. This combination unlocks a world of new creative possibilities for your instructional design and storytelling.

3. Animating the Masked Object

In the previous section, you animated the yellow circle, which served as a masking object (the *Matte*). You will now animate the masked object and explore even more creative possibilities.

When you used the *Corner Pin* mode in the previous chapter to fit the platform screenshots into the laptop screen, one image did not fit perfectly. You will now use the *Media Matte* effect to fix this problem.

1. In the timeline, position the playhead at timecode *0:00:20:00* to see the problematic screenshot.
2. Use the **Shapes** tab of the **Annotations** panel to add a rectangle over the screenshot (any color will do).

In the timeline, Camtasia places the rectangle at the playhead position on the first available track (Track 7 in this case).

3. Click the eye icon in the header of track 6 (the track which contains the screenshots) to temporarily hide it.
4. Switch to *Corner Pin* mode on the canvas.
5. Align each corner of the rectangle with the corners of the laptop screen.

*If you selected a rounded rectangle, set the **Corner Radius** to **0** in the **Annotations** tab of the Properties panel.*

6. Switch back to *Edit* mode when done.
7. Click the eye icon in the track 6 header to bring the screenshots back.
8. In the timeline, make the white rectangle appear and disappear at the same time as the screenshot on track 6.

9. Drag the **Media Matte** effect from the **Visual Effects** panel and drop it onto the new rectangle.

Your canvas and timeline should now look like the following screenshot.

06_41.png - The screenshot fits perfectly within the laptop screen

The Media Mate effect seamlessly trims any overhanging edges, creating the impression that the screenshot perfectly fits within the laptop screen.

10. Click the padlock icon in the header of Track 7 to protect the rectangle against any changes.
11. Click the screenshot to select it.
12. On the canvas, enlarge and move the screenshot so the first chart is visible on the laptop screen.

After this operation your canvas should look like the image below.

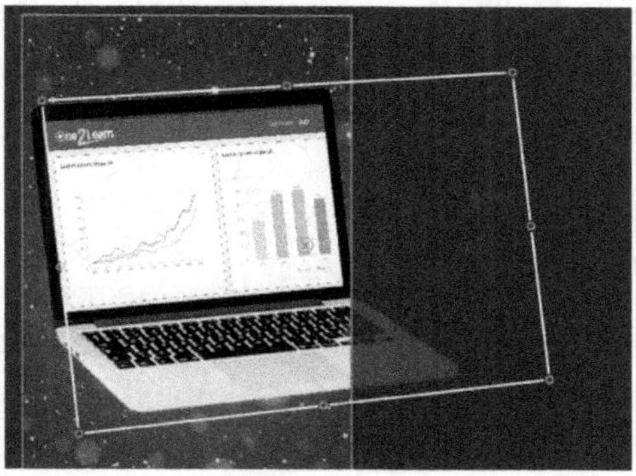

06_42.png – Move and resize the screenshot to see the first chart within the laptop screen.

The Media Matte effect keeps the screenshot confined within the rectangle covering the laptop screen, even when the screenshot is moved or resized.

13. Open the **Animations** panel on the left side of the screen.
14. [*Windows only*] Select the **Animations** tab.
15. Drop a **Custom** animation on the screenshot underneath the masking rectangle.
16. Position the playhead *after* the animation.
17. Move the screenshot until the second graph appears in the middle of the laptop screen.
18. Drop a second **Custom** animation after the first one.
19. Position the playhead *after* the second animation.
20. Move the screenshot over till you see the third graph on the laptop screen.
21. In the timeline, slightly shorten the duration of the animations and space them out across the screenshot, as shown in the following image.

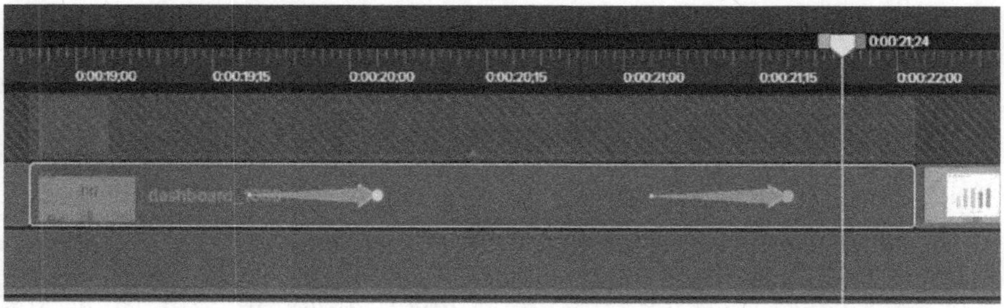

06_43.png - Distribute the animations over the duration of the screenshot.

It is now time to test-drive this new special effect!

22. Position the playhead a few seconds ahead of this sequence.
23. Play the video and enjoy the result!
24. Unlock track 7 and save the project.

In this section, you have animated the screenshot within the laptop screen. Thanks to the *Media Matte* effect, the screenshot remains perfectly cropped within the confines of the laptop screen, giving the static image the appearance of a video being played on the device.

4. Using a Video Matte

In the previous two sections, you applied the Media Matte effect to simple shapes and created engaging custom effects. In this section, you'll take it even further by using a video as the masking object. Get ready to explore a whole new world of possibilities.

1. Import the ***Chapter06/resources/flames.mov*** video into the Media Bin of the ***00_00_trailer*** project.
2. Move the playhead towards the end of the project at timecode *0:01:05;00*.
3. Drag the ***flames.mov*** video from the **Media Bin** and drop it onto track 5, so it overlaps both the narrator's video and the closing logo.

This action is illustrated in the following screenshot.

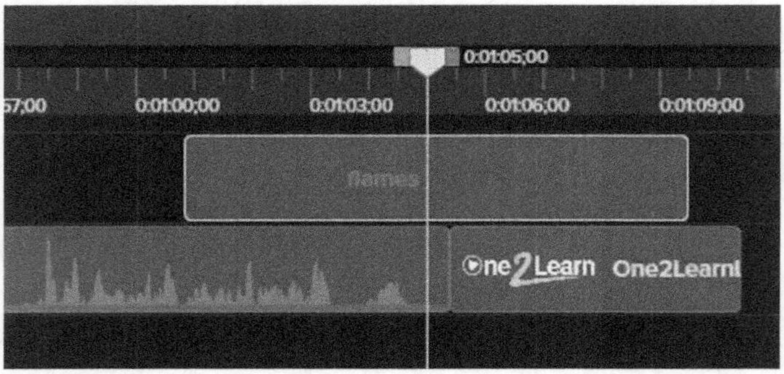

*06_44.png - Make the **flames.mov** clip overlap the narrator's video and the closing logo.*

There is more to this new video than meets the eye! Let's take a closer look to discover what makes it so unique.

4. Position the playhead slightly ahead of the new video.
5. Press play and watch the new video carefully.

The ***flames.mov*** video shows fire sweeping from left to right. Notice that areas without flames are *transparent*, thus revealing the narrator that sits behind.

> *This is why this video uses **.mov** rather than the standard **.mp4** format. One of the differences between the two formats is that **.mov** supports transparency, whereas **.mp4** does not.*

This feature is particularly useful when applying the Media Matte effect. Indeed, remember that the pixels of the masking object (in this case, the video) become transparent once the effect is applied.

6. On the canvas, resize the ***flames.mov*** video until it completely covers the narrator. Don't worry if the video extends beyond the edges of the canvas.
7. Position the playhead just before the logo appears at timecode *0:01:05;11*.
8. Shift the ***flames.mov*** video clip on the timeline so that the flames completely cover the narrator at the playhead position.

The result of these adjustments is shown in the image below.

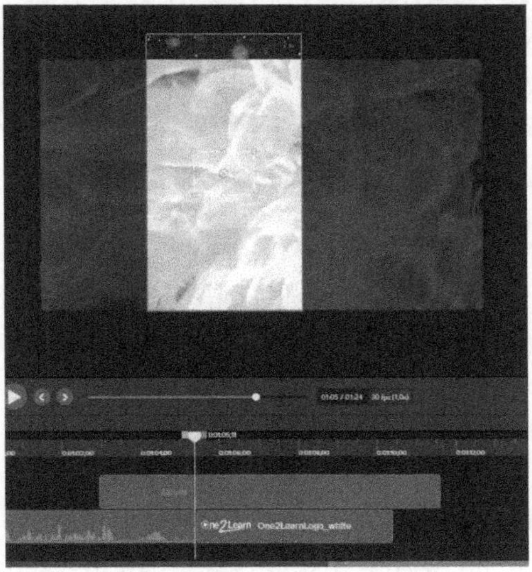

*06_45.png - Shift the **flames.mov** video clip so that the flames completely cover the narrator at the playhead.*

The next step is to apply the Media Matte effect and proceed with the final adjustments.

9. Drag the **Media Matte** effect onto the **flames.mov** video clip.
10. In the Properties panel, set the effect **Mode** to **Alpha Invert**.
11. Also apply the **Clip Speed** effect to the same video clip.
12. Scroll down the Properties panel to view the properties of the **Clip Speed** effect.
13. Increase the **Speed** to `2,00x` to double the playback speed of the ***flames.mov*** video.
14. In the timeline, reposition the ***flames.mov*** video so that the narrator is completely hidden at the playhead position.
15. Position the playhead slightly ahead of this sequence.
16. Press *play* and enjoy yet another very cool custom transition!

After completing these steps, the end of the timeline should look like the image below.

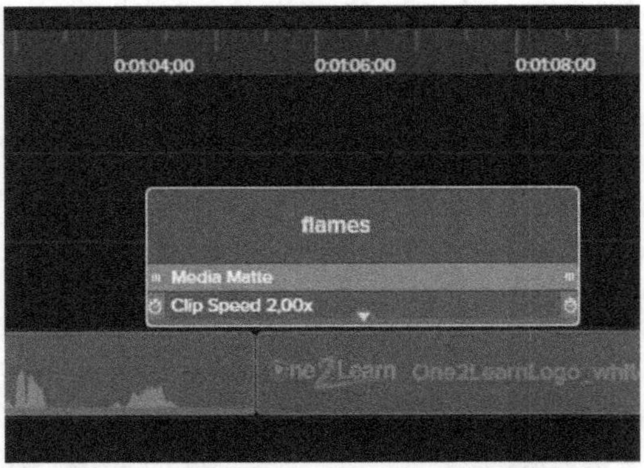

*06_46.png - The end of the timeline with two visual effects applied to the **flames.mov** video.*

By using a video as the masking object, you've successfully created a unique transition between the narrator and the logo. This example also demonstrates the ability to apply multiple visual effects onto a single element. The properties of these effects are easily accessible at the bottom of the Properties panel.

G. Conclusion

In this chapter, you moved deeper into post-production by bringing your visual elements to life with transitions, animations, behaviors and special effects.

Transitions can be applied at the beginning, the end, or between elements in the timeline. They determine how clips appear, disappear, and flow into one another.

Animations can be applied anywhere in the project. Use them to gradually adjust the properties of an element, smoothly taking it from one state to the next.

Behaviors are fully customizable animation presets. They are particularly well suited for text annotations, but you can apply them to any element in your project.

Finally, the visual effects panel include particularly powerful tools, such as background removal, precise speed manipulation, and static or animated track mattes, to create all kinds of unique transitions and animations.

These special effects breathe new life into your videos, making them a lot more engaging and enjoyable to watch. These visual enhancements don't just polish your video; they can also amplify your voice, ensuring your message is more vibrant and impactful than ever!

That said, you should use these features sparingly. Overusing these tools can lead to counterproductive visual clutter and will betray your lack of experience in the art of storytelling and teaching through video. To demonstrate true mastery of your medium, you must ensure that your tools support the narrative rather than obscure it.

Never lose sight of your primary objective: to *teach* and *communicate*. Every creative choice you make should serve this ultimate goal. Sometimes, the most effective choice is to not use any special effects at all. Next time you watch a movie or TV series, pay attention to the transitions between shots. You'll notice that *invisible* cuts are the norm and that eye-catching visual effects are only used to highlight key moments in the story.

Focus on the Mouse Cursor

The tools explored in previous chapters can be used to create all kinds of video content. Whether you are crafting a commercial, a marketing or political message, an internal communication, or even a feature-length film, Camtasia has you covered!

That said, Camtasia is primarily built for education and training professionals. As such, it includes many features specifically designed to create instructional video tutorials.

The mouse cursor is the silent narrator of any good tutorial. It plays a crucial role in driving your narrative and helps guide your audience through the content. This focal point captures the viewer's attention and helps them absorb the subject matter. When developing such a tutorial, it is therefore essential to pay close attention to the appearance, color, size, movements and behavior of the mouse cursor.

This chapter covers the features, effects, and tools in Camtasia that will help you make the mouse cursor the undisputed star of the show!

A. Preparing the Exercises

As in previous chapters, this one includes a variety of step-by-step instructions designed to work with the provided project files.

1. Download and unzip the exercises for Chapter 07.

These compressed projects must be imported into Camtasia using the process detailed at the beginning of Chapter 05 - Editing Your Video.

B. Modifying the Mouse Pointer

In Chapter 4 – Recording with Camtasia, you used Camtasia Recorder to record your screen. By default, Camtasia automatically saves your recordings as ***.trec*** files. This proprietary file format was specifically developed by TechSmith for use within Camtasia.

At first glance, using a proprietary format may seem like a drawback and raises a legitimate question: why forego a universal standard such as ***.mp4***, which offers seamless compatibility with virtually every video editing tool? The answer lies in how Camtasia Recorder captures the mouse cursor.

Camtasia Recorder doesn't actually record the mouse cursor. Instead, it captures a series of metadata, such as the position of the mouse, the shape of the cursor, and the location of the clicks. Camtasia uses this information to recreate a virtual mouse, which is then overlaid onto your screen recording. The ***.trec*** format was specifically designed to include this additional metadata, along with the audio and video streams also found in standard ***.mp4*** files. This clever trick gives you full control over the mouse cursor, movements, and actions during post-production.

It also means that the features covered in this chapter only work with ***.trec*** recordings created using Camtasia Recorder. Standard ***.mp4*** files imported into the media bin do not contain the necessary metadata for manipulating the cursor in Camtasia. In such files, the mouse is simply part of the footage and cannot be edited as a separate object.

To start exploring these features, you will now import the project you'll use in the next few sections.

1. Import the ***Chapter07/projects/01_02_dashboard.zip*** project into the ***Chapter07*** folder of the exercises.
2. When done, play the entire project in Camtasia.

As you watch this video, pay close attention to the shape, size, and movements of the mouse.

1. Changing the Pointer Size

In this project, the mouse pointer is sometimes hard to see, especially at the beginning, when it's still stationary. A simple fix is to make it bigger.

1. In the timeline, move the playhead before the first animation, somewhere around timecode *0:00:10:00*.
2. Click the screen recording to select it.
3. Make sure the Properties panel is open on the right side of the screen.

As shown below, the properties of this screen recording are divided into three tabs within the Properties panel.

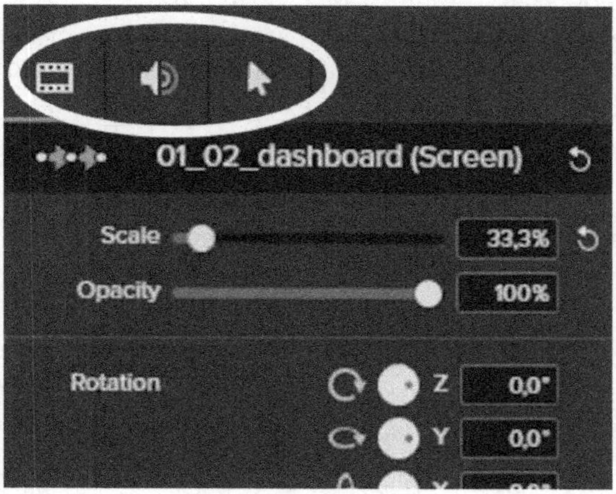

07_01.png - The properties of the screen recording are divided into three tabs.

The third tab (with the arrow icon) is specific to ***.trec*** recordings and lets you access the cursor properties.

4. Open the **Cursor properties** tab.

Use the **Scale** property to resize the mouse cursor. By default, Camtasia already scales it up to **225%** of its original size.

*You can change the default cursor scale in the preferences of Camtasia. Go to the **Project** (Windows) or **Recording** (Mac) tab of the preferences to change the **Default cursor scale**.*

Let's experiment with this feature.

5. Set the cursor scale way too high (around 1700%)!

Note that the mouse cursor does not get pixelated, even at this ridiculously high scale. This is because Camtasia does not use the original pointer, but generates its own high-resolution internal pointer based on the metadata contained in the *.trec* file.

The internal cursors generated by Camtasia are based on vector images. This type of image has the unique ability to always remain perfectly sharp regardless of the zoom level applied.

For this exercise, you will *slightly* enlarge the cursor to make it more noticeable on the screen.

6. Set the **Scale** property to approximately 420%.
7. Position the playhead around timecode *0:00:20:00*.
8. Take another look at the **Scale** property in the Properties panel.

Note that it has reverted to its default value of **225%**. This is due to the animation positioned slightly *ahead* of the playhead on Track 1 of the timeline. When adjusting the **Scale** property, the playhead was positioned *before* that animation, so the scale adjustment was applied only to the segment preceding the animation arrow on the timeline.

To maintain a consistent cursor size throughout the video, you must apply the same change to the entire screen recording.

9. Click the **Animation editing mode** icon in the upper left-hand corner of the Properties panel.

This step is depicted in the image below.

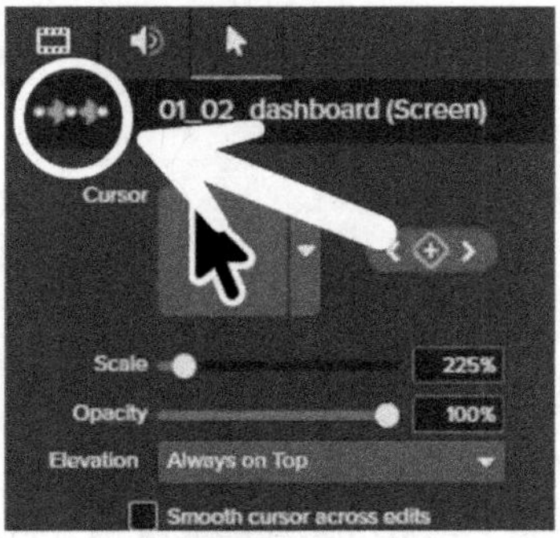

*07_02.png - Click the **Animation editing mode** icon.*

As stated in the pop-up message, this mode applies your changes to all animations in the selected media. In other words, your edits affect the entire clip as if there were no animations at all.

10. Click **Yes** to dismiss the message and switch to **Edit All Animations mode**.
11. Increase the scale of the cursor to **420%** again.

12. Click the **Animation editing mode** icon to switch back to the **Single Animation Mode.**
13. Move the playhead across the timeline while keeping an eye on the **Scale** property in the Properties panel.

You should notice that the cursor **Scale** is now set to **420%** for the entire duration of the screen recording.

Though easily missed, be sure to take note of the **Animation editing mode** icon. It's a powerful tool that will save you hours of work and a great deal of frustration!

2. Changing the Cursor Shape

By default, Camtasia tries to replicate the cursors captured by Camtasia Recorder. This works for most projects, but in some cases, it can be very useful to modify the cursor's shape during post-production.

- Erratic mouse movements during the recording cause unnecessary cursor changes.
- The original cursor lacks visibility.
- You want to standardize the appearance of the mouse cursor across multiple screen recordings created by different people using various computers and operating systems.
- You want to use a custom image, such as your logo, as a mouse cursor.

These are just some of the many reasons why Camtasia lets you customize the appearance of the cursor in screen recordings made with Camtasia Recorder.

1. Reviewing Recorded Cursors

To fully understand how this tool works, let's start by taking a closer look at the recorded cursors within this project.

1. Select the recording on track 1 of the *01_02_dashboard* project and open the Properties panel on the right side of the screen.
2. Open the **Cursor Properties** tab.
3. Position the playhead around timecode *0:00:10:00*.

As shown in the image below, the upper section of the Properties panel displays the appearance of the cursor at the playhead position.

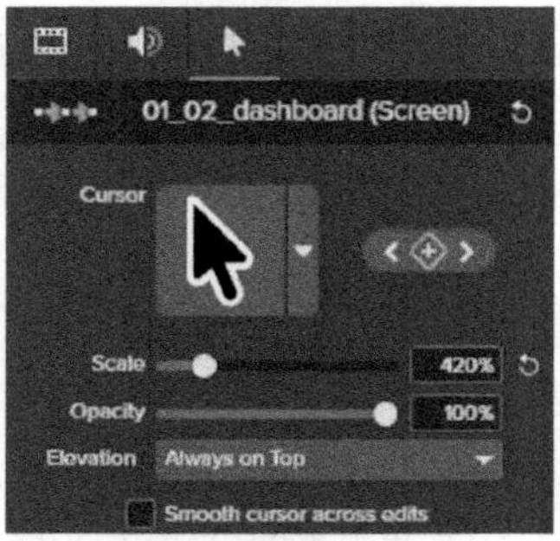

07_03.png - The upper section of the Properties panel shows the appearance of the cursor at the playhead position.

You will now move the playhead along the timeline and observe how the cursor changes throughout the project.

4. Position the playhead around timecode *0:01:26;00*.
5. Take another look at the Properties panel and notice the updated mouse cursor.

In the timeline, cursor changes are highlighted with a series of small icons scattered along the selected screen recording, as shown in the image below.

07_04.png - These small icons mark changes in the cursor's appearance.

Keep in mind that these icons are only visible if both the following conditions are met:

- The screen recording is selected in the timeline.
- The **Cursor Properties** tab is open in the Properties panel.

These cursors were captured by Camtasia Recorder during the recording.

2. Selecting a Recorded Cursor

Before you can customize a cursor, you must first select it. In this section, you will learn two methods for selecting a mouse cursor.

1. Select the screen recording on track 1 of the ***01_01_dashboard*** project.
2. Open the Properties panel and navigate to the **Cursor Properties** tab.

Remember, these are the two conditions for the cursor icons to be visible in the timeline.

3. [*Windows only*] In the timeline, double-click any cursor icon in the screen recording.

This action selects the cursor you double-clicked and moves the playhead to that position.

Alternatively, use the arrows at the top of the Properties panel to navigate across cursors, as shown in the image below.

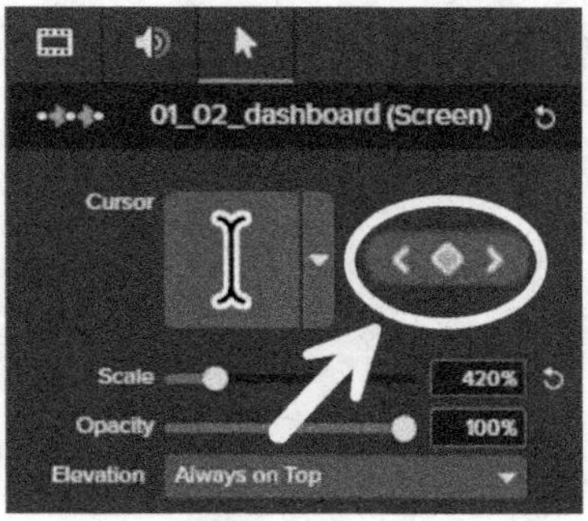

07_05.png – *You can navigate across cursors using the highlighted arrows.*

Clicking the right arrow selects the next cursor, while clicking the left arrow takes you back to the previous cursor. Every time you click, the playhead repositions itself accordingly.

4. Position the playhead at timecode *0:00:45:00*.

At this location, the mouse pointer appears as a black arrow, as shown in the upper section of the Properties panel.

5. Click once on the right-pointing arrow highlighted in the previous image.

This takes you to timecode *0:00:49;19*, where the cursor briefly changes to an *"I"* shape. This cursor is only visible for a very short time before the mouse pointer reverts to a black arrow.

3. Changing the Cursor Appearance

This minor visual change adds no educational value to your tutorial, but you're concerned that it might distract your viewers, especially after enlarging the cursor in a previous section. To maintain visual consistency and keep your audience focused, you'll now switch this cursor to a standard black arrow so that it retains its appearance.

1. In the Properties panel, click the arrow next to the cursor image to open the **Replace Cursor Image** drawer.

This action is depicted in the following screenshot.

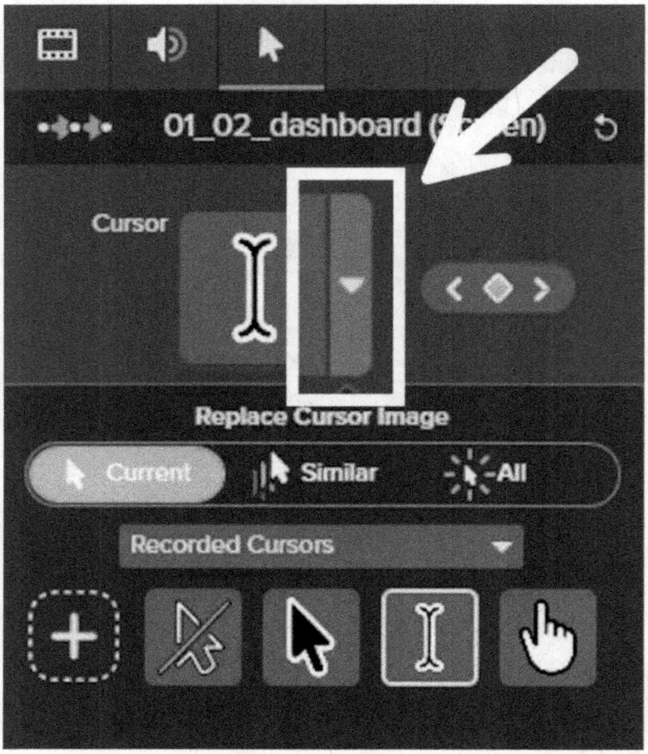

07_06.png - Open the ***Replace Cursor Image*** *drawer.*

Note that the I-shaped cursor is outlined in a thin yellow border to indicate it is the active cursor at the current playhead position.

2. Click the black arrow in the **Recorded Cursors** drawer.

The cursor on the canvas changes to a black arrow, confirming you have modified the appearance of a pointer within your project.

4. Changing Multiple Cursors at Once

The brief cursor change you fixed in the previous section was not an isolated incident; upon closer inspection of the rest of the project, you realize this visual glitch occurs repeatedly.

You will now replace all of these I-shaped cursors with black arrows in a single step.

1. Click twice on the right arrow next to the cursor icon in the upper section of the Properties panel.

This takes you to timecode *0:00:50;05*, where the cursor briefly changes to an I-beam shape again.

2. Click **Similar** in the **Replace Cursor Image** drawer of the Properties panel

This action is illustrated in the following screenshot.

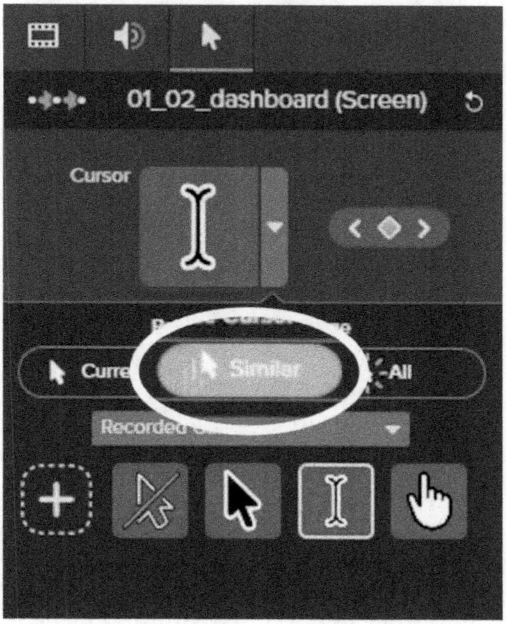

*07_07.png - Click **Similar** in the **Replace Cursor Image** drawer.*

This action selects all I-shaped cursors within the selected element and highlights them in yellow on the timeline.

3. With all these cursors selected, click the black arrow icon in the Properties panel.
4. Press the `spacebar` to start playing the project.

During playback, focus on the mouse cursor. The blinking I-shaped cursor has been eliminated, leaving only the steady black arrow.

5. Other Cursor Options

Before moving on, let's take a quick look at the other options in the **Replace Cursor Image drawer**. You don't need them for this specific project, but they come in handy in many situations.

The following image will serve as a visual guide for the options discussed in this section.

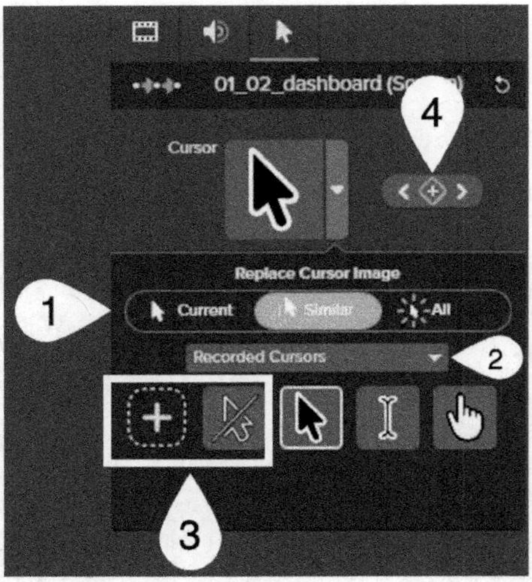

07_08.png – Use this image as a reference throughout this section.

First, let's look at the three selection buttons identified by number 1 in the above image.

- **Current** only selects the active cursor, i.e., the cursor visible at the current playhead position.
- **Similar** selects every cursor with the same appearance as the active cursor.
- **All** selects all cursors.

These selections only apply to the active multimedia element. For instance, clicking **All** selects every cursor *in the selected screen recording*, not every cursor in the project.

You can choose the cursor that will replace the selected one(s) from the dropdown menu identified by the number 2 in the preceding image. By default, only the cursors captured by Camtasia Recorder are displayed.

1. Open the **Recorded Cursors** dropdown and explore the available options.
2. Make sure to switch back to **Recorded Cursors** when done.

In the preceding image, number 3 identifies two special cursor options within the drawer.

- The crossed-out arrow icon lets you hide the selected cursor(s).
- The + icon enables you to use a custom graphic as the pointer. For example, using your company logo is a fun and easy way to uniquely promote your brand identity within your tutorial.

Finally, you can manually add additional cursor changes using the + button marked with number 4 in the above image.

With these options, you have everything you need to customize the appearance of the mouse cursor in your video tutorials. Just remember that this only works with ***.trec*** screen recordings made with Camtasia Recorder.

C. Applying Cursor Effects

Camtasia offers a wide range of effects to emphasize mouse movements and clicks. In the upcoming few sections, you will learn how to apply these cursor effects using the ***01_03_settings*** project from the exercises.

1. Save and close any open projects.
2. Import the ***Chapter07/projects/01_03_settings.zip*** project into the ***Chapter07*** folder of the exercises.
3. Watch the entire project to refresh your memory.
4. In the timeline, position the playhead around timecode *0:00:18;00* so that you can see the screen recording on the canvas.

You are now ready to explore Camtasia's cursor effects.

1. Working With the Cursor Color Effect

First, let's see how to customize the pointer's appearance using the *Cursor Color* effect. This approach proves very useful in many situations, including the following.

- Improve the cursor's visibility by using high-contrast colors against the background.
- Use your brand's official color scheme to reinforce your visual identity in a creative way.
- Optimize color usage for colorblind viewers.

Before you begin, remember that the **Screen** track in this project consists of multiple small segments. This was necessary to apply the *Clip Speed* effect only to specific portions of the recording. Since you want to apply the *Cursor Color* effect to the entire project, you must first select all these small segments using the following steps.

1. Right-click the **Screen** track header at the far left of the timeline.

2. In the context menu, click **Select All Media on Track** (Windows) or **Select All on Track** (Mac).

A thin yellow outline now surrounds every element on the **Screen** track, indicating they are all selected.

3. Click **Cursor Effects** on the left side of the interface to open the **Cursor Effects** panel.
4. Drag the **Cursor Color** effect from the **Cursor Effects** panel and drop it onto any of the currently selected clips in the timeline.

This action applies the effect to all selected multimedia elements. At the bottom of the Properties panel, you'll notice a new section for the **Cursor Color** effect.

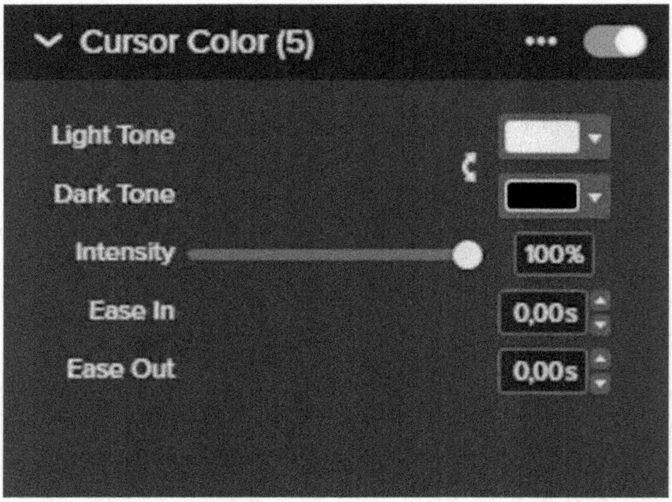

07_09.png - *The properties for the **Cursor Color** effect in the bottom of the Properties panel.*

On Windows, the number 5 in parentheses indicates the total number of selected items to which this effect is applied.

You can now choose the new colors for the mouse cursor.

5. Switch to **Edit All Animation** mode by clicking the **Animation editing mode** icon in the upper left-hand corner of the Properties panel.
6. Use the **Light Tone** and **Dark Tone** properties to select two colors of your choice.

The **Light Tone** color applies to the cursor's outline, while the **Dark Tone color** applies to the cursor's fill.

7. Also increase the **Scale** of the cursor to `420%`.

In Chapter 9 – Extending and Customizing Camtasia, you will create a custom theme to apply specific brand colors to the mouse cursor. But for now, let's experiment with another cursor effect.

2. Working with the Cursor Highlight Effect

The *Cursor Highlight* effect offers another practical way to emphasize the mouse cursor on screen.

1. Make sure all media items in the **Screen** track are still selected and that the **Edit All Animation** mode is still active.
2. Open the **Cursor Effects** panel on the left side of the screen.
3. Drag the **Cursor Highlight** effect from the **Cursor Effects** panel and drop it onto any one of the currently selected media items.

On the canvas, a yellow glow now highlights the mouse cursor, as shown in the image below.

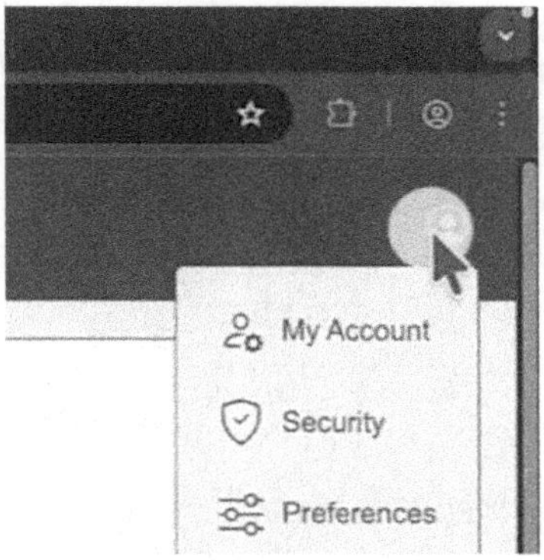

07_10.png - A yellow glow now highlights the mouse cursor.

You can adjust the properties of the **Cursor Highlight** effect in the corresponding section at the bottom of the Properties panel. Take some time to explore these properties and discover the full potential of this effect.

- Use the **Color** property to choose the color of the circle surrounding the mouse cursor.
- The **Size** property lets you change the size of the circle.
- The **Opacity** property lets you choose how transparent the circle is.
- The **Blur** property lets you blur the edges of the colored circle.

Also notice how the **Cursor Highlight** effect combines with the **Cursor Color** effect from the previous section. In the Properties panel, each effect has its own dedicated section.

3. Other Cursor Effects

While **Cursor Highlight** is one of Camtasia's most popular cursor effects, the **Cursor Effects** panel offers several variations that are worth exploring.

- Instead of using a solid color, the **Gradient** effect highlights the mouse cursor with a two-color circular gradient.
- The **Cursor Magnify** effect slightly enlarges a circular area around the mouse cursor.
- The **Cursor Spotlight** effect darkens everything except the area around the cursor.
- The **Cursor Isolation** effect is quite similar. It darkens the entire recording except for the cursor. Taken to the extreme, this effect leaves only the mouse cursor on the screen and completely hides everything else in the recording.
- The **Negative** effect inverts the colors of the screen recording within a circle surrounding the mouse cursor.
- The **Cursor Shadow** effect adds a drop shadow to the mouse cursor.

Finally, Camtasia offers two cursor effects designed to make cursor movements smoother, more natural, and more visible.

- The **Kinetic Cursor** effect simulates momentum making the cursor move in a more organic and natural way.
- The **Cursor Motion Blur** effect highlights mouse movements by blurring the cursor based on its speed: the faster the movement, the more pronounced the blur.

All these effects share a common goal: to help you highlight the mouse cursor so that your audience can easily follow each step of your tutorial.

D. Highlighting Mouse Actions

In the previous sections, you discovered many useful tools for customizing and enhancing the *appearance* of the mouse cursor. But the cursor is much more than a customizable icon; it is also the primary means by which you perform *actions* on your computer.

To maximize the educational effectiveness of your tutorial, your viewers must be able to identify, distinguish, and understand these actions.

This section demonstrates how to visually emphasize the mouse actions captured during the recording.

1. Ensure all items in the **Screen** track of the *01_03_settings* project are still selected and that the **Edit All Animation** mode is still active.
2. Position the playhead at timecode *0:00:10;00*.
3. Open the *Cursor Effects* panel on the left side of the screen.

As shown in the image below, the **Cursor Effects** panel has three tabs. So far, you have only explored the first one.

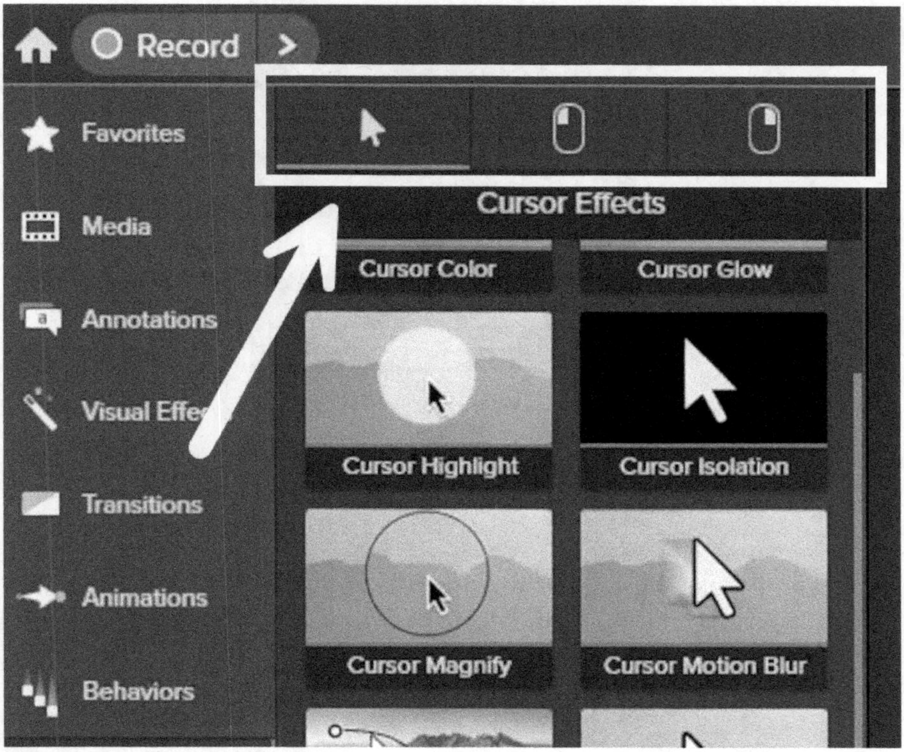

*07_11.png - The **Cursor Effects** panel has three tabs.*

The tools in the other two tabs are used to highlight *left-click* and *right-click* actions, respectively.

4. Open the **Left Click** tab of the **Cursor Effects** panel.
5. Take a moment to hover over each thumbnail to preview the corresponding effect.
6. Drag the **Rings** effect from the **Left Click** tab and drop it onto any of the selected clips in the **Screen** track.
7. Do the same with the **Sound** effect.

The latter adds a click sound to every left-click, demonstrating that mouse clicks can be enhanced with both visual and audio effects. The properties of these two effects can be found at the bottom of the Properties panel, as shown in the image below.

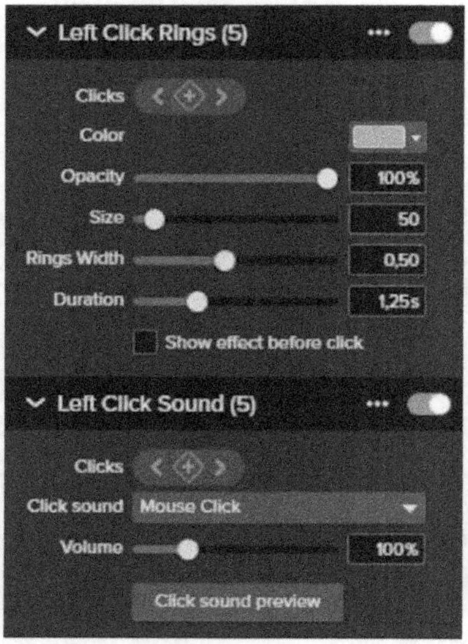

07_12.png - The properties of these effects can be found at the bottom of the Properties panel.

8. Take some time to explore these properties and discover the full potential of these effects.
9. When done, hit the `spacebar` to start playing the video.

To wrap up this section, examine the **Screen** track on the timeline. Each clip now has a small upward-pointing arrow, indicating that effects have been applied.

10. Click any one of these small arrows as illustrated in the image below.

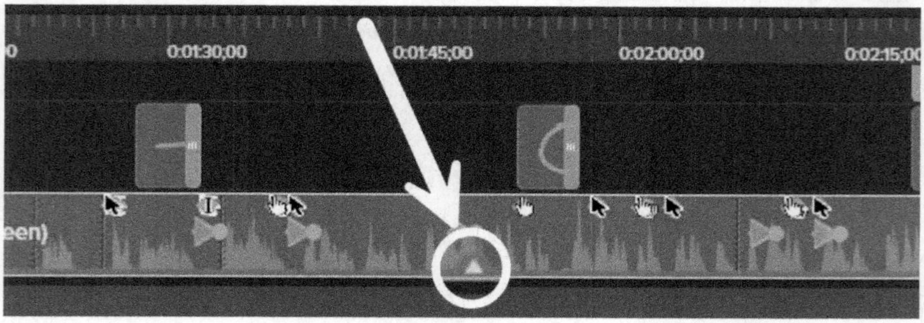

07_13.png - Click any one of these small arrows.

This reveals the effects that have been applied to this element. As you can see in the image below, the **Left Click Rings** and **Left Click Sound** effects provide visual indicators as of where clicks were made.

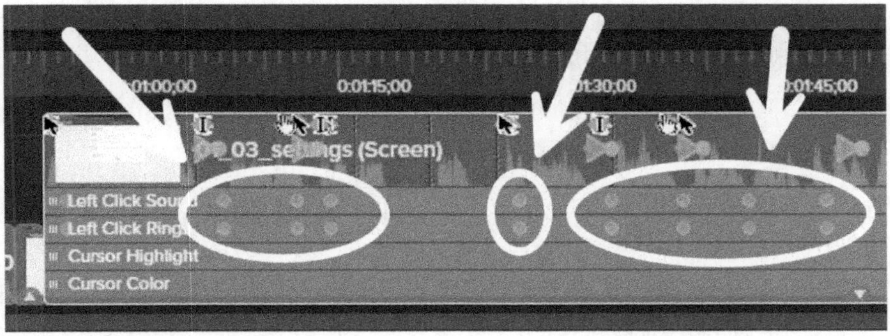

07_14.png – The effects and mouse clicks are visible in the timeline.

These cursor and click effects give you a wide range of options for highlighting the mouse cursor and its actions. Feel free to try out different combinations until you find your favorite.

E. Adjusting the Cursor Path

Let's now look at the cursor path—that is, the way the cursor moves across the screen. By default, Camtasia replicates the movements captured during recording but allows you to adjust the cursor trajectory during post-production. Here are a few common scenarios.

- Smooth out mouse movements to make them more fluid and less jerky.
- Hide a cut causing a sudden cursor jump.
- Remove unintended, distracting, or incorrect movements.
- Hide movements toward icons not captured by Camtasia, such as off-screen icons or items on the Camtasia Recorder toolbar.
- Reposition the cursor to make an action clearer and easier to spot.

The next few sections will walk you through the tools available in Camtasia for modifying the cursor path.

1. Using the Cursor Smoothing Effect

The *Cursor Smoothing* effect automatically removes unnecessary mouse movements. It analyzes the cursor path and eliminates jerks and jitters to ensure smooth, consistent cursor movement from one click to the next.

1. Make sure all items in the **Screen** track of project ***01_03_settings*** are still selected.
2. Position the playhead at timecode *0:00:55;00*.

At this point in the tutorial, the mouse pointer is hovering over the **Email** field of the **My Account** form.

3. Play the video and carefully watch how the cursor moves toward the **Save** button.

Notice how the cursor follows a curved path that makes it brush against the bottom edge of the canvas.

4. Open the **Cursor Effects** panel on the left side of the screen and navigate to the **Cursor Effects** tab.
5. Drag the **Cursor Smoothing** effect from the **Cursor Effects** panel and drop it onto any of the selected items in the **Screen** track.

This applies the effect to all selected items. Its properties can be found at the bottom of the Properties panel, as shown in the image below.

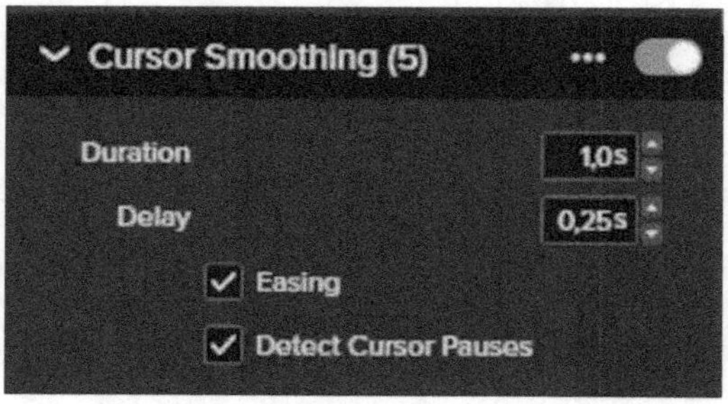

*07_15.png – The properties of the **Cursor Smoothing** effect.*

Unless you have specific requirements, you can safely stick with this default configuration.

6. Reposition the playhead at timecode *0:00:55;00*.
7. Restart the video and observe how the cursor moves from the **Email** field to the **Save** button.

The mouse now follows a straight path and no longer touches the bottom edge of the canvas.

The actual impact of this effect depends on the precision and smoothness of the mouse movements during recording. As you master the art of recording video tutorials, you'll get into the habit of avoiding unnecessary mouse movements, and your raw footage will naturally be a lot cleaner, reducing the need for major corrections in post-production.

*You can find more info on the **Cursor Smoothing** effect on the TechSmith website at https://www.techsmith.com/learn/tutorials/camtasia/cursor-smoothing/*

2. Manually Editing the Cursor Path

Even though the **Cursor Smoothing** effect settles most minor imperfections, certain scenarios require more advanced adjustments that go beyond its capabilities.

- When you want to change the position of a mouse click.
- When you don't want the mouse to move in a straight line.
- When you need to make significant changes to the cursor path.

In such cases, Camtasia lets you manually adjust the mouse path. This is what you will explore in the next exercise using the following steps.

1. Position the playhead at timecode *0:01:45;00* in the ***01_03_settings*** project.

At this point, the mouse pointer hovers over the **English** option of the **Preferences** dropdown menu.

2. Slowly drag the playhead to timecode *0:01:49;0*, keeping a close eye on the mouse movement and click.

The mouse pointer travels a long way before clicking the **Français** option. Your task is to minimize this movement so that the cursor clicks directly above its current position, without any unnecessary movement.

3. Select the screen recording located at the current playhead position on the **Screen** track.
4. Navigate to the **Cursor Properties** tab of the Properties panel.

To proceed, you would normally click **Edit Cursor Path**; however, this option is currently unavailable, as shown in the following screenshot.

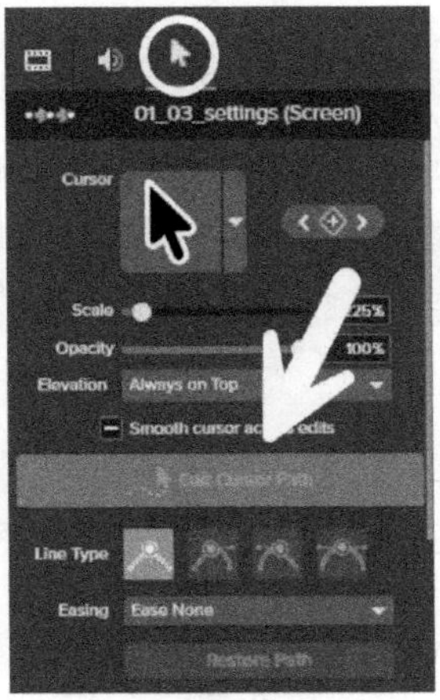

*07_16.png – The **Edit Cursor Path** option is currently unavailable.*

This is because the *Cursor Smoothing* effect is already applied to the selected item. To manually edit the cursor path, you must first remove this effect.

5. Scroll down the Properties panel until you see the **Cursor Smoothing** section.
6. [*Windows only*] Click the ellipsis icon in the upper right-hand corner of this section, then click **Delete Effect**.
7. [*Mac only*] Click the **Remove Effect** icon in the upper left-hand corner of this section.

These steps are illustrated in the following image.

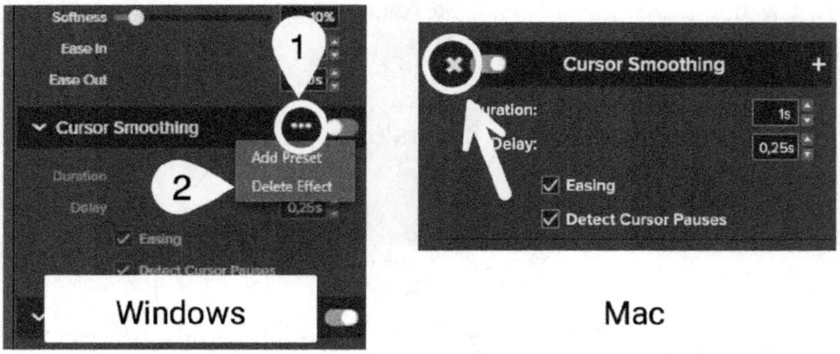

*07_17.png – Delete the **Cursor Smoothing** effect.*

Now that the effect has been removed, the **Edit Cursor Path** button becomes active.

8. Reposition the playhead at timecode *0:01:45;00*
9. Click **Edit Cursor Path** in the upper section of the Properties panel.

At this point, a window pops up, prompting you to either *Simplify Existing Path* or *Create New Path.*

10. Select **Simplify Existing Path** and click **Continue**.

The cursor path now appears on the canvas, as shown in the image below.

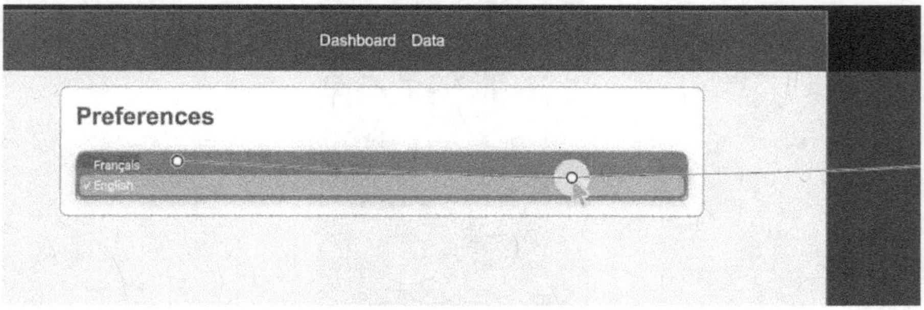

07_18.png - The cursor path now appears on the canvas.

You can now modify this path using the following steps.

11. Move the leftmost point to the right and position it near to the mouse cursor on top of the **Français** option of the dropdown menu.
12. In the Properties panel, click the first **Line Type** icon to create a straight path rather than a curved one.

The cursor path should now look like the following image.

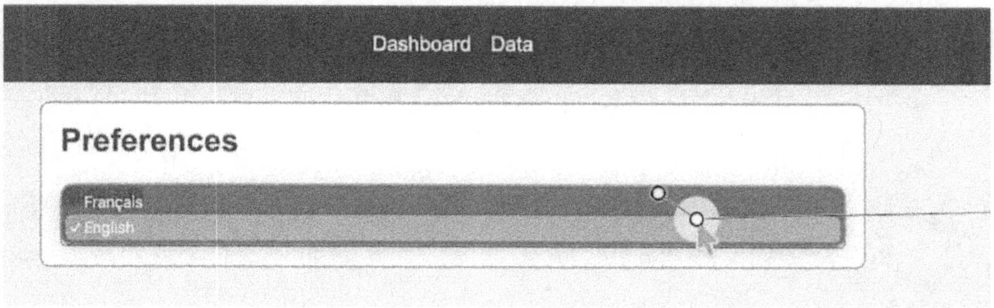

09_19.png - The new cursor path is visible on the canvas.

You will now test this sequence to ensure this adjustment goes unnoticed.

13. Click **Finish Editing** in the Properties panel.
14. Hit the `spacebar` to start playing the video and confirm the new mouse movement looks natural.
15. Save and close the *01_03_settings* project when done.

In this section, you modified an existing cursor path using the **Edit Cursor Path** feature of the Properties panel. Feel free to keep experimenting and adjusting the cursor path and click positions throughout the entire project.

F. Creating a New Cursor Path

Who said mouse cursors are exclusive to screen recordings? With Camtasia, you can add a mouse cursor to any object! In this section, you'll apply the *Cursor Path Creator* effect to a static image and design a custom mouse cursor path from start to finish.

But why on earth would anyone need that? Well, let me share a challenge I faced a few years ago. I was tasked with creating video tutorials for a secure internal application at a client's site. However, due to strict security protocols, I couldn't install their software on my device, and their IT department refused to allow Camtasia on their devices without a lengthy security audit. To get around this problem, I used the Windows `Print Screen` feature to take static screenshots, which I imported into the media bin of my Camtasia project. Using the *Cursor Path Creator* effect, I manually recreated the mouse movements and clicks over the still screenshots. This workaround allowed me to meet the deadline without installing any software and without breaking any security rules!

Now it's your turn to explore this feature. The first step is to import the project you'll be using for this exercise.

1. Save and close any open projects.
2. Import the ***Chapter07/projects/00_00_trailer.zip*** project into the **Chapter07** folder of the exercises.
3. Watch the entire project to refresh your memory.

Remember that the timeline for this project contains a lot of tracks. You may need to increase the height of the timeline to ensure all tracks are visible.

4. Position the playhead at timecode *0:00:10;00*.
5. Zoom in on the timeline to focus on the sequence between timecodes *0:00:08;00* and *0:00:25:00*.

The playhead is now positioned right after the appearance of the laptop image, which sits on track 5 of the timeline. Tracks 6 and 7 hold the elements inside the laptop screen, as shown in the image below.

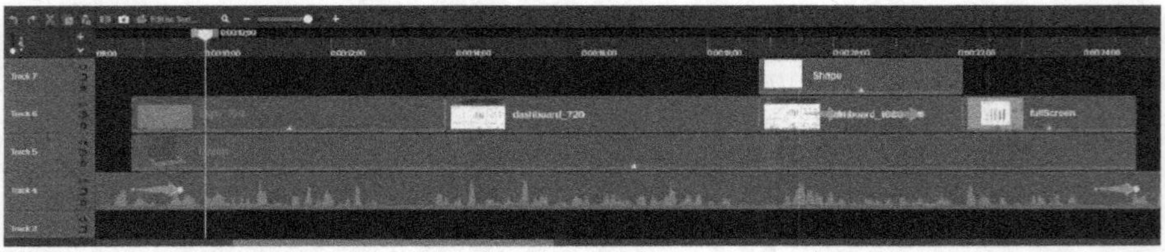

07_20.png - The playhead is now positioned after the appearance of the laptop image.

This is the sequence you'll be working with throughout this exercise. Before moving on, make sure these elements are clearly visible both in the timeline and on the canvas.

1. Applying the Cursor Path Creator Effect

Your task is to highlight the animations on the laptop screen with mouse clicks. Begin by applying the *Cursor Path Creator* effect to the laptop image.

1. Open the **Cursor Effects** panel on the left side of the screen.

2. Drag the **Cursor Path Creator** effect from the **Cursor Effects** panel and drop it onto the laptop image on track 5.

*The **Cursor Path Creator** effect can also be found in the **Visual Effects** panel , alongside the other visual effects.*

As shown in the image below, the Properties panel now features a **Cursor Properties** tab identified by an arrow icon.

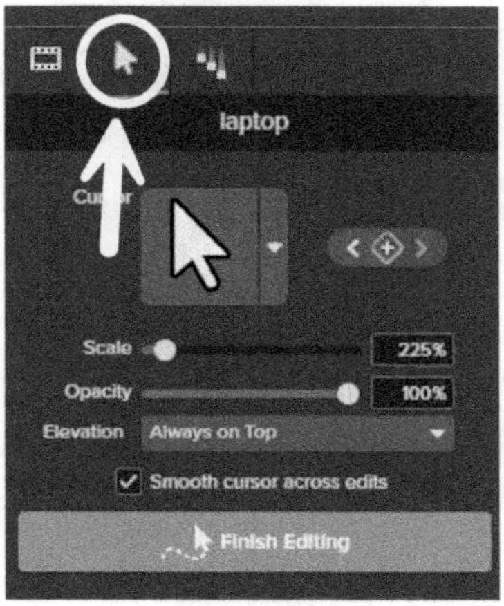

*07_21.png - The Properties panel now features a **Cursor Properties** tab.*

The cursor path is also visible on the canvas. However, the cursor itself is not clearly visible! There are two possible explanations for this:

- The cursor is covered by an element on an upper track.
- The cursor is too small.

In the next two sections, you'll learn how to fix each of these two problems.

2. Elevating the Cursor

You've applied the **Cursor Path Creator** effect to the laptop image on track 5. Keep in mind that any media on tracks 6 and 7 sits *above* this image and may block the cursor from view. Fortunately, this is very easy to fix using the Properties panel.

1. Select the laptop image to which you applied the **Cursor Path Creator** effect.
2. Open the **Elevation** dropdown in the **Cursor Properties** tab of the Properties panel.
3. Take a moment to review the available options, then select **Always on Top**.

This step is depicted in the screenshot below.

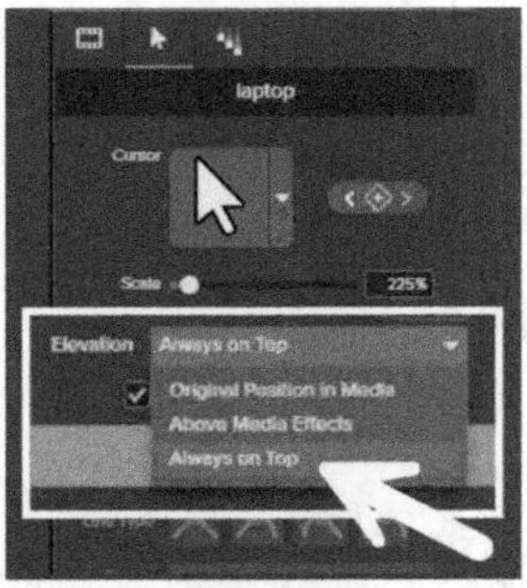

*07_22.png – Select **Always on Top** in the **Elevation** dropdown.*

With this option, Camtasia elevates the mouse cursor to the foreground, keeping it on top of everything else, which ensures that nothing will ever cover it again.

3. Increasing the Cursor Size

You also want to enlarge the cursor, as the default size is too small and makes it hard to see on the canvas.

1. Make sure the laptop image on track 5 is still selected.
2. In the Properties panel, increase the value of the **Scale** property until the pointer is clearly visible on the canvas.

Go ahead and increase the **Scale** to about `1000%`, as shown in the image below.

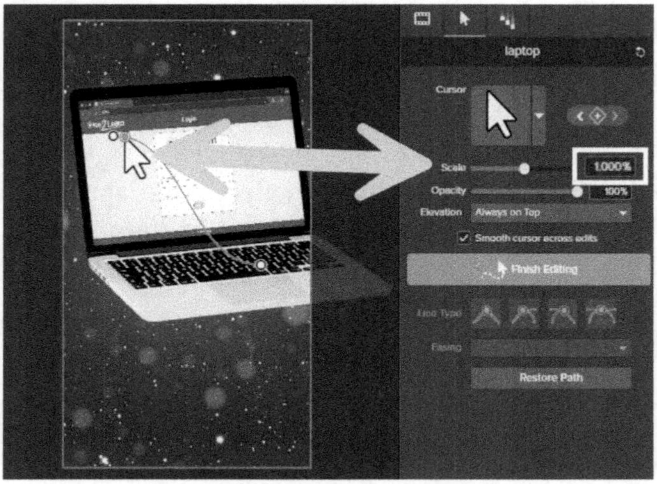

*07_23.png – Increase the **Scale** to `1000%`.*

Take this opportunity to select a cursor image using the steps outlined in the Changing the Cursor Shape section earlier in this chapter.

4. Defining the Cursor Path

At this point, the cursor is clearly visible on the canvas. The next step is to define its path by repositioning the points at each end of the cursor path on the canvas.

1. In the timeline, position the playhead before the mouse movement at timecode *0:00:09;20*.

On the canvas, the mouse cursor sits at its starting position in the upper-left corner of the laptop screen.

If you don't see the cursor path on the canvas, click **Edit Cursor Path** *in the Properties panel.*

2. Click the white dot just above the cursor. The dot turns yellow to indicate it is selected.
3. Move the dot to the left and position it off canvas, as shown in the image below.

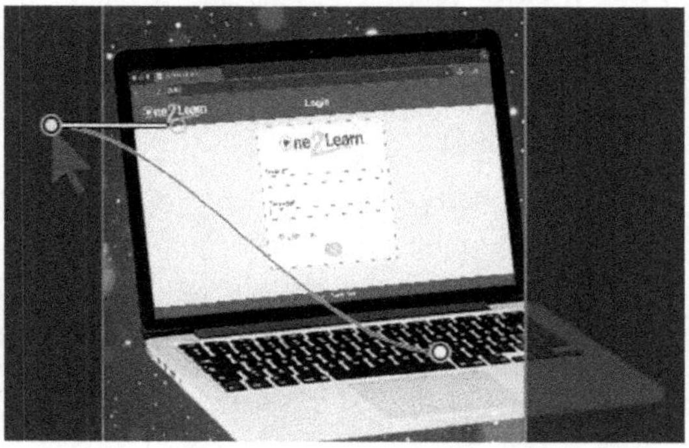

07_24.png - *Move the starting point of the cursor off canvas.*

You've just set the starting point of the cursor. You will now determine its destination by repositioning the other end of the line.

4. Select the dot at the other end of the curved line.
5. Position it in the center of the laptop screen.

After adjusting these two points, you have defined the cursor's entry path on the canvas. Your next task is to define the corresponding exit path that will guide the cursor out of the canvas to the other side.

6. Position the playhead at timecode *0:00:23;00*.
7. Right-click off the canvas, on the right side.
8. In the context menu, select **Extend Cursor Path to Here**.

Camtasia generates a second mouse movement, which starts where the previous movement ended and ends where you right clicked. Feel free to reposition the end of this second movement so it ends slightly outside the canvas on the right, as shown in the image below.

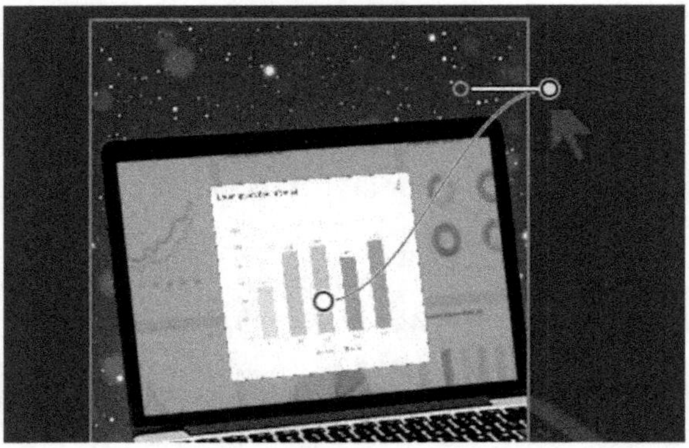

07_25.png - Position the end of the line outside the canvas, to the right.

In this section, you have defined the trajectory of the mouse cursor on the canvas. Here's a quick summary:

- The cursor will execute two movements: one to enter and another one to exit the canvas.
- The first movement begins off-screen, on the left side, and ends in the middle of the laptop screen.
- The second movement picks up where the previous one left off and ends off the canvas to the right.

You still need to determine exactly *when* these movements should occur.

5. Establishing the Timing and Speed of Movements

Remember that video editing requires positioning elements in both space and time. In the previous section, you positioned the mouse movement in *space* using the *canvas*. In this section, you'll use the *timeline* to position them in *time*, meaning you'll determine *when* and *how fast* these movements should occur.

1. Make sure the laptop image on track 5 is still selected and that the mouse cursor is still visible on the canvas.

2. Position the playhead at timecode *0:00:12;15*. This is the exact moment the mouse cursor should enter the canvas.

As shown below, the timeline marks these movements with dots connected by a series of right-pointing arrows.

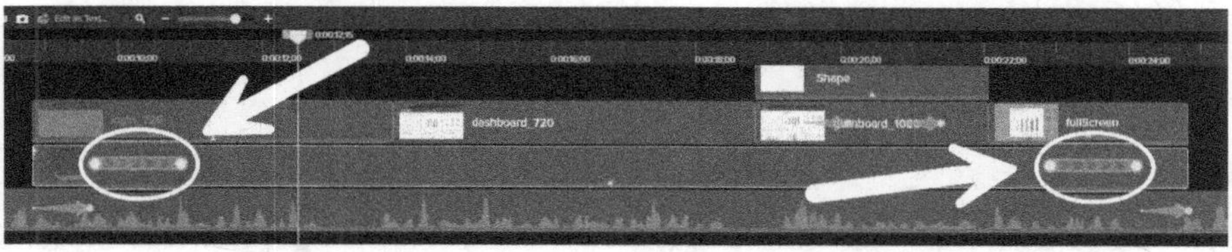

07_26.png - Cursor movements are also visible in the timeline.

3. In the timeline, drag the first mouse movement to make it start at the current playhead position.
4. Position the playhead at timecode *0:00:13;22*.

This is the exact moment when the first mouse movement must end.

5. Extend the first mouse movement so that it ends at the current playhead position

By extending the mouse movement in the timeline, you decrease the speed of the cursor. The result of these steps is shown in the image below.

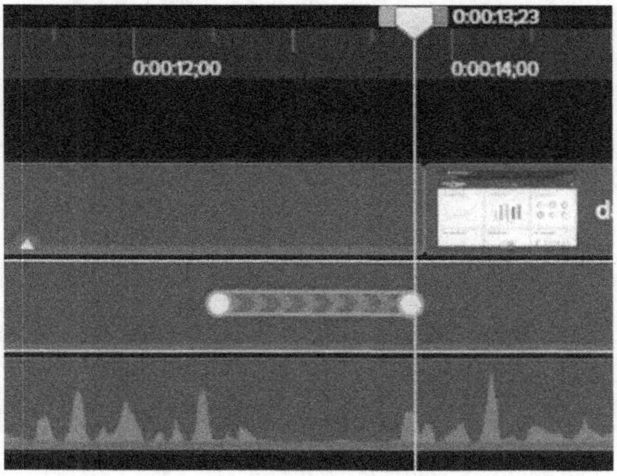

07_27.png - Stretching the mouse movement in the timeline reduces the cursor speed.

You will now use the same techniques for the second movement, which moves the cursor off the canvas.

6. Position the playhead just before the beginning of the **Out** behavior that removes the laptop image from the canvas at timecode *0:00:24;02*.
7. Move the second mouse movement so it ends at the playhead, keeping the speed unchanged.

Note that you just moved the second movement on the timeline, without stretching or shrinking it. This allows you to determine when the movement occurs without altering its speed.

Both movements are now correctly positioned in space (on the canvas) and in time (in the timeline).

6. Adding Mouse Clicks

Keep in mind that the mouse is much more than a visual pointer moving across the screen; it is also your primary tool for *interacting* with your computer. In this section, you will define the actions (the clicks) that should occur along the new cursor paths you just created.

1. Open the **Cursor Effects** panel on the left side of the screen.
2. Switch to the **Left Click** tab of the **Cursor Effects** panel.
3. Drag the **Sound** effect from the **Left Click** panel and drop it onto the laptop image on track 5 of the timeline.

The properties for this new effect can be found at the bottom of the **Cursor Properties** tab of the Properties panel, as shown in the following screenshot.

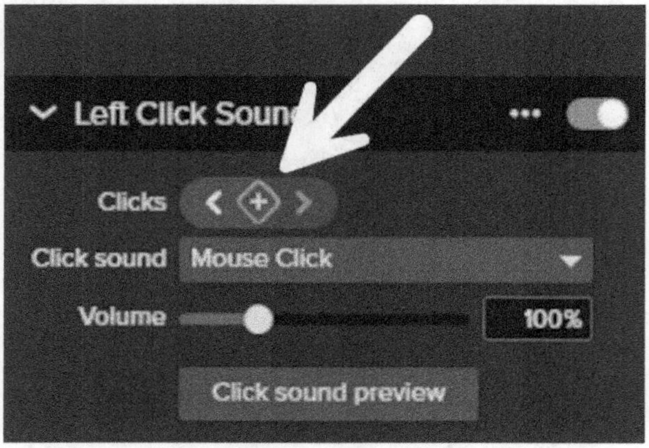

*07_28.png - The properties for the **Left Click Sound** effect.*

To define a click, just position the playhead at the desired location, then click the button identified by an arrow in the above image.

4. Position the playhead at timecode *0:00:13;22*.
5. Click the button identified by the arrow in the previous image.

This defines a first mouse click at the current playhead position. To visualize it, expand the effects drawer for the laptop image within the timeline.

6. Click the upward-pointing arrow in the middle of the laptop image on track 5 of the timeline.

This opens the effects drawer and reveals the active effects of this element, including the **Left Click Sound** effect. The click is clearly visible, as shown in the image below.

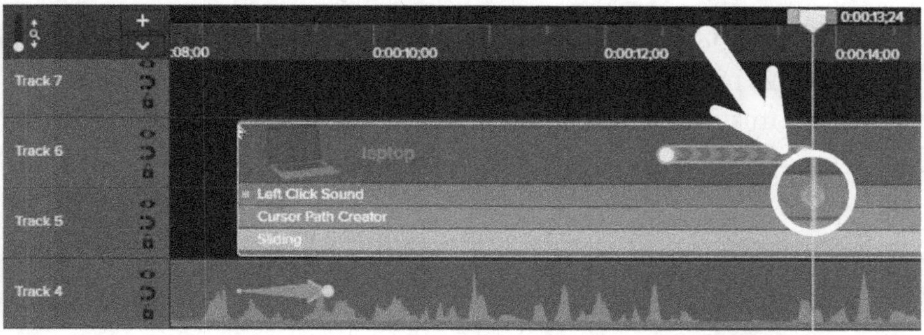

07_29.png - The click is clearly visible in the timeline.

You still have a few clicks to define to complete this first cursor path.

7. Define a second click at timecode *0:00:18;21*.
8. Repeat the same operations at the following three timecodes
   - *0:00:19;12*
   - *0:00:20;21*
   - *0:00:21;28*
9. Return to the **Left Click** tab of the **Cursor Effects** panel.
10. Drag the **Scaling** effect from the **Cursor Effects** panel and drop it onto the laptop image on track 5 of the timeline.

As shown below, this effect automatically inherits the same series of clicks as for the **Left Click Sound** effect.

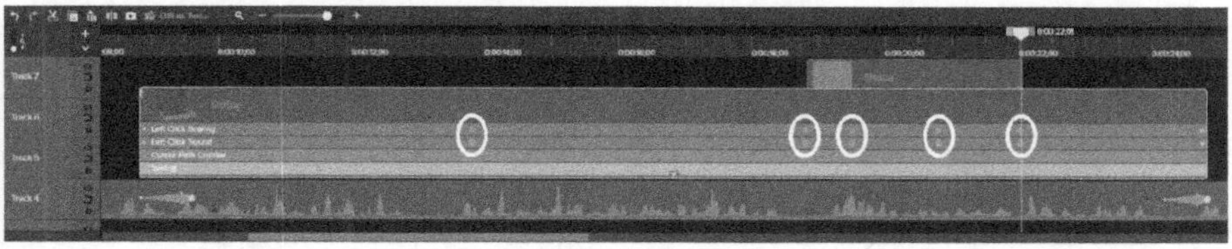

07_30.png - All click effects use the same clicks.

It is now time to test it all out using the following steps.

11. Position the playhead slightly ahead of this sequence around timecode *0:00:07;00*.
12. Play the project and enjoy the final version of your first fully customized cursor path!

At the end of this section, you have successfully created a custom cursor path directly within Camtasia. Keep in mind that this path has been applied to a still image, not to a screen recording as in previous examples.

7. Exercise – Creating a Cursor Path

Practice is key to unlocking the full potential of the **Cursor Path Creator** effect. In this hands-on exercise, you will create a second cursor path using the laptop image between timecodes *0:00:34;00* and *0:00:45;00*.

The main steps for this exercise are as follows:

- Apply the **Cursor Path Creator** effect to the second laptop image.
- Elevate the cursor so that it is always in the foreground.
- Increase the size of the cursor and choose the cursor image that works best for you.
- Define the entry path and the exit path of the cursor.
- Set the timing and speed of these two movements
- Apply the **Left Click Sound** effect to simulate two clicks just before each of the two image changes on the laptop screen.
- Also apply the **Left Click Scale** effect (or any other left-click effect of your choosing) to visualize the clicks on the canvas.

By the end of this exercise, you will have created a second cursor path and will be ready to move on to the next chapter.

G. Conclusion

You can, of course, use Camtasia as a general-purpose video editing tool and produce any type of video, whether it's a commercial, a news report, a documentary, or even a feature film.

But the features covered in this chapter establish Camtasia as the go-to tool for creating screen-based video tutorials. In this type of video, the mouse cursor plays a central role in your storytelling.

Camtasia offers a wide range of tools and effects designed to customize the appearance of the cursor, control its path, and highlight its onscreen actions. As an instructor, you can use these tools to reinforce the clarity and impact of your message to your learners.

By the end of this chapter, the sequences of your online training course are really starting to take shape. However, you still have one crucial aspect of video production to address. In the next chapter, you'll discover the Camtasia tools for producing the audio track for your videos.

Working with Audio

Post-production of your online course is now well underway. However, one crucial aspect of video production still needs to be addressed: the audio. Many novice video creators tend to focus solely on the visual quality of their work, at the expense of audio. Yet experienced creators all agree that sound is at least as important as the image.

Here's a simple experiment: play one of your videos with the sound turned off and ask a viewer to summarize the key information presented in the video. Then have someone else listen to the audio track only and ask the same question. You'll find out that the bulk of your message is actually conveyed through *audio*.

By the way, don't *you* also consider audio quality when choosing your next video to watch? In a recent TechSmith study (2024), participants ranked audio quality as one of the most important factors in determining the overall quality of a video. The survey also reveals that poor audio is one of the main reasons viewers drop out midway through.

See pages 20 and 28 of the survey, which you can download for free from https://www.techsmith.com/resources/research/video-viewer-report/

This chapter will guide you through the effects and features of Camtasia for producing the perfect audio track. You'll learn how to adjust the volume, add background music, mix the music with the narration, and record an alternate narration. You'll also learn how to incorporate different types of subtitles and closed captions to make your video content accessible and even more impactful.

A. Preparing the Exercises

As with previous chapters, the step-by-step exercises are based on the provided projects and files. You first need to import these compressed projects into Camtasia using the process described at the beginning of Chapter 05 – Editing Your Videos.

You will now get ready for the first few exercises of this chapter.

1. Download and unzip the exercises for Chapter 08.
2. Import ***Chapter08/projects/00_01_prerequisites.zip*** into the ***Chapter08*** folder of the exercise.
3. Review the entire project to refresh your memory.

Since you last worked on this project, several updates have been made. First, the green backdrop around the narrator has been removed using both the **Remove a Color** and **Background Removal** effects. Additionally, track 1 contains a group of ten elements that has been renamed **PowerPoint Slideshow**.

B. Adjusting the Audio Level

Audio is a critical yet often overlooked component of any video project. This section introduces you to the main audio features and properties in Camtasia. You will use them to adjust and harmonize the audio levels across all elements in your project.

1. Automatic Loudness Normalization

When a project includes multiple audio clips, you may notice significant sound level discrepancies between clips. These discrepancies typically occur when recordings are made separately, by different narrators, or using different audio equipment.

To mitigate these fluctuating audio levels, Camtasia automatically adjusts the loudness of all audio elements. Let's see it in action using the following steps.

1. Open the zoom dropdown menu at the top of the canvas.
2. Click **Project Settings** at the bottom of the menu.

In the **Project Settings** dialog, note the **Auto-normalize loudness** checkbox, as shown in the image below.

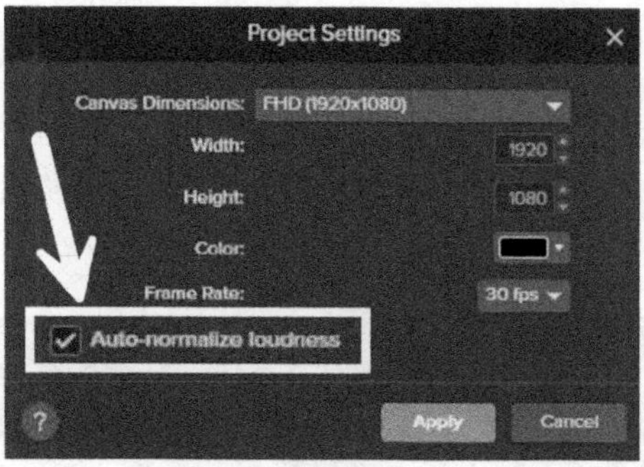

*08_01.png - The **Auto-normalize loudness** checkbox is enabled by default.*

This checkbox should be selected by default. It automatically adjusts the audio level of any clips on the timeline to the overall loudness of the project. In most cases, this default configuration works well and requires no further adjustment.

3. Click **Cancel** to close the **Project Settings** dialog box without making any changes.

With this configuration, the volume of all the audio clips in your project should be fairly consistent, and viewers shouldn't notice any significant volume variations.

2. Manually Adjusting the Audio Volume

Although the **Auto-normalize loudness** feature maintains relatively consistent audio levels, being able to manually adjust the audio volume in your projects remains essential. Here are a few practical examples.

- When you want to achieve a specific sound effect.
- When you need to mix multiple audio tracks playing simultaneously (for example, background music with narration).
- When Auto-normalize loudness is not sufficient or produces unwanted artifacts, such as hissing or digital distortion.
- When the volume of a clip needs to vary over time (for example, for fade in and fade out effects).

Clips containing audio data are clearly identified by the waveform displayed in the timeline. This visual indicator appears for both standalone audio files and video clips containing an audio track.

Use the following steps to discover the main audio properties available in the Properties panel.

1. In the ***00_01_prerequisites*** project, select the narrator video on track 2 of the timeline.
2. Open the Properties panel on the right side of the screen if necessary.
3. Click the speaker icon to navigate to the **Audio Properties** tab.

These steps are illustrated in the following image.

08_02.png - Click the speaker icon to open the ***Audio properties.***

There you find the **Gain** property, which defaults to **100%**. This means that the selected clip is played at its full original audio volume.

Although you don't need to make any manual adjustments to the audio volume in this project, let's experiment with this property, making sure to keep the audio volume unchanged by the end of this exercise.

4. Use the slider to significantly *reduce* the **Gain** of the selected clip while keeping an eye on the corresponding waveform in the timeline.

You will notice that the amplitude of the waveform decreases as you lower the **Gain** of the selected element.

5. Click the curved arrow icon next to the **Gain** property to restore its initial value.

The green line running across audio clips in the timeline provides another way to manually adjust the volume. This green line is known as the *Audio line*. It visually represents the sound level of the selected item.

Note that this volume indicator is only visible if the following two conditions are met.

- An item containing audio data is selected. It can be either a standalone audio file or a video clip with an audio track.
- For a video clip with an audio track, the **Audio Properties** tab is selected in the Properties panel.

You will now experiment with this *Audio line* using the following steps.

6. Drag the *Audio line* for the narrator's video down to lower the volume.

This reduces the volume of the selected media (and thus the height of the waveform in the timeline), but without affecting the **Gain** property in the Properties panel.

7. Use `Ctrl + Z` (Windows) or `Cmd + Z` (Mac) to undo the last action and restore the original volume.
8. Use the green and red handles on the playhead to select any section of the video.
9. Lower the audio line within the selection.

This operation is illustrated in the screenshot below.

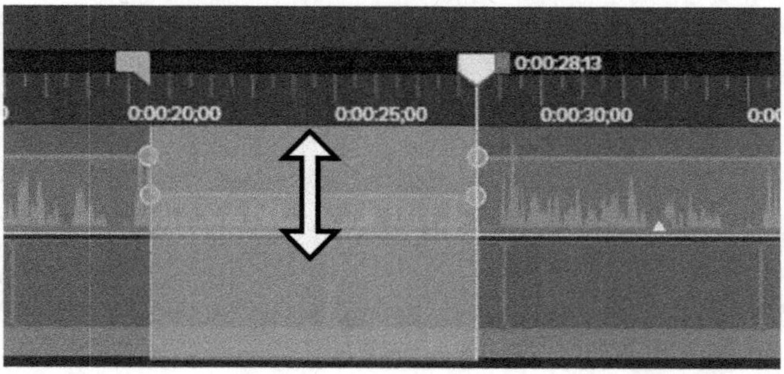

08_03.png - Drag the green line down to lower the volume within the selected segment.

This action reduces the volume within the selected segment only. To make this possible, Camtasia automatically adds four *Audio points* to the *Audio line* at the exact moments when the audio line changes direction.

10. Double click the triangle atop the playhead to cancel the selection.
11. Right-click any of the four audio points.
12. In the context menu, click **Remove All Audio Points** (Windows) or **Delete all audio points on media** (Mac)

After deleting the audio points, the audio waveform reverts to its original shape.

In this section, you have explored several methods for manually adjusting the audio volume of any media item containing audio data.

C. Applying Audio Effects

Similar to the cursor and visual effects discussed earlier, Camtasia offers several audio effects that you can apply to any clip containing audio. These can be found in the **Audio Effects** panel, on the left side of the screen.

1. Make sure the *00_01_prerequisites* project is still open in Camtasia.
2. Click **Audio Effects** on the left side of the screen to open the corresponding panel.

Windows users have access to six audio effects, while Mac users can choose from eight. In the next few sections, you'll apply several of these effects to the audio narration on track 2 of this project.

1. Applying Noise Reduction

When recording audio narration, your microphone doesn't just capture your voice. It also picks up a whole range of unwanted background noise. This includes the constant hum of your computer's fan, the whirring of your air conditioner or heater, traffic noise from the nearby street, or any other ambient noise from your workspace.

Since few Camtasia users have access to a dedicated, soundproof recording room, the application offers an AI-powered noise reduction effect. This technology intelligently distinguishes speech from background noise, helping you produce clear and polished audio tracks even when recording in less-than-ideal conditions.

3. Start playing the *00_01_prerequisites* project and listen very carefully to the audio narration.

The soundtrack for this sequence is fairly clean, yet upon closer listening, you can hear faint traffic noise coming from the nearby street, especially when wearing headphones.

4. Drag the **AI Noise Removal** effect from the **Audio Effects** panel and drop it onto the narrator's video on track 2 of the timeline.
5. Start playing the project from the beginning and carefully listen to the narration, preferably with headphones.

You shouldn't hear the slightest background noise anymore!

Powered by AI, this effect generally produces excellent results, even with recordings of average quality. *I strongly recommend consistently applying this effect to every audio recording you make.*

Another advantage of this effect is its remarkable simplicity. In the Properties panel, the only available option for this effect is the **Amount** property. In most cases, the default value of 80 works perfectly, so all you need to do is apply the effect and let AI magically remove all the background noise!

2. Applying Audio Compression

The purpose of audio compression is to reduce (compress) the dynamic range of your audio tracks.

Dynamic range refers to how much the volume varies between the quiet and loud parts of an audio recording. When compressing audio, you essentially even out the audio level across the entire recording.

Audio compression has nothing to do with data compression and does not affect the amount of disk space the audio file takes up on your computer.

1. Drag the **Audio Compression** effect from the **Audio Effects** panel and drop it onto the narrator's video on track 2 of the timeline.

As shown in the image below, a new section appears at the bottom of the Properties panel for the **Audio Compression** effect.

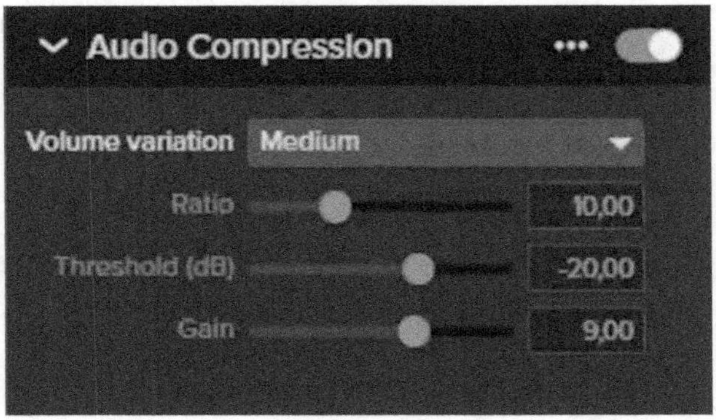

*08_04.png - The properties of the **Audio Compression** effect.*

The **Volume Variation** (Windows) or **Variation** (Mac) menu offers three audio compression presets (**High**, **Medium**, and **Low**). While these presets generally produce excellent results, advanced users typically go one step further and apply manual adjustments on top of the chosen preset.

2. Open the **Volume Variation** (Windows) or the **Variation** (Mac) dropdown menu.
3. Select **Low** to apply predefined values to the **Ratio**, **Threshold**, and **Gain** properties.

In the timeline, the waveform now displays a more uniform pattern, and the overall audio volume has been lowered. To recover the original audio volume, you will now increase the value of the **Gain** property using the following steps.

4. Reopen the **Volume Variation** (Windows) or **Variation** (Mac) dropdown and select **Custom**.
5. Increase the **Gain** until the height of the waveform reaches the audio line.

After applying the above steps, your audio waveform should look similar to the following illustration.

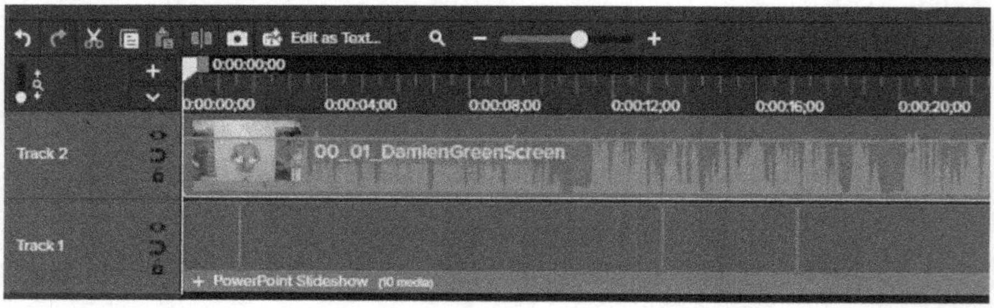

*08_05.png - The waveform after applying the **Audio Compression** effect.*

When playing the project, you should notice that the overall volume has been slightly increased and that the sound level remains constant throughout the entire clip.

3. Exercise

I typically apply both the **AI Noise Removal** and **Audio Compression** effects to every audio clip I import into my Camtasia project; the former removes all background noises, while the latter maintains consistent audio levels. Together, they transform my raw recordings into clean, production-ready audio tracks.

In this exercise, you will practice this technique and apply these two effects to another project. The main steps are as follows.

1. Save and close the ***00_01_prerequisites*** project.

2. Import the ***Chapter08/projects/02_02_conclusion.zip*** project into the ***Chapter08*** folder of the exercises.
3. Watch the entire project to refresh your memory.
4. Apply both the **AI Noise Removal** and **Audio Compression** effects to the narrator's video on track 2 of the timeline.
5. Open the **Volume Variation** (Windows) or **Variation** (Mac) menu of the Properties panel and select **Low**.
6. Reopen the same dropdown menu and select **Custom**.
7. Increase the **Gain** until the height of the waveform reaches the audio line that runs across the narrator's video clip in the timeline.

By consistently applying these two effects to your recordings, you'll almost always end up with a production-ready clear and consistent sound in all your projects.

4. Applying Fade In and Fade Out Effects

The **Fade In** effect gradually increases the volume from zero to 100% at the beginning of a clip. Conversely, the **Fade Out** effect gradually decreases the volume at the end of a clip until silence. In this section, you will apply and customize these two effects using the following steps.

1. Make sure the ***02_02_conclusion*** project is still open in Camtasia.
2. Open the **Audio Effects** panel on the left side of the screen.
3. Position the playhead at the beginning of the project, before the appearance of the narrator.
4. Zoom in on the timeline to get a close-up view of the beginning of your project.
5. Drag the **Fade In** effect from the **Audio Effects** panel and drop it onto the video of the narrator on track 2 of the timeline.

After applying this effect, the start of the audio line over the narrator's video is no longer horizontal, as shown in the image below.

08_06.png - The start of the audio line is no longer horizontal.

The audio line depicts the *variations* in sound level over time. Until now, the line was perfectly horizontal, meaning that the volume remained steady from start to finish. The **Fade In** effect alters the beginning of the audio line, creating a gentle slope that rises from silence (0%) to full volume (100%).

This effect softens the opening of the narration. It is also a very effective way to dampen any breath noise before the narrator starts speaking.

6. Start playing the video and hear the narration volume gradually increase from 0 to 100%.

In this instance, you realize that the first few words of the narration are barely audible because the fade-in is a little too slow. To fix this, you will manually speed up the fade-in effect by repositioning the audio points.

An audio point marks a turning point on the audio line, indicating exactly where the audio line changes direction. The **Fade In** effect automatically generates two audio points: one at the start of the audio line and another one a few seconds later.

The first of these two audio points is almost invisible, as it is located in the lower-left corner of the narrator's video clip in the timeline.

7. In the timeline, move the second audio point to the left to speed up the **Fade In** effect. As you do so, make sure to maintain the volume at **100%** after the effect.

This operation is illustrated in the image below.

*08_07.png - Move the audio point to the left to speed up the **Fade In** effect.*

*In this specific situation, you may feel like a fade in is unnecessary. To remove it, right-click any audio point, then select **Delete** from the context menu to remove that specific point only. You can also select **Remove All Audio Points** to reset the entire audio line. For more precise control, right click anywhere on the audio line to add additional audio points.*

You will now apply a **Fade Out** effect to the end of the same clip.

8. Go to the end of the project.
9. Drag the **Fade Out** effect from the **Audio Effects** panel and drop it onto the narrator's video.

Using a fade out effect prevents the sound from cutting off abruptly at the end of the narration. Feel free to manually adjust the position of the audio points in the timeline to control the speed of the **Fade Out** effect.

D. Recording an Alternate Narration

Every time I conduct a Camtasia training session, the same question always comes up: "*Is it better to record video and audio together or in separate recording sessions?*" My answer is always the same: "*It depends*". The best choice depends on many factors, such as the context, the complexity of the project, as well as how comfortable you are with both Camtasia and the application you're recording.

The standard approach is to record video and audio simultaneously using Camtasia Recorder. However, there are many situations where recording audio and video separately makes more sense.

- When the onscreen actions are particularly complex, it may be easier to focus solely on the video at first and record the narration later (or vice versa).
- If you're not happy with the audio quality of the original recording, you can re-record the narration in Camtasia during post-production.
- If you need to record a tutorial in a foreign language, it's often easier to record the audio track separately.
- When you want to use the same voice across multiple recordings made by different speakers.
- When you want to add additional voiceover comments to an existing video.

These are just a few examples of situations where recording audio and video separately gives you more control and often yields better results.

You will now explore the tools for recording audio directly within Camtasia.

1. Save and close any open projects.
2. Import the ***Chapter08/projects/01_02_dashboard.zip*** project into the ***Chapter08*** folder of the exercises.
3. Watch the entire project to refresh your memory.

For this exercise, your task is to replace my narration with your own voice. The first step is to disable the original audio track.

4. Right-click the screen recording on track 1 of the timeline.
5. Click **Separate Audio and Video**.
6. Click the eye icon in the header of track 2.

You can see the results of these steps in the image below.

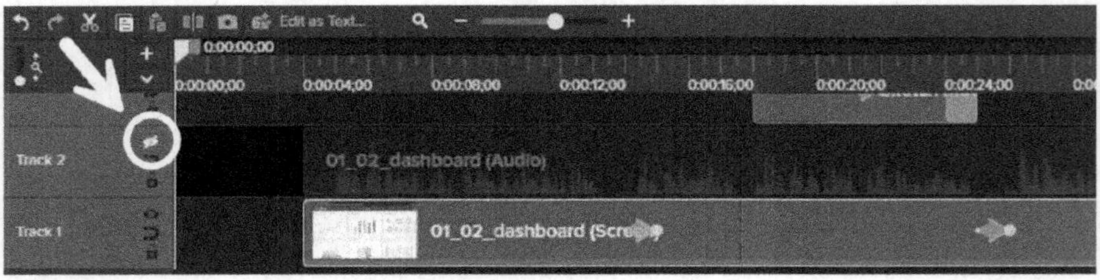

*08_08.png - **Separate audio and video**, then mute the track containing the audio.*

In Camtasia, hiding an audio track mutes the audio. Using this technique, you can keep the original soundtrack in your project and use it as a reference while recording your own version.

1. Preparing the Audio Recording

Although the AI Noise Removal effect is a powerful feature, it delivers the best results when your original recording is already of good quality. Before exploring Camtasia's audio recording tools, let's take a moment to prepare for your audio recording. These practical tips will help you avoid common recording pitfalls and achieve high-quality results.

1. Choosing the Right Recording Environment

Choosing your recording space is one of the most influential decisions for the quality of your recorded audio. You don't necessarily need a professional studio; any quiet room with minimal background noise works just fine.

Choose a room away from any noise disturbances and eliminate any potential sources of background noise. For example, turn off the air conditioning, put your phone on silent mode, and disable all notifications.

Next, try to minimize echoes and reverberations. Drawing the curtains and laying a rug on the floor help dampen sound reflections and go a long way in improving the acoustics of the chosen room.

Finally, inform those around you to avoid any unexpected interruptions. A note on the door is a good way to let others know that a recording is in progress.

2. Choosing the Right Recording Equipment

Your computer's built-in microphone is great for basic everyday tasks, such as joining video calls, taking online classes, or occasionally recording a video.

However, if creating videos becomes part of your daily work, I strongly recommend investing in a good microphone. It doesn't have to be expensive. You can find podcast microphones designed for recording audio narration at very affordable prices.

Here are some criteria to consider when choosing the right microphone.

- **Polar pattern**: An omnidirectional microphone picks up sound coming from all directions, while cardioid microphones prioritize sound originating directly from the front. Cardioid microphones therefore make it easier to isolate the sound you want to record and reject background noises.
- **Connection**: Most microphones plug directly into your computer via USB. You can also opt for a dedicated audio interface, which allows you to use professional-grade microphones and connectors.
- **Positioning**: Headset microphones move with you, keeping a steady distance between your mouth and the microphone, which ensures a consistent audio level.

Take the necessary time to try out several models before deciding which one is best for your voice.

3. Positioning Your Microphone

Generally speaking, you should position your microphone two to five centimeters from your mouth and keep that distance constant throughout the entire recording session.

Equally important is angling your microphone slightly to the side to avoid plosives. These unwanted noises are caused by sudden bursts of air hitting the microphone directly. This typically happens with letters P, B, D, and T. By positioning the microphone to the side, the airflow passes by rather than hitting head-on, dramatically reducing these unwanted distortions.

Most microphones come with a windscreen, which provides a first line of defense against plosives, but this protection is limited and barely solves the problem. Since it is very difficult, if not impossible, to fix plosives in post-production, the best approach is to eliminate them as much as possible when recording.

If you're working with a cardioid microphone, be mindful of the *proximity effect*. This inherent characteristic of cardioid microphones accentuates low frequencies as you move closer to the mic. This can make your voice sound muddy, muffled, and unclear. To mitigate this effect, you can slightly move away from the microphone or apply appropriate audio processing later in the audio chain. Note that such processing is not currently available in Camtasia.

4. Other Audio Recording Tips and Tricks

To wrap things up, here are a few simple tips and tricks that can significantly improve the quality of your audio recordings.

- Before you begin recording, write out your script and practice reading it aloud multiple times. This rehearsal serves two purposes: it naturally warms up your voice, and it helps you identify tricky sections that require extra attention to pronunciation.
- Speak slowly with a calm voice, especially if part of your audience speaks a different language.
- Keep a glass of water within reach to prevent the dry mouth effect, which is particularly unpleasant for those listening with headphones.
- Standing up and using gestures while recording helps produce clearer and more dynamic recordings.
- Remove any jewelry that might generate unwanted noise or bump against the microphone.
- Don't worry too much about getting the perfect take. Editing magic makes it easy to fix mistakes or piece together clips from different takes to create a seamless narrative.

With these tips and a little bit of practice, you'll soon be able to capture high-quality audio narrations.

In any case, never underestimate this aspect of your work. Remember that good sound often goes unnoticed, while poor sound alone can ruin an otherwise remarkable video production.

2. Using the Narration Panel

It is now time to return to Camtasia and replace the existing narration with your own version.

1. Make sure the *01_02_dashboard* project is still open.
2. Open the **Narration** (Windows) or **Voice Narration** (Mac) panel on the left side of the screen.

To make the text more readable, this panel will be referred to as the **Narration** *panel. Mac users should read* **Voice Narration** *in all references.*

The **Narration** panel houses the built-in tools for recording audio directly within Camtasia.

3. Open the dropdown menu at the top of the **Narration** panel.

This menu lists all the audio devices connected to your computer. The first step is to select the device you wish to use for this recording session.

4. Select the audio interface (microphone) you want to use for this recording session.
5. Speak normally into the chosen microphone.

If everything is properly connected and configured, the audio signal should modulate at the top of the **Narration** panel, as shown in the image below.

08_09.png - The sound modulates in the **Narration** *panel (Mac).*

Depending on the sensitivity of your microphone, the sound will modulate in the green, orange, or red zone of the meter.

6. Adjust the microphone's input sensitivity so that the recording level is at about two thirds of the meter's range between the green and the orange zone.

How to adjust the input level of your microphone depends on your specific audio equipment.

- Use the slider just below the meter in the **Narration** panel to adjust the gain of the microphone. Note that the availability of this option depends on your audio equipment.
- If this slider is disabled, you must adjust the gain directly on your audio interface or microphone.
- On Windows, click the magic wand icon to the right of the dropdown menu to automatically find the optimal gain setting for your audio device.

Once the gain is correctly set, the hardware is ready for recording. Now *you* need to get ready to record the narration for this project.

7. Open the ***Chapter08/resources/01_02_dashboard.txt*** file from the exercises in Notepad (Windows) or TextEdit (Mac).
8. Copy and paste the contents of this file into the **Narration** panel in Camtasia so that the script remains visible while you record.
9. Position the playhead at the beginning of the project.
10. In the **Narration** panel, make sure the **Mute timeline during recording** (Windows) or **Mute speakers during recording** (Mac) checkbox is selected.

This checkbox should be selected by default. When enabled, it mutes all project audio to prevent it from being picked up by the microphone during recording.

11. Time to focus! When you feel ready, click **Start Voice Recording**.

The recording begins and the playhead starts traveling across the timeline. With the video playing on the canvas, you can easily sync your voice narration with what you see on screen.

12. Click **Stop** when done.
13. [*Windows only*] Save your audio recording in the ***Chapter08/01_02_dashboard.tscproj*** folder of the exercises.

Recording a perfectly synchronized voice-over is not easy and definitely requires some practice. Don't worry if you don't get it right the first time; every professional started exactly where you are now, so there's no shame in messing up! If you made a mistake, you most likely don't need to start it all over again. Just stop the recording, move the playhead back to the start of the failed sentence, drag the end of the recorded audio clip to the current playhead position, and resume the recording from there.

3. Integrating the New Narration

By default, Camtasia places your audio recording on the first available timeline track, or on a new track if none is available. From there, feel free to rename and rearrange the tracks as you see fit.

I typically position my audio tracks at the bottom of the timeline, though this is a personal preference rather than a technical requirement. With time and practice, you'll also figure out the organization that works best for you.

If you recorded multiple takes and your audio narration is split into several different clips, make sure to group them into a single item in the timeline.

After you complete the recording, you may need to slightly adjust the synchronization between the new narration and the video. If so, use the editing tools covered in the Synchronizing Video and Audio section of Chapter 05 – Editing Your Video.

Finally, apply the audio effects mentioned at the beginning of this chapter to your new narration:

- The **AI Noise Removal** effect.
- The **Audio Compression** effect.
- Optionally, a **Fade In** and/or a **Fade Out** effect.

When you are completely satisfied with the result, you can safely delete the original narration still present in your project.

E. Adding Background Music

Background music serves as the emotional soundtrack of your video production. Upbeat, cheerful music energizes and uplifts the audience, while slower melodies foster introspection, concentration, or even melancholy.

For the next exercise, your task is to add background music to the trailer video. You must also ensure that the narration remains intelligible over the music.

1. Save and close the ***01_02_dashboard*** project.
2. Import the ***Chapter08/projects/00_00_trailer.zip*** project into the ***Chapter08*** folder of the exercises.
3. Watch the entire project to refresh your memory.

Since your last visit to this project, the **AI Noise Removal** and **Audio Compression** effects have been applied to the narrator's video on track 4 of the timeline.

You will now add a new track at the bottom of the timeline to accommodate the background music.

4. At the far left of the timeline, right-click the **Track 1** header.
5. In the context menu, click **Insert Track > Below**.
6. Rename the new track `Music`.

The result of these steps is shown in the following image.

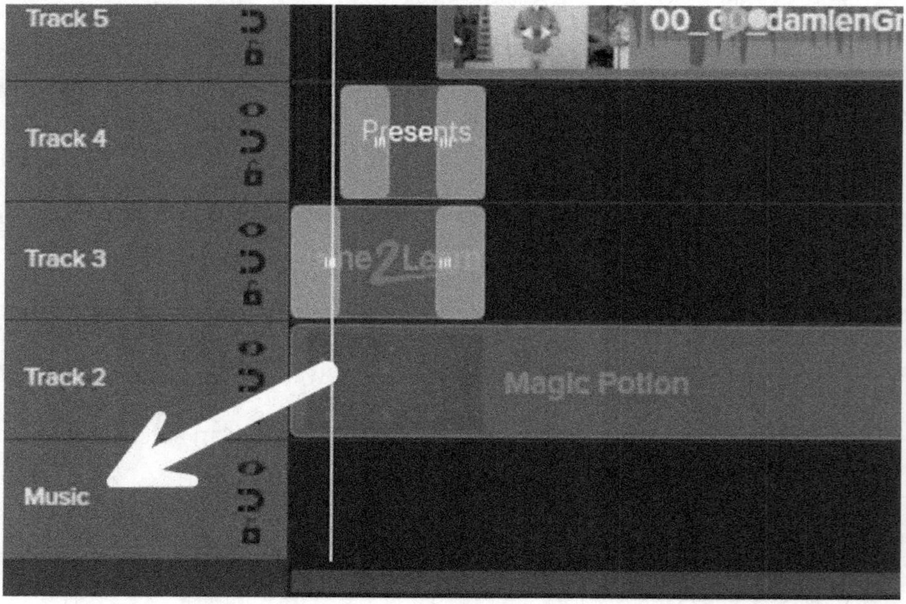

*08_10.png - Add the **Music** track at the bottom of the timeline.*

Remember that placing background music at the bottom of the timeline is a matter of personal preference, not a technical requirement.

The next step is to choose the right background music for this project. This is the perfect opportunity to explore the **Camtasia Assets**!

7. Open the **Media** panel on the left side of the screen.
8. Open the **Camtasia Assets** tab.
9. Click **See All** in the **Music** section of the **Camtasia Assets**.

These steps are depicted in the image below.

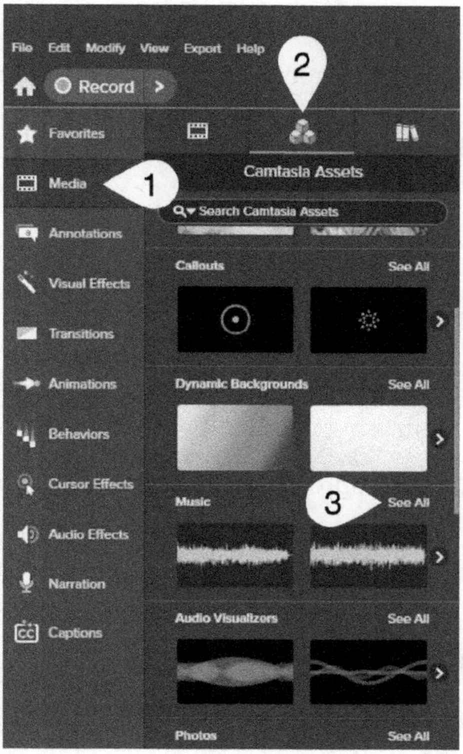

*08_11.png - Click **See All** in the **Music** section of the **Camtasia Assets**.*

Now all you have to do is browse through the **Camtasia Assets** and choose a background music file of your liking.

*As discussed in Chapter03 – Creating a new project, only a small portion of the **Camtasia Assets** is available for free. Full access to the entire assets library requires a Camtasia Pro subscription.*

10. Double-click any audio clip in the **Camtasia Assets** panel to open the **Preview** window and listen to it before importing.
11. Drag the chosen audio from the **Camtasia Assets** panel and drop it onto the **Music** track of the timeline.

Camtasia downloads the selected file and adds it to the timeline once the download is complete.

*In the final version of this exercise, I used **Synth Wave Special** as the background music.*

12. If necessary, reposition the downloaded music track so it starts at the very beginning of the project.

13. Play the entire project.

As you listen, pay close attention to the balance between the background music and the narration. You quickly notice that the music overpowers the voice and makes it difficult to understand. Let's fix that in the next section.

1. Using the Emphasize Effect

While background music can help set the overall tone of your video, you must ensure that it does not compete with the narration. This is precisely what is happening in the ***00_00_trailer*** project: the music is drowning out the narrator's voice, making it difficult to understand what is being said.

Camtasia offers several approaches to solving this problem.

- First, you can lower the volume of the background music in the Properties panel. While this method is straightforward, it lowers the volume throughout the entire music track, including when the narrator is not speaking.
- You can manipulate the audio line of the background music to manually adjust its volume. Using this method, you can lower the music only when the narrator is speaking. However, this manual approach is time-consuming, tedious, and error-prone.
- You can use the **Emphasize** effect to automatically duck the music only when the narrator is speaking.

In this section, you will explore the latter approach. You must apply this effect to the audio track you want to emphasize. In this example, apply it to the audio track of the narrator's video.

1. Open the **Audio Effects** panel on the left side of the screen.
2. Drag the **Emphasize** effect from the **Audio Effects** panel and drop it onto the narrator's video on track 5 of the timeline.
3. Reposition the playhead at the beginning and start playing the project

As the video plays, the music automatically lowers just before the narrator starts speaking, then returns to its original volume after the end of the narration.

The **Emphasize** effect automatically lowers the volume of every audio element in the project except the one to which it is applied, which remains at its original volume.

4. Select the narrator's video on track 5 of the timeline.

5. Open the Properties panel on the right side of the screen and navigate to the **Audio Properties** tab.

The properties for this effect can be found at the bottom of the **Audio Properties** tab in the Properties panel, as shown in the image below.

You may need to collapse the Auditate section of the panel to better view the properties of the ***Emphasize*** *effect.*

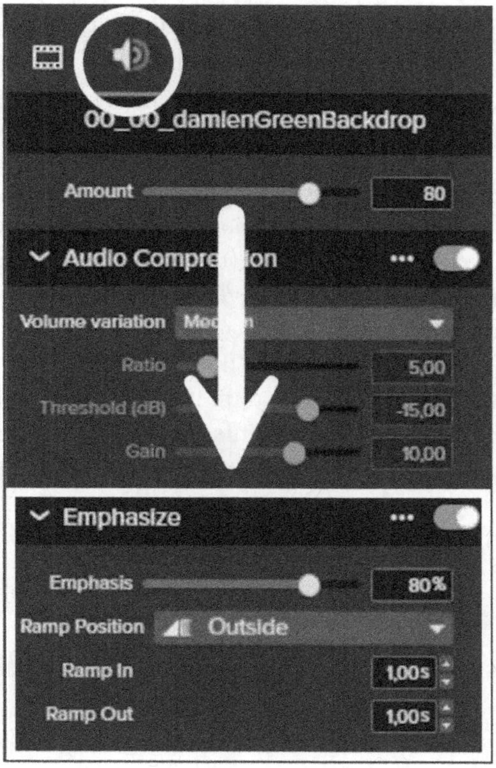

08_12.png - The properties of the ***Emphasize*** *effect at the bottom of the Properties panel.*

The default values yield excellent results and rarely need to be changed.

- The **Emphasize** property lets you set the amount of attenuation applied to the other tracks. The default value of 80% means the audio volume of all other tracks is reduced by 80%.
- The **Ramp Position** (Windows) or **Ramp** (Mac) property determines *when* the audio level should be lowered. **Outside** means it is lowered just before the narrator starts speaking and returns to normal just after the narration ends.
- **Ramp In** determines how quickly the audio volume decreases, and the **Ramp Our** property determines how quickly it returns to normal.

Thanks to the **Emphasize** effect, the mix between the background music and the narration is now well balanced.

One issue remains: the background music is much longer than the actual video. Let's fix that in the next section.

2. Shortening the Background Music

There's a good chance the track you picked for the background music is longer than the video. In this section, you'll trim the background music, so it ends at the same time as the video. Once again, there are multiple approaches to tackle this task.

- The easiest is to cut off the background music track where the video ends, optionally with a fade-out. While this approach is easy to implement, it frequently yields unsatisfying results. Since the music stops before reaching its natural conclusion, the ending feels awkward and leaves the viewer with a sense of incompleteness.
- Another approach is to use the **Clip Speed** audio effect to speed up or slow down the background music until it aligns with the video. This method works well for minor adjustments, but in this case, the necessary correction is far too extreme for the result to sound natural.
- The third approach is to remove material from the middle of the track, keeping the beginning and the end intact. This is the method that produces the best listening experience. The challenge is to ensure it goes unnoticed.

Your task in this exercise is to implement this third approach.

*The timecodes provided in this exercise assume you are using the **Synth Wave Special** audio clip from the Camtasia Assets. You'll need to adjust them if you use a different audio asset.*

The first step is to add yet another track at the bottom of the timeline.

1. Right-click the **Music** track header at the far left of the timeline.
2. From the context menu, select **Insert Track > Below**.
3. Position the playhead at timecode *0:00:30;00*.

At this point, the waveform suggests the background music remains relatively steady for quite a while.

4. Select the background music audio clip in the timeline.

5. Click the **Split** icon in the upper-left corner of the timeline. You can also press the `S` key (Windows) or use the `Cmd + T` (Mac) shortcut.

This action splits the selected audio clip at the playhead position.

6. Drag the ending portion of the background music to the newly created **Track 1**.
7. On **Track 1**, align the end of the background music with the end of the video. You may have to trim the beginning of the ending audio clip so that it fits within track 1 of the timeline.

These steps are depicted in the following image.

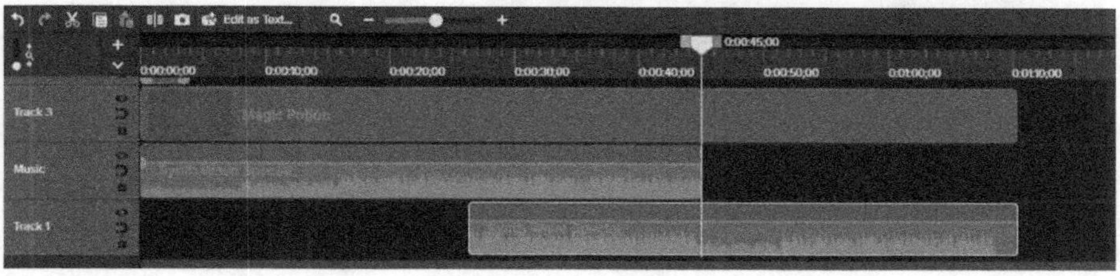

08_13.png - The beginning and end of the background music on two different timeline tracks.

As shown in the above image, the beginning and the end of the background music overlap for quite a while.

You will now shorten the audio clip on track 1 so that the two clips overlap for three seconds on Windows and one second on Mac. This corresponds to the default duration of the fade in and fade-out effects on these two platforms.

8. Zoom in on the timeline until you can clearly see the area where the two audio clips overlap.
9. Position the playhead at timecode *0:00:27;00* (Windows) or *0:00:29;00* (Mac)
10. Trim the beginning of the audio clip on track 1 to the current playhead position.

The final step is to fade the background music out on the **Music** track while fading it in on **Track 1**.

11. Open the **Audio Effects** panel on the left side of the screen.
12. Drag the **Fade Out** effect onto the audio clip on the **Music** track.
13. Drag the **Fade In** effect onto the audio clip on **Track 1**.

Looking at the timeline, you can see both fades happening at the same time, producing a seamless transition between the start and end of the background music, as shown in the image below.

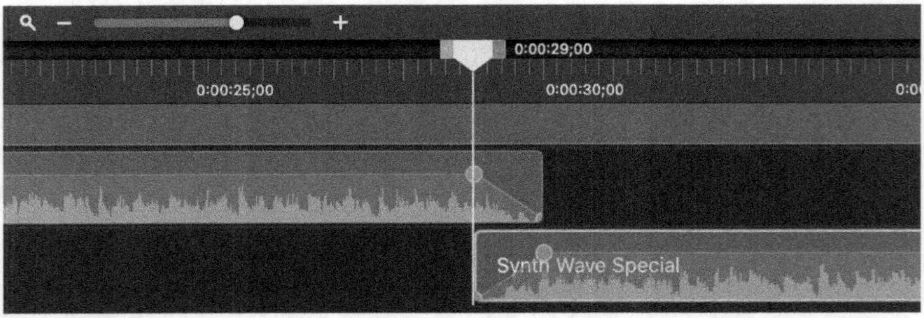

*08_14.png - The fade-out on the **Music** track occurs at the same time as the fade in on **Track 1**.*

To wrap things up, you'll now test the background music and clean up the timeline.

14. Position the playhead at the beginning of the project and watch the entire video.

While watching the video, pay close attention to the background music. As the playhead reaches the fade transitions, confirm that the edit goes unnoticed.

15. In the timeline, select both audio clips for the background music.
16. Right-click anywhere within the selection and select **Group** from the context menu.
17. Position the new group on the **Music** track, leaving **Track 1** empty.
18. Right-click the **Track 1** header at the far left of the timeline and select **Remove Track** from the context menu.
19. Save the ***00_00_trailer*** project.

After completing these steps, the background music is perfectly aligned with the project's duration, and the **Music** track contains a group comprising two audio clips.

F. Working With Captions

Post-production of the ***00_00_trailer*** project is almost complete! The only remaining step is to add subtitles.

Camtasia offers two types of subtitles, each serving a specific purpose.

- *Closed captions* can be turned on or off by the viewer. Their purpose is to make your video accessible, so that viewers with hearing impairments can access the content in optimal conditions.
- *Dynamic captions* are always visible. Their distinctive formatting and animated delivery make them very popular on social media, where they help capture viewers' attention and boost the visual impact of your message.

You will now explore both caption types, starting with *Dynamic captions.*

1. Exploring Dynamic Captions

Dynamic captions are very popular on social media. Whether in promotional videos or bite-sized influencer content, such as TikToks and Facebook Reels, these rolling text overlays capture viewers' attention, significantly amplifying the impact and engagement of your message.

It turns out the ***00_00_trailer*** project is designed to promote your online course on social media, making it an ideal candidate for experimenting with Camtasia's dynamic captions.

1. Generating Dynamic Captions

Generating dynamic captions in Camtasia is quick and easy. Just drop a caption item into the timeline and let AI magic do the rest.

For this example, you'll subtitle the narration on track 5 of the timeline. To keep things clear and organized, start by adding a new empty track at the top of the timeline.

1. Make sure the ***Chapter08/00_00_trailer*** project is open in Camtasia.
2. Right-click the **Track 8** header at the far left of the timeline.
3. In the context menu, click **Insert Track > Above**.
4. Click **Captions** on the left side of the screen to open the corresponding panel.

The **Captions** panel features two tabs. The first one is for **Closed Captions**, while the second is for **Dynamic Captions** (the order is reversed on Mac), as shown in the image below.

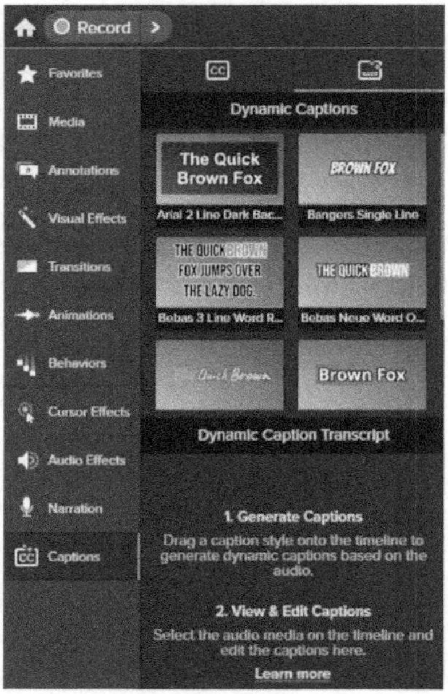

08_15.png - The ***Dynamic Captions*** *panel in Camtasia.*

For this exercise, make sure you are on the **Dynamic Captions** tab.

At the top of the **Dynamic Captions** tab, you'll find a selection of built-in caption templates. Choose whichever template you like the most.

5. Drag the selected template from the **Dynamic Captions** panel and drop it onto the newly created track 9.

Positioning dynamic captions at the very top of the track stack ensures that they will always stay in the foreground and will never be covered by another item in the project.

If this is your first time using dynamic captions, you may see the ***AI Information in Camtasia*** *message pop up. Take a moment to read it, then click* ***Enable****.*

You can toggle AI transcription on and off in the preferences of Camtasia. Go to the ***Program*** *(Windows) or* ***General*** *(Mac) tab of the preferences and look for the* ***Enable AI audio transcription*** *checkbox.*

Most AI features in Camtasia are powered by third-party technologies and services, which may require an internet connection. More information about the AI technologies and services used by TechSmith can be found at: https://support.techsmith.com/hc/en-us/articles/26140574750861-Third-Party-AI-Technology-Used-in-TechSmith-Products.

After adding the selected template to the project, Camtasia automatically transcribes the audio narration.

6. On track 9 of the timeline, adjust the duration of the dynamic captions item so it starts and ends with the narration on track 5.
7. Position the playhead at timecode *0:00:05;00* so you can see the dynamic captions on the canvas.
8. Resize and reposition the dynamic captions within the canvas so they span two lines and align along the bottom edge of the canvas.

After completing these steps, your project should look like the following image.

*08_16.png - **Dynamic Captions** are displayed on two lines at the bottom of the canvas.*

9. Start playing the video and enjoy the dynamic captions entirely generated by Camtasia's built-in AI!

The chosen template automatically applied default formatting to the generated dynamic captions, which may or may not suit your needs. In the next section, let's review some options for customizing the look and feel of these dynamic captions.

2. Formatting Dynamic Captions

Camtasia offers so many options for formatting dynamic captions that it is impossible to cover them all in this guide. Instead, you will focus on a selection of options that will help you explore the powerful capabilities of this tool.

1. In the ***00_00_trailer*** project, select the dynamic caption item on track 9 of the timeline.
2. If necessary, open the Properties panel on the right side of the screen.

The **Dynamic Captions** properties are found in the **Text Properties** tab of the Properties panel, as shown in the image below.

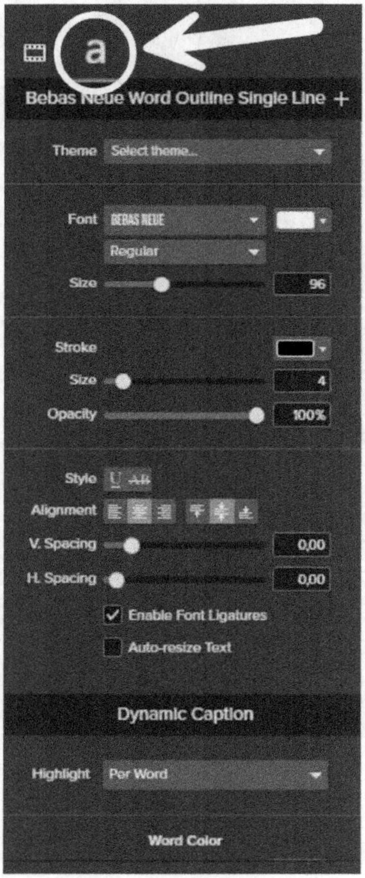

08_17.png - The dynamic captions properties in the Properties panel.

The upper section contains basic text formatting controls such as font, size, color, and alignment. The dedicated tools for customizing dynamic captions appear further down.

3. Scroll down the Properties panel until you reach the **Dynamic Caption** section.
4. Open the **Highlight** dropdown menu.
5. Select **Per Word**.

This option enables the caption highlighting effect, which you can customize using the tools in the lower section of the Properties panel.

6. Select any color you like in the **Stroke Color** section.

This determines the stroke color that highlights the word currently being spoken by the narrator.

7. In the **Word Opacity** section, reduce the opacity of **Future** words to around `50%`.

This option reduces the opacity of unread text on the canvas. The opacity of each word reverts to normal once the narrator reads it aloud.

8. In the **Advanced** section, increase the value of the **Scale** property to about `20`.

This feature expands the text word by word as the narration progresses, which helps highlight your message and makes it easier to follow along even when the audio is muted.

9. In the **Block** section, select the **Split captions by sentence** checkbox.

Enabling this option forces each sentence to start on a new line, ensuring a clean visual separation between statements.

10. Play the video and enjoy your custom dynamic captions.

The result of these steps is illustrated in the following image.

08_18.png - The Properties panel offers a wide range of options for customizing dynamic captions.

This tool offers a wide range of possibilities, so take a moment to discover the other available features and further explore its incredible potential.

3. Adjusting the Automatic Transcription

When you dropped the dynamic captions into the timeline, Camtasia automatically transcribed the audio using AI. Although this technology has made tremendous progress in recent years, you certainly noticed this automatic transcription is not error-free. This is particularly true for technical terms, proper nouns, or acronyms, which AI still struggles to transcribe correctly.

For this reason, you will now learn how to fix this automatic transcription using the **Dynamic Captions** panel.

1. In the *00_00_trailer* project, select the narrator's video on track 5 of the timeline.
2. Open the **Captions** panel on the right side of the screen.
3. If necessary, navigate to the **Dynamic Captions** tab.

With the narrator's video selected in the timeline, the lower section of the **Dynamic Captions** panel displays the AI-generated transcript.

4. Review the transcript and make any required corrections, including spelling and grammar errors.

*For your reference, you will find the transcript of this audio narration in the **Chapter08/resources/00_00_trailer.txt** file of the exercises.*

By following these simple steps, you can quickly and easily correct any transcription errors. But fixing the text isn't enough: you may also need to fine-tune the syncing between the dynamic captions and the narration.

Depending on the quality of the AI-generated audio transcript, your project may or may not require any adjustments. Just read through the following steps to get a general idea of the workflow, then use your best judgment to determine whether adjustments are needed in your specific case.

5. Position the playhead at timecode *0:00:04;00*.
6. Use the **View > Show Transcript** menu item to enable the transcript markers in the timeline.
7. Zoom in on the timeline until you see the transcript markers on the narrator's video.

After completing these steps, the timeline should look like the following image.

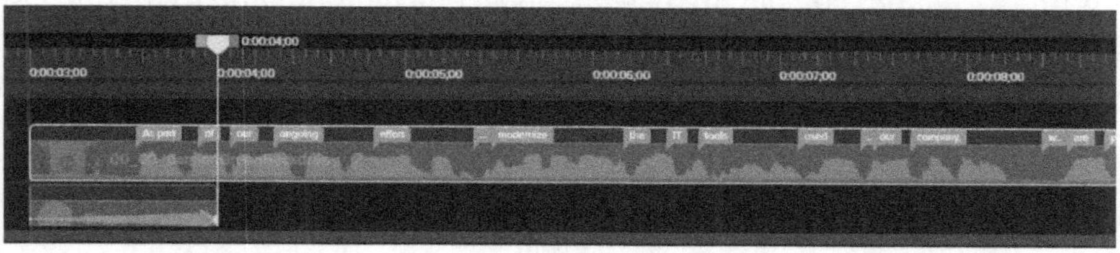

08_19.png – Zoom in on the timeline until you see the transcript markers.

When you zoom in close enough, the transcript appears on the timeline as a series of small purple bubbles. You can reposition these bubbles to fine-tune the syncing between the audio and the corresponding caption.

If needed, you can also perform the following actions on the transcript:

- To *remove* a transcription marker (a purple bubble), right-click the marker to remove then click **Delete** in the context menu.
- In the context menu, you can also click **Convert to Gap** to prevent captions from appearing when the narrator is not speaking.
- To *add* a transcription marker, position your cursor where you want to add the new marker and click the + icon.

This last action is illustrated in the image below.

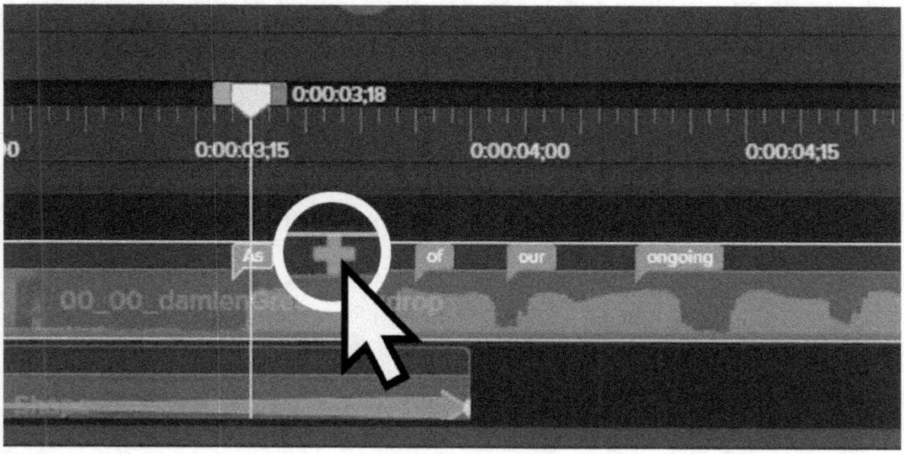

08_20.png - You can add transcription markers in the timeline.

You have now reviewed all the tools you need to create, edit, format, fix, and adjust dynamic captions in your Camtasia projects. In the next section, you will dive into closed captions.

2. Working with Closed Captions

While *Dynamic Captions* are used to boost engagement, the main purpose of *Closed Captions* is to make your video accessible.

- Closed captions allow those with hearing impairments to read the spoken content.
- They help viewers watch the video in a foreign language.
- They make it possible to follow along with the video in noisy environments, such as open spaces or public transportation.

Unlike dynamic captions, which are always visible no matter what, viewers can turn closed captions on or off during video playback.

Now, let's get ready to experiment with closed captions.

1. Save and close the ***00_00_trailer*** project.
2. Open the ***00_01_prerequisites*** project from the ***Chapter08*** folder exercises.
3. Use the **View > Hide Transcript** (Windows) or deselect the **View > Show Transcript** (Mac) menu item to hide the transcript markers in the timeline.

You already worked with this project earlier in this chapter while exploring audio effects. You will now add closed captions and learn how to sync them with the narration.

The process for adding and syncing closed captions greatly differs between the Mac and the Windows versions of Camtasia. Feel free to skip directly to the section that applies to your operating system.

1. Adding Closed Captions on Windows

On Windows, use the **CC** tab of the **Captions** panel to create and synchronize closed captions.

1. Open the **Captions** panel on the left side of the screen.
2. Switch to the **CC** tab of the **Captions** panel, as shown in the following screenshot.

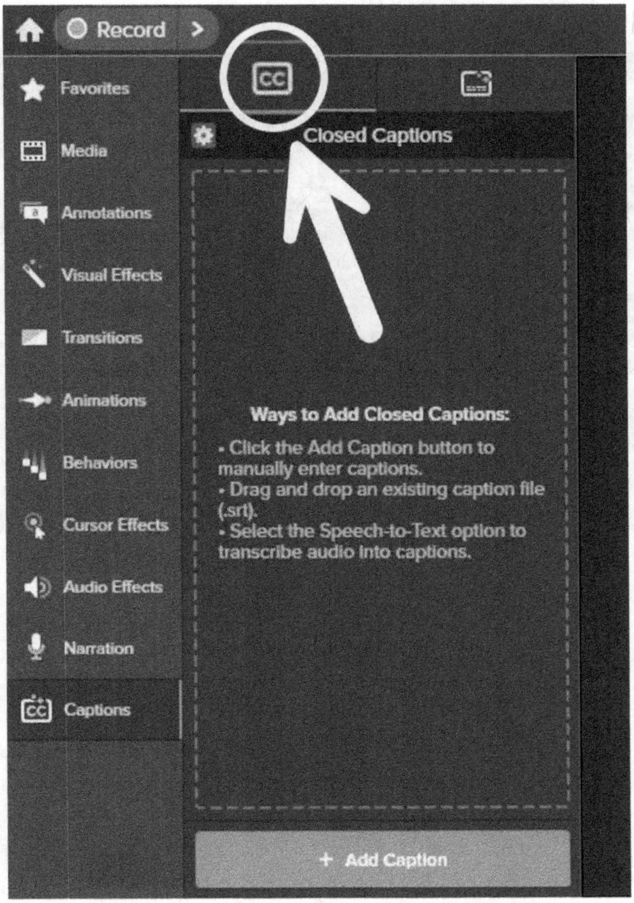

*08_21.png - Switch to the **CC** tab of the **Captions** panel.*

As stated in the **CC** panel, there are several ways to add Closed Captions to your Camtasia project.

- You can add and synchronize captions manually using the **Add Caption** button at the bottom of the **CC** panel.
- You can import a caption file in ***.srt*** format (see the Importing and Exporting Captions section later in this chapter).
- You can use the Speech-to-Text feature to automatically transcribe the audio into synchronized captions.

For this exercise, you'll leverage the third option and let AI do the heavy lifting before applying the finishing touches manually.

3. Select the narrator's video on track 2 of the timeline.
4. Click the gear icon in the upper left-hand corner of the **CC** panel.
5. Click **Speech-to-Text** in the menu that opens.

This action is illustrated in the following screenshot.

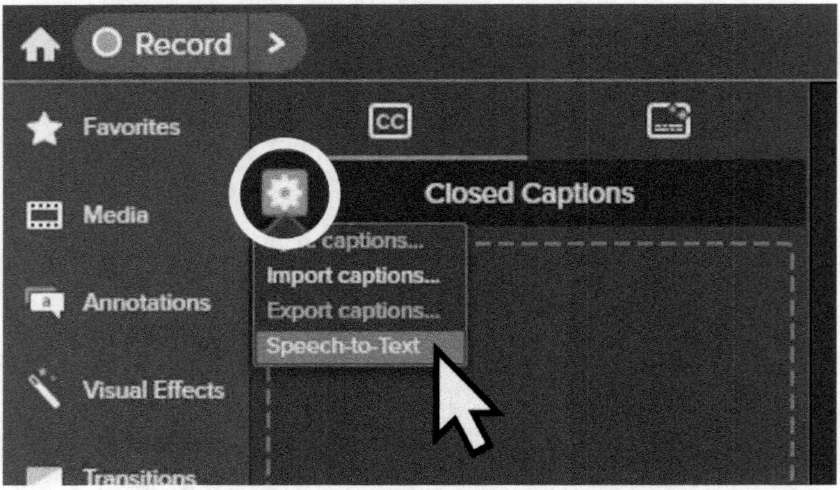

*08_22.png - Click **Speech-to-Text** in the menu that opens.*

Take a moment to read the **Speech-to-Text** message that appears on the screen and note how you can transcribe either the entire timeline or just the selected media clip. In this case, either choice produces the same result, since the selected clip is the sole audio source in the project.

6. Click any one of the two options in the **Speech-to-Text** message.

Once Camtasia finishes generating the transcription, you should see the following changes in your project.

- The generated transcription text is visible in the **CC** panel on the left side of the screen.
- The caption corresponding to the playhead position is displayed at the bottom of the canvas.
- Camtasia has inserted a new track into the timeline to accommodate the newly created closed captions.

It is now time to test the result using the following steps.

7. Reposition the playhead at the beginning of the project.
8. Click anywhere on the canvas to deselect the captions track.
9. Play the video.

During playback, keep a close eye on the generated captions. Although AI did the heavy lifting, you should notice some errors in the generated transcription. You will fix these issues later in the Fine-tuning the Automatic Transcription section.

2. Adding Closed Captions on Mac

If you work on a Mac, you can use either the **Captions** or **Audio Effects** panel to create and synchronize closed captions.

1. Open either the **Captions** or the **Audio Effects** panel on the left side of the screen.
2. If on the **Captions** panel, navigate to the **CC** tab as shown in the image below.

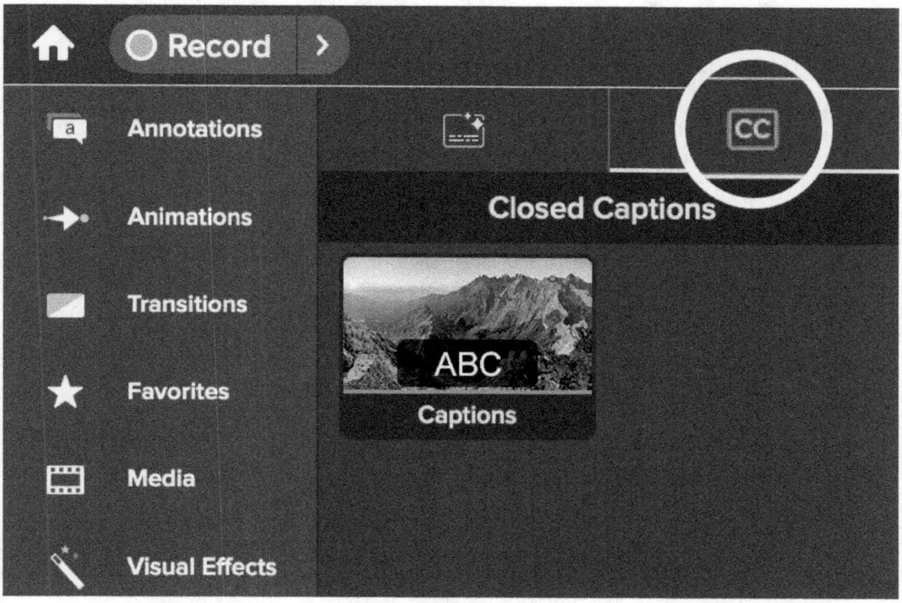

08_23.png - Navigate to the **CC** *tab of the* **Captions** *panel*

Whether you're in the **Captions** or **Audio Effects** panel, the **Captions** effect is available in both cases.

3. Drag the **Captions** effect from the left panel and drop it onto the narrator's video on track 2 of the timeline.

As soon as you drop the effect, a special caption track appears between the canvas and the timeline.

You can control the visibility of the caption track using the ***View > Show Caption Track*** *menu item.*

As shown in the image below, the caption track splits the audio narration into four-second segments, which corresponds to the average duration of a caption.

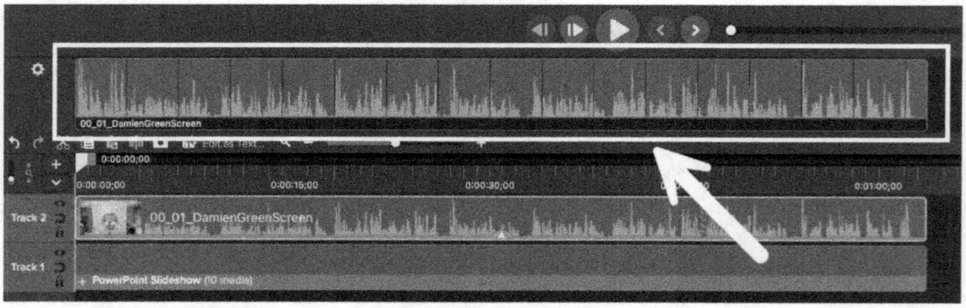

08_24.png - The caption track splits the audio into four-second segments.

The next step is to use AI to automatically transcribe the audio narration on which you dropped the **Captions** effect.

4. Click the gear icon in the upper left-hand corner of the captions track.
5. In the menu that opens, click **Transcribe Selected Media**.

It should take just a few seconds for Camtasia to transcribe this audio clip. When done, you can test the result using the following steps.

6. Reposition the playhead at the beginning of the project
7. Play the entire video.

During playback, keep a close eye on the generated caption. Although AI did the heavy lifting, you should notice some errors in the generated transcription. You will fix these issues in the next section.

3. Fine-Tuning the Automatic Transcription

Just as with dynamic captions discussed earlier, automatic transcription is prone to errors, especially with proper nouns, acronyms, and technical terms. You should always carefully review the generated transcript and manually apply any necessary corrections.

1. Select the first caption in the caption track to see the caption text on the canvas.
2. Take the necessary time to review the generated transcript and correct any errors, including spelling and grammar issues.
3. Move the playhead onto the next caption when done.
4. Repeat this process till the end of the project.

*For your reference, you can find the corrected transcript of this audio narration in the **Chapter08/resources/00_01_prerequisites.txt** file of the exercises.*

On Windows, you can also edit the generated transcript directly within the ***CC*** *tab of the* ***Captions*** *panel.*

Another common issue with automatic transcription is how Camtasia distributes the text across subtitles. In my opinion, there's often too much text in a single caption, and I don't like it when a new sentence starts in the middle of a caption.

To control how text is spread across captions, Camtasia offers two handy features, which you can access by right clicking any caption in the timeline (Windows) or in the caption track (Mac), as shown in the following screenshot.

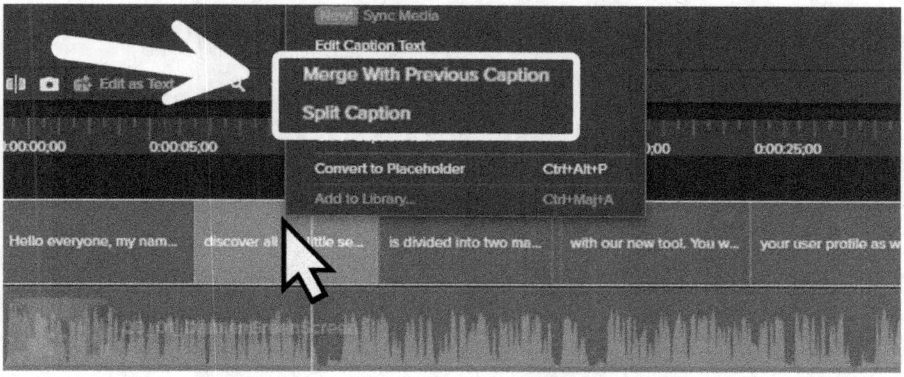

08_25.png – Right click a caption item to access ***Merge With Previous Caption*** *and* ***Split Caption****. On a Mac, you can choose between* ***Split Caption*** *and* ***Merge with next caption****.*

In addition to splitting and merging captions, you can also adjust the syncing of the captions with the corresponding audio by dragging the separator line between two captions in the timeline (windows) or in the caption track (Mac).

5. Take the necessary time to refine and resync the automatically generated captions using the aforementioned tools.

How much editing is needed depends as much on the quality of the automatic transcription as on your personal preferences. I personally use the following guidelines when making these kinds of adjustments.

- I try to limit each caption to two (sometimes three) lines of text.
- I try to make sure each sentence starts at the beginning of a new caption.
- I make sure each caption contains at least six or seven words, so they don't go by too fast and the viewer has enough time to read them comfortably.

After applying the necessary changes according to the above guidelines, the **CC** panel for your project should look like the following screenshot (Windows).

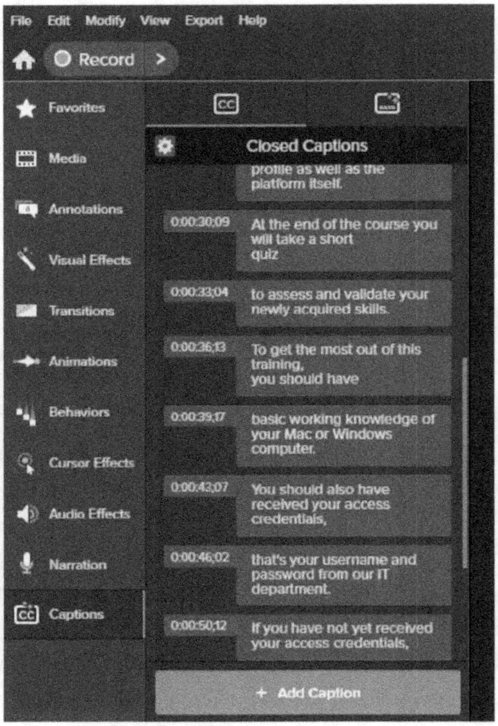

*08_26.png – The **CC** panel after rebalancing the text between the captions (Windows).*

Although Camtasia offers other methods for adding subtitles, the approach described in this section proves to be the most effective and straightforward solution.

4. Formatting Closed Captions

To ensure your captions meet accessibility requirements, you should adhere to established international captioning standards.

Camtasia complies with the guidelines of the *Americans with Disabilities Act* (ADA). According to these guidelines,

- Captions must not exceed 32 characters per line, and there must not be more than three lines of text displayed at the same time.
- The typeface and font size must ensure optimal readability for the viewer.
- Text color must contrast sharply with the background, so it remains legible for people with visual impairments or color blindness.

The caption formatting options slightly differ depending on whether you're running Camtasia on Mac or Windows.

On Windows

Use the following steps to format closed captions in Camtasia for Windows:

1. In the timeline, double-click any caption to reopen the caption editing window over the canvas.
2. Click the **A** (font) icon in the lower-left corner of that window.

The formatting properties for closed captions are available in the dropdown menu, as shown in the image below.

08_27.png - Click the A *(font) icon to open the closed caption formatting menu.*

This menu contains the necessary options for adjusting the appearance of the caption text (font, size, color, alignment, etc.).

3. Use these tools to format the captions as per your preferences.

This may cause the formatting of your captions to no longer comply with ADA standards. If so, a red **ADA** warning button appears next to the **A** (font) icon in the lower-left of the caption editing window, as shown in the following image.

08_28.png - Changes to caption formatting may result in broken ADA compliance.

Use the following steps to address this concern and ensure ADA compliance throughout the project.

4. Click the red **ADA** button in the lower-left corner of the caption editing window.

This button lists all formatting compliance issues for your closed captions.

5. Click **Make Compliant** to reset your captions' formatting and restore ADA compliance.

Generally speaking, you should avoid changing the default closed captions formatting to always maintain ADA compliance.

In Chapter 11—Exporting Your Videos, you'll learn how to export your project with or without closed captions.

On a Mac

On a Mac, the closed caption formatting tools are accessible only after you make the caption track visible.

1. Use the **View > Show Caption Track** menu item to display the caption track if necessary.
2. Click the gear icon in the upper-left corner of the caption track.
3. Select **Caption Settings** from the menu that opens.

These steps are illustrated in the following screenshot.

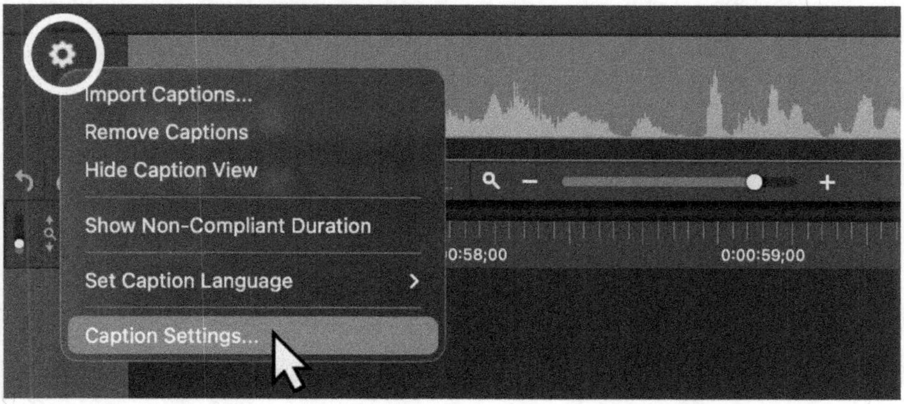

*08_29.png - Click the gear icon to access the **Caption Settings** (Mac).*

This opens a small dialog box where you can adjust closed caption formatting (font, size, color, etc.).

To ensure ADA compliance, the available choices are intentionally limited. For instance, the **Font** dropdown only includes ADA approved fonts.

Generally speaking, you should avoid changing the default closed captions formatting to always maintain ADA compliance.

In Chapter 11—Exporting Your Videos, you'll learn how to export your project with or without closed captions.

4. Click **Cancel** to close the **Captions Settings** dialog.
5. Click the gear icon again in the upper-left corner of the caption track.
6. Hover over the **Set Caption Language** menu item and make sure **English** is selected.
7. Click the gear icon one last time.
8. Select **Show Non-Compliant Duration**.

This automatically highlights any caption that does not comply with ADA duration guidelines. You will need to adjust the duration of the highlighted captions (if any) to ensure compliance.

5. Importing and Exporting Closed Captions

Camtasia provides robust caption import and export capabilities, opening numerous possibilities for your video projects and workflows.

Exporting captions serves multiple purposes, such as

- archiving captions as part of project documentation,
- reusing captions in various video editing tools or video hosting platforms (such as YouTube and Vimeo),
- sending captions to external translation services for localization.

Similarly, importing Captions addresses common production needs, such as

- importing captions created in third-party applications into Camtasia,
- seamlessly integrating translated captions into your projects,
- transferring captions between the Windows and Mac versions of Camtasia without compatibility issues.

This section walks you through the process of importing and exporting captions. Let's start with exporting.

1. Use the **Export > Export Captions** menu item.
2. Navigate to the destination folder and name the future caption file.
3. At the bottom of the export window, select the format for the captions file you want to generate.
4. Save the captions file.

You can export captions from Camtasia in either the SAMI (*Synchronized Accessible Media Interchange*), SubRip, or VTT format. These formats produce files with the ***.smi***, ***.srt***, and ***.vtt*** extensions, respectively. The chosen export format primarily depends on the import capabilities of the target platform or software.

Now let's review the steps for importing captions.

5. Use the **File > Import > Captions** menu item.
6. Navigate to the caption file you want to import.

Camtasia supports importing captions in the *SAMI* (***.smi*** or ***.sami***), *SubRip* (***.srt***) and *VTT* (***.vtt***) file formats.

6. Hand-on Exercise – Creating Closed Captions

Although AI does help a lot, adding closed captions in Camtasia remains a hands-on task that demands focus and precision. Success requires careful attention to details, a bit of experience, and a good deal of patience. In this exercise, you will go through the same process again and add closed captions to the ***01_02_dashboard*** project, in which you recorded your own voice earlier in this chapter.

The main steps for this exercise are the following.

- Save and close ***00_01 prerequisites***, then open the ***Chapter08/00_01_dashboard*** project.
- Open the **Captions** panel and navigate to the **CC** tab.
- Use the captioning workflow specific to your operating system (Mac or Windows) to generate closed captions.
- Sync and format the closed captions in accordance with ADA standards.

G. Conclusion

This chapter walked you through the audio tools in Camtasia; an essential yet often overlooked aspect of any video production. Don't fall into this trap: poor sound always undermines even the most visually stunning video content. Neglect either of these two aspects, and your entire message is compromised!

Your journey started with exploring the main audio properties and effects available in Camtasia. You used these tools to reduce background noise and fine-tune the audio volume for your entire project.

Then, you used the **Narration** (Windows) or **Voice Narration** (Mac) panel, to record an alternate voiceover directly within Camtasia. Along the way, you also learned some tips and tricks to help you choose the right recording equipment and improve the overall quality of your audio recordings.

Then, you incorporated background music and used the **Emphasize** effect to ensure the music doesn't compete with the narration.

Finally, you explored *dynamic captions* and *closed captions,* two types of captions available in Camtasia.

Dynamic captions are very popular on social media platforms, where they boost engagement, while closed captions make content accessible for viewers with hearing impairment or those watching your video in a language other than their own.

In the next chapter, you'll finalize your video projects by designing and implementing branded intro and outro sequences. You'll learn how to customize and expand Camtasia to create a consistent visual identity across all your content, all while optimizing your video production workflow.

Extending and Customizing Camtasia

After integrating audio in the previous chapter, post-production of your online training course is almost complete. However, you still need to finalize several key visual elements, such as intros, outros, banners, and titles. These elements must comply with your organization's (or client's) brand identity and deliver a professional viewing experience that builds user trust and reinforces your credibility.

Moreover, you'll soon realize that, depending on your project requirements and personal preferences, you'll tend to use roughly the same tools over and over again. Keeping a customized toolset within easy reach will help you streamline your workflows, resulting in a more efficient and satisfying video editing experience.

In this chapter, you will pursue three main objectives: streamlining your workflows, improving teamwork, and maintaining visual consistency across all your videos. To achieve these objectives, you will explore tools such as themes, custom libraries, and templates. You will also learn how to customize your workspace by configuring tool panels and keyboard shortcuts to fit your personal preferences.

A. Preparing the Exercises

The step-by-step instructions in this chapter are based on the provided projects and files. Before using these projects, you need to import them into Camtasia using the process described at the beginning of Chapter 05 – Editing Your Videos.

You will now import the first project used in this chapter using the following steps:

1. Download and unzip the exercise files for Chapter 09.
2. Import the ***Chapter09/projects/01_02_dashboard.zip*** project into the ***Chapter09*** folder of the exercises.
3. Watch the entire project to refresh your memory.

Note that the closed captions you created in the previous chapter do not appear in this project. The reason for this is a compatibility issue. Closed captions created in Camtasia for Windows do not transfer to Camtasia for Mac, and vice versa. Therefore, we had to remove the captions to ensure the exercise files work on both platforms. But don't worry, they aren't lost! Before removing them from the project, they were first exported to an ***.srt*** file, so they can easily be reimported using the following steps.

4. Go to **File > Import > Captions**.
5. Navigate to the ***Chapter09/resources*** folder of the exercises.
6. Import the ***01_02_dashboard.srt*** file.
7. Save the project.

*On a Mac, you may need to use the **View > Show Caption Track** menu item to display the caption track between the timeline and the canvas.*

Importing closed captions in this way creates an additional track in the timeline. Make sure to position it above all other tracks so that the captions are never obscured by any other element.

B. Working With Themes

Camtasia themes help you stay on brand by ensuring consistent use of colors and fonts across all your video projects.

To create a new theme, start by importing the style guide for this video training series into the ***01_02_dashboard*** project. Note that this preliminary step isn't strictly necessary, but it will make it a lot easier to create a custom theme in subsequent steps.

1. Position the playhead at the beginning of the project.
2. Import **Chapter09/resources/02lBrandGuide.pdf** into the media bin.
3. In the media bin, right-click the brand guide you just imported.
4. Click **Add to Timeline at playhead** in the context menu

The brand guide is now visible in the center of the canvas. In the timeline, it is located on the first available track, at the playhead position. This element serves a single purpose: to give you a visual reference when creating a custom theme in the next section. Once the theme is created, you can safely remove this guide from the project, so don't worry too much about its exact location—it really doesn't matter.

1. Discovering the Components of a Theme

Camtasia comes with a single theme that is automatically applied to all new projects. In fact, you've been using this default theme all along. To fully understand what a theme is, you'll first take a look at the elements making up this default theme.

1. Go to **File > Manage Themes** (Windows) or **Camtasia > Manage Themes** (Mac) to open the **Theme Manager**.

*If this is your first time opening the **Theme Manager** window, a message will appear explaining what a theme is. Click **OK** to acknowledge the message and open the **Theme Manager**.*

The **Theme Manager** is divided into two columns. The right column displays a live preview of the currently selected theme. On the left, you find three tabs for the three components of a Camtasia theme.

2. At the top of the **Theme Manager**, make sure the **Default** theme is currently selected. If you see a different theme, open the **Theme** dropdown and select **Default**.

The Theme Manager window should now look like the following image.

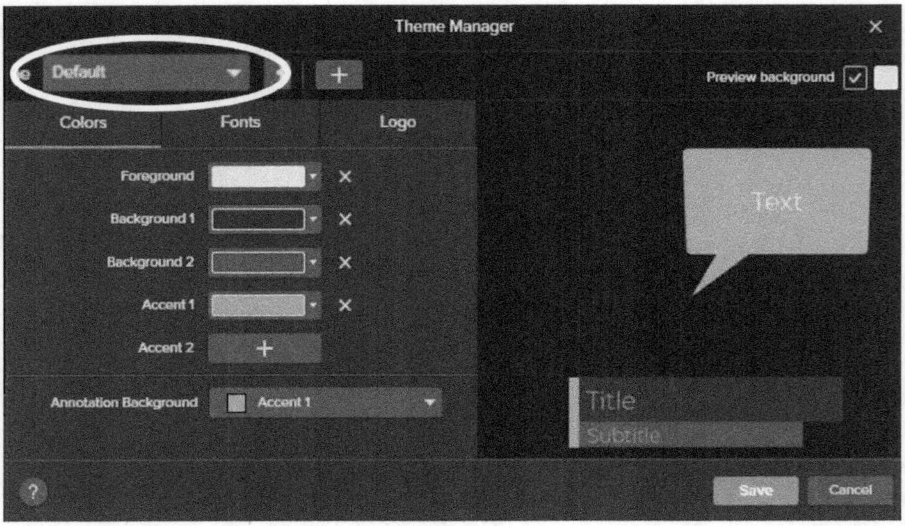

*09_01.png - The **Theme Manager** window with the **Default** theme selected.*

The first component of a Camtasia theme is a color palette of up to five different colors. You don't have to use all five colors; in fact, the **Default** theme uses only four.

3. Select the **Fonts** tab from the left column of the **Theme Manager**.

The second element is a set of up to two fonts. As with colors, you don't have to select two fonts. The **Default** theme actually uses only one.

4. Finally, open the **Logo** tab from the left column of the **Theme Manager**.

The third element of a Camtasia theme is a logo. Note that the **Default** theme does not include a logo. Just as with colors and fonts, you are not required to include a logo in a Camtasia Theme.

2. Creating a Custom Theme

Now that you have a better idea of what a Camtasia theme is, it's time to create your own based on the style guide you imported into the project.

1. Click the **+** icon at the top of the **Theme Manager**.
2. Type `One2Learn` in the **New Theme** window and click **OK**.
3. Reposition the **Theme Manager** window so the imported brand guide is fully visible on the canvas.
4. In the **Colors** tab of the **Theme Manager**, click the **Foreground** color to open the color picker.

5. Click the eyedropper icon.

The Eyedropper tool lets you pick any color visible on the screen, which makes it super easy to select a specific color, such as one from your brand guide.

6. With the eyedropper tool active, click the first color square from the brand guide (dark blue) to set that color as the **Foreground** color.
7. Repeat the same process to set the other four colors of the theme based on the four remaining color squares from the brand guide.
8. Select **Accent 2** (White) as the **Annotation Background** color.

The **Colors** tab of your new theme should now look like the image below.

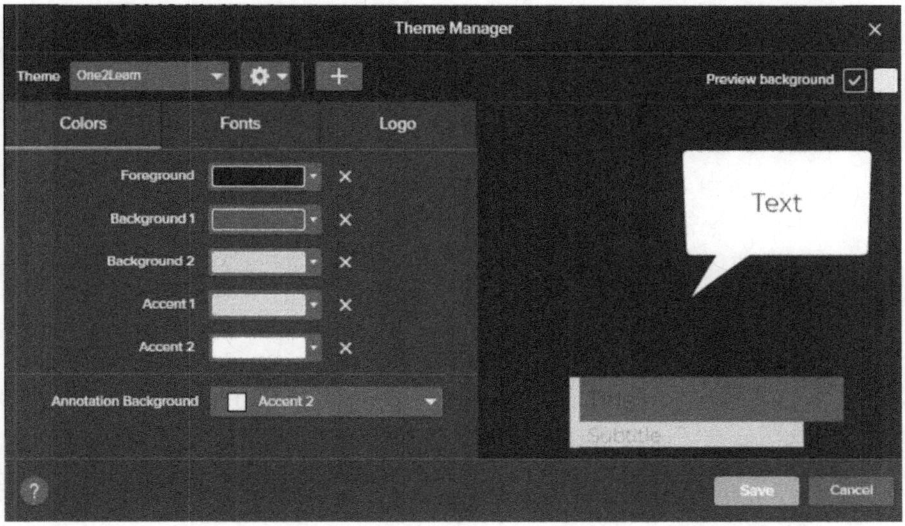

09_02.png - Add the colors from the color guide using the eyedropper tool.

The next step is to select the fonts for this new theme.

9. Open the **Fonts** tab of the **Theme Manager**.
10. As per the style guide, select **Roboto** as **Font 1** and **Verdana** as **Font 2**.

Finally, let's import the One2Learn logo into the new theme.

11. Open the **Logo** tab of the **Theme Manager**.
12. Click **Browse** and import ***Chapter09/resources/o2l-icon.png***.
13. Click **Save** in the lower right-hand corner of the **Theme Manager**.

This final step saves the new theme and closes the **Theme Manager**.

Now that you have saved the new theme, the style guide that you imported earlier is no longer needed and can safely be deleted.

14. Select the style guide on the canvas and press `Delete`.
15. Right-click anywhere within the media bin.
16. Click **Delete Unused Media** from the context menu.

In the next section, you'll use this new theme to style various visual elements throughout the project.

3. Using a Custom Theme

The ***01_02_dashboard*** project includes several graphic components, such as sketch motion annotations and cursor effects, which you can now style using your new theme.

1. Position the playhead at around timecode *0:00:20;00*.

At this point, a red arrow pointing to the upper right corner of the chart is visible on the screen.

2. Select the red arrow on the canvas.
3. If necessary, open the **Properties** panel on the right side of the screen.
4. Go to the **Annotation Properties** tab of the Properties panel.
5. Click the **Animation Mode** icon in the upper-left corner of the Properties panel to apply changes across all animations.

The first property in the Properties panel is the annotation **Color**. Now that you've created a theme, you won't be choosing colors at random anymore. Instead, you'll use your theme to select a specific color from your brand guide.

6. In the Properties panel, click the red rectangle to open the color picker.
7. In the color picker, open the dropdown menu and select the **One2Learn** theme from the previous section.

You now have preferred access to the five colors defined in your theme, as shown in the image below.

09_03.png - You have preferred access to the colors in the ***One2Learn*** *theme.*

These are the exact colors defined in your organization's brand guide.

8. Click the third theme color (orange) to apply it to the currently selected annotation.
9. In the timeline, position the playhead around timecode *0:0:45;00*.
10. Select the double arrow in the middle of the canvas.
11. Open the **Annotations** tab in the Properties panel.
12. Use the same technique to apply the same orange color to the double arrow.
13. Repeat these steps to apply the same orange color to the remaining two annotations on track 3 of the timeline.

Thanks to the new theme, it has been very easy to apply *the exact same color* to all annotations. But using a theme isn't limited to annotations. For example, let's use it to finalize the cursor effects in this project.

14. Select the screen recording on track 1 of the timeline.
15. Open the **Cursor Properties** tab of the Properties panel.
16. Make sure the **Edit All Animations** icon is still *on* in the upper-left corner of the Properties panel

Scrolling down the Properties panel, you should see three cursor effects applied to this clip: **Cursor Highlight**, **Left Click Scaling**, and **Left Click Sound.** The properties of these effects are available in the lower section of the Properties panel.

17. Select the second color in the theme (blue) for the **Cursor Highlight** effect.
18. Set the opacity of this effect to 50% and adjust its Size to 73.

In this section, you used your new theme to finalize the annotations and cursor effects in the ***01_02_dashboard*** project.

After completing these steps, the mouse cursor should look like illustrated in the image below.

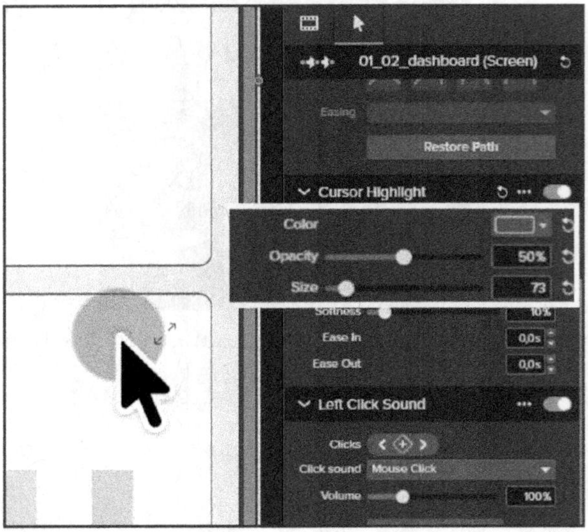

09_04.png - The mouse cursor and the Properties panel after applying the theme colors.

The beauty of themes is that they are saved in Camtasia rather than tied to a specific project. This means you can reuse the same theme across multiple projects, thus maintaining a consistent brand identity across all the videos in your online training course.

4. Other Theme Manager Options

To wrap up this exploration of themes in Camtasia, you will now look at the other options available in the Theme Manager. None of these options are necessary for the current exercise, so you will simply review them without applying any changes.

1. Use the **File > Manage Themes** (Windows) or **Camtasia > Manage Themes** (Mac) menu to reopen the **Theme Manager**.
2. From the **Theme** dropdown, select the **One2Learn** theme you created earlier.
3. Click the gear icon to the right of the **Theme** dropdown.

As shown in the following image, this icon contains the tools you need to **Rename**, **Delete**, and **Export** the selected theme. Also note the **Import Theme** option at the end of the menu.

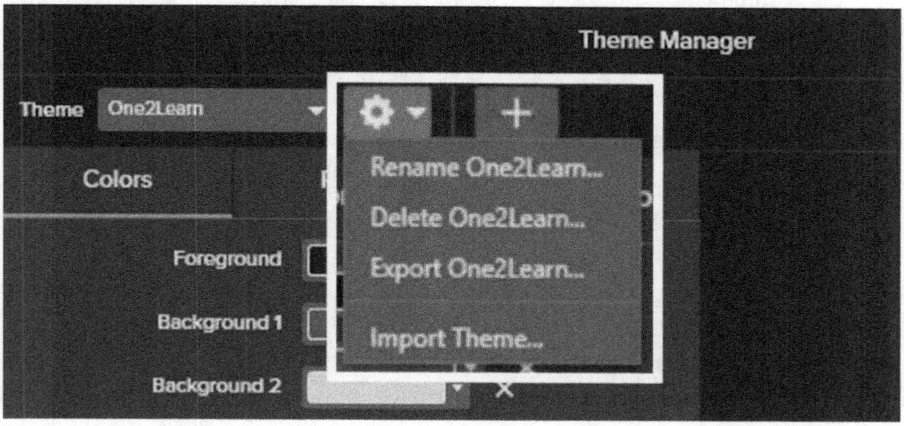

*09_05.png - This icon contains the tools to **Rename**, **Delete**, and **Export** the selected theme.*

The ability to export and import themes allows you to share themes with other Camtasia users. This promotes collaboration and ensures all team members stick to the same style guide.

C. Exploring Camtasia Libraries

Ensuring a consistent visual identity across all the videos in your online course goes far beyond just the colors and fonts of your custom theme. You should also include other branding elements, such intros, outros, titles and banners.

For example, the intro for each video of your online course should have the same layout, design, and animations. Only the content —such as the title and background image—is specific to each video.

Libraries let you save any number of items for reuse in different projects. They work in much the same way as the *Camtasia Assets* you used in the previous chapter to add background music. The main difference is that libraries are stored on your computer, whereas *Camtasia Assets* are hosted online by TechSmith.

In short, the items you use in your projects stem from the following three main sources.

- Elements imported into the media bin are specific to the current project.
- Library resources are stored on your computer and can be reused in any project edited with this installation of Camtasia.
- Camtasia Assets are hosted online by TechSmith and are accessible to all Camtasia users.

These three sources are grouped together in the **Media** panel on the left side of the interface.

1. Save and close any open projects.
2. Import the ***Chapter09/projects/00_01_prerequisites.zip*** compressed project into the ***Chapter09*** folder for the exercises.
3. Import the project captions from the ***Chapter09/resources/00_01_prerequisites.srt*** file.
4. Watch the entire video to refresh your memory.
5. Open the **Media** panel on the left side of the screen.

This panel comprises three tabs: the **Media Bin**, the **Camtasia Assets**, and the **Library**, as shown in the following screenshot.

*09_06.png – The three tabs in the **Media** panel.*

You will now explore in detail the third tab of the **Media** panel, which provides access to Camtasia libraries.

In previous versions of Camtasia, a default library was automatically installed with the application. Starting with the 2026 version, this default library has been replaced by the free tier of the Camtasia Assets. If you upgraded from a previous version, you may still have access to this older library, even after updating to the new version.

1. Creating an Outro

You'll start by creating the outro for the ***00_01_prerequisites*** project.

1. Position the playhead at the end of the ***00_01_prerequisites*** project, at timecode *0:01:05;22*.
2. Import the ***Chapter09/resources/00_01_cover.jpg*** and ***Chapter09/resources/One2LearnLogo.png*** images into the media bin.
3. Drag the ***00_01_cover.jpg*** image from the media bin and drop it onto track 1 of the timeline immediately after the PowerPoint slideshow.
4. Drag a white rectangle from the **Shapes** tab of the **Annotations** panel and drop it onto Track 2 of the timeline, just above the background image you added in the previous step.
5. On the canvas, resize the rectangle and position it in the center of the screen, as illustrated in the image below.

09_07.png – Enlarge the rectangle and position it in the center of the canvas.

*You can use the automatic snapping behavior to position the rectangle precisely at the center of the canvas. This feature should be enabled by default. If it isn't, use the **View > Enable Canvas Snapping** menu item to turn it on.*

You will now add the One2Learn logo as well as two text annotations to this outro.

6. Drag the ***One2LearnLogo.png*** image from the media bin and drop it onto the canvas above the white rectangle.

In the timeline, Camtasia places the logo on the first available track (Track 3) at the current playhead position.

7. On the canvas, slightly reduce the size of the logo and center it within the upper portion of the white rectangle.
8. Open the **Callouts** tab of the **Annotations** panel on the left side of the screen.
9. At the top of the **Annotations** panel, open the **Theme** dropdown and select the **One2Learn** theme you created in the previous section.

Selecting the theme in the annotations panel lets you set the font and the color of the new text caption even before it is inserted into your project!

10. Drag any simple text annotation (i.e., one with no shape or outline) from the **Annotations** panel and drop it onto the canvas just below the logo.

In the timeline, Camtasia positions this new element on track 4, above the logo.

11. Make sure the new text annotation is selected and the Properties panel is open.
12. In the **Text Properties** tab, apply the second color from the **One2Learn** theme (blue) to the text.
13. Set the font size to `65`.
14. Double-click the new annotation and type **`Introduction`**.
15. Drag a second text annotation from the **Annotations** panel and drop it onto the canvas below the first annotation.
16. In the Properties panel, set its font size to `45` and apply the third color of the **One2Learn** theme (orange) to the text.
17. Double-click the new text annotation and type **`Next video: <Enter> Logging In and Out`**.
18. Arrange these two text annotations, as shown in the image below.

09_08.png - The elements of the outro properly arranged on the canvas.

After completing these steps, the elements of the outro are correctly positioned in space (on the canvas). You will now arrange them in time (in the timeline) and apply a transition effect.

19. In the timeline, adjust the duration of the second text annotation so it appears at timecode *0:01:06;22* and remains on screen until the end of the project, for a total duration of four seconds.
20. Open the **Transitions** panel on the left side of the screen.
21. Apply a **Fade In** transition to the second text caption.

In the timeline, the last few seconds of the project should now look like the following image.

09_09 – Your outro in the timeline.

The outro for this project is now complete. To test it, rewind the playhead by a few seconds and play the video.

Don't forget to save your work every now and then. After all, creating such a branded sequence takes time, not to mention that you'll need to include a similar outro in every video of your online course. Enter the *library*! Instead of recreating the same outro in every video, you'll save it as a library item so you can easily reuse it in other videos.

2. Grouping Assets

Your outro sequence consists of five separate items: a background image, a white rectangle, the logo, and two text annotations. In the library, they will be stored as a single reusable item. You must, therefore, group them into a single entity.

1. In the timeline, select all five elements making up the outro sequence you created in the previous section.
2. Right-click anywhere in the selection.
3. Select **Group** in the context menu or use `Ctrl + G` (Windows) or `Cmd + G` (Mac).

The five components of the outro have now been grouped into a single element on track 1 of the timeline, as shown in the following screenshot.

09_10.png – The five elements of the outro are combined into a single item.

You will now rename this new group using the following steps.

4. Right-click the new group in the timeline.
5. Select **Rename Group** in the context menu.
6. Type `o21-outro` as the group name and press `Enter`.

Grouping items in this way has many advantages:

- It simplifies the timeline, making it easier to manage complex projects with numerous elements spread across multiple tracks.
- Groups let you move, resize, or even duplicate many items at once.

- You can apply animations, behaviors, transitions, and other effects to a group. These group-wide effects combine with any effects already applied to individual elements within the group.

You can create as many groups as needed, each containing an unlimited number of items. You can also nest groups together to create multiple levels of organization within your timeline.

You are now ready to move on to the next step, but before that, let's take a quick look at how you can access individual group items without breaking the group apart.

7. In the timeline, click the + icon in the lower left-hand corner of the **o2l-outro** group.

Clicking this icon opens the group, which appears as a new tab in the timeline, as shown in the image below.

09_11.png – The group appears as a separate tab in the timeline.

This tab gives you access to each individual group member, which you can edit using the standard tools in Camtasia.

8. Open the **Main Timeline** tab to return to the project timeline without closing the group.
9. Click the cross icon on the **o2l-outro** tab to close the group.

You are now back to the initial situation with the **o2l-outro** group sitting on track 1 of the timeline.

3. Configuring Quick Properties

Remember that your goal is to create a reusable outro sequence—one that is consistent enough to maintain your brand identity, yet flexible enough to accommodate new content. Core elements, such as the duration and overall layout of the outro, will remain the same from project to project, while the background image and caption texts will be different in each video.

In this section, you will define the properties that should be accessible in the Properties panel when the group is selected.

1. Position the playhead at the end of the ***00_01_prerequisites*** project so that the outro sequence is visible on the canvas.
2. Select the **02l-outro** group on track 1 of the timeline.
3. If necessary, open the Properties panel on the right side of the screen.

As shown in the following screenshot, three properties are visible in the first tab of the Properties panel when the group is selected.

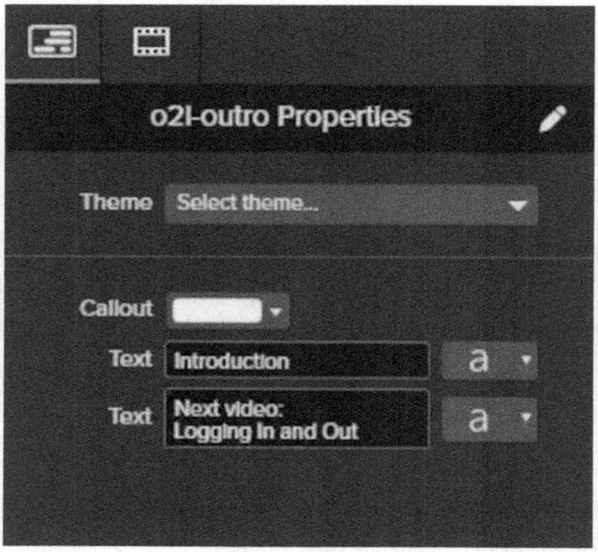

09_12.png – By default, three properties are available in the Properties panel

Camtasia automatically configures these properties based on the contents of the selected group. This means that each group has unique properties directly related to the elements within it.

In this example, the properties of your outro sequence are as follows:

- The **Callout** property controls the color of the white rectangle enclosing the logo and the two text annotations. In this example, it should always be white, so this property should *not* appear in the Properties panel.
- The remaining two properties control the text content of the annotations. Since these values are specific to each instance of the outro, you must keep them visible in the Properties panel. However, you should rename them to avoid having two properties with the same name.

With this in mind, you will now customize the properties displayed in the Properties panel when the group is selected.

4. Click the pencil icon in the upper-right corner of the Properties panel.

This opens the **Quick Property Editor**, as shown in the image below.

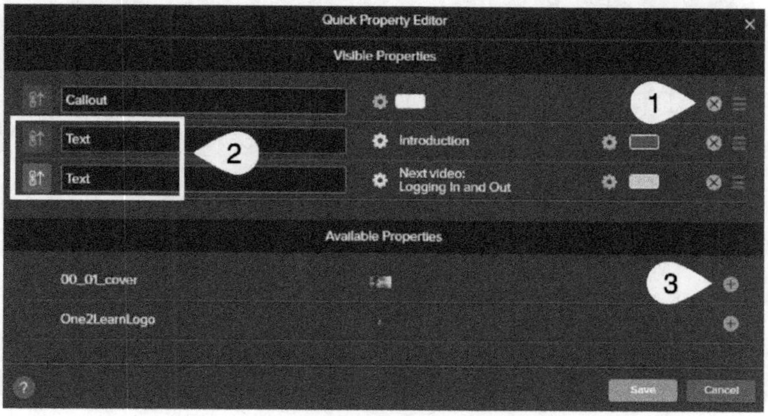

*09_13.png – The **Quick Property Editor** window.*

This window is divided into two sections. The top section shows the properties that are currently visible in the Properties panel. In the lower section, you'll find the remaining properties that are not currently available in the Properties panel.

5. Click the red **X** for the **Callout** property (number 1 in the above image) to remove it from the Properties panel.
6. Rename the two **Text** properties (number 2 in the above image). Enter `Title` for the first property and `Next Video` for the second.
7. In the lower section of the window, click the green + for the **00_01_cover** property (number 3 in the above image).
8. Rename this property `Background Image`.
9. Use the three-line (hamburger) icon on the right of each visible property to move the **Background Image** property to the top.

The **Quick Property Editor** window should now look like the image below.

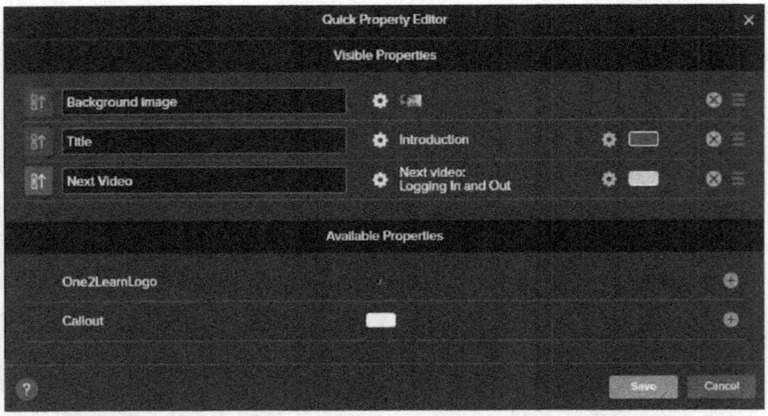

*09_14.png – The **Quick Property Editor** after making changes.*

10. Click **Save** to save the changes and close the **Quick Property Editor**.

The Properties panel now reflects the choices you made in the **Quick Property editor**, making it easy to edit what you need, without accidentally altering properties that must remain the same across all projects.

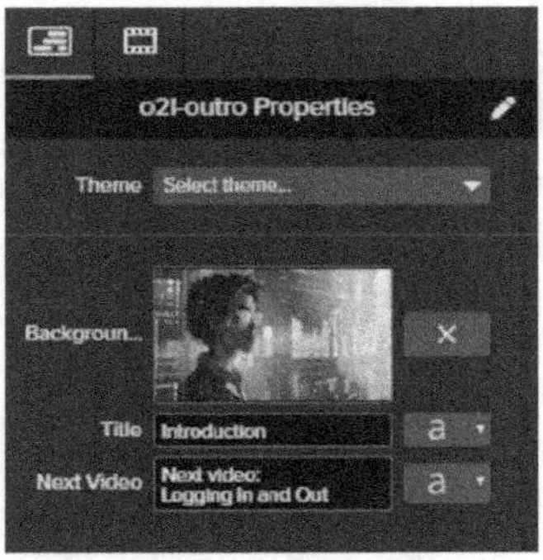

09_15.png – The properties in the Properties panel have been customized.

The **o2l-outro** group is now ready to be stored in a library.

4. Creating a New Library

You are now ready to save the **o2l-outro** group as a library item, so let's navigate to the **Library** panel using the following steps:

1. Click **Media** on the left side of the interface.
2. Open the third tab to access the **Library** panel.

Upon installation, Camtasia automatically creates an empty **Default** library, as shown in the image below.

*09_16.png – The **Default** library is initially empty.*

You could save the **02l-outro** item in this library, but you'll save it in a new library instead. Creating your own libraries allows you to organize your reusable assets however you need—by project, client, department, or even by video type.

3. At the top of the **Library** panel, open the **Library** dropdown menu.
4. Click **Create New Library**.
5. In the dialog, type `Camtasia Book` as the library name.
6. Keep **Start From** set to **Blank** (the default).
7. Click **Create**.

This creates a new empty library and opens it in the **Library** panel. You will now save the **02l-outro** group into this new library.

8. Right-click **02l-outro** on track 1 of the timeline.
9. In the context menu, click **Add to Library**.

When the **Add to Library** window opens, it uses the name of the group as the default item name. The selected library corresponds to the currently active library within the **Library** panel. This is exactly what you need for this exercise.

10. Click **OK** (Windows) or **Add** (Mac) in the lower-right corner of the **Add to Library** window.

As shown in the following screenshot, the **Camtasia Book** library now contains a first item named **02l-outro**.

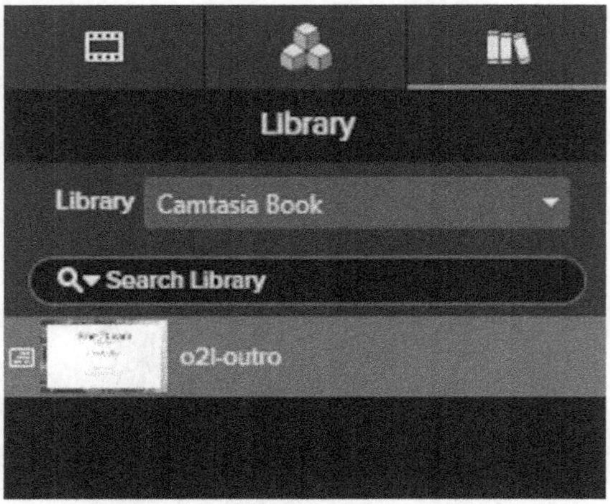

*09_17.png - The **Camtasia Book** library contains the **o2l-outro** item.*

You can now reuse this group as many times needed, both in this project and in any other Camtasia project.

5. Reusing Library Items

It's finally time to take advantage of the work you've done in previous sections by integrating your new outro into the ***01_02_dashboard*** project.

1. Save and close the ***00_01_prerequisites*** project.
2. Open the ***Chapter09/01_02_dashboard*** project.
3. Position the playhead at the end of the ***01_02_dashboard*** project.
4. Open the **Library** tab in the **Media** panel on the left side of the screen.
5. Make sure the **Camtasia Book** library is selected.
6. Drag **o2l-outro** from the **Library** panel and drop it track 1 of the timeline directly after the screen recording.

After completing these steps, the end of the timeline should look like the image below.

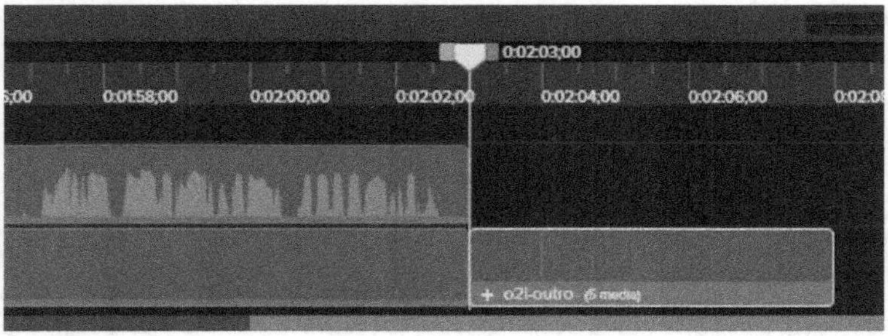

*09_18.png - Place **o2l-outro** on track 1 of the timeline right after the screen recording.*

Thanks to this library, integrating the outro into this other project is easier than ever. You will now customize it using the *Quick Properties* available in the Properties panel.

7. Position the playhead so you can see the outro on the canvas.
8. Make sure the **o2l-outro** item is selected in the timeline.

With **o2l-outro** selected, the Properties panel displays the *Quick Properties* you configured in the previous section.

9. Click the cross next icon to the **Background Image** property to remove the default image.
10. Click **Import File**.
11. Import the ***Chapter09/resources/01_02_cover.jpg*** image.
12. Enter `The Data Dashboard` in the **Title** field of the Properties panel.
13. Enter `Next Video: <Line break> Customizing the Platform` in the **Next Video** field.

> *To create a line break, use* `Shift + Enter` *(Windows) or* `Option + Enter` *(Mac).*

The *Quick Properties* let you customize every **o2l-outro** instance on the fly, as shown in the image below.

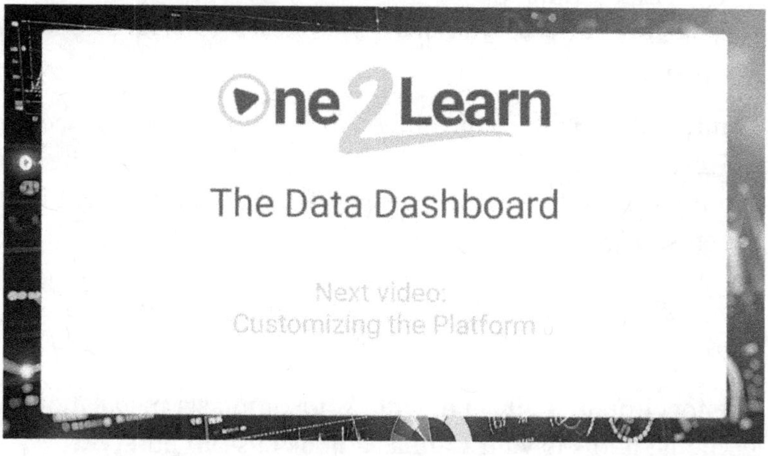

09_19.png – o2l-outro has been customized in the ***01_01_dashboard*** *project.*

You will now add a smooth transition between the screen recording and **o2l-outro** using the following steps:

14. Open the **Transitions** panel on the left side of the screen.
15. Drag the **Fade** transition from the **Transitions** panel and drop it onto the timeline between the screen recording and **o2l-outro**.

This last step demonstrates how you can apply a transition to a group rather than individually to each member of the group.

To see the result, rewind the playhead by a few seconds and start playing the video.

6. Importing and Exporting Libraries

Many organizations use libraries to provide their users with ready-to-use assets that comply with internal policies and corporate branding guidelines. In this section, you'll learn how to export a library so you can share it with other Camtasia users. You'll also import a library into your Camtasia installation to easily bring additional brand-compliant assets into your video projects.

1. Still in the ***01_02_dashboard*** project, reopen the **Library** tab of the **Media** panel on the left side of the screen.
2. Open the **Library** dropdown.
3. Hover over the **Manage Library** option.

Here, you find several options to *rename, delete,* and *export* the active library.

4. Click **Export Library**.
5. Navigate to the ***Chapter09*** folder in the exercises and save the library under a name of your choice.

The resulting ***.libzip*** file contains the entire library as well as some Camtasia-specific metadata. You can now share this file with other users so they can import it into their Camtasia installation and benefit from your library items.

.libzip files created on a Mac can be imported into the Windows version of Camtasia, and vice versa.

You will now import a ***.libzip*** file into your Camtasia installation to add a few additional items to your **Camtasia Book** custom library.

6. Reopen the **Library** drop down at the top of the **Library** tab of the **Media** panel.
7. Click **Manage Library > Import Zipped Library**.
8. Import the ***Chapter09/resources/CamtasiaBook_EN.libzip*** file.
9. In the **Import To Library** dialog box, select the **Camtasia Book** library you created earlier.

10. Click **Import**.

As shown in the image below, the **Camtasia Book** library now includes two additional items: **o2l-intro** and **o2l-slide**.

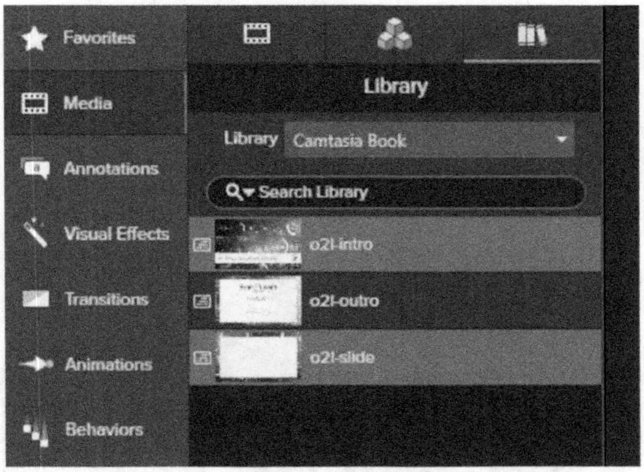

09_20.png – The ***Camtasia Book*** *library includes two additional items.*

These two elements come from the ***CamtasiaBook_EN.libzip*** file you just imported, demonstrating how Camtasia users can share library elements with one another.

7. Organizing Libraries

You can store as many items as you want in each of your libraries, including background music, stock images, video clips, logos, icons, and short animations. To keep track of all this content and make it easier to find, you can organize your libraries using a folder structure similar to what you're used to on your computer.

1. Return to the **Library** tab of the **Media** panel.
2. Make sure **Camtasia Book** is the active library.
3. Right-click anywhere in the **Library** panel.
4. Select **New Folder** from the context menu.
5. Name the new folder `Titles` and validate with the `Enter` key.
6. Drag **o2l-intro** and **o2l-outro** in the **Titles** folder

On Windows, Camtasia won't let you move **o2l-outro** into the **Titles** folder because it is already in use in the active project. The easiest solution is to close the current project and rearrange the library from an empty project.

7. [*Windows only*] Save and close the ***01_02_dashboard*** project.
8. [*Windows only*] Restart Camtasia and create a **New Project**.

9. [*Windows only*] Return to the **Library** tab in the **Media** panel.
10. [*Windows only*] Drag **o2l-outro** into the **Titles** folder of the **Camtasia Book** library.
11. [*Windows only*] Close the new empty project without saving.
12. [*Windows only*] Restart Camtasia.
13. [*Windows only*] Reopen the ***01_02_dashboard*** project from the **Recent Projects** section of the welcome screen.

After completing these steps, the **Camtasia Book** library should look like the image below.

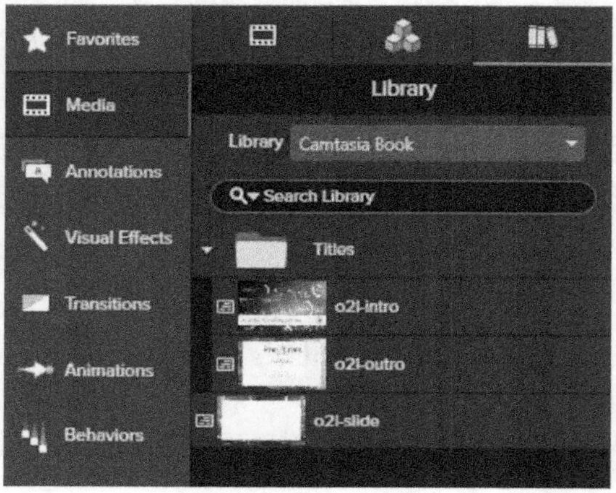

*09_21.png – Both items are stored in the **Titles** folder of the **Camtasia Book** library.*

8. Libraries: Hands-On Exercise

To conclude this section on Camtasia libraries, you will now insert the **o2l-intro** library item into the ***01_02_dashboard*** project. The main steps for this exercise are as follows:

1. Position the playhead at the beginning of the ***01_02_dashboard*** project.
2. Hold down the `Shift` key while moving the playhead to the right to create a gap of at least five seconds at the beginning of the project.

Holding down **`Shift`** moves the entire project to the right, creating a few seconds of empty space at the beginning of the project. You will now insert **o2l-intro** into this empty space.

3. Drag **o2l-intro** from the **Library** panel and drop it onto track 1 of the timeline at the very beginning of the project.
4. Position the playhead in the gap between **o2l-intro** and the rest of the project.

5. Hold **`Shift`** while moving the playhead to the left until the gap between the intro and the rest of the project is filled.
6. Drop a **Fade** transition between **02l-intro** and the screen recording on track 1 of the timeline.

When done, the first few seconds of the timeline should look like the following image.

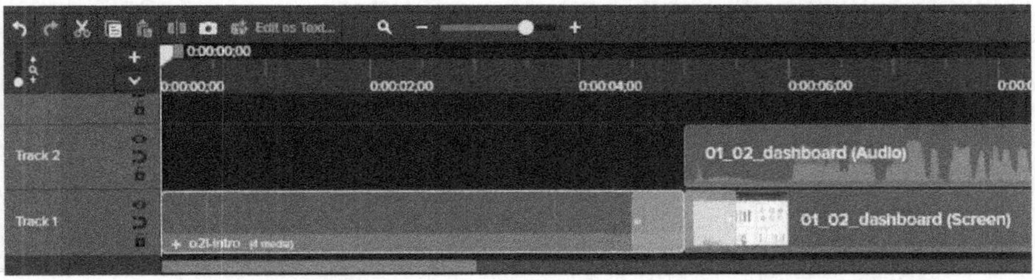

*09_22.png – **02l-intro** at the beginning of the timeline on track 1.*

This exercise wraps up your exploration of libraries in Camtasia. They let you build custom collections of reusable assets that you can instantly drop into any project. This significantly boosts your productivity while helping you maintain visual consistency across all your videos. Share them with your team to ensure everyone stays on brand without starting from scratch every time.

D. Customizing Tool Panels

The panels on the left side of the screen offer an extensive range of tools designed to meet a wide variety of needs. In practice, however, most users always use the same few tools and settings. In this section, you will learn how to customize these panels so that the tools and settings you use most often are always just a click away.

1. Using the Favorites Panel

The **Favorites** panel lets you gather your favorite tools in one place, making it easy to add animations, behaviors, transitions, and special effects without having to switch between panels.

1. Click **Favorites** on the left side of the screen to open the **Favorites** panel. You can also use the **F** key on your keyboard.

The **Favorites** panel starts completely empty. It's up to you to add the tools you use most often. This way, every Camtasia user can keep their personal selection of tools just a click away!

2. Open the **Transitions** panel on the left side of the interface.

Camtasia offers a huge selection of transitions, but in practice, you'll always end up using the same few.

3. Type **Fade** into the search field at the top of the **Transitions** panel.
4. Hover over (Windows) or click (Mac) the **Fade** transition thumbnail until a star appears in the upper right-hand corner.
5. Click that small star.

This action adds the **Fade** transition to the **Favorites** panel and the star turns yellow to indicate it is selected.

6. Repeat these steps with the other few transitions you use regularly.
7. Open the **Animations** panel on the left side of the interface.
8. [*Windows only*] Select the **Animations** tab.
9. Click the star icon associated with the **Custom** and **Restore** animations.
10. Keep browsing the other panels and use the same process to add additional items to the **Favorites** panel.
11. When done, return to the **Favorites** panel.

As shown in the image below, the **Favorites** panel now lists all thumbnails you have favorited by clicking the star icon.

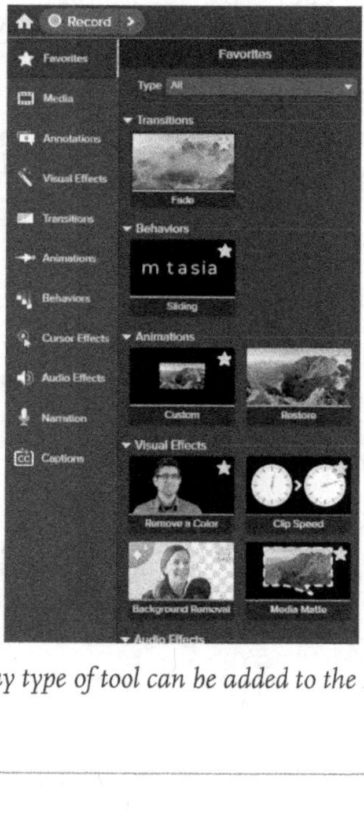

*09_23.png – Any type of tool can be added to the **Favorites** panel.*

Use the **Type** dropdown to display only a specific tool category. By default, all categories are shown.

To remove a tool from the favorites, just click the yellow star again. It turns back to gray to indicate it is disabled.

2. Adding Presets

When using Camtasia, you often find yourself making the same adjustments in the Properties panel. For example, you consistently change the font, text size and color every time you add a new text annotation. So why not save these custom presets in the **Annotations** panel so they're always just a click away?

1. Position the playhead at the end of the project to see **02l-outro** on the canvas.
2. Double click the outro sequence on the canvas.

Double-clicking **02l-outro** opens the group, allowing you to access each of its individual members without having to ungroup it.

3. Select **The Data Dashboard** title to see its properties in the Properties panel.

Earlier in this chapter, you adjusted the font size and color of this item in the Properties panel. You will now save these changes in the **Annotations** panel by creating a reusable custom preset.

4. In the upper right-hand corner of the Properties panel, click the + icon to add a preset.

This action is illustrated in the image below.

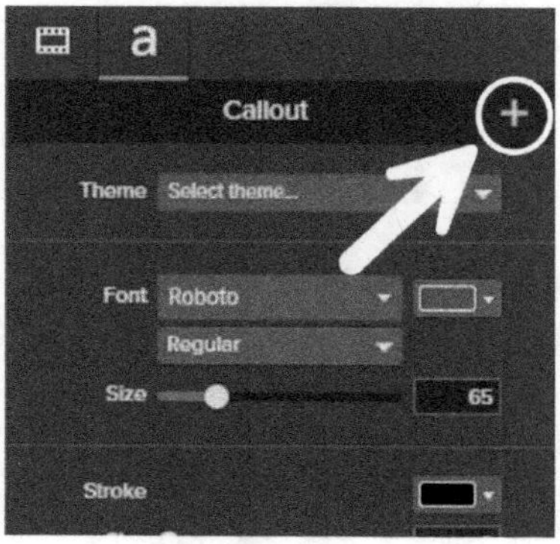

09_24.png – Click + in the upper right-hand corner of the Properties panel.

This adds a new preset to the **Callouts** tab of the **Annotations** panel.

5. Repeat these steps with the other text annotation of the outro.
6. Open the **Annotations** panel and go to the **Callouts** tab.
7. Open the **Style** dropdown and select **User**.

As shown in the image below, two new presets have been added to the **Callouts** tab of the **Annotations** panel.

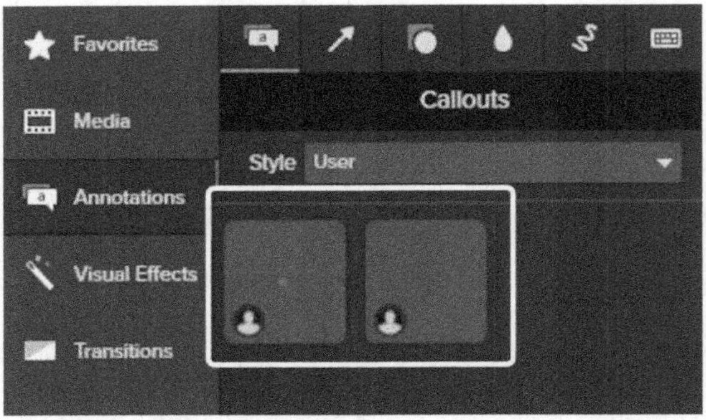

09_25.png – Two additional presets are available in the ***Callouts*** *panel.*

You can use the exact same process to add presets to the other tool panels as well. In no time, you'll have a whole custom collection of behaviors, cursor effects, visual effects, audio effects, and other creative tools at your fingertips.

8. Hover over one of your two custom presets in the **Callouts** panel.
9. Click the star that appears in the upper-right corner of your custom caption to add it to your **Favorites**.
10. Repeat the same process for the other caption preset.

The **Favorites** panel, combined with custom presets, gives you easy access to your own custom toolset that fits your unique workflow and visual style.

E. Customizing Keyboard Shortcuts

No matter the editing software, videographers love using keyboard shortcuts. So much so that virtually all of Camtasia's tools can be accessed using a keyboard shortcut. You can even customize these shortcuts, which can be very useful in many situations.

- If you use multiple video editing applications, you can standardize the keyboard shortcuts across all of them.

- ➢ You can assign easier shortcuts to your favorite tools, thereby customizing the software to fit your workflows.
- ➢ Customizing keyboard shortcuts can help reduce muscle fatigue and minimize repetitive movements.

You will now open the Camtasia preferences window and review all available keyboard shortcuts.

1. Use **Edit > Preferences** (Windows) or **Camtasia > Settings** (Mac) to open the **Preferences** window.
2. Open the **Shortcuts** tab of the preferences.

This window lists all Camtasia tools in one column, with the corresponding keyboard shortcuts in the other. To make navigation easier, the tools are grouped by category in the left column.

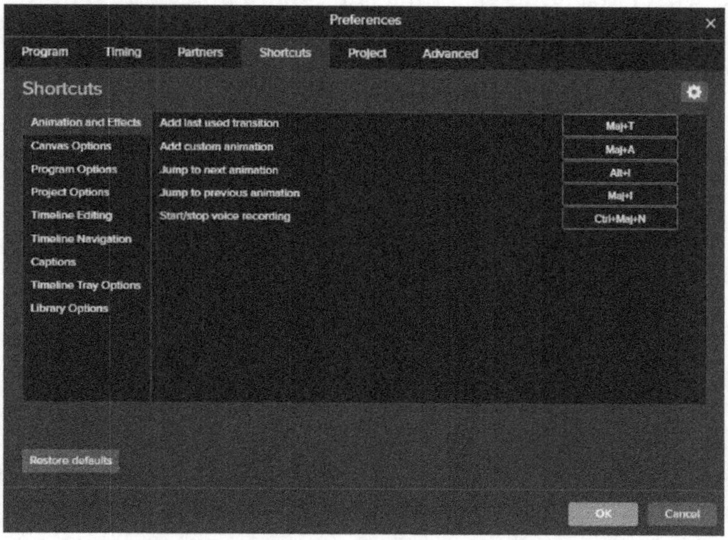

*09_26.png – The **Shortcuts** tab in the **Preferences** window.*

You can also use this window to customize keyboard shortcuts.

3. Use the categories in the left column to select the tool whose shortcut you want to change.
4. In the right column, click the keyboard shortcut to be changed.
5. Type the new shortcut on your keyboard.

If the selected shortcut is already assigned to another command, a warning appears at the bottom of the window.

6. To restore the default shortcut for a specific command, click the curved arrow icon next to the custom shortcut.

7. On Windows, you can also click **Restore Defaults** in the lower-left corner of the **Preferences** window.

Because Camtasia has so many features, manually configuring keyboard shortcuts for each is tedious. Fortunately, you can export and import shortcut configurations, allowing you to easily share your custom shortcuts with other users or take advantage of configurations created by your colleagues.

8. Click the gear icon located at the top of the **Shortcuts** tab in the **Preferences** window.

This is where the options for importing and exporting keyboard shortcuts are located.

Camtasia saves keyboard shortcuts in ***.camshortcuts*** files on Windows and ***.camsc*** files on Mac. Note that importing shortcuts exported from the Windows version of Camtasia into a Mac (or vice versa) is not supported.

Future exercises and step-by-step instructions assume that the default keyboard shortcuts have not been changed.

*From the Camtasia welcome screen, click **Support** to view a list of the most commonly used keyboard shortcuts.*

F. Working With Templates

A template is a reusable project blueprint. Any element that can be included in a standard project can also be integrated into a template. Every new project derived from this template automatically inherits these elements, allowing you to speed up your production processes and maintain a consistent look and feel across all your videos.

In this section, you will first explore the existing templates before creating a custom template.

1. Exploring Out-of-the-Box Templates

Camtasia comes with a dozen predefined templates to help you get started with creating different kinds of videos, such as tutorials, presentations, and content for social media. These templates are readily accessible from the Camtasia welcome screen.

1. Save any open files and close Camtasia.
2. Restart Camtasia.
3. Once on the welcome screen, open the **Templates** tab.

As shown in the image below, this tab contains a dozen or so templates.

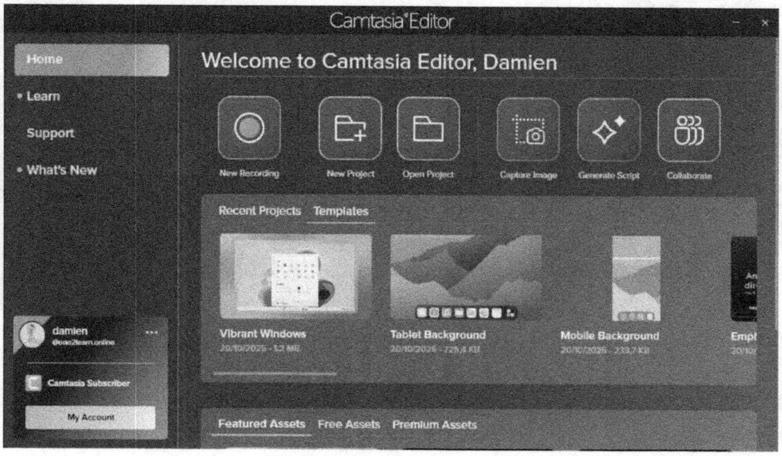

*09_27.png – The **Templates** tab of the welcome screen.*

Some of these templates let you create landscape videos, optimized for desktop viewing, while others generate portrait videos, better suited for social media.

4. Use the horizontal scroll bar to scroll through the available templates.
5. When ready, double-click the **Floating Screen** template

Camtasia then creates a new project based on this template.

*If the **Floating Screen** template isn't available on your computer, you'll find a copy of it in the **Chapter09/resources** folder of the exercises. Just double-click the **Floating Screen.camtemplate** file to import the template into Camtasia and create a new project from it.*

When the new project opens, you'll quickly notice it is not empty. The elements already contained in the project are inherited from the template and provide a solid foundation for getting started.

6. Start playing the video to view this content on the canvas.
7. Pause the video after a few seconds.

As shown in the following screenshot, the **Floating Screen** template contains two elements. These appear both in the media bin and on the first two tracks of the timeline.

*09_28.png – The **Floating Screen** template contains two elements.*

It's worth noting that the timeline tracks have already been renamed, which is another element carried over from the template.

- The **Dynamic Background** track contains a group of two elements, which also appear in the media bin. These assets are not specific to templates and can be used in any Camtasia project.
- In contrast, the **Screen Content** track contains a special item called a *placeholder*. A placeholder is a temporary element meant to be replaced by a permanent element during editing.

Also notice that transitions have been added at the beginning and end of these two elements.

8. Select the placeholder object on the **Screen Content** track of the timeline.
9. Navigate to the **Placeholder Properties** tab of the Properties panel.

Here you find a note left by whoever designed this template, with instructions on the intended use of the selected placeholder.

The next step is to replace the placeholder with something else. In this example, you will use a video clip that you must first import into the media bin.

10. Import the ***Chapter09/resources/lessIsMore.mp4*** video into the media bin.
11. Drag the ***lessIsMore.mp4*** file from the media bin and drop it onto the placeholder on the **Screen Content** track.

The ***lessIsMore.mp4*** video runs for 4 minutes 52 seconds, whereas the placeholder in the template is only one minute long. Camtasia provides four options to resolve this duration discrepancy.

- **Replace from Start** retains the duration of the placeholder (one minute in this example) and keeps only the first minute of the inserted video. The remaining footage is discarded.
- **Replace from End** also retains the duration of the placeholder but uses the last minute of the inserted video rather than the first.
- **Replace with Clip Speed** uses the Clip Speed effect to adjust the playback speed of the imported video so that it fits entirely within the one-minute placeholder.
- **Ripple Replace** adjusts the duration of the placeholder to the duration of the inserted video.

You will use the latter option in this example.

12. Click **Ripple Replace**.
13. If necessary, adjust the zoom level of the timeline so that you can see the entire project.
14. Adjust the duration of the **Dynamic Background** item to that of the **Screen Content** track.

The project should now be 4 minutes and 52 seconds long, and its timeline should look like the image below.

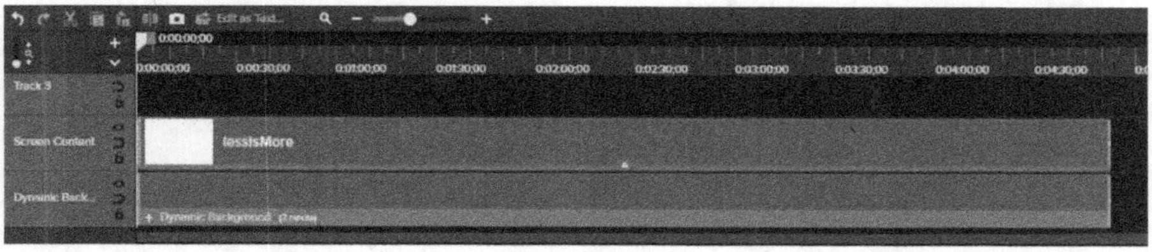

09_29.png – The project is now 4 minutes and 52 seconds long.

After replacing the placeholder with actual footage, you could consider the project complete. However, to demonstrate the ability to modify any part of the template, you will continue editing this project and add a background music track.

15. Right-click the header of the **Dynamic Background** track at the far left of the timeline.
16. Select **Insert Track > Below**.
17. Open the **Camtasia Assets** tab of the **Media** panel.
18. Drag your preferred music track from the **Camtasia Assets** panel and drop it at the beginning of track 1.

19. If the background music track is shorter than the project, duplicate it as many times as needed so that there is music from the beginning to the end of the project.
20. Stop the music a few seconds after the video ends and apply a fade-out effect so it gently fades away.

Although you started this project from a template, you were able to add an extra track to the timeline and incorporate background music. This demonstrates that using a template does not limit the range of tools at your disposal when working with Camtasia. With or without a template, you have complete freedom to customize the project to suit your needs.

Passionate about photography, I recently completed four years of evening classes to sharpen my skills and meet other photographers. The ***lessIsMore.mp4*** *slideshow is my final course assignment on minimalist photography. I hope you enjoy it!*

2. Creating a New Template

Now that you know more about templates, it's time to create your own. In doing so, you'll be working toward the following two objectives:

- **Save time** on video production, both for you and your colleagues.
- **Implement consistent styles and standards** across all the videos you and your team produce.

In fact, a template is nothing more than a standard Camtasia project. It only becomes a template when you explicitly save it as one.

1. Save and close any open projects.
2. Restart Camtasia and create a **New Project**.
3. Open the zoom dropdown above the canvas and select **Project Settings**.
4. Select **HD (1280 x 720)** as the canvas size and click **Apply**.
5. Open the **Library** tab of the **Media** panel on the left side of the screen.
6. Make sure the **Camtasia Book** library created earlier in this chapter is selected.
7. Drag **02l-intro** from the **Library** panel and drop it onto the timeline at the beginning of Track 1.
8. Use the **Edit > Add Placeholder** (Windows) or **Edit > Add Placeholder to Timeline** (Mac) menu or use the **P** key on your keyboard to add a new placeholder to the project.
9. Position the new placeholder on track 1 immediately after **02l-intro**.
10. Drag **02l-outro** from the **Library** and drop it onto track 1, immediately after the placeholder.

Keep in mind that a placeholder is a temporary item meant to be replaced by actual multimedia content later on. Anything you add to the placeholder (such as styles, animations, transitions, effects, or behaviors) will automatically be applied to the final footage.

11. Drag two transitions of your choosing from the **Transitions** panel. Drop the first one between the intro and the placeholder, and the second one between the placeholder and the outro.
12. Also drag the **AI Noise Removal** audio effect onto the placeholder.

The project timeline should now look like the image below.

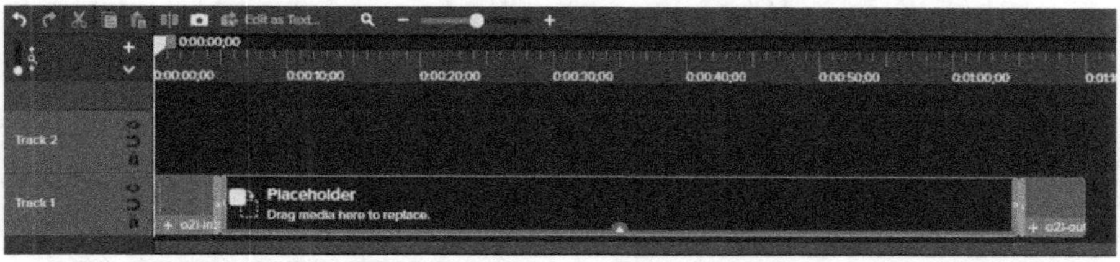

09_30.png – The project timeline with an intro, a placeholder, and an outro.

Finally, take a moment to name and describe the placeholder to help the template user understand your intent and use it according to your organization's policies and best practices.

13. Select the placeholder on track 1 of the timeline.
14. Open the **Placeholder Properties** tab of the Properties panel.
15. Enter `Screen Recording` in the **Title** field.
16. Enter `Drag a screen recording here. Use a 16:9 aspect ratio and 1280 x 720 (HD) or 1920 x 1080 (FHD) resolution` into the **Note** field.

You now have a basic template with an intro, a placeholder, and an outro. You could add many other things to this template, such as cursor effects, or even dynamic captions. However, for the purposes of this exercise, you will consider this template complete and save it as a new template in Camtasia.

17. Position the playhead at around timecode *0:0:03;00* to see all the elements of the intro on the canvas.

The image displayed on the canvas when saving the template is used as the template thumbnail in the Template Manager.

18. Navigate to **File > Save Project as Template**.
19. Type `021-Tutorial` as the template name and click **OK**.

Your project is now saved as a template in Camtasia. To create a new project based on this template, you can use either the **File > Create Project from Template** menu item or the **Templates** tab of the welcome screen.

3. Using the Template Manager

This section guides you through the *Template Manager*, which provides a complete suite of tools for managing and maintaining your Camtasia templates.

1. Use the **File > Manage Templates (Windows)** or **Camtasia > Manage Templates** (Mac) menu to open the **Template Manager**.

As shown in the image below, the **Template Manager** lists all templates available in your Camtasia installation, including the template you created in the previous section.

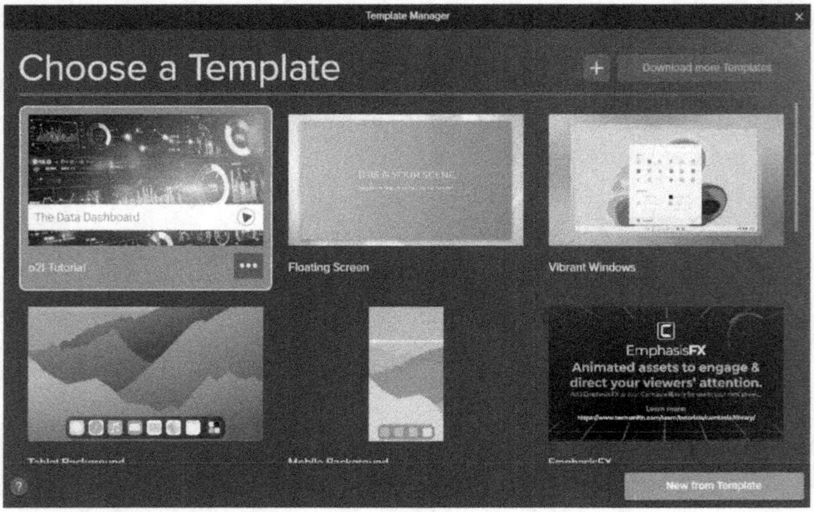

*09_31.png - The **Template Manager** lists all templates available in your Camtasia installation.*

You can use the Template Manager to create a new project based on the selected template. To do this, select a template and click **New from Template** in the lower-right corner of the window, or double-click the selected template.

You can also do the following from the **Template Manager** window:

- In the upper right-hand corner, **Download More Templates** takes you to https://library.techsmith.com, where you can access a wide selection of additional templates available for download.

- In the lower-right corner of every template, click the three-dot icon to rename, delete, or export the selected template. Exporting saves the template on your computer as a ***.camtemplate*** file.
- In the upper-right corner of the **Template Manager**, the + icon lets you import ***.camtemplate*** files shared by other users.

Note that you cannot open an existing template for editing. To edit a template, start by creating a new project based on the template you want to edit, make the necessary changes in the newly created project, and save it as a new template. You can then delete the old version of the template from the **Template Manager**.

G. Importing and Exporting Packages

In this chapter, you discovered a wide range of tools designed to enhance and customize your Camtasia installation: themes, custom libraries, favorites, presets, keyboard shortcuts, and templates. Each of these elements can be exported individually and shared with other users.

In this section, you'll discover a unique way to easily export these resources and make sharing them a breeze.

1. Make sure you have a project open in Camtasia. It can be a new, empty project.
2. Navigate to **File > Export > Package**.

This opens the **Export Package** dialog, as shown in the following image.

*09_32.png – The **Export Package** dialog.*

A *package* is a single export file that lets you bundle templates, themes, custom libraries, keyboard shortcuts, favorites, and custom presets. Just select the items you want to include in the package and click **Export** in the lower-right corner of the window. The resulting ***.campackage*** file can be shared with other Camtasia users, who will use the **File > Import > Package** menu item to import all items included in the package in a single step.

H. Conclusion

The tools covered in this chapter are all designed to increase your productivity and help you maintain visual consistency across multiple projects.

You started by saving the key pieces of your brand identity in a theme. This gives you instant access to your organization's colors, fonts, and logo in the Properties panel of Camtasia.

Next, you explored libraries. These let you save an unlimited number of reusable elements, which you can then use in any project. The **Quick Properties Editor** lets you choose which properties are displayed in the Properties panel, so you can quickly adapt these library items to your current project.

You can also customize the tool panels on the left side of the interface using your custom presets. Populating the **Favorites** panel with your unique set of preferred tools is another way to customize Camtasia and streamline your workflows.

Finally, templates let you speed up and standardize creating new projects.

Whether you're a beginner or a seasoned Camtasia user, themes, libraries, shortcuts, presets, favorites, and templates will quickly become valuable allies that facilitate teamwork while helping you rapidly create high-quality projects that align with your organization's visual identity.

Making Your Videos Interactive

Active learning boosts retention, sharpens focus, and fuels engagement, regardless of the delivery modality. Whether face-to-face or virtual, it is essential for instructors and teachers to embed interactivity at the heart of every training program they design and deliver.

However, videos typically offer a linear, non-interactive experience. Your audience watches without interacting; they consume without participating. The video plays from start to finish, with no branching options, no clickable elements, and no built-in assessments.

Fortunately, Camtasia offers several tools for adding interactivity to your video projects. For example, you can provide your audience with an interactive table of contents for instant navigation, use *Interactive Hotspots* to pause the video until the learner clicks, and even embed quizzes directly into the video.

These interactive elements only work when the video is played using the Smart Player, a special video player provided by Camtasia. Publishing to YouTube or Vimeo removes this interactivity, as these platforms replace the Smart Player with their own video player, which does not support Camtasia's unique interactive features.

The tools presented in this chapter are primarily intended for eLearning developers who have access to a SCORM compliant LMS (Learning

Management System) capable of hosting this type of interactive learning content.

SCORM (Sharable Content Object Reference Model) is a set of standards and specifications used in the eLearning industry to enable communication between learning content and the Learning Management System (LMS) on which it is hosted. We'll delve further into SCORM and into creating SCORM packages with Camtasia in *Chapter 11 – Exporting your videos*.

A. Preparing the Exercises

The hands-on exercises in this chapter are based on the provided exercise files. These are compressed projects that you must first import into Camtasia using the import process described at the beginning of Chapter 5 – Editing Your Video.

1. Download and unzip the exercises for Chapter 10.
2. Import the ***Chapter10/projects/01_02_dashboard.zip*** project into the ***Chapter10*** folder of the exercises.
3. Also import the closed captions from the ***Chapter10/resources/01_02dashboard.srt*** file.
4. Watch the entire project to refresh your memory.

You are now ready to start exploring the interactive features of Camtasia.

B. Working with Markers

Markers are reference points that you can insert anywhere in your project. Although not interactive on their own, they are essential for creating a clickable table of contents and for defining *Interactive Hotspots.*

1. Use the **View > Show Markers** menu item or the `Ctrl + M` keyboard shortcut (Mac and Windows) to display the marker tracks.

After enabling the marker tracks, focus your attention on the timeline at the bottom of the screen.

- Every clip on the timeline now includes a narrow marker track (1 in the image below)
- The project has its own marker track, located just below the timecode ruler (2 in the following image).

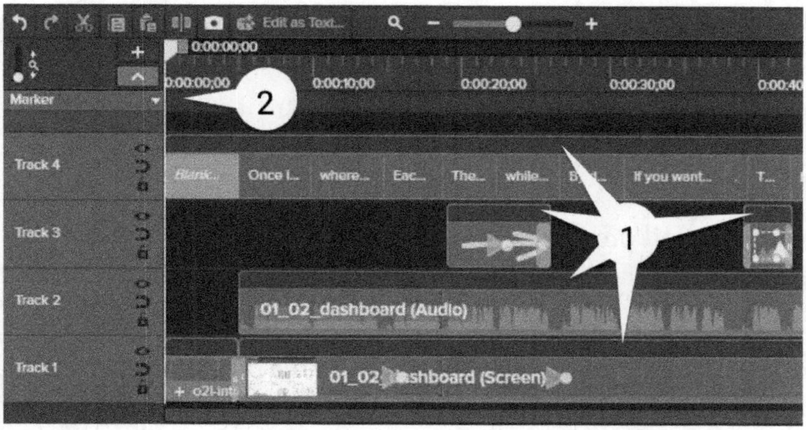

10_01.png - The marker track for each clip (1) plus that for the timeline (2).

You will now define new markers within these marker tracks.

2. Position the mouse in the project marker track, just below the timecode ruler.

When doing so, a blue diamond and a vertical line appear on the timeline at the current mouse position.

3. Move the mouse along the marker track in order to position the vertical blue line immediately after the transition between the intro and the screen recording.
4. When the blue vertical line is around timecode *0:00:05;15*, click to create a first marker.
5. If necessary, drag the marker on the timeline to adjust its position.

After completing these steps, a new marker is visible on the timeline, as shown in the image below.

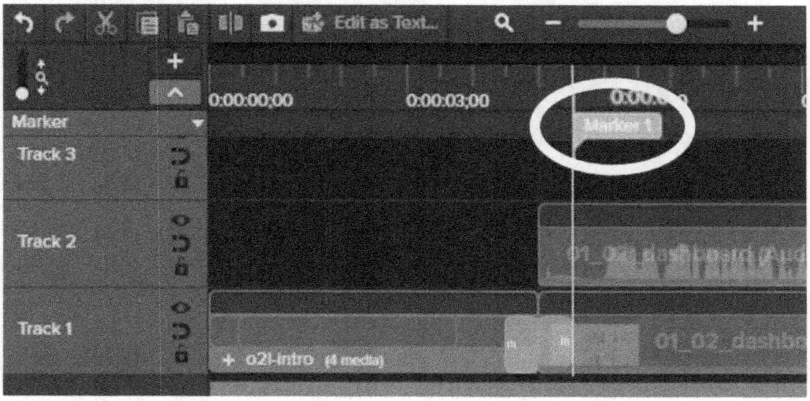

10_02.png - A first marker is visible in the timeline.

You will now change the name of the marker in the Properties panel.

6. Make sure the Properties panel is open on the right side of the screen and that the new marker is currently selected in the timeline.
7. Type **Dashboard** in the **Marker name** field of the Properties panel and press **Enter** to validate.

The **Thumbnail** property shows the image that appears on the canvas at the marker. Camtasia automatically updates the thumbnail whenever you move the marker in the timeline.

Since you placed this first marker just below the timecode ruler, the marker is linked to the project. You can also link a marker to a specific clip in the timeline using the following steps:

8. Position the playhead at timecode **0:00:57;00**.
9. Position the mouse pointer in the marker track of the screen recording on track 1 of the timeline at the playhead position.
10. Click to drop a second marker.
11. Enter **Enlarging a Chart** in the **Marker name** field of the Properties panel and press **Enter**.

As shown in the image below, the marker is located in the screen recording marker track rather than in the main project marker track.

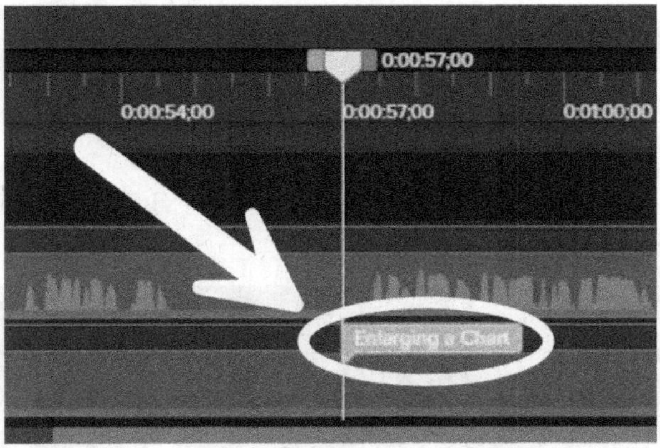

10_03.png - The second mark is linked to the screen recording.

Since the marker is linked to the screen recording, moving this clip on the timeline also moves the marker, which keeps the marked event in sync with the flow of the video.

You will now add one last marker to this project using the following steps:

12. Position the playhead at timecode *0:01:14;00*.

13. At this point, create an additional marker linked to the screen recording.
14. Name it `Data Page` in the Properties panel.

Three markers are now visible in the timeline. The first one is linked to the project, while the other two are linked to the screen recording that sits on track 1.

You shouldn't notice anything different when playing the video. Remember that markers aren't interactive elements per se. For now, their only benefit is to help you better structure and organize the timeline.

15. Use **View > Hide Markers** (Windows) or deselect the **View > Show Markers** menu item (Mac) to hide the marker tracks in the timeline.

Even though marker tracks are hidden, the markers themselves are still visible on the timeline. Look for the tiny blue triangles scattered throughout the project at the marker positions.

When using Camtasia Recorder to capture a PowerPoint presentation, markers are automatically added for each new slide in the presentation.

In the next chapter - Exporting your Videos, you'll use these markers to automatically generate a table of contents for this project. But for now, let's explore another interactive feature of Camtasia.

C. Working With Interactive Hotspots

This section walks you through the *Interactive Hotspot* effect in Camtasia. Let's kick things off by importing a new project.

1. Save and close any currently open projects.
2. Import the ***Chapter10/projects/01_03_settings_interactive.zip*** file into the ***Chapter10*** folder in the exercises.
3. Also import the closed captions from the ***Chapter10/resources/01_03_interactive_settings.srt*** file.
4. Watch the entire project.

This project is a modified version of the ***01_03_settings*** project you worked with in previous chapters.

- Some animations have been removed.
- Annotations have been added in various places throughout the project.
- Five markers are visible in the timeline, just below the timecode ruler.

The *Interactive Hotspot* effect lets you turn any element in your project into a clickable button. By default, this button pauses the video and waits for the viewer to click. Clicking the button triggers an action, which typically resumes the video either from where it left off or from a marker.

5. Position the playhead at timecode *0:00:12;00*.
6. Zoom in on the timeline to get a clear view of the specific elements present at this stage of the project.

At this point in time, a prompt inviting the viewer to click the icon in the upper-right corner is displayed on the canvas, as shown below.

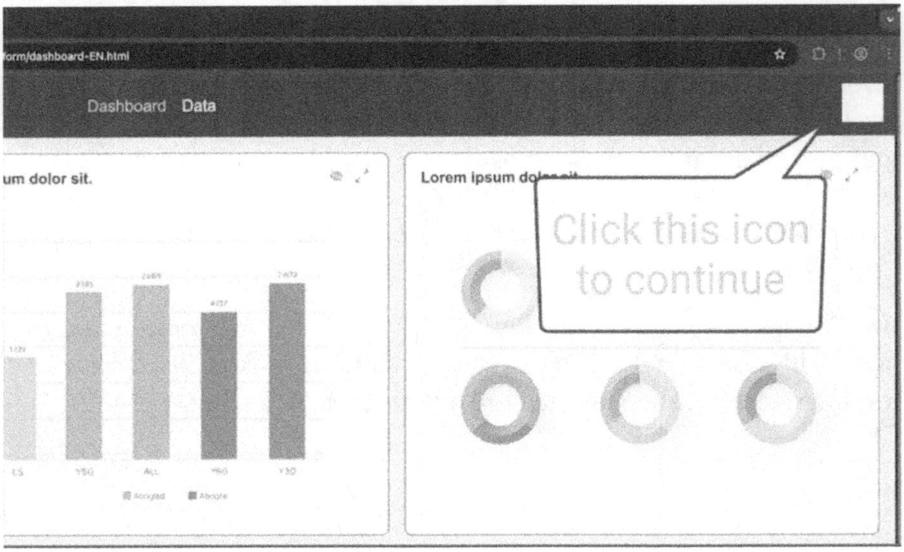

10_04.png - A prompt asking the viewer to click is displayed on the canvas.

The annotation sits on track 3 of the timeline. Track 4 contains a white square covering the icon you want the user to click. You will now use the *Interactive Hotspot* effect to turn that white square into a clickable button.

7. If necessary, zoom in to get a comfortable view of the upper-right portion of the canvas.
8. Open the **Visual Effects** panel on the left side of the screen.
9. Scroll down the panel and locate the **Interactive Hotspot** effect.
10. Drag the **Interactive Hotspot** effect from the **Visual Effects** panel and drop it onto the white square that sits on track 4 of the timeline.

The white square is now an interactive clickable element! Use the Properties panel to configure what happens when the viewer clicks it.

11. Make sure the white square is selected and open the Properties panel on the right side of the screen.

The properties for the **Interactive Hotspot** effect are located at the bottom of the Properties panel, as shown in the image below.

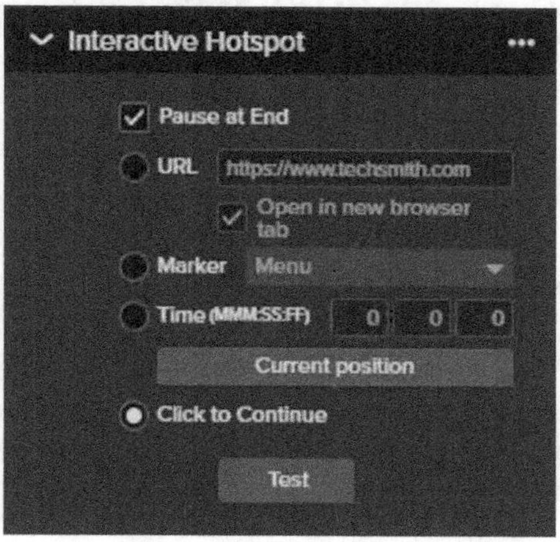

10_05.png - The properties of the ***Interactive Hotspot*** *effect.*

Pause at End is enabled by default. This option pauses the video when the playhead reaches the end of the white square.

The remaining options control what happens when the viewer clicks the button. In this example, you can keep the default **Click to Continue** action, which resumes video playback from where it left off.

The final step is to make the white square invisible.

12. At the top of the Properties panel, set the **Opacity** of the white square to 0%.

This creates the impression that users are clicking the icon, when they are actually clicking the transparent square directly above.

13. Position the playhead at timecode *0:00:18;00*.
14. Increase the height of the timeline so you can see all nine tracks.

At this point, two text annotations and four white rectangles have been added to the project. These rectangles cover the four menu items located in the upper-right corner of the canvas.

15. Drag the **Interactive Hotspot** effect from the **Visual Effects** panel and drop it on the canvas onto the topmost white rectangle on track 4.
16. In the Properties panel, select the **Marker** action.

17. Open the dropdown menu and select **Account**.

After completing these steps, the properties for the **Interactive Hotspot** should appear as shown in the image below.

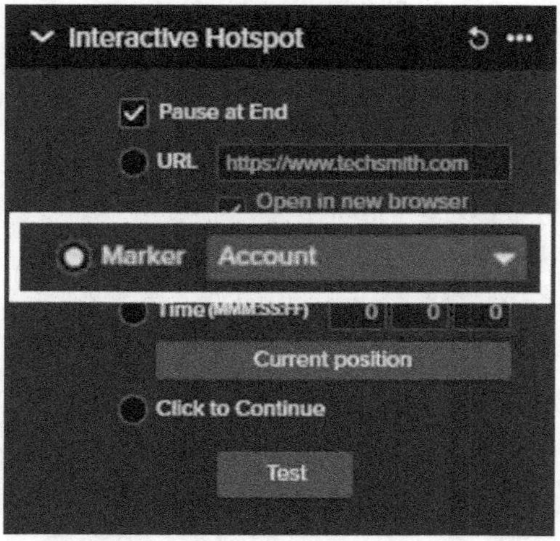

*10_06.png - The properties of the **Interactive Hotspot** after selecting **Account**.*

With this configuration, clicking the button positions the playhead at the **Account** marker (at timecode *0:00:18;04*) and resumes video playback from that point.

18. Reduce the **Opacity** of the selected rectangle to **0%** so you can see the menu item below.
19. Repeat these steps to make the other three white rectangles clickable:
    - The second rectangle goes to the **Security** marker.
    - The third one goes to the **Preferences** marker.
    - The last one goes to the **Logout** marker.
20. Also make the **Conclusions** text annotation clickable. Clicking this button takes the viewer to the **Conclusions** marker at the end of the project.

With these interactive hotspots, viewers can click the menu items to navigate the video. To ensure this navigation system works properly, each segment ends with a **Back to Menu** button, which you will now make clickable using the following steps.

21. Reduce the height of the timeline, or zoom out so you can see the entirety of the canvas.
22. Play the video.

Note that the interactive hotspots you defined earlier do not function within Camtasia, so the video does not pause, and the hotspots are not clickable.

23. Manually pause the video when you encounter the first **Back to Menu** button (at timecode *01:02:09*).
24. Use the **Interactive Hotspot** effect to make the button clickable.
25. In the Properties panel, configure the **Interactive Hotspot** so that clicking this button takes the viewer back to the **Menu** marker.
26. Repeat these steps for the other three **Back to Menu** buttons.
27. Save the project when done.

By enabling viewers to click menu items and buttons, you've created a navigation system that transforms the video into a fully interactive experience.

To wrap up this section, here is a brief recap of all the actions supported by the **Interactive Hotspot** effect.

- **URL** opens a web page when the viewer clicks the button.
- **Marker** positions the playhead to the selected marker and resumes video playback from that point.
- **Time** positions the playhead at a specified timecode. You can enter this timecode manually within the Properties panel or click **Current Position** to automatically populate the timecode for the current playhead position. Video playback then resumes from the selected timecode.
- **Click to Continue** simply un-pauses the video, so playback resumes from where it left off. This is the default action.

The **Test** button at the bottom of the Properties panel offers a quick way to check the selected action. But testing these interactions in real-world conditions (i.e., within a web browser) requires exporting the project with the Camtasia Smart Player, which you'll do in the next chapter.

D. Working With Quizzes

No matter what you teach or how you deliver your courses, you will inevitably face the challenge of student assessment. Virtually every eLearning authoring tool addresses this universal need with the ability to create interactive assessments that learners can take online.

Camtasia is no exception and provides the ability to add quizzes directly into your videos. Just like interactive hotspots discussed in the previous section, quiz questions pause the video until the viewer provides an answer.

To explore this feature, you will first import the ***02_01_quiz*** project into Camtasia.

1. Save and close any open projects.
2. Import the ***Chapter10/projects/02_01_Quiz.zip*** project into the **Chapter10** folder of the exercises.
3. Also import the ***Chapter10/resources/02_01_Quiz.srt*** captions file.
4. Watch the entire project.

This is the only project you haven't worked with yet. Take the necessary time to inspect its components, behaviors, transitions, and effects. You should recognize many of the features covered in previous chapters.

1. Inserting a Quiz

The process for inserting a quiz into your project is very similar to the process for inserting markers.

1. Position the playhead at timecode *0:00:41;10*.
2. Use **View > Show Quizzes** or the `Ctrl + Q` keyboard shortcut (Mac and Windows) to show the *Quiz Tracks*.

Just like the Markers Tracks mentioned earlier, *Quiz tracks* can be found at the following two locations within the timeline.

- Each multimedia element has its own dedicated *Quiz Track*, allowing you to associate quizzes with any clip in the timeline.
- The project has its own *Quiz Track*, which appears just below the timecode ruler.

In this example, you will attach a quiz to the background image that sits on track 1 of the timeline.

3. Position the mouse within the *Quiz Track* for the background image on track 1 of the timeline at the playhead position.
4. Click to create a new quiz.

As shown in the image below, a green marker highlights the location of a quiz.

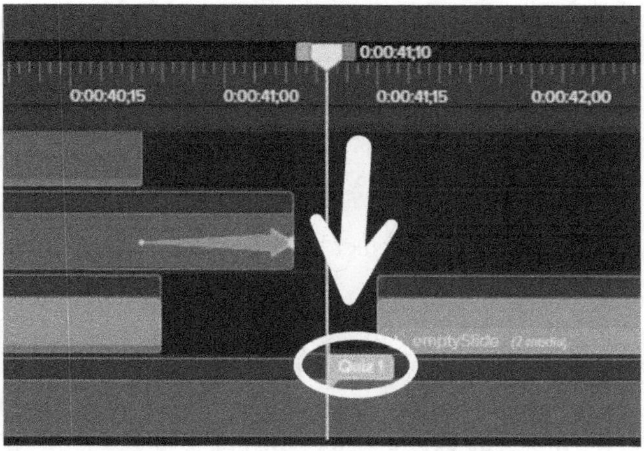

10_07.png - A green marker highlights the location of a quiz.

You can have multiple quizzes in a single Camtasia project, each with an unlimited number of questions.

2. Configuring Quiz Properties

In this section, you will review the properties of the new quiz, which are available in the Properties panel.

1. Click the green marker to select the quiz you created earlier.
2. Open the Properties panel on the right side of the screen.

The quiz properties are organized into two tabs, as shown in the image below.

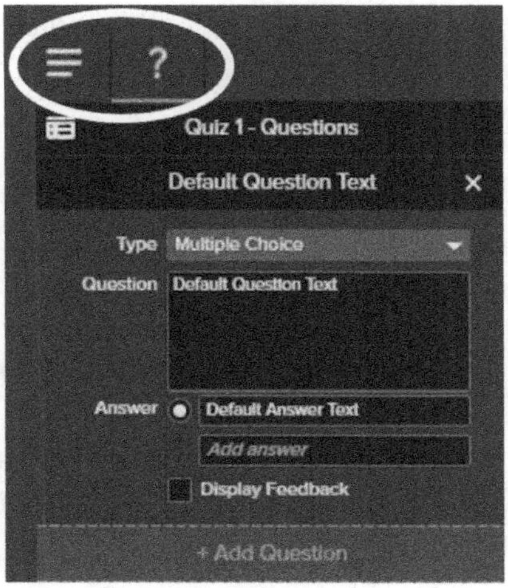

10_08.png - The quiz properties are organized into two tabs.

Use the first tab to configure the quiz properties and the second to define and organize the quiz questions. Note that the second tab is selected by default.

3. Select the first tab to see the quiz properties.
4. Type `Final Quiz` in the **Quiz Name** field and press `Enter`.

The other two properties are selected by default.

- The **Score Quiz** checkbox lets you define a graded assessment. Deselect it to create quizzes that do not need to be graded (i.e., with no right or wrong answers), such as satisfaction surveys.
- Deselecting **User can view their results** prevents Camtasia from displaying the quiz results at the end of the quiz. However, this does not affect the data transfer to your LMS, so learners may still be able to view their scores on your learning platform.

For this exercise, leave both boxes selected to use the default settings, creating a graded quiz that allows learners to view their results immediately after completing it.

3. Defining Quiz Questions

Now that the quiz properties are configured, let's add some questions.

1. Select the second tab in the Properties panel, identified with a question mark icon.
2. Open the ***Chapter10/resources/02_01_questions.pdf*** file in your default PDF reader.
3. Open the **Type** dropdown and take note of the four question types supported by Camtasia.
4. Select **Multiple Choice**.
5. Copy the first question stem from the PDF file and paste it into the **Question** field of the Properties panel.
6. Similarly, copy and paste the four answer choices.
7. Select the third choice as the correct answer.
8. Select the **Display Feedback** checkbox.
9. Copy and paste the *Positive feedback* from the PDF file into the **If correct** field and the *Negative feedback* into the **If incorrect** field.

As shown in the image below, the first question is now correctly defined in the Properties panel.

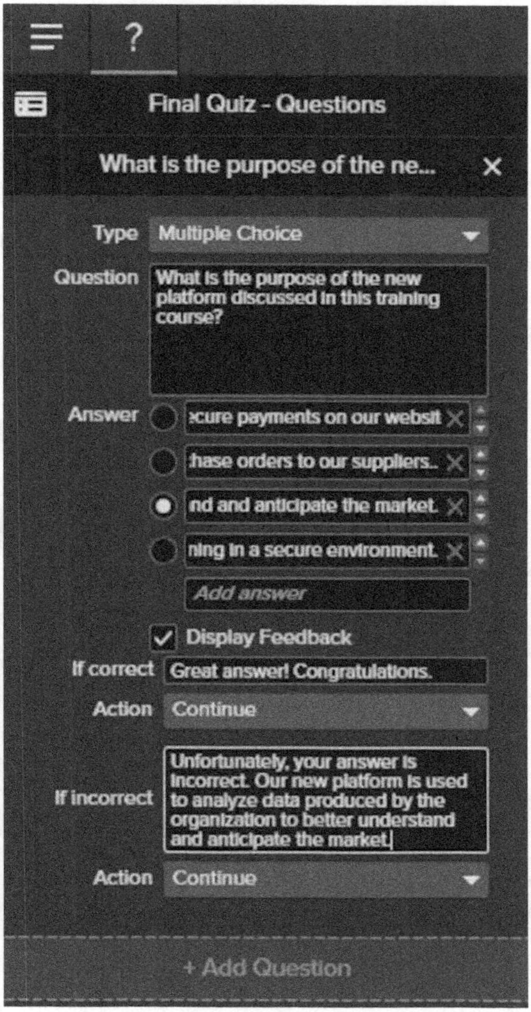

10_09.png - The first quiz question is defined in the Properties panel.

You will now use the same process to define the other two questions.

10. Click **Add question** at the bottom of the Properties panel.
11. Use the instructions in the PDF document to select the appropriate question type and copy the content into the corresponding fields of the Properties panel.

Note that the form in the Properties panel varies according to the question type. For example, when defining a *Fill in the blank* question, you must include a comprehensive list of all acceptable answers. Camtasia will compare the learner's response against this list and consider the answer correct when an exact match is found.

4. Editing and Deleting Questions

To edit or delete existing questions, select the desired quiz (green marker) in the timeline and navigate to the second tab of the Properties panel.

1. In the timeline, click the **Final Quiz** green marker to select your quiz.
2. Navigate to the second tab of the Properties panel.

From here, you can edit existing questions or add new ones.

You can also reorder the questions or even delete them using the buttons shown in the image below (on a Mac, the buttons are reversed).

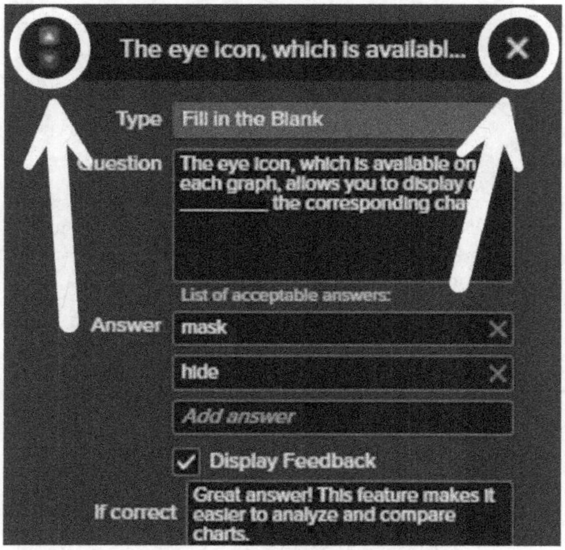

10_10.png - These icons let you reorder or delete questions.

5. Testing the Quiz

Just as with interactive hotspots, a specific video player is required to test the quiz under real-world conditions. However, you can perform an initial test directly within Camtasia using the following steps:

1. Make sure the quiz is selected in the timeline and the Properties panel is open on the right side of the screen.
2. Select the first tab in the Properties panel to access the quiz properties.
3. Click **Preview**.

The quiz pops up in a floating window, giving you a first glimpse of the experience awaiting your viewers.

E. Conclusion

The vast majority of video tutorials available online offer a passive viewing experience: the content is played in the order set by the video creator in the timeline of their editing software. It is this linear, non-interactive experience that prevails on most major video hosting platforms.

The tools covered in this chapter give you the power to completely redefine this user experience. Making your videos interactive puts the viewer in the driver's seat. In the most advanced examples, each viewer follows their own path through the video, depending on the interactive hotspots they click and how they answer quiz questions. This means that viewers will not necessarily watch the video in the order defined in the video editing application's timeline. In fact, viewers may not even see all the sequences or, conversely, they may view certain parts of the project multiple times. The experience is said to be *non-linear* and *interactive*.

Camtasia offers several tools to let you build this interactivity. First, you learned about *Markers*, which allow you to place reference points in your project. These reference points are linked either to the project itself or to a specific media clip. Next, you discovered the *Interactive Hotspot* effect, which allows you to turn any element in the project into a clickable area that triggers an action when clicked by the user. Finally, you inserted a *Quiz* into your project.

By the end of this chapter, you probably feel both excited and frustrated. Excited by the world of new possibilities offered by these interactive tools, and frustrated that you haven't yet been able to fully test and experiment with them. Remember that these interactive features require a special video player provided by Camtasia, known as the *Smart Player*. This interactive video player, along with other options for exporting and producing your videos, will be covered in the next chapter.

Exporting Your Videos

All the sequences for your online training course are now fully finalized within Camtasia. To get to this point, you went through three major steps. It all began with the *pre-production* step, where you met with subject matter experts (SME), scripted the content, sourced visuals, and defined the best instructional approach. Next came the *Recording* step, during which you produced the raw footage for your videos (the rushes). This includes footage shot in a studio or on location, as well as screen recordings made with Camtasia Recorder. Finally, during the *post-production* step, you trimmed errors, organized clips on the timeline, added effects, polished narration, inserted background music, created subtitles, and more.

Your work is currently saved as Camtasia projects (with a ***.tscproj*** file extension on Windows or ***.cmproj*** on Mac), which can only be opened with Camtasia. The final step of the workflow is to export your projects to a universal video format so your audience can view your videos and take the course without installing Camtasia on their computer.

Most of the time, you'll export your projects as ***.mp4*** files, but there are many variations and options available to help you optimize the exported video. Let's explore these options more closely in this chapter.

A. Producing a Local File

First, let's look at the most common export method. It generates a standard ***.mp4*** video file directly on your computer, which can then be uploaded to any hosting service supporting the ***.mp4*** format.

1. Download and unzip the exercises for Chapter 11
2. Import the ***Chapter11/projects/00_00_trailer.zip*** project into the ***Chapter 11*** folder of the exercises.
3. Watch the entire project to refresh your memory and to double-check one last time that everything is ready for export.

This project is a social media trailer for your online course and includes *Dynamic Captions*. Remember that this type of caption is always visible to all users, so there is no need for a specific button to turn them on or off.

4. Click **Export** in the upper-right corner of the interface.
5. Select **Local File**.

The dialog box that opens lets you define the name and location of your ***.mp4*** file. Camtasia automatically uses the project name as the default file name, which is perfectly fine for this exercise.

6. Select the ***Chapter11/export*** folder of the exercises as the export location.
7. Leave all other options at their default and click **Export**.

The duration of this resource-intensive rendering process largely depends on the length of the video and on the available hardware resources. Exporting long videos on an older computer can take several dozen minutes.

8. When the export completes, click **Open File Location** (Windows) or **Reveal in Finder** (Mac).
9. Double-click *00_00_trailer.mp4* to open the video.

The exported file no longer opens in Camtasia, but directly within your computer's default media player. This demonstrates the ability to play the video outside of Camtasia using any ***.mp4*** compatible media player.

If you reimport the exported ***.mp4*** back into Camtasia, you will no longer be able to access its individual components separately. During export, all tracks in the timeline are merged into a single video file. To edit this video, reopen the corresponding Camtasia project, make your edits, then export a new ***.mp4*** file.

Congratulations on completing your first Camtasia project! The ***00_00_trailer*** project has gone through every stage of the production process: from pre-production through recording and editing to final export.

1. Exploring the Export Options

In the previous section, you exported a first video using Camtasia's default export settings. These defaults work fine for most projects, but you can adjust several options to optimize the resulting file.

1. Save and close any open projects.
2. Import the ***Chapter11/projects/01_01_loginLogout.zip*** project into the ***Chapter 11*** folder of the exercises.
3. Watch the entire video to refresh your memory.

This is the project you created in Chapter 02 – A First Video with Camtasia Rev. This version of the project includes the intro and outro you created in Chapter 09 – Expanding and Customizing Camtasia, and the audio compression effect has been applied to the audio track. However, it does not include any closed captions.

4. Click **Export** in the upper right-hand corner of the screen.
5. Select **Local File.**
6. Select the ***Chapter11/export*** folder of the exercises as the export location.

Before clicking **Export**, let's take a moment to explore the main options in this dialog box. These are slightly different depending on your operating system.

1. On Windows

Let's start by exploring the options available on Windows. If you work on a Mac, you can skip ahead to the next section.

1. Open the **File Type** dropdown.

As shown in the image below, Camtasia offers several export formats for your project.

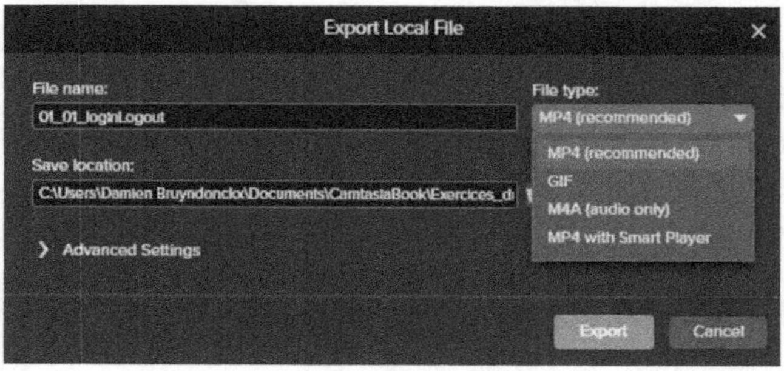

11_01.png - Camtasia offers several export formats for your project.

For example, you can export just the audio track as a ***.m4a*** file, which is useful for editing the audio in a dedicated application or converting this project into an audio podcast.

MP4 with Smart Player exports the video along with Camtasia's proprietary media player. Remember that this player is required to enable the interactive features discussed in the previous chapter. You'll learn more about it in the Using the Smart Player section later in this chapter.

2. For this exercise, stick with **MP4 (recommended)**.
3. Click **Advanced Settings** in the lower-left corner of the **Export Local File** dialog.

As shown in the image below, this gives you access to three tabs containing the advanced export options available in Camtasia for Windows.

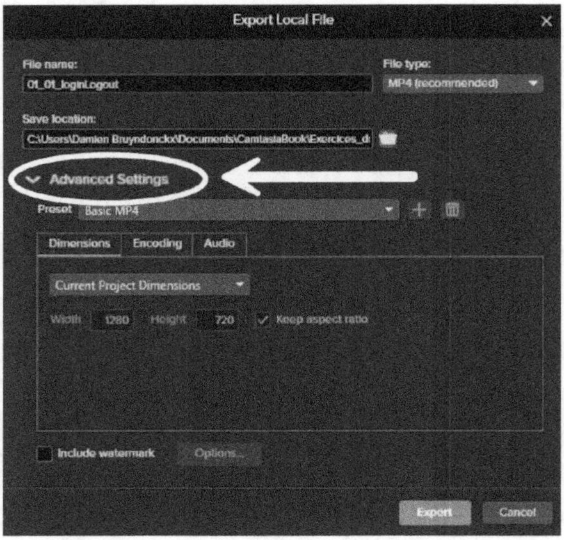

11_02.png – The advanced export options in Camtasia for Windows.

Take a moment to review these options. Most of the time, these defaults work just fine.

- By default, the exported video automatically adopts the same **Dimensions** as the canvas.
- The **Encoding** tab lets you configure the encoding settings for your ***.mp4*** video. If your video hosting service has specific technical requirements, you can adjust them here to ensure compatibility.
- The **Audio** tab lets you adjust the audio bitrate. A higher bitrate yields better audio but produces larger files. Conversely, a lower bitrate saves space at the expense of audio quality.

At the bottom of the dialog box, notice the ability to include a watermark, such as a logo or copyright notice, to your videos.

If you're using the free trial edition of Camtasia, a watermark is automatically added to all your videos. This is the only difference between the free trial and the licensed version of the application.

For the purposes of this exercise, you can keep all these settings at their defaults.

4. Keep all settings at their defaults and click **Export**.

The export process for your second video now begins. It should take anywhere from a few seconds to several minutes, depending on your computer's performance.

2. On Mac

On a Mac, you'll find the export settings at the bottom of the export window, as shown in the following screenshot.

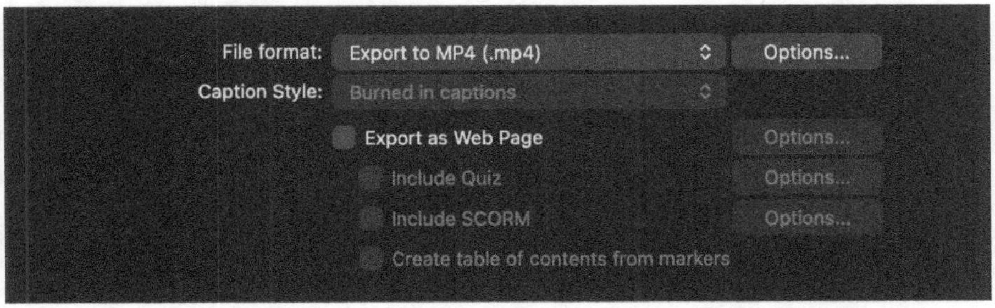

11_03.png - The advanced export options in Camtasia for Mac.

Let's explore some of them using the following steps:

1. Open the **File Format** dropdown and take note of the available options.
2. For this exercise, choose **Export to MP4 (.mp4)**.
3. Click **Option** next to the **File Format** dropdown.

This opens the **Advanced Export Options** dialog in Camtasia for Mac. Take a moment to review the available options. In most cases, the default configuration works just fine.

- By default, the exported video automatically adopts the same **Dimensions** as the canvas.

- The **Video** section of the dialog lets you configure the encoding settings for your ***.mp4*** video. If your video hosting platform has specific technical requirements, you can adjust them here to ensure compatibility.
- The **Audio** section lets you adjust the audio bitrate. A higher bitrate yields better audio but produces larger files. Conversely, a lower bitrate saves space at the expense of audio quality.

For the purposes of this exercise, you can keep all these settings at their defaults.

4. Leave all settings at their default values and click **OK** to close the **Advanced Export Options** dialog.
5. Click **Export** in the bottom right-hand corner of the window.

The export process for the second video has now begun. It should take anywhere from a few seconds to several minutes, depending on your computer's performance.

2. Exporting With Burned-In Captions

In Chapter 08 – Working with Audio, you've added captions and subtitles to several videos in your online course. As a reminder, Camtasia supports the following two types of captions.

- Eye-catching *Dynamic Captions* are widely used on social media to boost the visual impact of your message. They are always visible and cannot be turned off by viewers.
- *Closed captions* improve the accessibility of your videos, especially for hearing-impaired viewers. They can usually be toggled on and off by the viewer during playback.

In this section, you'll explore one option for displaying closed captions in the exported video.

1. Make sure the ***Chapter11/01_01_loginLogout*** project is open in Camtasia.
2. Import the ***Chapter11/resources/01_01_loginLogout.srt*** caption file into the ***01_01_loginLogout*** project.
3. Click **Export** in the upper right-hand corner of the screen.
4. Select **Local File.**
5. Select the ***Chapter11/export*** folder of the exercises as the export location and type `01_01_loginLogout_captions` as the file name.
6. [*Windows only*] Open the **Advanced Settings** at the bottom of the **Export Local File** window.

Windows users will now see a **Captions** tab in the **Advanced Settings** panel, while on Mac the **Caption Style** dropdown is enabled in the lower section of the export window.

7. Select the **Captions** tab of the **Advanced Settings** (Windows) or open the **Caption Style** dropdown (Mac)

When playing the video, the button allowing the viewer to turn the captions on and off is built into the Smart Player. If you choose to export your video without the Smart Player, you can enable closed captions in two different ways.

- One option is to export the video without any caption and save the closed captions separately using the **File > Export > Captions** menu item. Most video hosting services (such as YouTube, Vimeo, and most LMSs) allow you to upload this caption file along with the video, giving viewers the option to turn captions on or off using the controls built into the media players used by these platforms.
- The other option is to export the video with *Burned-in captions.* These are permanently embedded in the video, just like any other element in the timeline. This means they are always visible and cannot be turned off by the viewer during playback.

For this exercise, you will explore *Burned-in* captions. In the next section, you'll use the *Smart Player* to let viewers toggle captions on and off during playback.

8. Select the **Render video with open (always visible) captions** (Windows) or select **Burned in captions** in the **Caption Style** dropdown (Mac).
9. Click **Export**.
10. [*Windows only*] Click **Continue** to acknowledge the warning and start the export process.
11. When the export process completes, click **Open File Location** (Windows) or **Reveal in Finder** (Mac).
12. Double click the *01_01_loginLogout_captions.mp4* file.

During playback, the closed captions remain visible throughout the entire video, as shown in the image below.

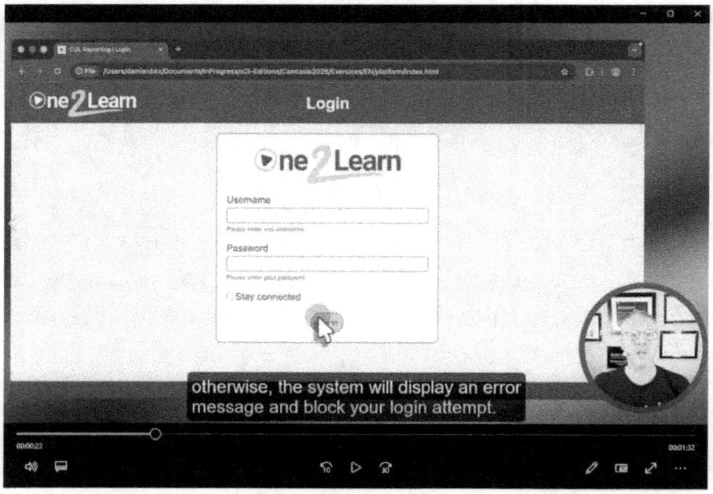

11_04.png - Burned-in captions in Windows Media Player.

B. Working With the Smart Player

So far in this chapter, you have learned how to export ***.mp4*** videos directly to your computer. Because the ***.mp4*** format does not support interactivity, learners can only watch these videos passively from start to finish.

In this section, it is finally time to discover the *Smart Player*, a special video player designed to support the interactive features offered by Camtasia.

1. Working with Interactive Closed Captions

In the previous section, you exported your video with *burned in captions*, meaning captions that are permanently baked into the ***.mp4*** file and cannot be hidden during playback. In this section, you will export the same project again, but with interactive closed captions that viewers can toggle on and off.

1. Open the ***Chapter11/01_01_loginLogout*** project in Camtasia.
2. Click **Export** in the upper right-hand corner of the screen.
3. Select **Local File**.
4. Select the ***Chapter11/export*** folder of the exercises as the export location.

From this point on, the steps differ depending on whether you're on Mac or Windows. Refer to the section corresponding to your operating system for further instructions.

1. On Windows

Here are the next steps if you're using Windows:

1. Open the **File Type** dropdown and select **MP4 with Smart Player**.
2. If needed, open the **Advanced Settings** section at the bottom of the **Export Local File** dialog.
3. Select the **Smart Player** tab of the **Advanced Settings**.
4. Click **Additional Smart Player Options**.
5. Make sure the **Captions** checkbox is selected.
6. Open the **Caption Type** dropdown and select **Closed Captions**.

At this point, the **Smart Player Options** dialog should look like the image below.

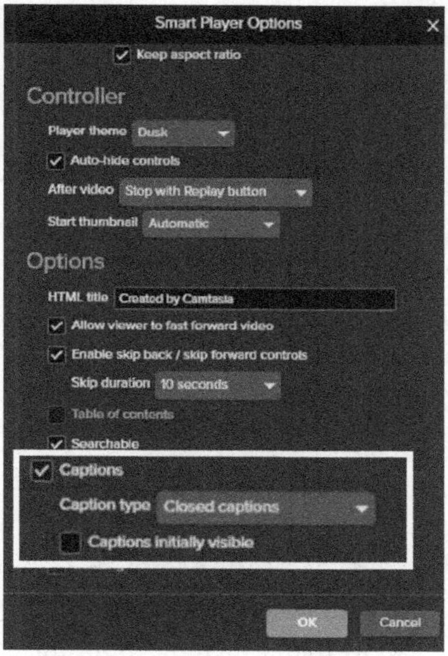

11_05.png - The Smart Player options for exporting closed captions on Windows.

Before moving on, take note of the **Captions initially visible** option, which lets you decide whether captions are visible by default or not. The other available options will be covered later in this chapter.

7. Click **OK** to validate these choices and close the **Smart Player Options** window.
8. Click **Export**.
9. When the export is complete, click **Open File Location**.

You can now proceed directly to the Testing Closed Captions section.

2. On Mac

Here are the next steps if you're using a Mac:

1. Select **Export as Web Page** in the lower section of the export window.

This is the checkbox that enables *Smart Player* export in Camtasia for Mac.

2. Open the **Caption Type** dropdown and select **Closed Captions**.

At this point, the export settings on your Mac should look like the image below.

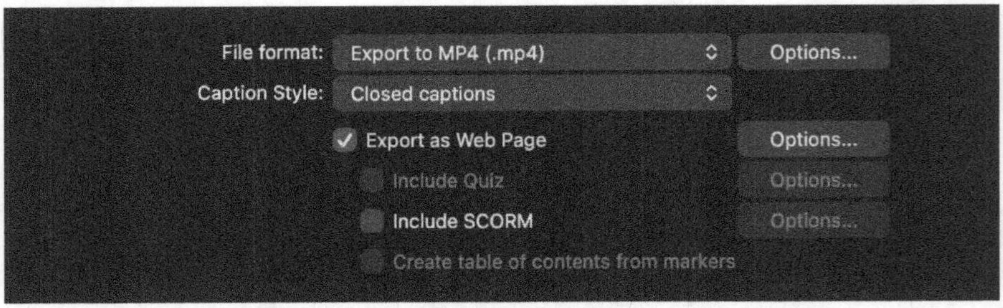

11_06.png - The options for exporting closed captions with the Smart Player on Mac.

The other Smart Player options will be covered later in this chapter.

3. Click **Export**.
4. When the export completes, click **Reveal in Finder**.

In the next section, you'll test these closed captions in real-world conditions.

3. Testing the Closed Captions

Selecting **MP4 with Smart Player** (Windows) or **Export as Web Page** (Mac) instructs Camtasia to generate both the ***.mp4*** video *and* the Smart Player. Because of that, the export folder includes both the standard video file as well as several other files used by the Smart Player.

To ensure proper operation of the Smart Player, all the files and subfolders contained in the export must remain exactly as is. Renaming, moving, or modifying any of these items will prevent the Smart Player from working properly.

The Camtasia *Smart Player* is an HTML5 application that runs natively in most modern web browsers and mobile devices. All the additional files generated by Camtasia are required for this application to work properly.

1. Navigate to the ***Chapter11/export/01_01_loginLogout*** folder of the exercises.

2. Double-click the ***01_01_loginLogout.html*** (Windows) or ***index.html*** (Mac) file.

As shown in the following image, the project opens in your default web browser rather than in a standard media player.

11_07.png - The project opens in your default web browser.

You will now explore the basic features of the Camtasia Smart Player using the following steps:

3. Click Play in the middle of the screen to start playing the project.
4. Hover your mouse over the playing video to reveal a set of icons at the bottom of the Smart Player.

Use these icons to control playback (play/pause), adjust the audio volume, change the playback speed and enable full-screen. The icon highlighted in the image below lets you toggle the closed captions on and off.

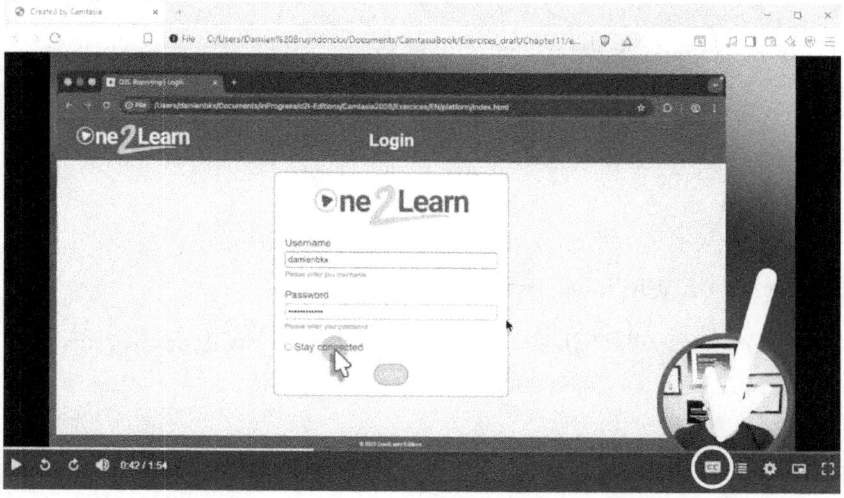

11_08.png - The highlighted icon lets you toggle the closed captions on and off.

At the end of this section, you've had a first glimpse of the Smart Player and viewers can now toggle captions on and off during playback.

2. Generating a Table of Contents From Markers.

You'll now revisit the ***01_02_dashboard*** project, in which you added markers in the previous chapter. These markers will now be used to automatically generate a table of contents for the video. Viewers will be able to click the TOC entries to navigate the project, so it must be exported with Camtasia's Smart Player.

1. Save and close any open projects.
2. Import the ***Chapter11/projects/01_02_dashboard.zip*** project into the ***Chapter11*** folder of the exercises.
3. Also import the closed captions from the ***Chapter11/resources/01_02_dashboard.srt*** file.

Here's a quick recap of the interactive elements you incorporated into this project in previous chapters:

- In Chapter 08 – Working with Audio, you added Closed Captions.
- In Chapter 10 – Making Your Videos Interactive, you dropped three markers onto the project timeline.

You will now export this project with the Smart Player and generate a clickable table of contents based on these three markers.

4. Click **Export** in the upper-right corner of the screen.
5. Select **Local File.**
6. Select the ***Chapter11/export*** folder of the exercises as the export location.

Once again, the steps are significantly different, depending on your operating system.

1. On Windows

If you work on Windows, use the following steps:

1. Open the **File Type** dropdown and select **MP4 with Smart Player.**
2. If needed, open the **Advanced Settings** section.
3. Navigate to the **Smart Player** tab of the **Advanced Settings** and click **Additional Smart Player Options.**
4. Make sure the **Table of Contents** and **Searchable** checkboxes are selected.

Selecting **Table of Contents** instructs Camtasia to generate a table of contents based on the markers you inserted into the project. Selecting **Searchable** adds a search field, allowing users to find a marker with a text search.

Now let's take this opportunity to explore a few additional Smart Player options on Windows.

5. In the **Controller** section of the **Smart Player Options** dialog, deselect **Auto-hide controls**.
6. In the **Options** section, enter `Data Dashboard` in the **HTML Title** field.
7. Open the **Caption Type** dropdown and select **Under video captions**.
8. Click **OK** to save and close the **Smart Player Options** dialog.
9. Click **Export**.
10. Click **Open File Location** when the export completes.

You can now skip directly to the Testing the Table of Contents section.

2. On Mac

Use the following steps if you work on a Mac.

1. Select **Export as Web Page** to export the video with the Smart Player.
2. Also select **Create table of contents from markers**.

Let's take this opportunity to discover yet another method for exporting closed captions.

3. Open the **Caption Style** dropdown and select **Under video captions**.
4. Click **Export** in the lower-right corner of the window.
5. Click **Reveal in Finder** when the export completes.

In the next section, you will test the interactive table of contents in real-world conditions.

3. Testing the Table of Contents

Once again, Camtasia generated the Smart Player files in addition to the ***.mp4*** video file.

1. Double-click ***01_02_dashboard.html*** (Windows) or ***index.html*** (Mac) to open the project in your default web browser.
2. Click play to start playing the video.

As shown in the image below, closed captions now appear under the video. Also note that the playbar button for toggling them on and off is gone, which means closed captions are always visible.

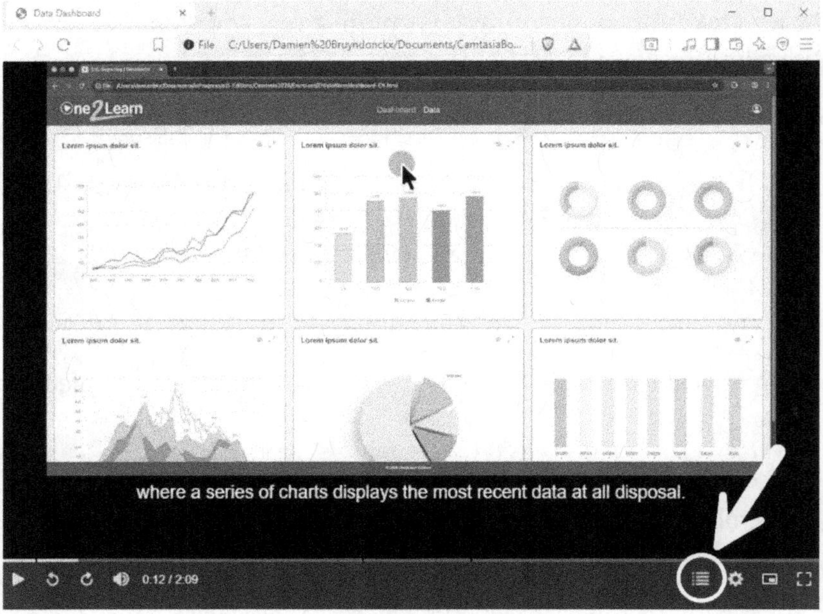

11_09.png - Closed captions now appear under the video.

To view the table of contents, just click the icon highlighted in the above image.

3. Click the highlighted icon to open the table of contents.

The clickable table of contents opens on the left side of the video. It contains one entry for each of your three markers.

*On Windows, Camtasia has also generated the **Introduction** entry at the top of the table of contents.*

4. Click the table of contents entries to navigate through the video.
5. Enter a keyword in the search field to filter the table of contents entries, then use the search results to navigate through the video.

*On Windows, the browser tab displaying your video has been renamed using the title you entered in the **HTML Title** field of the **Smart Player Options**. Unfortunately, this option is not available on Mac.*

In this section, you leveraged the markers defined in the previous chapter to create an interactive table of contents for your video.

3. Exporting an Interactive Video

In Chapter 10 – Making Your Videos Interactive, you created an interactive version of the ***01_03_settings*** project using Camtasia's *Interactive Hotspot* effect. You will now export and test this project using the Smart Player.

1. Save and close any open projects.
2. Import the ***Chapter11/projects/01_03_settings_interactive.zip*** project into the ***Chapter11*** folder of the exercises.
3. Also import the ***Chapter11/resources/01_03_settings_interactive.srt*** caption file.
4. Watch the entire project to ensure everything is ready for export.
5. Click **Export** in the upper right-hand corner of the screen and select **Local File.**
6. Select the **Chapter11/export** folder as the export destination.
7. Choose the **MP4 with Smart Player** File Type (Windows) or select **Export as Web Page** (Mac).
8. [*Windows only*] Open the **Advanced Settings** section at the bottom of the export window.
9. [*Windows only*] Navigate to the **Smart Player** tab and click **Additional Smart Player Options.**
10. [*Windows only*] Deselect the **Table of Contents** and **Searchable** checkboxes.

On Windows, these options are selected by default, but in this example, viewers will use Interactive Hotspots to navigate the video; the table of contents is therefore unnecessary.

11. Open the **Caption Type** dropdown and select **Under video captions.**
12. [*Windows only*] Click **OK.**
13. Click **Export** in the lower right-hand corner of the window.
14. After the export completes, click **Open File Location** (Windows) or **Reveal in Finder** (Mac).
15. Double-click ***01_03_settings_interactive.html*** (Windows) or ***index.html*** (Mac) to open the project in your default web browser.
16. Play the project.

As the project plays, notice how Interactive Hotspots pause the video and offer viewers a unique way to navigate the project. In addition, the *Under video captions* prevent closed captions from overlapping with the project.

4. Exporting a Quiz

In this section you'll export the ***02_01_quiz*** project you created in the previous chapter.

A quiz is a highly interactive feature where learners must be able to answer questions and receive instant feedback based on their responses. For this reason, you need to use the Smart Player when exporting a Camtasia project containing a quiz.

1. Save and close any open projects.
2. Import the ***Chapter11/projects/02_01_Quiz.zip*** project into the **Chapter11** folder of the exercises.
3. Also import the ***Chapter11/resources/02_01_Quiz.srt*** caption file.
4. Watch the entire project one last time to make sure everything is ready for publication.
5. Click **Export** in the upper-right corner of the screen and select **Local File**.
6. Select the ***Chapter11/export*** folder of the exercises as the export location.
7. [*Windows only*] Open the **Advanced Settings** section at the bottom of the **Export Local** File window.
8. [*Windows only*] Open the **Preset** dropdown menu and select **Basic MP4 with Smart Player**.

On Windows, using this preset restores all Smart Player settings to their default values and automatically exports any Quiz included in your project.

On a Mac, if the project you're exporting includes a quiz, the **Export as Web Page** and **Include Quiz** checkboxes are automatically selected.

9. Click **Export**.
10. After the export completes, click **Open File Location** (Windows) or **Reveal in Finder** (Mac).
11. Double-click the file *02_01_quiz.html* (Windows) or ***index.html*** (Mac) to open the project in your web browser.
12. Play the entire project and answer the quiz questions.

After completing this exercise, you've finally experienced your quiz in real-world conditions using the Camtasia Smart Player.

1. Editing Quiz Properties (Mac only)

Camtasia for Mac lets you edit the text labels in quiz captions and buttons. Unfortunately, this capability is missing from the Windows version.

1. With the *02_01_quiz* project open in Camtasia for Mac, click **Export** in the upper right-hand corner and select **Local File.**
2. At the bottom of the export window, click **Options** next to the **Include a Quiz** checkbox.

As shown in the image below, the **Quiz Settings** dialog allows you to modify button labels and edit the captions learners will see while taking the quiz.

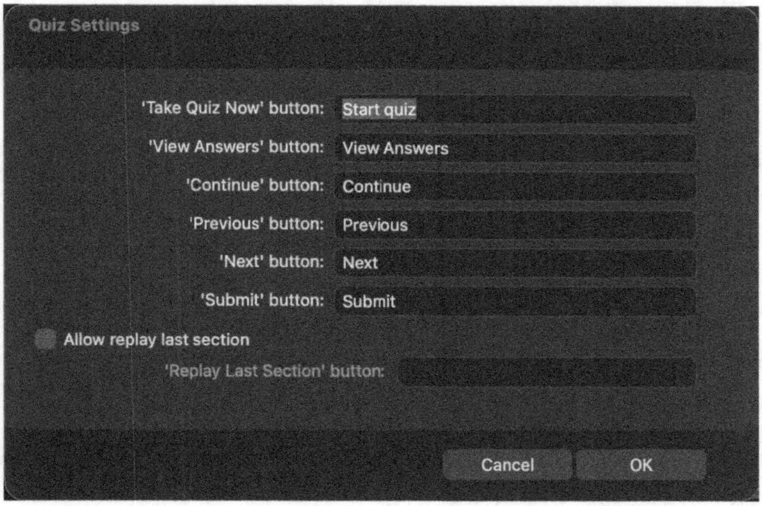

*11_10.png - The **Quiz Settings** dialog is only available in Camtasia for Mac.*

In this exercise, you can keep all the default values and cancel the project export.

2. Exporting a SCORM Package

If you want to track quiz results on your LMS, you must export your project as a SCORM package.

SCORM (*Sharable Content Object Reference Model*) is a technical specification that enables data exchange between eLearning modules and their host LMS. Two versions of the SCORM specification are in use today:

- **SCORM 1.2** was released in October 2001. To this day, countless authoring tools and LMS platforms still use SCORM 1.2.
- **SCORM 2004** is the most recent version. It has four editions, but only the 2nd, 3rd and 4th editions remain in common use today. SCORM 2004, 4th Edition, was released in March 2009.

Camtasia can generate SCORM packages compatible with all current versions and editions of the SCORM specification.

You can find more information about SCORM on the official website at https://scorm.com.

Use the following steps to export ***02_01_Quiz*** as a SCORM package.

1. Click **Export** in the upper-right corner of the screen and select **Local File.**
2. Select the ***Chapter11/export*** folder of the exercises as the export location.
3. Enter `02_01_Quiz_SCORM` as the **File name**.
4. [*Windows only*] Open the **Advanced Settings** section at the bottom of the **Export Local File** window.
5. [*Windows only*] Open the **Preset** dropdown menu and select **Basic MP4 with Smart Player.**
6. [*Windows only*] Navigate to the **Smart Player** tab of the advanced settings.
7. [*Windows only*] Select **Report Using SCORM**, then click **SCORM Options**.
8. [*Mac only*] Select **Include SCORM** at the bottom of the export window, then click the associated **Options** button.

A valid SCORM package must comply with strict rules. One of those rules is to provide a manifest file that precisely describes the eLearning module to the LMS. The window you just opened lets you configure that manifest.

The most important piece of information in the manifest file is the SCORM version used by this module. Ask your LMS administrator which version or SCORM your organization uses.

9. Open the **Version** dropdown and select the appropriate SCORM version for this module. For this exercise, the chosen version does not matter.
10. Take a moment to enter a **Title** and a **Description**.

This metadata is used by your LMS to make the content more discoverable.

11. Enter `50%` in the **Passing Score** field.

This setting is very important because it tells the LMS whether the learner has passed or failed. The LMS can use this information to grant the learner access to the next module in the learning path or to issue a certificate.

The SCORM Options window should now look like the following image.

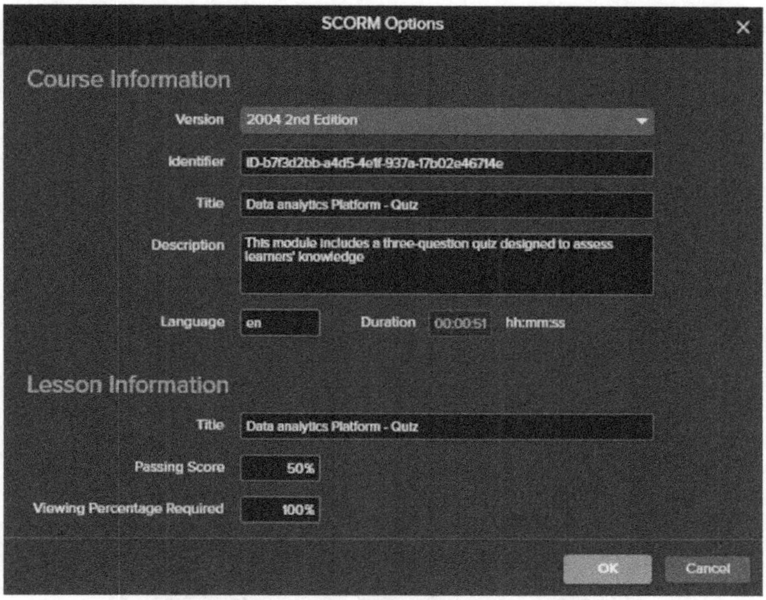

*11_11.png - The **SCORM Options** dialog box on Windows.*

While the **Manifest Options** dialog on Mac looks a little different, it offers identical properties and functionality.

*The **Identifier** field is required to ensure compliance with the SCORM specification. Camtasia automatically generates one that is guaranteed to be unique. In virtually all cases, this default identifier is perfectly valid; you can also enter a custom identifier if necessary.*

12. Leave all other options at their defaults and click **OK** to close the **SCORM options** dialog.
13. Click **Export** in the lower-right corner of the window.
14. After the export completes, click **Open File Location** (Windows) or **Reveal in Finder** (Mac).
15. [*Windows only*] Select all generated files and compress them into a ***.zip*** package using Windows Explorer.

*On Windows, make sure to compress the files created by Camtasia, not the parent folder containing them. If you compress the parent folder, the manifest file (**ims-manifest.xml**) will not be at the root of the compressed package, and the LMS will not be able to deploy your content.*

The resulting ***.zip*** file is a SCORM package ready to be deployed on your LMS. A SCORM-compliant LMS will be able to unzip this file, locate the manifest, and automatically deploy your content.

C. Other Export Options

As shown in the image below, the Camtasia **Export** menu includes several other export options worth mentioning.

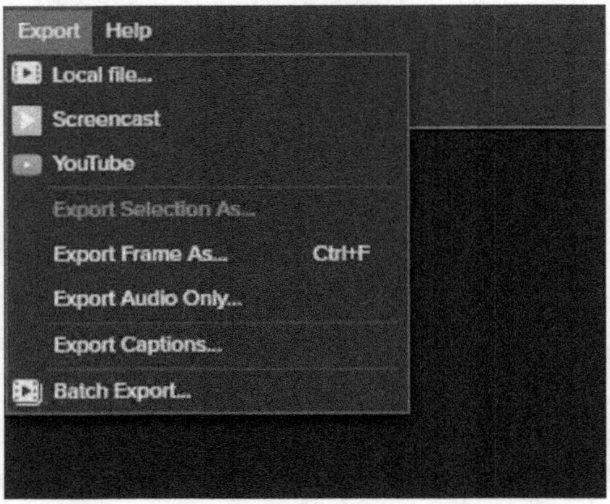

*11_12.png - The **Export** menu in Camtasia for Windows.*

On a Mac, the **Export** menu is slightly different but offers essentially the same options.

- Camtasia can export your video straight to your YouTube channel. Just remember that YouTube doesn't support the Smart Player, so any interactive features will be removed.
- **Screencast** is TechSmith's own video hosting and collaboration platform. Screencast uses the Smart Player, which means interactive features are preserved when you use this option. You'll learn more about Screencast in the next chapter.
- **Export Frame As** allows you to export the image currently displayed on the canvas.
- **Export Audio Only** extracts just the audio track from your project, allowing you to edit the audio in an external application or create audio podcasts.
- On Windows, **Export Selection As** allows you to export the portion of the project currently selected on the timeline.
- Exporting longer videos can take hours, even more so on slower computers. With **Batch Export**, you can render several videos in a single operation. Run this process in the evening before leaving the office or during your lunch break. When you return, you'll find a ready-to-use ***.mp4*** file for each of your projects.

These powerful export options give you precise control over how Camtasia exports and publishes your video projects.

D. Conclusion

Now that the export step is complete, your videos are finally ready to begin their new life, supporting your learning and communication efforts. In this chapter, you discovered the many options available in Camtasia for rendering high-quality video files.

First, you explored the options for exporting your videos locally as ***.mp4*** files. This universal export format is supported by virtually all hosting providers and learning management systems, making it the default export format for most use cases.

If your Camtasia project contains interactive elements, such as interactive captions, markers, hotspots and quizzes, you must export the *Smart Player* in addition to the video file. Camtasia can also generate SCORM packages, which makes uploading your projects to an LMS a breeze and lets you track quiz results.

Upon completing this chapter, you have reviewed the entire video creation process with Camtasia, from pre-production to final export. But Camtasia is just one piece of a larger ecosystem that includes a suite of applications and online services, which you will explore in the next and final chapter.

Exploring the Camtasia Ecosystem

As you begin this final chapter, you have already gone through every step of the video production process with Camtasia. The tools you've learned in previous chapters enable you to produce all kinds of videos, such as instructional videos, demonstrations, marketing videos, promotional videos, shorts for social media, and even feature films.

You could stop here and use Camtasia as a standalone solution. But Camtasia is just one piece of a broader ecosystem designed to speed up production, simplify distribution, and facilitate collaboration.

This is what you will learn in this final chapter. You will start with Screencast, TechSmith's free image and video hosting platform. You will then explore Camtasia Online, a browser-based tool that makes it easy to create simple videos without any installation. Finally, you'll take your first steps with Camtasia Audiate, which provides AI-powered features such as automatic transcription, text-based editing, text-to-speech, translation, script generation, and even avatar creation.

A. Hosting Videos on Screencast

Screencast is TechSmith's image and video hosting platform. Built right into Camtasia, it takes just a few clicks to publish to Screencast and share your videos with a wide audience. Its built-in discussion module makes it easy to collect feedback, ideas, and comments from all stakeholders, fostering an iterative review cycle for your videos.

All TechSmith account holders enjoy a free version of Screencast, which can store up to 25 videos. As a reminder, creating a TechSmith account is free of charge and is required to download and activate the Camtasia trial version.

Learn more about Screencast and find your perfect subscription at https://www.techsmith.com/screencast/

1. Publishing to Screencast

In this section, you will publish the ***02_02_conclusion*** project to Screencast directly from within Camtasia.

1. Download and unzip the exercises for Chapter 12
2. Import the ***Chapter12/projects/02_02_conclusion.zip*** project into the ***Chapter12*** folder of the exercises.
3. Also import the closed captions from the ***Chapter12/resources/02_02_conclusion.srt*** file.
4. Watch the entire project to ensure everything is ready for publishing.
5. Click **Export** in the upper-right corner of the screen.
6. Select **Screencast**.
7. If necessary, sign in to your TechSmith account.

As shown in the following screenshot, you can now enter a title for your video along with a brief description. The system automatically uses your project name as the default title, which is perfectly fine for this exercise.

12_01.png - *Enter the video title and description.*

The **Description** is optional and can be edited after the video is published.

8. Click **Export** (Windows) or **Share** (Mac)

As in the previous chapter, Camtasia exports the project in ***.mp4*** format, but the resulting file is uploaded to Screencast rather than stored on your computer.

9. [*Windows only*] Once the upload completes, your video opens automatically in your web browser.
10. [*Mac only*] Once the upload completes, the URL for your video is automatically copied to the clipboard. Open your browser and paste the link into the address bar to view the video.

*On a Mac, you can find the URLs for all videos uploaded to Screencast in the export history. Click **Export** in the upper-right corner of the screen and select **Export History**.*

After completing these steps, your video is available on Screencast and can be shared with your audience.

2. Sharing Your Video

By default, anyone with the link can view your video without restrictions. This works well in most cases, but for enhanced security, you can make your video private or password-protect it.

To change the access permissions for your video, you must first log in to Screencast.

1. Click **Sign In** in the upper-right corner of Screencast and enter the username and password for your TechSmith account.
2. Click the blue **Share** button underneath your video.

This opens the **Share Media** dialog, as shown in the following screenshot.

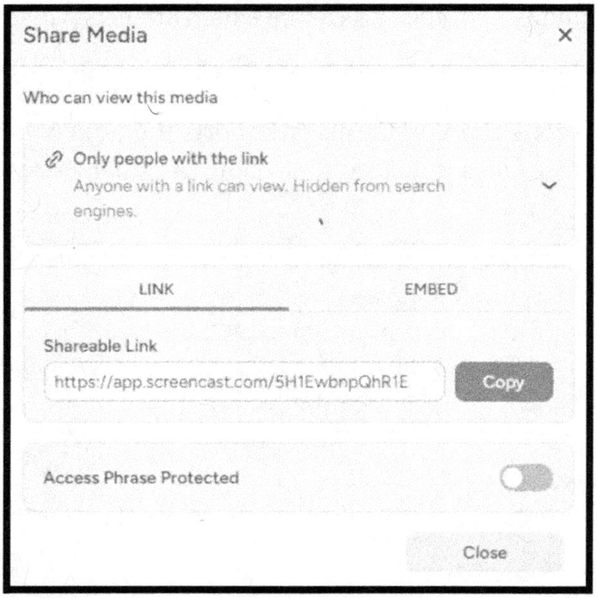

*12_02.png - The **Share Media** dialog on Screencast.*

The first option in this dialog box lets you choose whether your video is private or public.

3. Open the **Who can view this media** dropdown and review the available options.
4. For this exercise, select **Only people with the link**.

Next, you find the URL to share with your audience. If you prefer to embed the video on an existing web page, use the HTML code provided in the **Embed** tab.

5. Enable **Access Phrase Protected** and enter a password.
6. Click **Close**.
7. To test this password, open an incognito window in your current browser (or switch to a different browser entirely) and paste the link to your video.

In this section, you discovered how Screencast lets you share and protect your videos.

3. Editing Video Details

After uploading your video to Screencast, you can still edit the title and description you entered in Camtasia. Use the following steps to edit this information after the video has been published.

1. Navigate to screencast at https://app.screencast.com.
2. Log in to the platform.
3. Open the video you want to edit.
4. Click **Edit Details** underneath the video.

As shown in the screenshot below, you can then edit the title and description of the selected video.

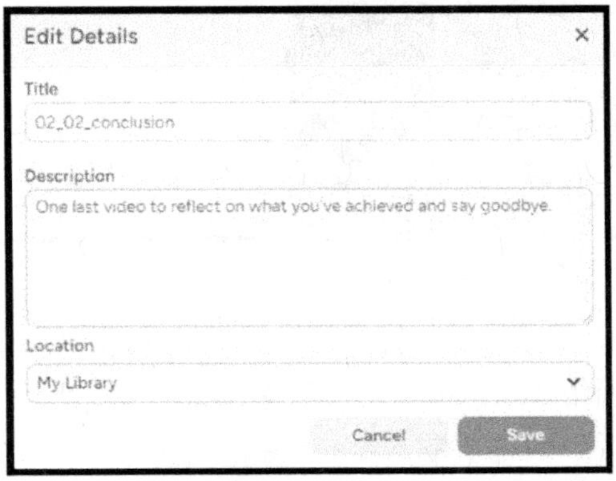

12_03.png - You can edit the title and description for your video.

For this exercise, you don't need to modify this information.

5. Click **Cancel** to close the **Edit Details** window.

Additional options, such as changing the video thumbnail and replacing the media file, are available under **More** below the video.

4. Commenting on a Video

By default, Screencast gives every viewer the ability to contribute. Using the built-in annotation and commenting tools, stakeholders can share feedback, report issues, or suggest improvements, thereby fostering a true collaborative process.

1. Go to your Screencast account and open the video you want to comment on.
2. Start playing the video.
3. To add a comment, just pause the video and use the annotation tools in the panel on the right.

Each comment is attached to a specific timecode. You can also like and reply to any comments, sparking asynchronous conversations with anyone watching your video.

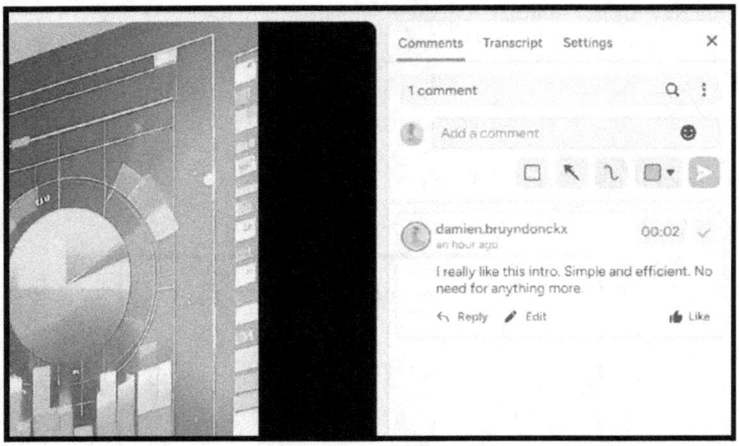

12_04.png - The commenting and review tools are located to the right of the video.

You don't need a TechSmith account to participate in these discussions; anonymous contributors will be prompted to enter their name when posting their first comment.

4. Navigate to the **Settings** tab on the right of your video.
5. At the bottom of the panel, you find the option to disable the **Conversation**.

This process is illustrated in the image below.

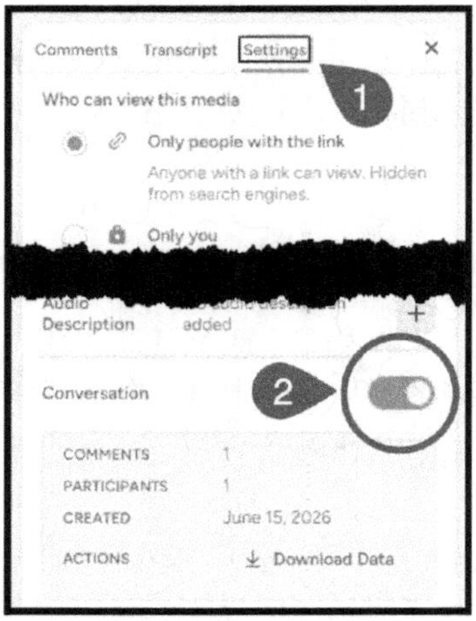

*12_05.png - You can disable the conversation in the **Settings** tab.*

Take some time to explore everything else Screencast has to offer. You'll discover a powerful yet easy-to-use hosting platform. If you've signed up for a paid Screencast Pro subscription, you'll get unlimited storage and access to additional AI-powered tools, such as automatic captioning and chapter creation.

B. Discovering Camtasia Online

Camtasia Online is a browser-based, lightweight version of Camtasia Rev that is available free of charge to all TechSmith account holders.

As of this writing, Camtasia Online is not supported on Safari. To access Camtasia Online on your Mac, use Google Chrome or Microsoft Edge.

To familiarize yourself with Camtasia Online, you will now use it to re-record the ***01_01_loginLogout*** project that you created in Chapter 02 – A First Video with Camtasia Rev.

1. Open ***platform/reset.html*** from the exercises in your web browser to reset the platform.
2. Click **Back to login page**.
3. Open the ***Chapter12/resources/01_01_loginLogout_scenario.pdf*** file and take a moment to review the scenario.
4. Open another browser tab and navigate to https://camtasia.techsmith.com.
5. Click **Sign In** in the upper-right corner of the Camtasia Online interface and log in to your TechSmith account.

When you log in to Camtasia Online for the first time, you are taken directly to a new project. Returning users are taken to the home screen instead.

6. If necessary, click the Camtasia logo in the upper-left corner of the screen to return to the home page.

As shown in the image below, the Camtasia Online home screen lists your existing Camtasia Online projects.

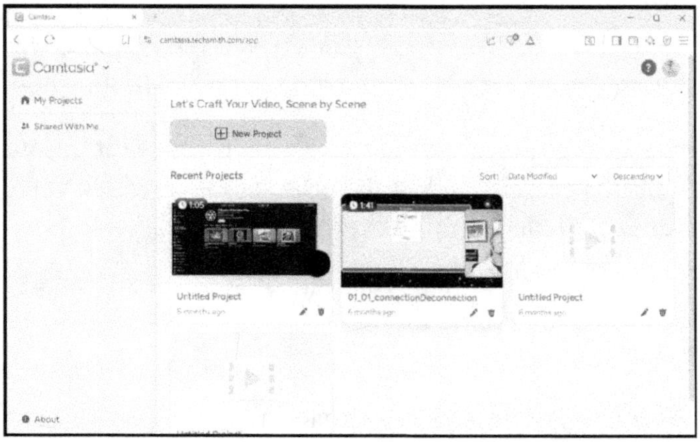

12_06.png – The Camtasia Online welcome screen.

From this screen, you can open or delete any existing projects. For this exercise, though, you'll start fresh and create a new blank project.

7. Click **New Project**.
8. In the upper-left corner of the screen, click the **Untitled Project** title.
9. Type `01_01_loginLogout` as the new project title and press **`Enter`** to validate.

Everything is now ready for you to proceed with the recording of your project using Camtasia Online.

1. Recording With Camtasia Online

A Camtasia Online project is organized into scenes. The **Scenes** panel, at the bottom of the screen, lets you add, delete, and reorder scenes. When you start a new project, one empty scene is created automatically. For technical reasons, each scene cannot exceed five minutes, but there is no limit to the number of scenes you can include in a project.

Each scene can be either a Camtasia Online recording or a video you import from your computer. For this particular exercise, you'll record a new scene using Camtasia Online.

1. Click **Record** on the left side of the screen.
2. Select **Screen and Webcam** to record both the onscreen action and your webcam.

Next, your browser asks you to allow access to your webcam and microphone. Note that this prompt originates from your browser, not from Camtasia Online.

3. Select the webcam and microphone you want to use for your recording and authorize access.

Now you must select the tab, window, or screen you want Camtasia Online to record. For this exercise, select the browser tab in which you opened the ***platform/index.html*** file from the exercises.

4. Select the **O2L Reporting | Login** tab.
5. Deselect **Also share tab audio**.
6. Click **Share**.

These actions are illustrated in the image below.

Remember that this prompt originates from the browser, not from Camtasia Online. Depending on the browser you're using, this dialog box may look slightly different, and the options may have different names, but the available features should be essentially the same.

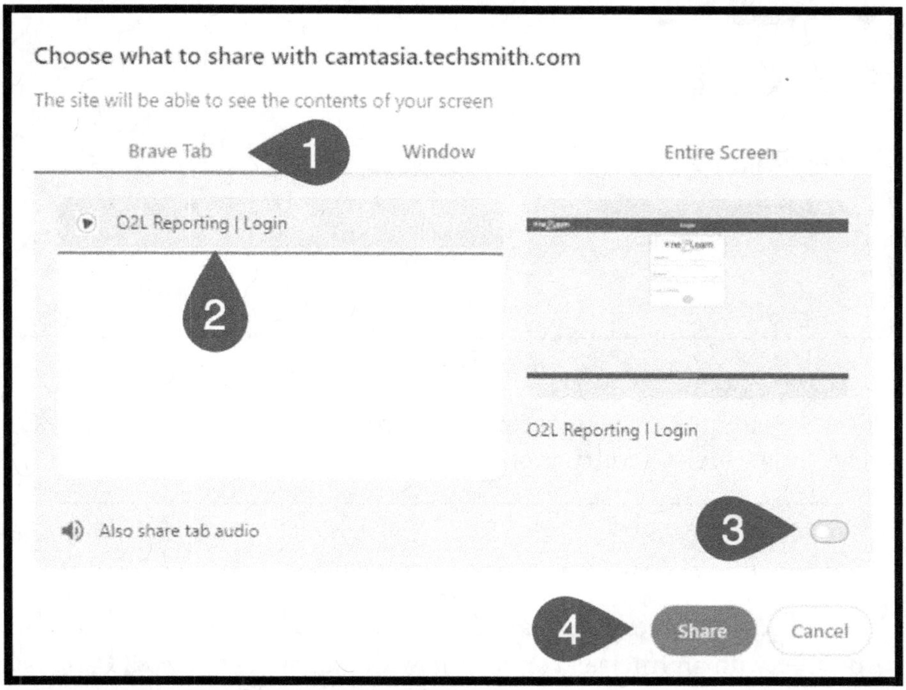

12_07.png - *Select the tab you want to record.*

A live preview of the scene appears on the canvas. Use the toolbar beneath the canvas to toggle your microphone, webcam, and screen recording on or off.

7. When everything is ready, click **Start Recording** beneath the canvas. After a brief five-second countdown, the recording begins.
8. Navigate to the tab displaying the platform.
9. Record the tutorial using the scenario included in the PDF file.
10. After you finish recording, click **Stop Sharing** at the top of the interface.
11. Return to the Camtasia Online tab in your browser.

As shown in the following screenshot, your recording is now visible on the canvas.

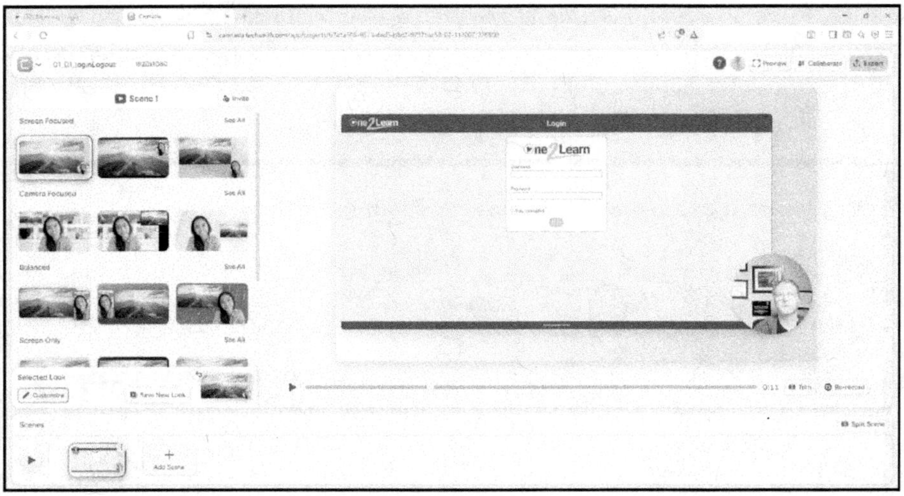

12_08.png - The completed recording appears on the canvas.

Press Play to preview your recording. If you're not happy with the result, create a new scene and try another take.

You could also delete the existing scene and start from scratch, but creating a new scene lets you compare your takes and choose the best one.

The key advantage of Camtasia Online is that you can record from any computer with an Internet connection without having to install Camtasia.

- You can capture screen activity on computers that don't support Camtasia, such as Linux machines.
- In highly controlled IT environments, strict internal policies often prevent the installation of third-party software. Since Camtasia Online requires no installation, you can still record screen activity on those locked-down machines.

After the recording is complete, you can proceed to the editing phase of your project using Camtasia Online.

2. Post-production With Camtasia Online

The post-production tools in Camtasia Online are very similar to those available in Camtasia Rev. You'll start by trimming the unwanted sections at the beginning and end of your recording.

1. Click **Trim** in the lower-right corner of the canvas.

2. Drag the green handles at the beginning and end of your recording to select the portion you want to keep.
3. Click **Done** when ready.

Note that Camtasia Online cannot cut out a middle section out of your recording.

*To work around this limitation, you can use the **Split Scene** button to split the scene at the playhead position. You'll then be able to trim the beginning and end of each resulting scene separately.*

Once you've finished trimming, use the tools in the left column to select and customize a layout.

4. Browse the **looks** listed in the left column and choose the one you like most.

Some looks focus on the webcam, while others prioritize screen recording or offer hybrid configurations by combining both sources. As shown in the image below, each section includes a **Show All** button providing access to even more options.

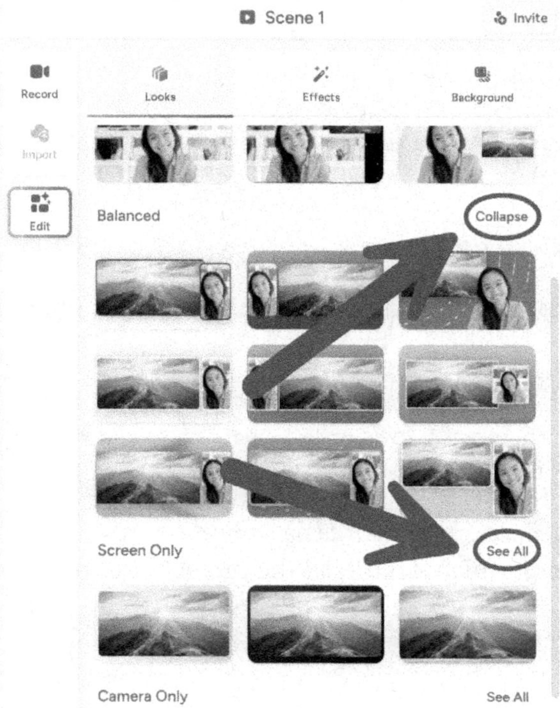

*12_09.png – **See All** gives you access to even more options.*

You can now customize the selected look.

5. Click **Customize** in the lower-left corner of the left column.
6. Browse through the available options and choose the one that works best for you.
7. Click **Close** when done.
8. Navigate through the **Effects** and **Background** tabs and explore the available options.

These tabs should look pretty familiar, as they offer roughly the same tools as Camtasia Rev.

If your project contains multiple scenes, you can give each scene its own layout. Select the scene you want to edit at the bottom of the screen, then change its properties in the left column.

When done, you can proceed to the export step of the process.

3. Exporting With Camtasia Online

At this point in the process, Camtasia Online offers the following three options:

- If you're happy with the result, you can export your project as an ***.mp4*** file and download it to your computer.
- You can share your project on *Screencast* to reach a wide audience and gather feedback from viewers.
- You can export the project to Camtasia Editor and continue working on it with all the tools discussed in previous chapters.

All these options are available under **Export** in the upper-right corner of the screen.

1. Click **Export** in the upper-right corner of the screen.
2. Take a moment to review the available options, then **click Open in Camtasia Editor**.

Once the project opens in Camtasia Editor, you can use the entire Camtasia toolset to continue working on the project you began online.

4. Enabling Collaboration with Camtasia Online

In the previous sections, you've gone through the entire video production process with Camtasia Online, from recording footage to post-production and export. These tools make it easy for anyone to create short videos for free.

But Camtasia Online has another trick up its sleeve: you can use its built-in collaboration features to invite others to work on the project with the option to give them edit access to the entire video or restrict edits to a particular scene.

1. Return to https://camtasia.techsmith.com/ and open the ***01_01_loginLogout*** project you created previously.
2. Select a scene at the bottom of the screen.
3. Click **Invite** in the upper-right corner of the left column.

This action is depicted in the following image.

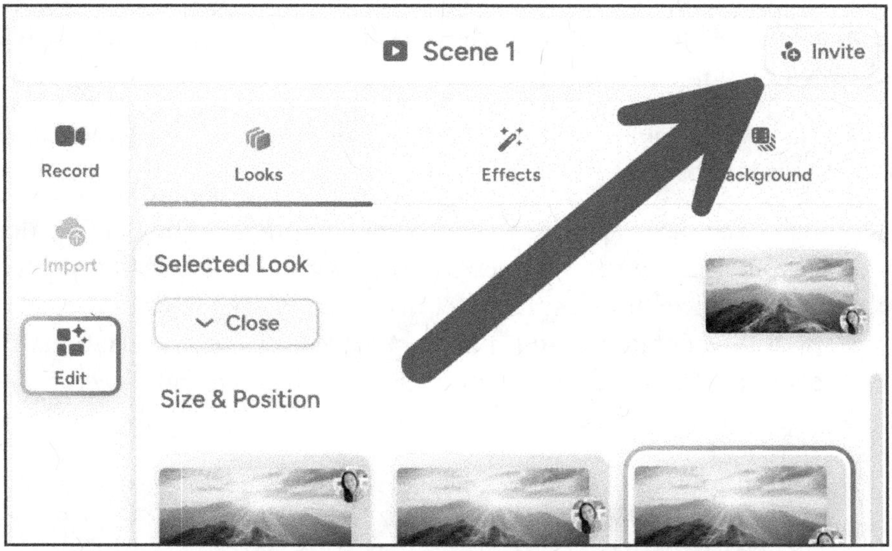

*12_10.png – Click **Invite** in the upper-right corner of the left column.*

You must now enter the email address of the contributor you wish to invite. If your project includes multiple scenes, this contributor only has access to the currently selected scene.

4. Enter the email address of the contributor you want to invite and click **Invite**.

The system then sends an invitation to the provided email address.

You will now learn how to invite a contributor so they can access the entire project.

5. Click **Collaborate** in the upper-right corner of the screen.

The window that opens has two tabs. Collaborators invited via the first tab have full **Project Access** so they can add, edit, and even delete any scene.

Remind any collaborators you invite that they must have a TechSmith account and sign in before accessing your Camtasia Online project.

Thanks to real-time collaboration and the convenience of recording directly in the browser with no additional installation, Camtasia Online has become an essential part of TechSmith's video production suite.

C. Working With Camtasia Audiate

The last tool covered in this chapter is *Camtasia Audiate.* Its basic tier is available to all individual Camtasia users after downloading and installing the application.

Business users need to purchase Camtasia Audiate separately. Please contact your Camtasia reseller for more details.

Originally, Camtasia Audiate was just an audio transcription application that let you clean up raw recordings by editing the transcribed text. Over time it has evolved into a suite of AI-driven tools used to draft an polish scripts, auto-generate closed captions, produce voice-over narrations via text-to-speech, translate projects into different languages, and even create video avatars.

Although Camtasia Audiate is installed locally on your computer, many of its features rely on online services. You must, therefore, be connected to the Internet when using Camtasia Audiate.

1. Text-Based Video Editing with Camtasia Audiate

In this section, you will use Camtasia Audiate to trim unwanted parts out of a raw recording. This text-based editing workflow was Audiate's primary use case when it first launched back in 2019.

1. Import the ***Chapter12/projects/01_02_dashboard_rushes.zip*** project into the ***Chapter 12*** folder of the exercises.
2. Watch the entire project.

The only clip in this project has not yet been edited. At this point, you could use the tools covered in Chapter 5 - Editing Your Video to clean up this raw footage. Instead, you will now export this clip to Camtasia Audiate and use *text-based editing* to perform this task.

3. Select the video clip that sits on track 1 of the timeline.
4. Go to the **Audio Properties** tab of the Properties panel.
5. Click **Edit in Audiate.**

This last step is depicted in the image below.

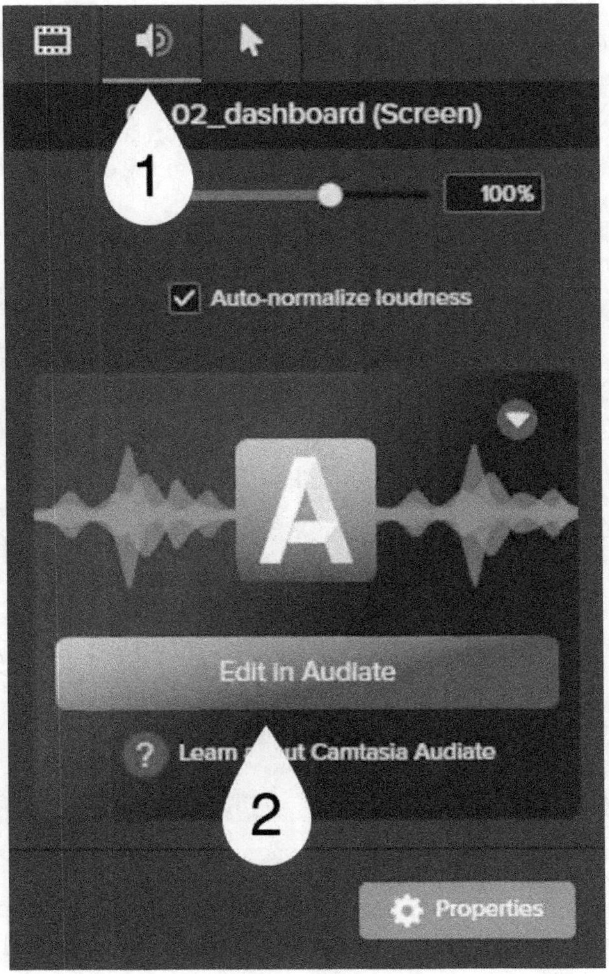

*12_11.png - Click **Edit in Audiate**.*

Note that this button is only available if Camtasia Audiate is installed on your computer.

After a short wait, Camtasia Audiate opens, asking if you'd like to import the project as a single scene or split it into multiple scenes.

6. For this exercise, select **Import as One Scene** and click **Import**.

Audiate converts your project's audio track into text, using the same language as the previous transcription.

7. If the transcription language is not English, go to **Settings > Transcription Language** and select **English**.

Take this opportunity to explore the list of languages supported by Audiate.

> *Although the app can handle all the languages in the menu, the user interface is currently available in English only.*

8. Once you've selected the correct transcription language, go to **File > Transcribe Project** to restart the transcription in the chosen language.

A few moments later, the transcript of your narration appears on the screen, as shown in the image below.

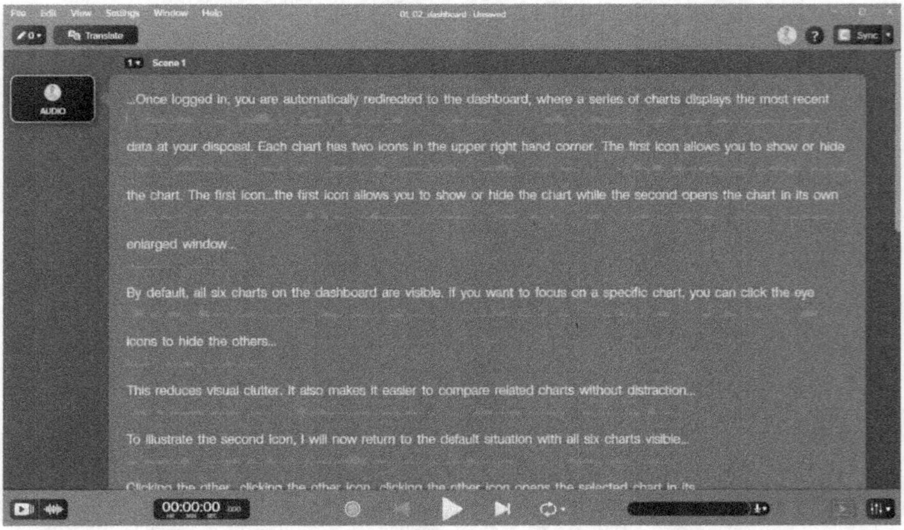

12_12.png - The transcript of your narration appears on the screen.

Audiate relies on third-party services to perform this transcription. This is the reason why you must be connected to the Internet when using Camtasia Audiate.

You can find a complete list of all third-party AI services used by TechSmith products under the following URL: https://support.techsmith.com/hc/en-us/articles/26140574750861-Third-Party-AI-Technology-Used-in-TechSmith-Products.

You will now test the results of this transcription.

9. Click the play button at the bottom of the Audiate interface to start playing the project.

During playback, you'll notice that Audiate doesn't just transcribe the narration; it also syncs each word with the corresponding audio.

10. Select the ellipsis (...) at the very beginning of the transcription.

In Audiate, ellipses mark silences. By selecting the ellipses at the beginning of the transcript, you actually select the silence at the start of the audio track, before the narration begins.

11. Hit `Delete` on your keyboard.

Since the text is synchronized with the underlying audio, deleting the ellipsis automatically deletes the corresponding silence in the audio file. In other words, you've just trimmed the beginning of your footage, but you did it as if you were using a word processor rather than video editing software.

12. Use the same steps to remove any errors and hesitations in the transcription: select the text to remove and hit `Delete`.
13. If you spot a spelling, capitalization, punctuation or transcription error, select the text to modify, right-click the selection, and choose **Custom Word** or **Combine into Custom Word**. Enter the corrected text and click **OK**.

This method lets you edit the transcript while preserving the synchronization between the text and the underlying audio.

14. When done, position the cursor at the beginning of the transcript and play the entire project.

The narration should now be cleared of unnecessary silences, as well as of any errors or hesitations present in the original recording. All you need to do now is transfer these changes back to your Camtasia project.

15. Click the small arrow next to the **Sync** button in the upper-right corner of the interface.

This reveals the Camtasia sync options, as shown in the following image.

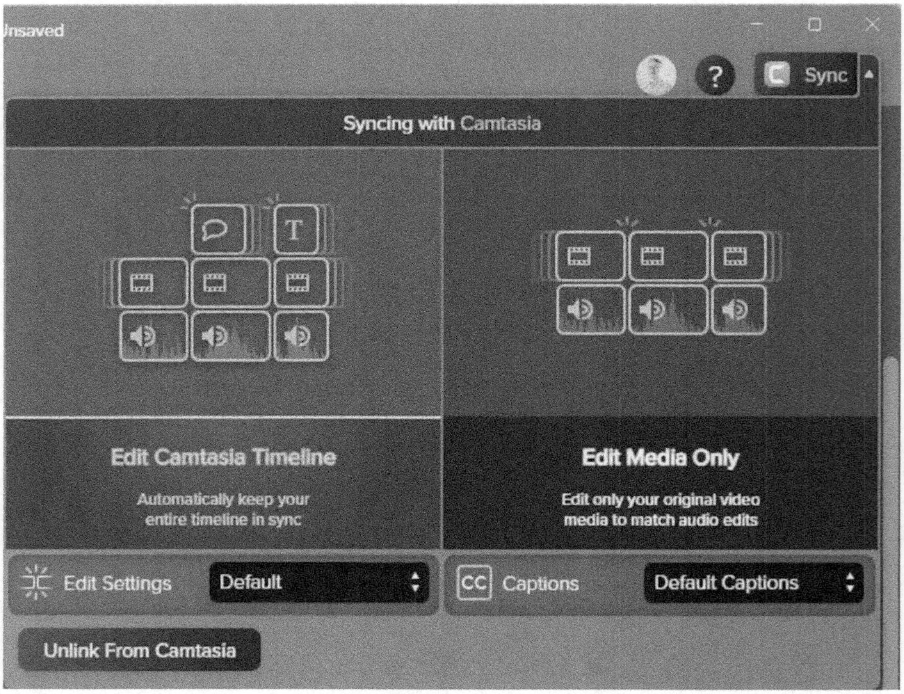

12_13.png – The Camtasia sync options in Audiate.

For this exercise, you will select the following export options.

16. Select **Edit Camtasia Timeline**.
17. Open the **Captions** dropdown and select **Default Captions**.
18. When done, click **Sync** in the upper-right corner of the screen.
19. Save the Audiate project as ***Chapter12/01_02_dashboard.audiate***.
20. Return to Camtasia.

Take a close look at the Camtasia timeline and notice that the cuts made in Audiate have been transferred to your Camtasia project. This is the result of the **Edit Camtasia Timeline** option you selected in Audiate. Also note the new caption track added to the Camtasia timeline.

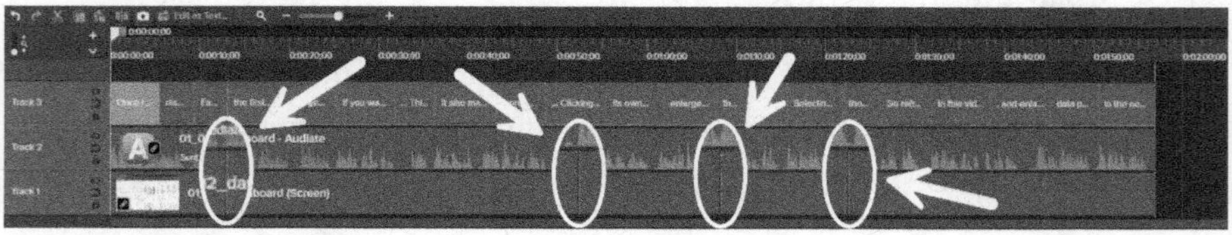

12_14.png - The cuts made in Audiate have been transferred over to Camtasia.

Thanks to the automatic transcription feature in Camtasia Audiate, you have been able to edit your video as easily as you would a text document.

Audiate also automatically generates and synchronizes closed captions for your Camtasia project.

At this point, you could continue editing this project using all the tools available in Camtasia. However, for the purposes of this exercise, you'll stop here and move on to exploring more Camtasia Audiate features in the next section.

2. Localizing Videos with Camtasia Audiate

In this section, you will start from a fully completed Camtasia project and use Camtasia Audiate to translate it into another language. In doing so, you will explore several tools, such as automated translation, text-to-speech, and video avatar generation.

> *Translation and voice-over generation are available to Camtasia Create and Camtasia Pro subscribers. Avatar generation requires a Camtasia Pro subscription. Please refer to the following page for more information on the available subscription plans and pricing: https://www.techsmith.com/store/camtasia*

You will now generate the French version of the ***02_02_conclusion*** project you already worked with earlier in this chapter.

1. Open the ***Chapter12/02_02_conclusion*** project.
2. Use the **File > Save As** menu item to save a copy of this project under ***Chapter12/02_02_conclusion_FR***.
3. Select the narrator's video that sits on track 2 of the timeline.

This is the only multimedia element in the project that shows an audio waveform. This is the audio track you will now export to Audiate.

4. Navigate to the **Audio Properties** tab of the Properties panel.
5. Click **Edit in Audiate**.
6. Once Audiate opens, select **Import as One Scene** and click **Import**.

Audiate converts your voice recording into text. Because your configuration persisted, the transcription language should already be set to English.

7. Take the necessary time to review and correct this transcription using the tools mentioned in the previous section.
8. When done, click **Translate** in the upper-left corner of the screen.

> *As a reminder, this button is only available to users with a Camtasia Create or Camtasia Pro subscription.*

9. Pick **French** as the target language for this exercise.
10. Click **Translate** to confirm.

Once the translation is complete, Audiate gives you the option to automatically produce the corresponding audio file.

11. Click **No** to close the message without generating the audio.

Before generating the French-speaking narration, you should first check the quality of the translation and make any necessary changes using the following steps.

12. Double-click anywhere in the translation to switch to edit mode.
13. If you know some French, take the necessary time to proofread, edit, and improve this translation.

Since you'll soon be generating a new audio narration track in French using text-to-speech, there's no need to worry about the synchronization between the text and the underlying audio.

14. When you're happy with the translation, click the **Done Scripting** button at the bottom of the screen.
15. Return to the beginning of the text, then click **Audio** in the upper-left corner of the workspace.

As shown in the screenshot below, clicking this button gives you access to a suite of AI-powered features.

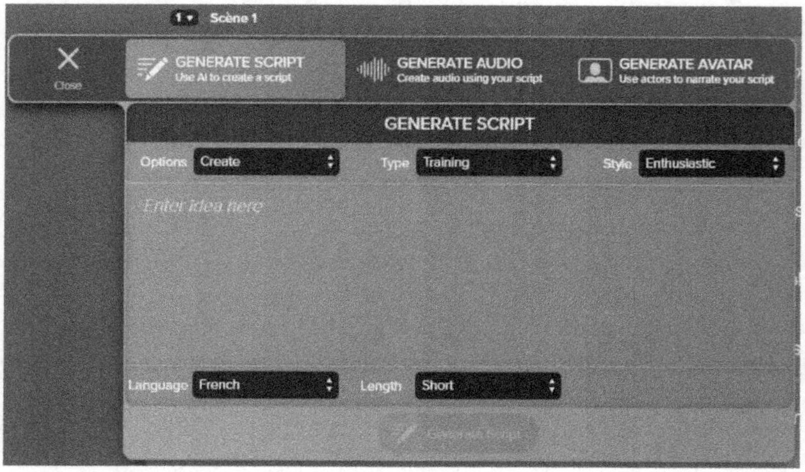

12_15.png - This gives you access to a suite of AI-powered features.

Please note that some of these tabs may not be available depending on your subscription plan.

16. Select the **Generate Audio** tab.
17. Use the play buttons to hear samples of the available text-to-speech voices.
18. Select your preferred speech agent and click **Generate Audio**.
19. When the process is complete, click play at the bottom of the interface to listen to the result.

If you're not satisfied with the result, feel free to revise the text and try out other speech agents until you find something that works for you.

Finally, let's generate a video avatar to substitute for the original narrator in your Camtasia project.

20. Return to the beginning of the text and click **Generate** in the upper-left corner of the workspace.
21. Select the **Generate Avatar** tab.
22. Browse through the available avatars and choose the one that suits you best.

If you selected a female voice for the narration, only female avatars will appear. Conversely, if you selected a male voice, you'll only see male avatars.

23. Click **Generate Avatar**.

Once again, Audiate relies on third-party services to generate the avatar. After a short wait, the avatar should appear in Audiate, as shown in the image below.

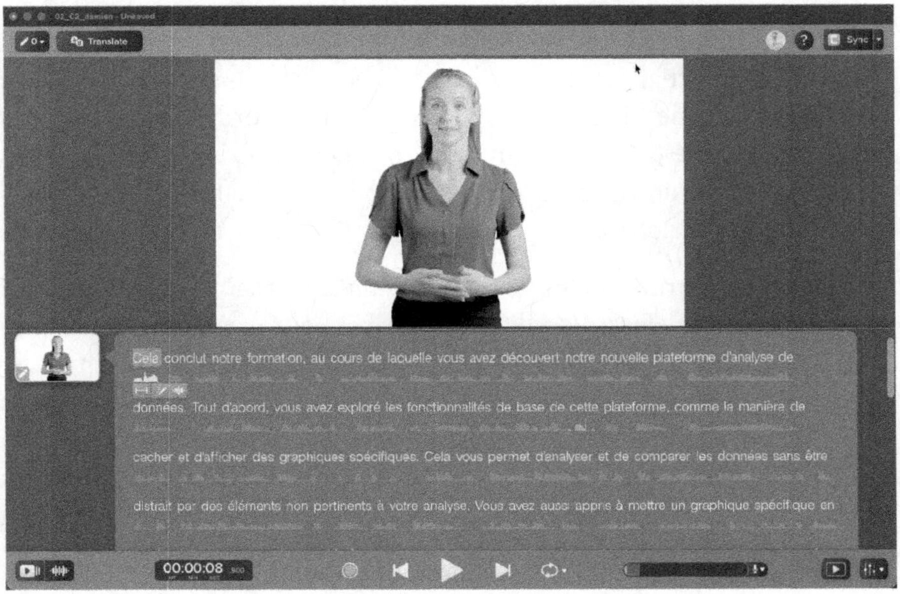

12_16.png - The avatar appears in Audiate.

Before sending this data back to Camtasia, play the project in Audiate to verify that the avatar's lip synchronization accurately aligns with the generated text-to-speech audio.

24. When everything is ready, click the **Sync** button in the upper-right corner of the interface.
25. Save the Audiate project as ***Chapter12/02_02_conclusion_FR.audiate.***
26. Return to Camtasia.

You can now use the tools in Camtasia to finalize the French version of this project. This task includes hiding the original narrator, removing the background from the avatar, and translating the onscreen captions.

You can find the final French translation I produced with these tools in the ***Chapter12/resources/02_02_conclusions_FR.mp4*** *video file of the exercises.*

D. Conclusions

By the end of this final chapter, you should have a much better understanding of the online services and apps that make up the Camtasia ecosystem.

First, you explored *Screencast,* TechSmith's free video-hosting and collaboration platform that integrates seamlessly with Camtasia, making publishing your videos to Screencast a breeze.

Next, you discovered *Camtasia Online,* a browser-based lightweight version of Camtasia Rev that's accessible for free without any installation. This service allows anyone to create simple videos and record screen activity on computers where Camtasia cannot be installed. This includes Linux systems and locked-down machines in environments that restrict the installation of external software.

Finally, you've learned about *Camtasia Audiate.* Its main features are available to all Camtasia users. Audiate transcribes your narration into text, lets you edit audio clips as if you were using a word processor, automatically synchronizes the text with the audio, and creates captions for your videos. Other AI-powered features, such as script generation, translation, text-to-speech, and video avatar creation, are available only to Camtasia Create and Camtasia Pro subscribers.

But no matter which subscription plan you choose, you have access to powerful yet easy-to-use tools that let you create a wide variety of video projects.

By the end of this book, you have acquired the necessary skills to put those tools to work for teaching, communicating, and expressing your creativity.

As we wrap up, I'd like to thank you for joining me on this learning journey. I hope you enjoyed exploring Camtasia and I look forward to seeing the videos *you* will produce with these tools and your new skills.

Damien Bruyndonckx – August 2026.

Index

D

E

F

I

K

L

M

N

P

Q

R

S

www.ingramcontent.com/pod-product-compliance
Lightning Source LLC
LaVergne TN
LVHW060543061126
851857LV00017B/1880
9782960412727